Microsoft

W9-DIW-314

Troubleshooting
Microsoft
Office XP

Nancy Stevenson and Elaine Marmel

PUBLISHED BY
Microsoft Press
A Division of Microsoft Corporation
One Microsoft Way
Redmond, Washington 98052-6399

Library of Congress Cataloging-in-Publication Data pending.

Printed and bound in the United States of America.

1 2 3 4 5 6 7 8 9   QWT   7 6 5 4 3 2

Distributed in Canada by Penguin Books Canada Limited.

A CIP catalogue record for this book is available from the British Library.

Microsoft Press books are available through booksellers and distributors worldwide. For further information about international editions, contact your local Microsoft Corporation office or contact Microsoft Press International directly at fax (425) 936-7329. Visit our Web site at www.microsoft.com/mspress. Send comments to *mspinput@microsoft.com*.

FrontPage, Hotmail, Microsoft Press, MS-DOS, MSN, NetMeeting, the Office logo, Outlook, PivotChart, PivotTable, PowerPoint, SharePoint, SmartShapes, Visual Basic, Windows, Windows Media, Windows NT, and Wingdings are either registered trademarks or trademarks of Microsoft Corporation in the United States and/or other countries. Other product and company names mentioned herein may be the trademarks of their respective owners.

The example companies, organizations, products, domain names, e-mail addresses, logos, people, places, and events depicted herein are fictitious. No association with any real company, organization, product, domain name, e-mail address, logo, person, place, or event is intended or should be inferred.

Acquisitions Editor: Alex Blanton
Project Editors: Judith Bloch and Aileen Wrothwell
Technical Editor: Curtis Philips

Body Part No. X08-41924

Acknowledgments

The authors would like to thank all the folks at Microsoft Press for their support in getting this book done. We'd especially like to thank Alex Blanton for providing the opportunity to write this book, Aileen Wrothwell and Judith Bloch for shepherding the entire process so diligently, and Tory McLearn for juggling about a thousand files with efficiency and grace.

Quick contents

Contents

Part 1: Common elements   3

AutoRecover and file repair   4

Clip art   14

Drawing   24

Contents

Contents

Contents

Part 4: PowerPoint   293

Contents

Contents

About this book

Troubleshooting Office XP is designed to help you avoid spending lots of time sifting through information to find the answer to a problem. Instead, the design of the book helps you quickly cut to the chase and find the answer to the problem you're experiencing.

How to use this book

The book covers the four most widely used Office XP products: Excel, Outlook, PowerPoint, and Word. Because Office is a suite of products, we've begun the book with a section that deals with common elements—problems that relate to functions such as menus and toolbars that you'll find in all the applications. In this first section—"Common elements"—we've discussed problems related to sharing data between these Office applications—and even a few problems related to sharing data between these Office applications and other Office applications such as Access and FrontPage. Then we've covered what we think are the most common problems encountered when using each of these applications in a section devoted specifically to that application. You'll find chapters within each application's section organized alphabeti-

cally by categories of information, such as Formatting or Printing.

We didn't intend for you to read this book from cover to cover; instead, we think you'll refer to it when you encounter a problem. As you review the Table of Contents, you'll notice that the topic headings describe problems you might encounter. Each topic covered contains information that describes the problem and how to fix it.

Flowcharts

At the beginning of each chapter, you'll find a flowchart that helps you diagnose the problem and takes you to the correct topic. On the flowchart, you'll see questions with yes or no answers. As you follow the arrows on the chart, you'll find yourself directed to the topic that covers your problem.

Also on the flowchart, you'll find "quick fixes"—problems that require only a few steps to solve. Instead of directing you to another page in the book, you'll find the description of the problem as well as its solution in the "Quick fix" box right there on the flowchart.

You'll also find, on the flowchart, a list of chapters that contain related information to further help you find solutions to your problem.

Solutions spreads

After the flowchart helps you find the right page, you'll turn to a solution topic. Each solution is organized in the same way. At the top, you'll find the "Source of the problem" section, which contains information that describes what caused the problem. Following that section, you'll find a way to solve the problem in the "How to fix it" section, complete with screen shots that show you what you should be seeing while you fix the problem.

Although each solution is designed to minimize your reading to get you back to work quickly, you will occasionally find additional information that might explain the problem further, address a related problem, or help you avoid the problem in the future. You will also find tips and notes with valuable material, and "Before you start" sections containing cautionary information crucial to helping you avoid getting into trouble when following the steps presented to fix a problem.

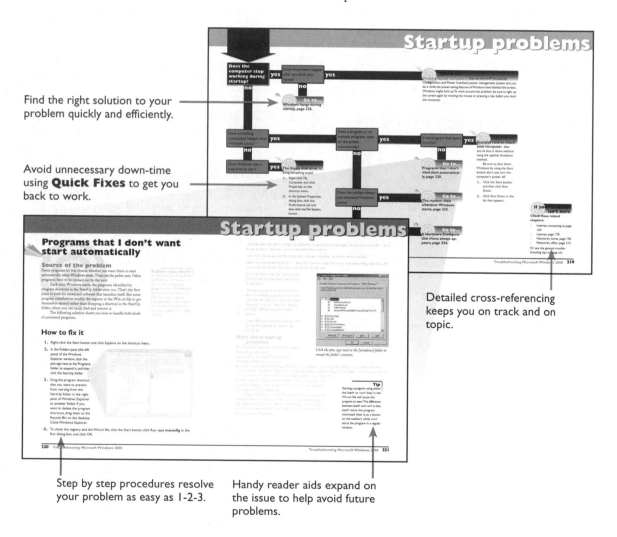

Find the right solution to your problem quickly and efficiently.

Avoid unnecessary down-time using **Quick Fixes** to get you back to work.

Detailed cross-referencing keeps you on track and on topic.

Step by step procedures resolve your problem as easy as 1-2-3.

Handy reader aids expand on the issue to help avoid future problems.

Troubleshooting Tips

The word troubleshooting can bring to mind the image of a battered frontiersman riding shotgun on a stagecoach headed west. A modern-day troubleshooter has some things in common with those pioneering souls. A troubleshooter by definition is someone who sits around waiting for trouble to show up (traditionally with machinery or equipment of some kind) and finds ways to fix it. *Troubleshooting Office XP* is the resource you can call on whenever you encounter trouble using Word, Excel, Outlook, or PowerPoint.

Trouble with computing can come from many sources: some problems are a result of the way you're trying to use a program, your specific hardware setup, problems on the Internet or your company network, or a setting in Office. Does this book cover every possible problem you could encounter with Office XP? No. But it covers the most common issues—the ones you're likely to run into in your day-to-day work.

This is the book you can open when you need it, so you can solve your problem and get back to work.

How to troubleshoot

Successful troubleshooting consists of a series of logical steps. To use this book efficiently, you have to find the broader category of your problem, and then narrow it down to the specific problem you've encountered.

With Office XP, you first need to identify the application that has the problem. Of course, you know if you're working in Word or Excel, but are you working with the main program or a shared application, such as Microsoft Graph? This book offers a section the deals with common problems, some of which relate to shared applications, as well as sections for the most often used Office programs.

Once you are sure which application to look under, you need to identify the broadest category of the problem. For example, if your e-mail messages keep coming back as undeliverable, when you look in the Outlook section of this book, you will probably turn to the "Sending and receiving e-mails" chapter.

Next, review the flowchart at the beginning of the appropriate chapter. We've filled these with problems that paraphrase the questions you'll come up with when you encounter trouble. Often these questions include a symptom, such as "an error message appears," "a color printout comes out black and white," or "my e-mail was deleted." Some problems can be fixed in a few steps, so we've covered them in "Quick fix" boxes within the flowchart itself. Others require more information; those problems are listed with a page number where you can go to get detailed help.

Office XP integration considerations

Remember, Office XP is an integrated suite of products. It also includes shared applications such as WordArt and Clip Organizer. In addition, Office has many tools and features that allow you to interact with the Internet and even other programs. Some problems might originate because of the integration of several computer programs within Office or between Office and another source. We've tried to include coverage of integration issues in this book, so look in the "Common Elements" part of the book first.

If the problem is between two Office applications, consider it from both sides. For example, if you're exporting information from Excel to Word, look in the Excel section under exporting and in the Word section under importing. Your solution might have been placed under one application but not both to avoid redundancy.

In some cases, you might also have to look to another software product, your operating system, or a hardware manufacturer for information and help.

If you're still stuck

With a software product as robust as Office XP, a single book cannot possibly cover every problem you might encounter. We've tried to offer the most common issues, but now and then you'll run into trouble we just didn't shoot for you. When that happens, use the following resources for further information:

- *http://microsoft.com/office*, the Microsoft Office product family Web page

- *http://search.support.microsoft.com/kb*, the searchable Microsoft Knowledge Base

- *http://www.zdnet.com*, a useful Web site that provides technology tips

- *http://communities.msn.com/MSOffice/ _whatsnew*, a good place to discuss Office products with fellow users to see if they've encountered the same issue

Common elements

Part I

Did your system crash while you were working on an Office document?

yes

Do you want to recover the file you were working on?

yes

no

Were other files damaged that you want to repair?

yes

Go to...

I need to restore a file that was damaged, page 6.

no

Do you want to be able to locate previous versions of a file?

yes

Quick fix

...up files. If you want to be able to maintain the version prior to the changes you most recently saved, you can set up Word to create backup files.

1. On the Tools menu, click Options and then click the Save tab.

2. Select the Always Create Backup Copy check box to activate it.

3. Click OK.

Do you see your file in the Document Recovery task pane?

yes → Are the changes you thought would be saved missing?

yes → **Go to...** My file was recovered but it doesn't contain my changes, page 10.

no

Did you enable AutoRecover before the system problem occurred?

yes → **Go to...** The AutoRecover feature doesn't recover my file when I restart, page 8.

no

Quick fix

Enabling AutoRecover.
If you didn't activate AutoRecover, the application will not have saved a version of the file when it crashed; do so now to avoid future losses.

1. On the Tools menu click Options and display the Save tab.

2. Select the Save AutoRecover Info Every check box to enable the feature.

If your solution isn't here, check these related chapters:

- Searching, page 76
- Opening and saving files, page 444

Or see the general troubleshooting tips on page xix.

I need to restore a file that was damaged

Source of the problem

Files can get damaged in a number of ways: your system can crash in the middle of saving a file, a virus can infect a file and eat some of your information, or you might put a computer disk through the washing machine (trust me, this happens). Not all damaged files can be recovered, but Office does offer a few tools that will work with some files. One tool opens and repairs a file; the other lets you open a file and retrieve only text. If a file contains damaged graphics, this might at least save you the trouble of re-creating any text.

Whichever method you choose, once you open a damaged file, you should immediately save it in whatever format you wish. With either of the recovery methods suggested here, text in paragraphs, headers, footers, footnotes, endnotes, and fields are recovered. With the Recover Text method, document formats, graphics, fields, and drawing objects are not recovered.

To open a document and recover just the text, you have to install a Recover Text Converter. This converter is part of a typical Office installation, but if you find that for some reason it's not on your computer, you can install it from your Office CD.

How to fix it

One recovery option, Open And Repair, only works in Word and Excel. Follow these steps to repair a file:

1. On the File menu, click Open.

2. In the Look In list, click the drive, folder, or Internet location that contains the file that you want to open.

3. In the folder list, locate and open the folder that contains the file.

4. Select the file that you want to recover.

5. Click the arrow next to the Open button, and then click Open And Repair. ▶

If you want to open a file and retrieve only text, you can do so using the Recover Text Converter and this procedure:

1. On the Tools menu, click Options, and then click the General tab. ▶

2. Make sure the Confirm Conversion At Open check box is selected, and then click OK.

3. Click File, Open.

4. In the Files Of Type box, click Recover Text From Any File. ▶

5. Click Open. All recovered text is displayed in a Word document.

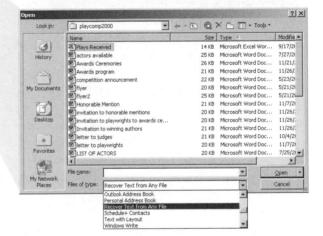

More about the Document Recovery task pane

The Document Recovery task pane appears whenever an Office application is unexpectedly interrupted. The pane may offer you several versions of a document to choose from and will tell you what repairs were made to the files, if any. You can open all the documents to compare versions, open and save one or more of the versions, or save all versions for later review.

The AutoRecover feature doesn't recover my file when I restart

Source of the problem

If you think of your computer as a three-ring circus with multiple applications running, messages streaming into your Inbox, and behind-the-scenes utilities backing up and checking your system, AutoRecover is the safety net that can save you from a painful fall. AutoRecover is a feature that works in all Office products to automatically save your documents periodically as you work on them. AutoRecover keeps these documents in a Windows folder. If your system crashes because of a power failure or computer glitch, the last AutoRecover file should be available when you restart your computer and open the Office application you were working in. This file may not contain all your changes—it will include everything you did up to the point when AutoRecover last saved your document before the crash occurred.

Your Office application should display the last saved file in the Document Recovery task pane when you open an application that recently crashed. If your document doesn't appear in the Document Recovery task pane, it does not necessarily mean that there aren't saved versions of the file on your hard disk—there probably are. You can use the following method to manually find the last saved version of your file.

Before you start

If you lose a file or changes to a file that you haven't saved because of a computer crash or other disaster, use AutoRecover. You can't hurt anything by trying to locate the AutoRecover file—and you might save yourself the trouble of re-creating everything you lost. However, be aware that any recovery files that you don't save when offered that option are deleted when you quit an Office application.

Tip

AutoRecover is simply a safety feature; it is not a replacement for saving your work frequently. Get in the habit of saving your work every time you finish writing a paragraph, creating a slide, or filling in a row or column of numbers.

How to fix it

If the Document Recovery task pane does contain the recovered document, simply follow these steps to save it:

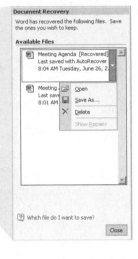

1. Click the arrow to the right of the recovered document version you'd like to save, and click Open. ▶

2. Review the document; if it's the one you want to save, click the Save button on the toolbar.

3. Locate the current document in your folders and click the file name to select it.

4. Click Save. A message appears asking whether you want to replace the existing document; click Yes.

If the document doesn't appear in the Document Recovery task pane, you can open it from its location on your hard disk by doing the following:

1. Start the Office application.

2. Click Open.

3. Locate the folder that contains your recovery files (for example, for Word it would be c:\Documents And Settings\User Name\Application Data\Microsoft\Word). ▶

4. In the Files Of Type box, click All Files. Recovery files are always named "AutoRecovery save of file name" and have the file name extension .asd.

5. Open the recovered file and save it.

My file was recovered but it doesn't contain my changes

Source of the problem

The whole point of AutoRecover is to periodically save the file you're working in. Then, if a power outage occurs in your neighborhood, or your computer suddenly decides to take a coffee break, you can be sure there is a saved version containing at least some of your most recent changes.

You can set AutoRecover to run at specified intervals, which might be as frequent as every minute to as long as hundreds of minutes. However, as with many things in life, timing is everything. If you set AutoRecover to save your file every 15 minutes and you've only been working for 10, no changes will be saved to your AutoRecover file, and if a crash occurs, you won't have anything to recover.

How do you determine the right interval to set for AutoRecover? Here's a useful rule of thumb: how much work are you willing to retype? Would 10 minutes of work prove difficult to redo? Or are you the type who turns pale at the thought of reliving even two minutes worth of work? Whatever your answer, that's the number of minutes you should set the AutoRecover interval to.

The following solution takes you through the steps involved in changing AutoRecover settings.

> **Before you start**
>
> To ensure that more recent versions of files are saved by AutoRecover, you can modify the frequency of your saves. However, if you opt for frequent saves, especially with larger documents, there can be a moment or two each time an AutoRecover runs when you won't be able to work in your application. The trade-off for this short delay is feeling more secure that you won't lose several minutes worth of work.

How to fix it

To change the AutoRecover save interval, follow these steps:

1. Open PowerPoint, Word, or Excel. (Outlook doesn't use AutoRecover.)

2. On the Tools menu, click Options, and then click the Save tab.

3. Select the Save AutoRecover Info Every check box.

ver and file repair

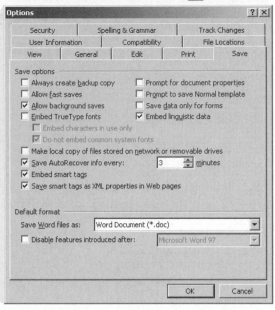

4. Use the spinner control next to the Save AutoRecover Info Every check box to adjust the interval setting. ▶

5. Click OK to save the new setting.

If you want to specify a different location for Windows to save recovered files, follow these steps:

1. On the Tools menu, click Options.

2. In Excel and PowerPoint, simply click the Save tab in the Options dialog box, and type in a location for saving AutoRecover files. ▶

or

1. In Word, click the File Locations tab.

2. In the File Types list, click AutoRecover files.

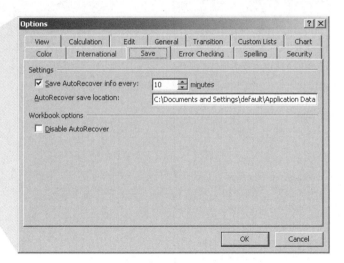

My file was recovered but it doesn't contain my changes

(continued from page 11)

3. Click Modify. ▶

4. If you want to store recovered files in a different folder, locate and open the folder.

5. Click OK twice to accept the new location, and close all dialog boxes.

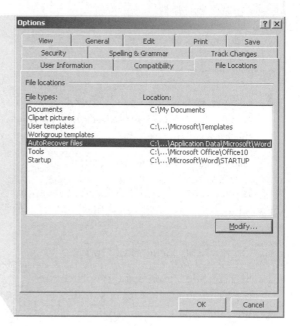

More about saving

Fast Saves is an interesting feature you can use to save files quickly. If you select the Allow Fast Saves check box in the Options dialog box, only changes to your document will be saved each time the file is backed up—not the entire document. This makes saving faster, especially with very large documents, though it does present you with several saved versions should your computer crash and enter Auto Recovery mode. When you're done with your changes and want to save the whole document again, clear the Allow Fast Saves check box.

Did you try to use Clip Organizer and run into a problem?

yes → Did you find the clip you wanted? **yes** →

no

Did you add a picture to Clip Organizer but now you can't find it? **yes** →

Go to...
I don't see the pictures I added to Microsoft Clip Organizer, page 16.

no

Do you have a picture you'd like to use but it's not in Clip Organizer? **yes** →

Go to...
The clip I want isn't in Clip Organizer, page 22.

no

Did you get different results than you expected? **yes** →

Go to...
When I search for clips I get too many results and they aren't what I want, page 20.

no

Did you have trouble getting Clip Organizer to work? **yes** →

Do you want to edit the clip?

yes

Are the pieces of the clip separate objects and hard to work with?

yes

Go to...

I can't select all the pieces in my clip, page 18.

no

Is the clip the wrong size for your document?

yes

Quick fix

Resizing clip art. Often, when you insert clip art, the clip is too large or small to fit your document. Try these methods to resize it:

1. Click the object to select it, then drag any of the selection handles that appear to enlarge or reduce it.

2. To retain the proportions of the object, only drag corner handles.

3. To expand or shrink the object in two directions (for example both the left and right sides simultaneously), hold down Ctrl while dragging a side handle.

Quick fix

When you can't get Clip Organizer to work. If you install Windows 2000 and you don't choose to retain the FAT32 file system on your hard disk, this causes a problem with Clip Organizer. To fix the problem:

1. Using the Add/Remove Programs feature in the Control Panel, click Change, Add Or Remove Features, and remove Clip Organizer under Office Shared Programs.

2. Using the same feature, reinstall Clip Organizer.

3. Restart Windows and Clip Organizer should work.

If your solution isn't here, check these related chapters:

- Drawing, page 24
- Drawing objects and pictures, page 310

Or see the general trouble-shooting tips on page xix.

I don't see the pictures I added to Microsoft Clip Organizer

Source of the problem

Clip Organizer uses a couple of methods to organize clips. One is to assign keywords. A keyword is like a name tag you wear at a convention that helps identify you to other convention attendees. Keywords are associated with a clip art file and are then used in clip art searches. When you search for clip art, you enter a keyword that relates to the category of art you're looking for, such as "buildings" or "food." Clip Organizer returns a set of clips that have that keyword attached.

Clip Organizer also allows you to organize clips into collections. You might create a collection of business art and personal art, for example. Any clip art that does not have a keyword attached to it is stored in the Unclassified Clips collection. If you perform a search or look through Office collections or collections you created, you won't find such unclassified clips.

Once you add a keyword to the clip or move the clip to another collection, it will no longer be stored in Unclassified Clips. It can then be found by using its keyword in a search or by looking in the appropriate collection using the Insert Clip Art task pane.

How to fix it

To add a keyword to a clip, you need to edit it by following these steps:

Note

If you can't find a clip that was added by another user on the same computer, it is because the clips you import or change are only visible to you when personal user profiles are enabled. If you do not have profiles enabled, all clips are shared among all of the users of the computer.

1. Display the Insert Clip Art task pane by clicking the Insert menu and clicking Picture, Clip Art. ▶

2. In the Search In list, make sure that the Everywhere check box is selected (this includes files that have keywords associated with them and those in the Unclassified Clips folder).

3. Clear the Search Text text box, and click Search to display the Unclassified Clips folder, or enter a search term for a clip that has keywords associated with it.

4. Locate the clip you want to associate a keyword with, click the arrow on its right side, and click Edit Keywords.

5. Type a term in the Keyword text box and click Add. Repeat this step with other keywords, and then click OK to save your additions. ▶

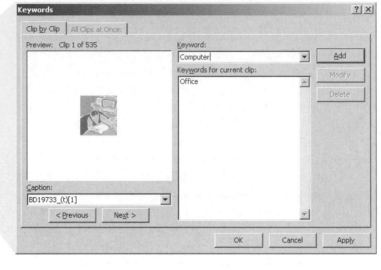

Tip

If you want to create a new collection in which to place clips, use the Clip Organizer link in the Insert Clip Art task pane. Click File, New Collection. Then cut and paste clips into the collection using Clip Organizer.

I can't select all the pieces in my clip

Source of the problem

If you've ever drawn a picture, you know that you typically draw several objects to create the whole image. A cat might have a circle for a head, an oval for a body, lines for whiskers, and a long, curly tail. Although a piece of clip art might also be compiled from several pieces, it is inserted into your document as a single object. Objects can be moved, resized, rotated, and formatted. Most of the time, this makes life very easy because you only have to perform actions on one object.

However, there are also times when you only want to perform a simple action, such as moving one leaf on a tree or changing the color of the cat's eyes to green. You can do this with drawing objects. You can group and ungroup drawing objects to work on a single object or separate objects to make changes to individual pieces.

With most clip art formats, you cannot ungroup elements. There is an exception: quite a few of the line drawing type clips you see in the Clip Organizer are actually Windows Metafile Format (WMF) metafiles, which use a .wmf file extension. Metafiles are saved in a vector graphics format for Windows-compatible computers. They are used mostly for word-processing clip art. Metafiles can be converted to drawing objects. If you do convert a metafile image and ungroup it, you might then have a bunch of little pieces that are hard to work with.

Fortunately, the drawing program shared by all office applications makes it easy to deal with grouping.

How to fix it

To group all the pieces of a clip, perform these steps:

1. Display the Drawing toolbar in your Microsoft Office program, and click Select Objects.

2. Hold down the mouse button and drag across all pieces of the object to draw a selection rectangle around the entire clip. ▶

3. On the Drawing toolbar, open the Draw menu, and then click Group.

If you want to ungroup the pieces at a later time to edit the picture in some way, follow these steps:

1. Click the grouped object.

2. On the Drawing toolbar, open the Draw menu, and then click Ungroup. ▶

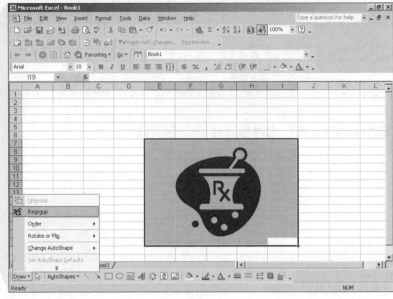

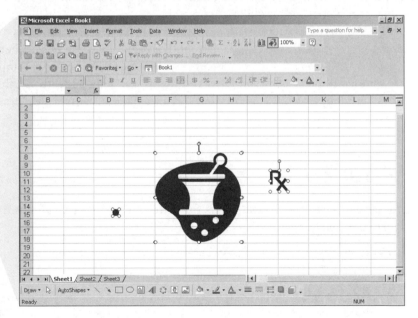

Tip

If you want to work with just some of the pieces of a graphic, you can hold down the Shift key and click just the ones you want, then make a formatting choice or rotate, move, or resize the pieces.

When I search for clips I get too many results and they aren't what I want

Source of the problem

To search for clips, you use keywords. If you're not finding the clips you need, you might be keyword challenged, but don't worry, there's help. All you have to do is become a more proficient keyword user.

For example, if you search by the keyword *food* when you want pictures of cookies, you'll have to sort through pies, candies, and cakes to find the clip you need (and this could even be fattening). If the clips returned in the Results box don't match the criteria you set, try using more keywords to narrow down your search. In addition, you can reduce the number of collections that are searched or choose to return a smaller set of media types (for example, don't retrieve sounds when all you need are pictures— what does a cookie sound like, anyway?).

Alternatively, you can also try using fewer keywords if the clips returned in the Results box don't seem to match the criteria you set. For example, if you've searched by the keywords *business*, *computer*, and *women*, and you don't get a clip of a woman using a computer in a business setting, try removing the keyword *business*. You might just get a perfectly useable clip of a woman sitting at a computer, which wasn't previously returned because the word *business* was not associated with the clip.

How to fix it

To narrow down search parameters for better success in finding clips that meet your needs, try these steps:

1. To display the Insert Clip Art task pane, on the Insert menu click Picture, Clip Art.

2. Type a single keyword in the Search Text text box, or type one keyword followed by a semicolon, and then type a second keyword. ▶

3. Open the Search In list, and clear the check boxes of the collections you don't want to include in the search (a check mark next to a collection indicates it's selected to be searched). When you're done, press Tab or click the arrow in the list to close it. ▶

4. Open the Results Should Be list, and clear any check boxes for media types you don't want to include in the search. ▶

5. Click Search. If you don't get the results you want, click the Modify button located just under the search results to change your keyword choices.

Searching for a specific clip

Perhaps you know the name of a graphic you want to insert; if so, you can find it by entering the file name in the Insert Clip Art task pane Search Text box. If you aren't sure of the exact file name, you can use wildcard characters. Wildcard characters are placeholders you use in a search that represent any text that might come after the text you enter.

Here's how wildcard characters work:

● Use the asterisk (*) as a substitute for zero or more characters in a file name. For example, type **writ*.jpg** to locate file names like writing.jpg or writer.jpg. The asterisk (*) must come at the end of the string, but before the file extension; you can't use it at the beginning or in the middle of the string; for example, ***can.wmf** or **wom*n.jpg** wouldn't work.

● Use the question mark (?) to represent a single character in a file name. For example, type **men?.jpg** to locate file names like mend.jpg or men3.jpg, but not mending.jpg.

The clip I want isn't in Clip Organizer

Source of the problem

Search through the Clip Organizer and you'll see hundreds of images. If you want a picture of a computer, you'll find a few dozen of all styles and colors. Need a picture of people playing sports? No problem—Microsoft has provided enough athletes to fill several playing fields. Don't see anything you like? Just download a whole new collection of clip art from the Web.

There will be times when you have a specific image that you'd like to include in your collection, so it's readily available to insert into any Office document. For example, it's useful to be able to place your company logo in Clip Organizer to retrieve and insert into business documents. The tool you use to insert new files into a collection is Clip Organizer. This is a type of cataloging system for clip art, where you can group clips in collections. You can place a graphic file in an existing collection or create new collections as you need them.

How to fix it

If the clips you want aren't in Clip Organizer, you can use a couple of methods to add them. You can add all graphics contained in specified folders by following these steps:

1. Display the Insert Clip Art task pane, and click the Clip Organizer link in the See Also section at the bottom of the task pane to open Clip Organizer. ▶

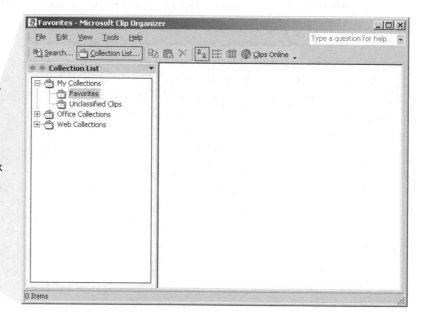

2. On the File menu, click Add Clips To Organizer. Click Automatically and do one of the following: ▶

- If you want to specify folders to be scanned, click Options. Select the check boxes next to the folders you want to be scanned for new clips, and then click Catalog. ▼

- If you want all folders to be scanned for media files, click OK.

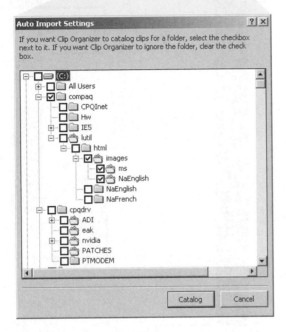

Note

New clips are added to Clip Organizer in the My Collections folder. If you scan a CD to retrieve a clip, the Clip Organizer creates a folder that reflects the name of the folder in which the clip was stored on the CD.

More about Clip Organizer

Clip Organizer is a great place to organize all your graphic files. You can store clips in collections, search for clips, view thumbnails, and go directly to Web sites for additional clip collections and tools for working with images.

If you only want to add one specified graphic file or set of files to a collection, follow these steps:

1. On the Clip Organizer File menu, point to Add Clips To Organizer, and then click On My Own.

2. Locate the folder that contains the clip you want to add, and then click the clip.

3. To store the clip in a collection, click Add To, click the collection where you want to store the clip, and then click OK.

4. Click Add.

Are you having trouble working with drawings? yes

Are you working with borders and colors? yes

Are you having difficulty with the fill colors in your drawing? yes

no

no

Are the colors in your drawing object uneven? yes

no

Did you add a border, but it doesn't appear? yes

Are you having trouble resizing an object? yes

Go to...
I can't resize an object, page 30.

no

Did you add a drawing but now you don't see it? yes

Go to...
I inserted a drawing, but I don't see it, page 28.

Are the colors in your drawing object uneven? **yes**

Quick fix

Getting smooth colors.
If your computer is only capable of showing 16 colors, colors might not appear smooth. Objects are best displayed on systems that can display more than 256 colors. You can:

1. Use a different system.

2. Be aware that the printed output of your drawing should be fine, even though your on-screen version is less than perfect.

Quick fix

Using fill effects. Sometimes it's better to fill a drawing object with something other than a solid color. Use this method to use various fill effects:

1. Click the Fill button on the Drawing toolbar.

2. At the bottom of the pop-up palette, click Fill Effects.

3. Use the settings on the Gradient, Texture, Pattern, or Picture tabs to add fill effects to your object.

Go to...
I can't see the border around an object, page 26.

If your solution isn't here, check these related chapters:

- Borders and numbered lists, page 402

- Drawing objects and pictures, page 310

Or see the general troubleshooting tips on page xix.

I can't see the border around an object

Source of the problem

The use of borders began when the first caveman drew a line in the sand and grunted to show that everything on one side was his and everything on the other side wasn't. Just as people use borders to separate pictures and countries, you can use borders to set off text, drawings, clip art, or other objects from everything else on your page.

In a drawing such as a circle or AutoShape, the border is actually the outer line that defines the drawing object. Making changes to that border involves choosing a setting for the border (such as a simple box, a shadow, or a 3-D effect) and applying a line style, thickness, and color. So far, so good. But sometimes borders around objects in your documents can disappear. This can have a few different causes:

- The border might have been removed by choosing the None setting in the Borders And Shading dialog box, or it might be the same color as the background.

- A 3-D effect might have been applied to the object. Applying this effect to an object turns off its border.

How to fix it

If the line color of your border is the same as the background color of your document:

1. Click the object, and then display the Drawing toolbar.

2. Click the arrow next to Line Color, and then click a color from the palette that appears. ▶

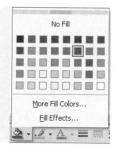

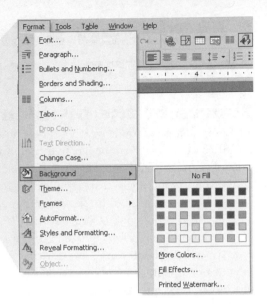

3. If you'd rather keep your text the same color, you can change your background color to make the text stand out against it more clearly. You do this by clicking Format, Background (in Excel click Sheet, then Background), and then clicking a color or image in the palette that appears. ▶

If you have applied a 3-D effect that has caused your border to disappear, simply remove the 3-D effect by following these steps:

1. Click the object.

2. Display the Drawing toolbar, and click the 3-D Style button.

3. Click No 3-D to remove the 3-D effect and restore any border that was previously assigned to the object.

Warning

There are other effects that can't be used in combination; for example, you can't apply a shadow and a 3-D effect to the same object.

I inserted a drawing, but I don't see it

Source of the problem

They say that a picture is worth a thousand words, but pictures in Office documents can be worth a thousand seconds of your valuable time. Graphics can enlarge the size of a file and can take several moments to display on screen, causing irritating delays. Microsoft has built in several features that suppress graphics from displaying to prevent these delays and has even provided a couple of views where graphics are banned from ever appearing. If you can't see a drawing you know you created in your document, the problem could be with one of the following settings in the Options dialog box.

- It's possible that you selected the Picture Placeholders View check box. Selecting this option helps you scroll through any document that includes graphics more quickly because your program displays placeholders (empty boxes) instead of pictures.

- Perhaps you cleared the Drawings View check box in Word. Clearing this option makes scrolling faster when a document contains drawing objects or other graphics because Word doesn't display graphics in Print Layout or Web Layout views.

Drawing objects aren't displayed at all in Normal or Outline views. To work with drawing objects, you must work in Print Layout view. You can also work in Web layout view with the Drawings View check box cleared in the Options dialog box, or work in Print Layout view.

In addition, there are times when you'll only see a portion of a picture on your screen, which is something else entirely. This problem occurs when the line spacing in your document is set to an amount that is smaller than the height of the graphic.

How to fix it

Let's deal with line spacing first. If your line spacing setting is too small, you might only see part of a drawing or graphic. To adjust line spacing so that an entire drawing is displayed, follow these steps:

1. Click anywhere within the paragraph that contains the graphic (but not on the graphic itself), and then click Paragraph on the Format menu.

2. Click the Indents And Spacing tab. In the Line Spacing box, click Single. ▶

3. If you click Exactly in the Line Spacing box, be sure to increase the measurement in the At box to match the height of the graphic.

4. Click OK to save the new setting; your graphic should display correctly.

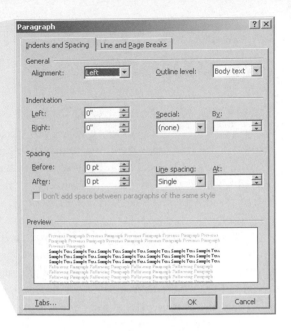

Note

Paragraph formatting works in Word and Outlook. In Excel, you can have a drawing object set to move and resize along with the cell it's in by adjusting the Object Positioning setting on the Properties tab of the Format AutoShape dialog box, and it will resize according to the size of the cell. In PowerPoint, placeholders will resize to accommodate graphics.

If you do not see your drawing, check these settings in the Options dialog box:

1. Click Options on the Tools menu.

2. Click the View tab, and then clear the Picture Placeholders check box in Word or the Show Placeholders check box in Excel. ▶

3. To display drawings, select the Drawings check box.

4. Click OK to save these settings.

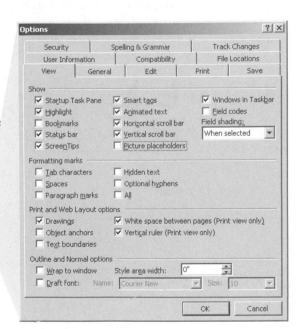

I can't resize an object

Source of the problem

Just as you don't want your waist to get too big or your bank account to get too small, you might also have preferences for the way drawing objects should resize. Office has some built-in restrictions that you can place on how objects resize. If you're not aware of the existence of these restrictions, they can cause you problems.

If you're working with text boxes, you can apply a setting so that the text box object resizes to accommodate the amount of text you enter. This can be very helpful, saving you the trouble of manually resizing the box. However, if you decide to change the text box shape for some reason, this setting can restrict what you can do.

You might also get unexpected results when resizing because of the aspect ratio setting. This setting controls the height and width of your object, which change in direct relation to each other. This setting keeps your objects in their original proportion. If you want to resize without retaining that proportion, however, you have to clear the Lock Aspect Ratio check box.

Before you start

There are certain constraints you can apply or remove from objects that control how you can size them. Removing these constraints lets you manipulate the objects freely, but you can also cause text to fit awkwardly on your page next to your object or distort your picture in some way.

How to fix it

If you're having trouble resizing a text box, check to see if the Resize Object To Fit Text check box is selected by doing the following:

1. Click the text box.

2. On the Format menu, click Text Box.

Tip

You must click the text box before opening the Format menu in order for the Text Box command to appear on the menu.

3. In the dialog box that appears, click the Text Box tab. ▶

4. Clear the Resize AutoShape To Fit Text check box.

If an object only resizes in proportion, the Lock Aspect Ratio check box is selected. You can clear the check box by following these steps:

1. Click the object.

2. On the Format menu, click the command for the type of object you are working with—for example, AutoShape or Picture.

3. Click the Size tab, and then clear the Lock Aspect Ratio check box. ▶

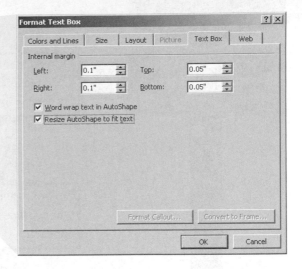

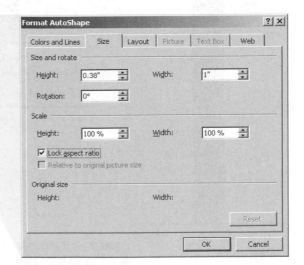

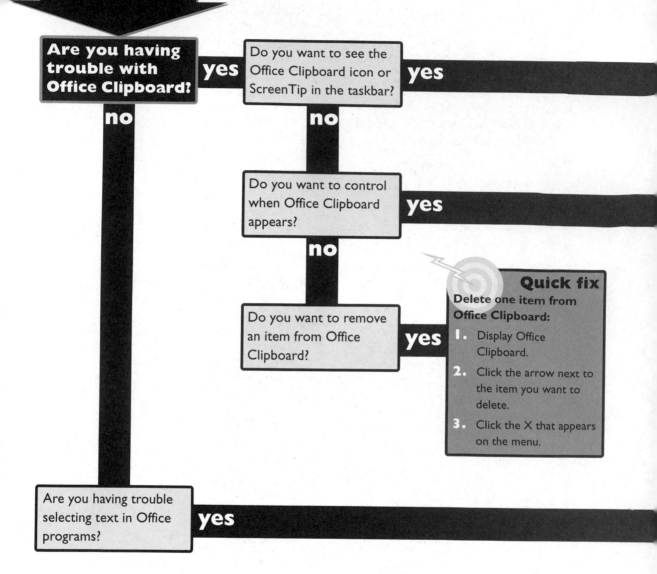

Are you having trouble with Office Clipboard?

yes → Do you want to see the Office Clipboard icon or ScreenTip in the taskbar? **yes** →

no ↓

Do you want to control when Office Clipboard appears? **yes** →

no ↓

Do you want to remove an item from Office Clipboard? **yes** →

no (from first box) ↓

Are you having trouble selecting text in Office programs? **yes** →

Quick fix

Delete one item from Office Clipboard:

1. Display Office Clipboard.
2. Click the arrow next to the item you want to delete.
3. Click the X that appears on the menu.

Go to...
I want to change the behavior of Office Clipboard, page 34.

Go to...
I want to change the behavior of Office Clipboard, page 34.

Go to...
Office programs are not selecting text the way I expect, page 36.

If your solution isn't here, check these related chapters:

- Editing data, page 134
- Entering and selecting data, page 144
- Copying, pasting, and moving, page 302
- Text editing, page 482

Or see the general trouble-shooting tips on page xix.

I want to change the behavior of Office Clipboard

Source of the problem

Sometimes it shows up, sometimes it doesn't. What's going on? The automatic appearance and behavior of Office Clipboard depends on the way you set Office Clipboard options.

Office Clipboard stores each item you copy while you work in any Office program. Office Clipboard can appear automatically, or you can force it to appear only when you decide you want to see it. Even if you choose not to display Office Clipboard, you can make the Office Clipboard icon appear in the system tray at the right of the Windows taskbar, letting you know that Office Clipboard contains elements that you can paste. You also can make the Office Clipboard ScreenTip appear so that you can keep track of the number of elements stored on Office Clipboard. If you prefer, you can disable the feature entirely.

How to fix it

To set Office Clipboard options, follow these steps:

1. Click the Edit menu of an Office program.

2. Click the Office Clipboard command. Office Clipboard appears.

3. Click the Options button.

4. Take one of the following actions to accomplish your goal:

   ● To show Office Clipboard as you collect items, select the Show Office Clipboard Automatically command. ▶

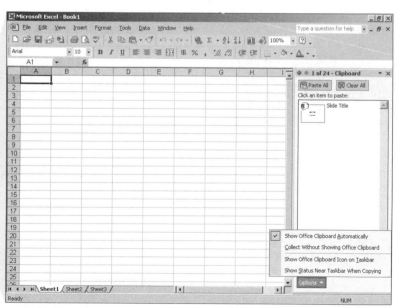

● To collect items without displaying Office Clipboard, select Collect Without Showing Office Clipboard, and clear the Show Office Clipboard Automatically command. ▶

| Show Office Clipboard Automatically |
| ✓ Collect Without Showing Office Clipboard |
| Show Office Clipboard Icon on Taskbar |
| Show Status Near Taskbar When Copying |

● To make the Office Clipboard icon appear in the system tray, select Show Office Clipboard Icon On Taskbar. ▶

| Show Office Clipboard Automatically |
| ✓ Collect Without Showing Office Clipboard |
| ✓ Show Office Clipboard Icon on Taskbar |
| Show Status Near Taskbar When Copying |

● To display a ScreenTip near the Office Clipboard icon in the system tray each time you copy, select the Show Status Near Taskbar When Copying command. ▶

| Show Office Clipboard Automatically |
| ✓ Collect Without Showing Office Clipboard |
| ✓ Show Office Clipboard Icon on Taskbar |
| ✓ Show Status Near Taskbar When Copying |

● To disable Office Clipboard entirely, make sure that no check marks appear next to the Collect Without Showing Office Clipboard command and the Show Office Clipboard Automatically command. ▶

| Show Office Clipboard Automatically |
| Collect Without Showing Office Clipboard |
| Show Office Clipboard Icon on Taskbar |
| Show Status Near Taskbar When Copying |

Note

When you disable Office Clipboard, the system Clipboard continues to function, storing only the last item you copied.

When you can't add more items to Office Clipboard

You can store no more than 24 items on Office Clipboard. When you try to copy the twenty-fifth item, Office Clipboard deletes the first item copied to accommodate the added item.

Even if Office Clipboard contains fewer than 24 items, you might notice that items you copy aren't added to it. Office Clipboard can hold up to 4 MB of information if your computer system has 64 MB RAM or less. If your computer system contains more than 64 MB RAM, Office Clipboard can hold up to 8 MB of information. If you try to add a large item to Office Clipboard, there simply might not be enough space.

Collected items remain on Office Clipboard until you close all Office programs running on your computer. To begin copying items again, delete some items, or click the Clear All button on Office Clipboard to empty it.

You might also find that even after you empty Office Clipboard, it won't store a particular item. In this case, you might be attempting to copy an item with a format that Office Clipboard doesn't support.

Office programs are not selecting text the way I expect

Source of the problem

You've tried your best and you just can't get Word or PowerPoint to select text the way you want. You keep highlighting whole words when you're trying to select characters only—or, in Word, you want to select all text except the paragraph mark—but you can't!

Based on the way you configure certain settings, you might find that you can select only whole words in PowerPoint or Word. Or, you might find that Word is selecting paragraph marks when you don't want to select a paragraph mark. You might also have trouble with drag-and-drop editing. You can control the way Office programs select text by changing certain settings.

How to fix it

To set options that control the way Office programs select text, follow these steps:

1. Click the Tools menu.

2. Click Options.

3. In the Options dialog box, click the Edit tab.

4. To control the way Word or PowerPoint selects whole words or single characters, select or clear the When Selecting, Automatically Select Entire Word check box. ▶

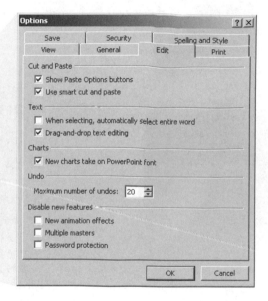

5. To avoid selecting paragraph marks in Word, clear the Use Smart Paragraph Selection check box. ▶

6. To enable drag-and-drop editing, select the Drag-And-Drop Text Editing check box—in Excel, the option is called Allow Cell Drag And Drop. ▶

Other drag-and-drop editing problems

To successfully *drag and drop*, make sure that the pointer appears over the selected text. When you press the mouse button to drag the text, you'll see a small, empty gray box attached to the mouse pointer. When you drag to highlight a line of text, pay close attention. If your pointer drops slightly below the current line, you will also highlight the line below the current line. To correct the selection, move the pointer back up while you continue to drag.

If you want to change the formatting of a specific part of a paragraph, make sure that you highlight only the text you want to change. If you select an entire paragraph, the changes you make affect all text in the paragraph. Also, be aware that some formatting changes, such as line spacing, alignment, bullets, and tabs, affect the entire paragraph: you can't apply these types of changes to part of a paragraph.

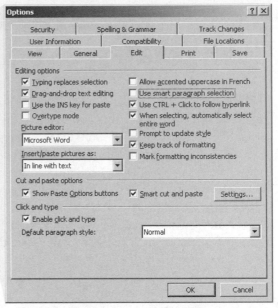

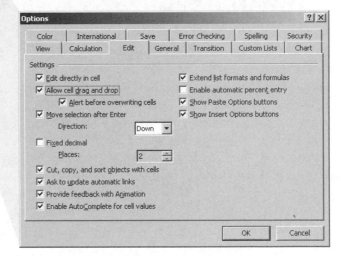

AutoCorrect isn't functioning as I expect

Source of the problem

The AutoCorrect feature can be helpful and save you time, or it can be the bane of your existence. To ensure that the feature helps you more than it angers you, double-check the options you set for AutoCorrect. The options that you set for AutoCorrect in Word, Excel, and PowerPoint are the source of most problems you might encounter with the AutoCorrect function. You can enable or disable AutoCorrect and control its behavior in a variety of ways. For example, you can control capitalization of text and correction of common typing mistakes.

With the AutoCorrect function enabled, you can choose to display a button immediately after making a correction, which allows you to reverse the correction. You also can disable the AutoCorrect function entirely.

How to fix it

You can control AutoCorrect options from the AutoCorrect dialog box. To display the AutoCorrect dialog box, click Tools, AutoCorrect Options. The AutoCorrect dialog box contains very similar options in each program. In the figure, you see the AutoCorrect dialog box from Word 2002, which contains two options that you won't find in any of the other programs: Automatically Use Suggestions From The Spelling Checker and Correct Keyboard Setting. ▶

Whenever the AutoCorrect feature has made a correction, a small, fairly flat, blue box appears under the corrected word; if you

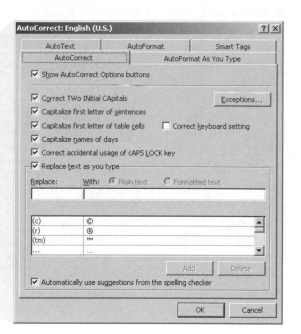

move your mouse pointer over the box, an AutoCorrect Options button appears. When you click the button's arrow, you see the AutoCorrect choices available to you. ▶

> The
> 乥 ▾
> ↰ Undo Automatic Corrections
> Stop Auto-capitalizing First Letter of Sentences
> Stop Automatically Correcting "teh"
> 乥 Control AutoCorrect Options...

If you don't want to see these buttons, clear the Show AutoCorrect Options Buttons check box in the AutoCorrect dialog box.

If you don't want to correct words with two initial capital letters, clear the Correct Two Initial Capitals check box.

You can control corrections to capitalization by selecting or clearing three check boxes: Capitalize First Letter Of Sentences, Capitalize First Letter Of Table Cells, and Capitalize Names Of Days.

When you select the Correct Accidental Usage Of Caps Lock Key check box, the Office program will monitor your typing for words you type in title case (initial capitalization and the rest of the letters lowercase) with the Caps Lock key engaged. In these cases, the Office program will correct the typing by switching uppercase letters to lowercase and lowercase letters to uppercase— and turn off the Caps Lock key.

You can disable the AutoCorrect feature entirely by clearing all of the check boxes on the AutoCorrect tab.

If AutoCorrect seems to miss a word that you frequently mistype, you can add the word to the AutoCorrect list by typing the incorrect version in the Replace box and the correct version in the With box of the AutoCorrect dialog box.

If one of the Office programs continues to incorrectly change an unusually spelled word or acronym that you frequently use, you can stop this behavior. Click the Exceptions button in the AutoCorrect dialog box, and type the acronym or unusually spelled word exactly as it should appear.

Tip

Office programs do not automatically correct errors in hyperlinks or in the first word that follows each hyperlink.

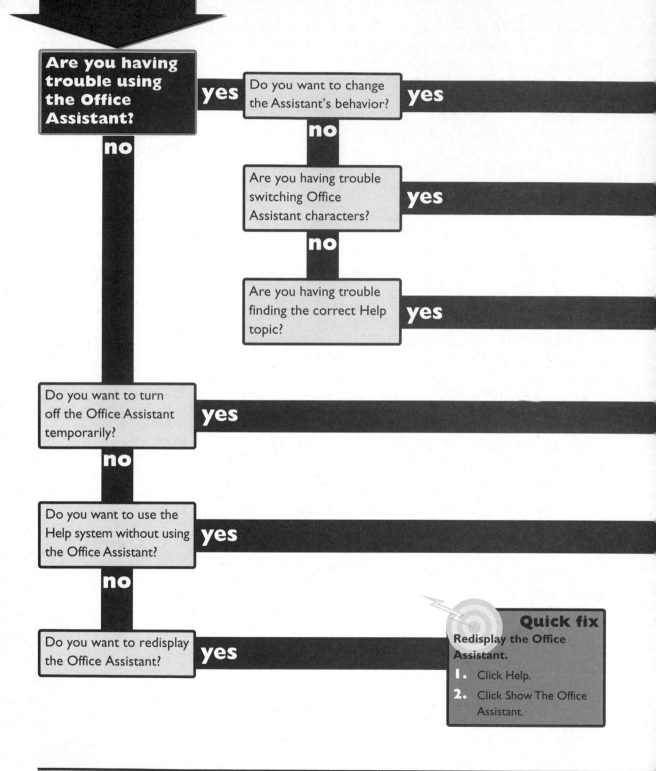

Are you having trouble using the Office Assistant?

yes → Do you want to change the Assistant's behavior? **yes**

no ↓

Are you having trouble switching Office Assistant characters? **yes**

no ↓

Are you having trouble finding the correct Help topic? **yes**

no ↓

Do you want to turn off the Office Assistant temporarily? **yes**

no ↓

Do you want to use the Help system without using the Office Assistant? **yes**

no ↓

Do you want to redisplay the Office Assistant? **yes**

Quick fix

Redisplay the Office Assistant.

1. Click Help.
2. Click Show The Office Assistant.

Go to...
I want to adjust the behavior of the Office Assistant, page 42.

Go to...
My Office program won't let me switch to a different Office Assistant, page 44.

Go to...
I can't find the Help topic I want in the Office Assistant, page 46.

Quick fix
Hide the Office Assistant until the next time you ask for help.

1. Click Help.
2. Click Hide The Office Assistant.

Quick fix
Disable the Office Assistant and use only the Help window.

1. Click the Assistant character.
2. Click Options and clear the Use The Office Assistant check box.

If your solution isn't here, check this related chapter:

- Security and macro warnings, page 472

Or see the general trouble-shooting tips on page xix.

I want to adjust the behavior of the Office Assistant

Source of the problem

You might find the Office Assistant's behavior somewhat distracting or unpredictable. You can modify the behavior of the Office Assistant in a couple of ways, which might make the Assistant easier to use:

- Turn off the Assistant's sounds

- Limit the movement of the Assistant

- Choose a different (perhaps less active) Assistant

> **Note**
> Limiting the movement of the Office Assistant also limits the movement of floating toolbars and menus.

How to fix it

To turn off the sounds the Office Assistant makes, follow these steps:

1. Click the Office Assistant.

2. Click the Options button. ▶

3. On the Options tab, clear the Make Sounds check box. ▶

4. Click OK.

To limit the movement of the Office Assistant, follow these steps:

1. Click the Office Assistant.

2. Click the Options button.

3. On the Options tab, clear the Move When In The Way check box.

4. Click OK.

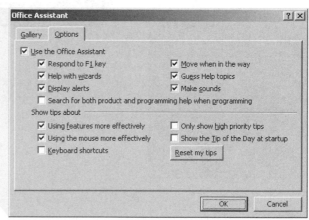

To choose a different Assistant, follow these steps:

1. Click the Office Assistant.

2. Click the Options button.

3. Click the Gallery tab. ▶

4. Click Next or Back to view each of the available Assistants.

5. Once you decide on an Office Assistant you want to use, click OK. If the Office Assistant you choose isn't already installed, you'll see a message that tells you that the selected Assistant is not currently installed—and you'll be asked if you want to install it. Click Yes. Office XP will begin the installation; you might be prompted to insert your Office XP CD.

Tip

The Office Logo Assistant has the least movement of all the Office Assistants.

Have you tried this?

If the Office Assistant only gets in your way occasionally, you can move it by dragging it. Just point the mouse pointer at the Office Assistant character (not the balloon), press and hold the left mouse button, and move the mouse. Once you have moved the Office Assistant to a nondistracting location, release the mouse button. Be aware that the Office Assistant will only remain in the new location temporarily; eventually, it will move somewhere else on your screen.

My Office program won't let me switch to a different Office Assistant

Source of the problem

This problem can occur in any Office program. Here's the situation.

When you try to switch to a different Office Assistant that you haven't yet installed, you get a message about the Office Assistant being unavailable because macros are set to not allow the Install On First Use feature. You double-check macro security in the application (click Tools, point to Macro, and click Security) and discover that you've already set security to low. In all probability, your problem is being caused by an add-in that is loading when you open your Office program.

How to fix it

You can solve this problem in any of three ways.

You can switch to a different Office application and install and change the Assistant. Once installed and selected, you can use the Assistant in the program where you received the message about macros. See the steps provided in "I want to adjust the behavior of the Office Assistant" on page 42.

You can use your Office XP CD to install the Assistant you want; it will then be available in the program in which you're trying to use it.

1. Quit any Office applications that are running.

2. Insert the Office CD, double-click the Setup program, select the Add Or Remove Features option, and click Next.

3. Click the plus sign next to Office Shared Features.

4. Click the plus sign next to Office Assistant.

5. Click the icon to the left of the Assistant you want to install.

6. Click Run From My Computer. ▶

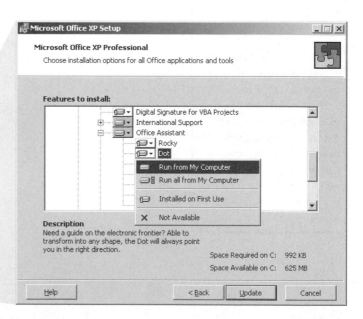

Help

You can also (temporarily or permanently) disable the add-in that is causing the problem. You'll find add-ins loading from one of two locations, and those locations depend on the operating system you're running. Follow these steps to disable add-ins that might be causing your problem:

1. Quit any Office applications that are running.

2. Start Windows Explorer.

3. Regardless of your operating system, find the C:\Program Files\Microsoft Office\Office10\Startup folder and move any files you find in this folder to another folder or rename them (by changing the extension). ▼

4. If you're working in Windows 2000, also look for and move or rename add-in templates in C:\Documents & Settings*UserName*\Application Data\Microsoft*ApplicationName*\ Startup, where *UserName* is your name and *ApplicationName* is the name of the application in which you get the error message. In Excel, the startup folder is named XIstart.

5. After moving or renaming the startup add-ins, restart the program in which you were getting the error and change the Assistant.

6. If you want to re-enable the add-in after installing the Assistant, repeat Steps 1–5. If you moved the add-in, put it back in the appropriate startup folder. If you renamed the add-in, rename it again, using its original extension.

> **Before you start**
>
> In this section, we suggest that you move or rename add-in programs. If you plan to enable the add-in again, be careful to note original names and locations as well as locations where you temporarily place add-ins. If you "lose" them on your computer, you won't be able to re-enable them.

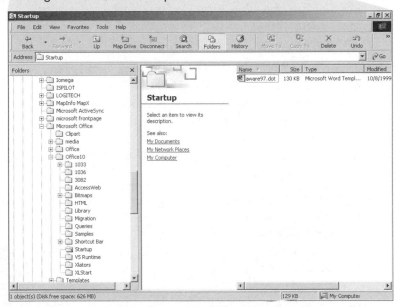

What are add-ins and where do they come from?

Add-ins are templates that load when you open an Office program. You don't need these add-ins to run the Office program, but they might add some functionality to the Office program that will disappear if you disable the add-in permanently. How do you get these add-ins? Add-ins are usually installed when you install another software program or even a printer driver. You might not even realize you've loaded an add-in.

I can't find the Help topic I want in the Office Assistant

Source of the problem

You might not find answers to the questions you type in the Office Assistant balloon. You are not limited to the topics the Office Assistant suggests; other sources of help exist.

How to fix it

Try these steps:

1. If you don't see the Help topic you want on the first screen of the Office Assistant balloon, click See More; if you still don't see what you want, click the link titled None Of The Above, Search For More Help On The Web. A Help window appears and displays the topic Finding Help Topics, which will help you search for additional assistance on the Web.

2. If you want to search the Office application's Help system, type a phrase in the What Would You Like To Do box that appears on the Answer Wizard tab, and then click the Search button. Topics appear in the Select Topic To Display list: double-click one to read about the topic. ▶

3. If you want to search the Web for help, click the Search On Web button. You'll see the same Help pane displayed that you saw after completing Step 1.

Note

If the left pane of the Help window doesn't appear, click the Show button on the Help pane toolbar.

Tip

If you want help narrowing the list of topics in the Help system list, click the Search Tips link that appears in the Help pane immediately after it opens.

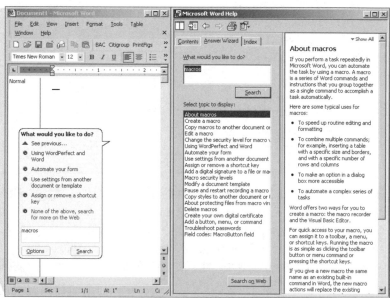

4. In the Finding Help Topics pane, you'll see a text box where you can type a question or send a comment to Microsoft about the Help topic you were trying to find. ▶

5. Click Send And Go To The Web. The topic you entered in the What Would You Like To Do box will be searched on the Web, and any comments you provided in the Finding Help Topics pane will be collected and used by Microsoft to improve future versions of the Help system.

Tip

You can identify other Help topics that are available on the Web by their titles, which will appear in the Answer Wizard in the form WEB: <title>.

Note

A firewall is software that protects the files and programs on one network from users on another network. A proxy server is an Internet server that acts as a firewall and monitors traffic between a protected network and the Internet.

Internet help doesn't seem to be available

If you see a "Page Not Found" message in your browser when you click on a Web-based Help topic, you are probably not connected to the Internet. You will also have trouble visiting the Microsoft Office Tools On The Web site (click the Help menu, and then click Office On The Web) if you are not connected to the Internet. If you are having trouble connecting to the Internet, one of the following might be causing your problem:

- The settings to connect your computer to the Internet might not be correct. To make sure they are, double-click the Internet Options icon in the Microsoft Windows Control Panel and check your settings.

- Your company's firewall or proxy server could be preventing access to this site.

- Your modem might not be working correctly. For more information, run the Modem Troubleshooter in Windows Help (locate it in the Windows Help index).

- The Microsoft Office Web site might be temporarily unavailable. If you can access other Web sites, wait awhile, and then try again. A

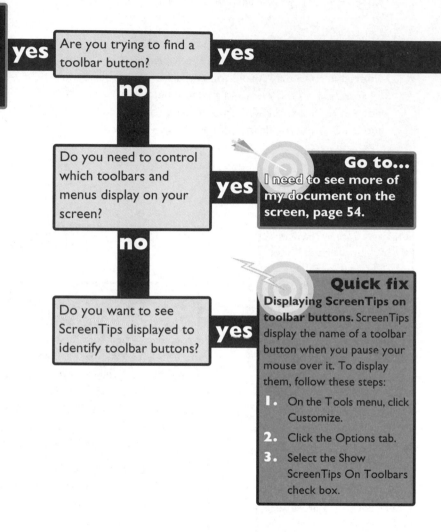

Do you need to control the display of toolbars or menus?

yes

Are you trying to find a toolbar button?

yes

no

Do you need to control which toolbars and menus display on your screen?

yes

Go to...

I need to see more of my document on the screen, page 54.

no

Do you want to see ScreenTips displayed to identify toolbar buttons?

yes

Quick fix

Displaying ScreenTips on toolbar buttons. ScreenTips display the name of a toolbar button when you pause your mouse over it. To display them, follow these steps:

1. On the Tools menu, click Customize.

2. Click the Options tab.

3. Select the Show ScreenTips On Toolbars check box.

Menus and toolbars

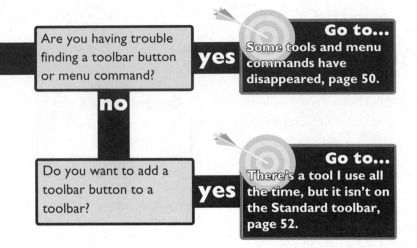

Are you having trouble finding a toolbar button or menu command?

yes → **Go to...** Some tools and menu commands have disappeared, page 50.

no

Do you want to add a toolbar button to a toolbar?

yes → **Go to...** There's a tool I use all the time, but it isn't on the **Standard** toolbar, page 52.

If your solution isn't here, check this related chapter:

● Templates and styles, page 106

Or see the general trouble-shooting tips on page xix.

Some tools and menu commands have disappeared

Source of the problem

Microsoft Office XP has become a candy store full of tasty tools and menu commands. These numerous features reflect the hearty functionality of the programs, but they also create dilemmas. Just as you can't eat every piece of candy in a candy store (well you could, but you'd get *very* sick), you can't have all the tools and menus in an Office program displayed simultaneously and still be able to see your document.

Microsoft has devised a few ways to juggle all these items. Personalized menus were created to initially show only your most frequently used commands. If you open a menu but you don't see the command you want, it might just be temporarily hidden. There's an easy way to check this: if an arrow appears at the bottom of a menu, the menu is not expanded. You can set up Office programs to always display full menus or to display personalized menus initially, but after a few moments expand them.

Office also manages these many tools by placing them on several different toolbars. By default, Office programs only display one or two of the most commonly used toolbars most of the time. Typically, when you initiate a function, such as a mail merge in Word, Office displays the relevant toolbar. However, you can easily display any toolbar whenever you need it.

In addition, you can use the Toolbar Options feature to expand Office toolbars to see temporarily hidden tools, just as you can expand menus to see more commands.

Before you start

There are so many tools available in Office programs that you have to decide which ones to display on your computer screen. Should you choose to display a button that is hidden, be aware that another button will be hidden in its place.

Tip

If you can't find the tool you want, the Microsoft Office program you're working with might not be maximized. Some toolbar buttons will be hidden when your program window isn't maximized. Click the Maximize button to enlarge the program window.

How to fix it

If you open an Office menu and there's an arrow at the bottom, the menu is not fully expanded. To expand an Office menu, follow these steps:

1. Click a menu to display it. ▶

Format	Tools	Table	Window
A	Font...		
三	Paragraph...		
三	Bullets and Numbering...		
	Borders and Shading...		
	Background		▶
	Theme...		
	Styles and Formatting...		
	Reveal Formatting...		
	Object...		
	✕		

Menus and toolbars

2. When the initial menu appears, do any of the following:

- Wait a few seconds, and the entire menu will appear.
- Expand the menu right away by clicking the arrow at the bottom of the menu.
- Double-click the menu to expand it immediately.

To display a toolbar, follow this procedure:

1. On the View menu, click Toolbars.

2. Click the name of the toolbar you want to display. ▶

To see more buttons on a toolbar that's already displayed, follow these steps:

1. Click the Toolbar Options arrow at the end of the toolbar. ▼

2. Click the menu item you want.

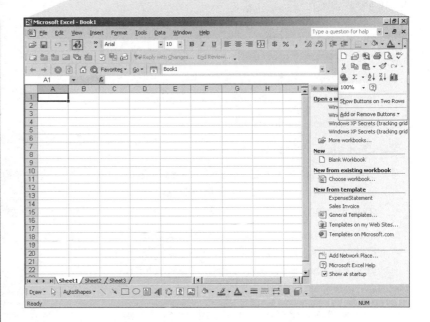

There's a tool I use all the time, but it isn't on the Standard toolbar

Source of the problem

Imagine you were handed the cash to build your own dream workshop. You could include any tools and equipment you like, from a high-end table saw to the finest woodworking tools. Now imagine you could do the same thing with your computing environment. As a matter of fact, in Office XP you *can* modify application toolbars by assembling the commands you find most useful. Office allows you to add commands to any toolbar by using a Customize feature.

How to fix it

You can add any available tool to any toolbar using the Office Customize feature. To customize a toolbar, follow these steps:

1. On the View menu, point to Toolbar, and click the toolbar for which you want to add a toolbar button.

2. On the Tools menu, click Customize.

3. Click the Commands tab.

4. Select an item in the Categories list that contains the command you want to add to the toolbar you're customizing. ▶

5. In the Commands list, drag the button you want to add to the toolbar you're customizing. You can drag each button to the location you prefer on the toolbar.

6. Repeat this procedure to add additional tools.

7. Click OK when you're done to close the Customize dialog box.

Before you start

Making any changes to menus or toolbars can be potentially dangerous: some of the advice from Office Help can be rendered incorrect relative to features you've reconfigured to work differently from the default functionality. Also, anybody else using your Office program might be confused by the nonstandard components on your toolbars and menus.

Tip

Another way to open the Customize dialog box is to right-click a displayed toolbar that you want to customize, and then click the Customize command that appears at the bottom of the menu.

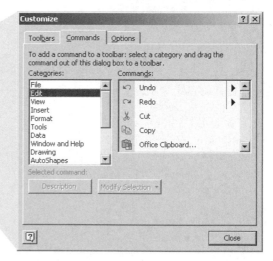

Menus and toolbars

Note

If you make changes to toolbars or menus and want to return them to their original settings, you can do so by clicking View, Toolbars, Customize. On the Toolbars tab of the Customize dialog box, click the name of the toolbar, and then click Reset.

Deleting tools from toolbars

You can also delete tools you don't want to appear on a toolbar. Display the toolbar you want to modify, and then follow either of these methods:

- Click the Toolbar Options button at the toolbar's right edge, and then click Add Or Remove Buttons. Select the toolbar you want to modify from the submenu that appears. All the buttons on the toolbar are displayed. Clear the check mark for each button you want to delete from the toolbar.

- Alternatively, you can display the toolbar you want to modify, right-click it, and choose Customize from the menu that appears. Drag any buttons you don't want off the toolbar.

I need to see more of my document on the screen

Source of the problem

When you think about it, there's only so much real estate available on your computer screen into which you can cram your document as well as all the toolbars, menus, rulers, scrollbars... well, you get the idea. If you want to see more of your document, you can use the Zoom feature to zoom out and see more on a page. However, this feature shrinks your text and graphics, and there are times when you need to see everything at its full size. What do you do?

At those times when you want to be able to see more of an actual document and less of the features Office programs offer to work with a document, you have several options:

- You can remove some toolbars from your display.

- You can combine two rows of tools into one.

- In Word and Excel, you can change to a Full Screen view, which removes toolbars and menus entirely.

Before you start

Removing toolbars and menus allows you to see more of your document, but can result in useful tools being moved out of sight. Still, being able to manipulate the elements of your display provides great flexibility as you work.

Note

Of course, you can also use the Print Preview feature to see more of your document on screen, but you can't make changes to the contents of a document from this view.

How to fix it

To remove a toolbar from your display, follow these steps:

1. Right-click any displayed toolbar.

2. From the list of toolbars that appears, click the one you want to hide to remove it from your screen (the check mark will disappear).

3. Repeat Steps 1 and 2 for each toolbar you want to hide. ▶

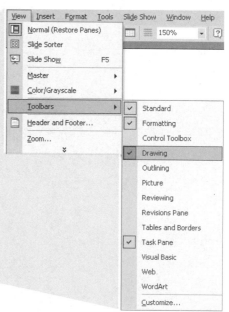

Menus and toolbars

Most Office programs include a Standard and a Formatting toolbar. The Standard toolbar typically includes tools for working with a document, such as saving a file, cutting and pasting text, and so on. A Formatting toolbar contains tools to format text and graphics. You can display all of these commonly used toolbar buttons in one row instead of two. Do so using this procedure:

1. Display both toolbars on screen by right-clicking either toolbar and making sure that both Standard and Formatting toolbars are selected.

2. Click the Toolbar Options button at the right edge of either toolbar.

3. Click Show Buttons On One Row. ▶

4. If you want to access more tools than will fit on your screen, click the Toolbar Options arrow again, and all the hidden buttons become available to you.

Displaying your document using the Full Screen view in Word or Excel is a breeze. Here's how:

1. On the View menu, click Full Screen. All your toolbars and menus disappear. ▶

2. To return to the regular display, press Escape or click the floating Close Full Screen button.

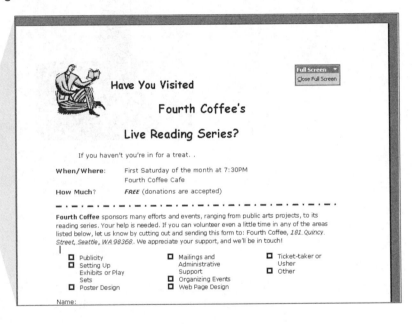

Note

To see more of your document in PowerPoint, you can close the Outline and Slides display on the left side of the screen in Normal view, and then close any open task panes to see more of your slides.

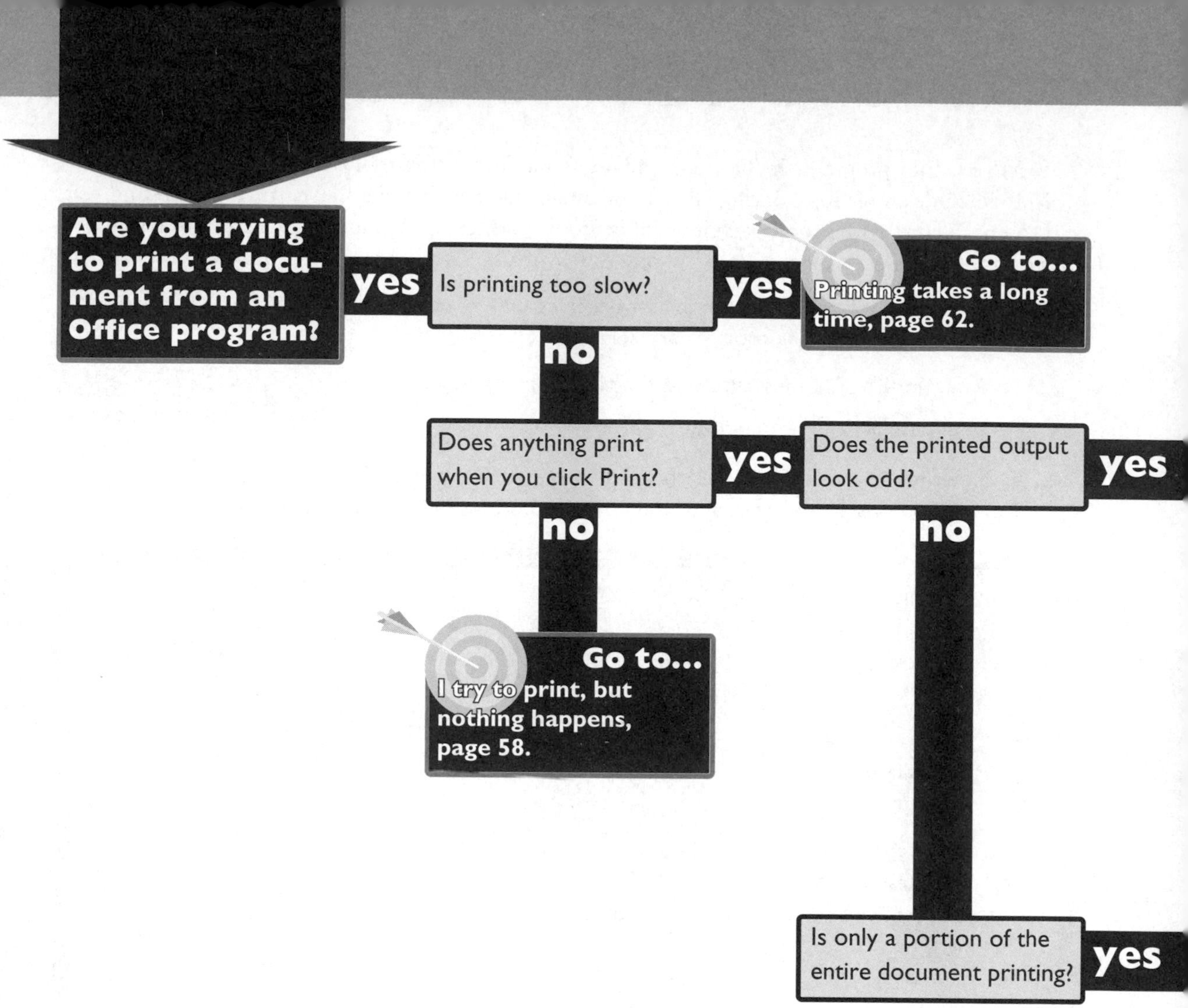

Are you trying to print a document from an Office program? yes → **Is printing too slow?** yes → **Go to...** Printing takes a long time, page 62.

no ↓

Does anything print when you click Print? yes → **Does the printed output look odd?** yes →

no ↓

Go to... I try to print, but nothing happens, page 58.

Does the printed output look odd? no ↓

Is only a portion of the entire document printing? yes →

Does text run off the page of the printed document?

yes

Go to... When I print, the text runs all the way to the edge of the paper, page 60.

no

Quick fix

Changing page orientation. You can print with either a landscape or portrait orientation, essentially controlling which direction across the paper document elements appear. To change the page orientation, follow these steps:

1. On the File menu, click Page Setup.

2. Each Office application has a slightly different Page Setup dialog box. Click the setting for either Landscape or Portrait orientation.

3. Click OK to accept the new setting.

Does text run across the page in the wrong direction?

yes

Quick fix

Selecting what to print. If you choose to print only the current page of a document, or selected text, the entire document will not print. Try this:

1. On the File menu, click Print.

2. In the Print dialog box, make sure that All is selected for the Print Range.

3. Click OK to print the entire document.

If your solution isn't here, check these related chapters:

- Printing (PowerPoint), page 350
- Printing (Word), page 462

Or see the general troubleshooting tips on page xix.

I try to print, but nothing happens

Source of the problem

Printing from your computer can be very complex because there are so many components involved—the printer itself, print drivers you install on your hard disk, cables that run from your computer to your printer, and connections to printers on your network. The settings you make to print a specific document in software such as Office applications might need some tweaking.

You should first check each of the following connections and settings to determine if in fact you do have a problem:

- Make sure your printer is turned on and is on line. There might be a button on the printer labeled "Online" that you should press.

- Check both ends of the cable that runs between your computer and printer to make sure the connections are tight.

- Check to see that the printer has paper. (Okay, this seems obvious, but we've all made this mistake!)

- Check the status of your print job in the Microsoft Windows Printers folder (from the Windows Start menu click Settings, Printers).

- Try printing another document. If that document prints, the problem might have something to do with the content of your first document (for example, your printer might not have enough memory to print very large graphic files).

- If you're printing over a network, you'll probably have to check with your network administrator to make sure your computer is configured to print to the designated printer. You may think you can't print only to discover that all your documents printed out—not once but seven times—to the printer three floors up.

If all these connections and settings are okay, it's time to check a few settings in your Office software.

Before you start

Printing problems can be caused by the printer itself, the connection from your printer to your computer, printer settings in Windows, or choices you make in the software you're printing a document from. You need to invest some time getting all of these components set up correctly. Make a note of these settings so you can duplicate them if you ever need to in the future.

Tip

If the printer you want to print to isn't listed in the Name list, it means the printer hasn't been set up on your computer. In Windows, on the Start menu click Settings, then Printers. Click the Add A Printer icon and follow the steps of the wizard. You might be asked to insert the Windows 2000 CD or provide a driver from your printer manufacturer during this process. When the wizard is completed, the printer will appear in the Print dialog box in the Name list.

How to fix it

Although you set the default printer for all your printing jobs in Windows, you can also choose a printer from the Print dialog box in your software program each time you print. Follow these steps to check your printer settings:

1. Open the document you want to print, click the File menu, and then click Print. The Print dialog box essentially looks like the one shown here in Excel. ▶

2. In the Printer section at the top of the dialog box, make sure that the Print To File check box is cleared. If the check box is selected, your document will not print to a printer, but will instead be saved to a file.

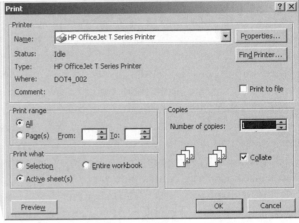

3. Check which printer is selected in the Name list in the Printer area. If the wrong printer is listed, click the arrow to display other printer choices, and click the one you want. If the correct printer is selected, click the Properties button to make sure it's set up properly. ▶

4. The items you see in the Printer Properties dialog box will vary somewhat depending on the printer you're working with. Make sure that the paper size and orientation are appropriate for your document, and then select or clear other settings as needed, such as two-sided printing or color management settings for a color printer.

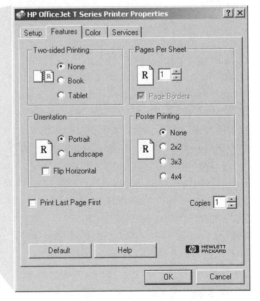

5. Click OK to apply your settings. Click OK again in the Print dialog box to print your document.

Have you tried this?

If your computer is connected to a network, the Find Printer button in the Print dialog box will help you view the printers available on the network and show which one you're currently set up to print to.

When I print, the text runs all the way to the edge of the paper

Source of the problem

We've all been through it: you print out a page or two (or 60) of a document and find that half the document text disappeared somewhere along the way. If text runs off the edge of the paper when you print, there could be two sources of the problem. First, the wrong printer might be selected. See the previous solution in this chapter for help with setting up your printer. Second, your page setup might be incorrect.

If you make a change to the margins or page orientation that causes text to fall outside of the printable area, a warning message is displayed, which allows you to click a button labeled Fix to fix this problem. If you click the Ignore button instead, your problematic settings will remain as is, and the text will be omitted from the printed document.

To fix this problem, check the orientation of the pages in your document. Portrait orientation prints with the shorter part of the page across the top and bottom similar to a painted portrait: portrait is the orientation used in standard business letter format. Landscape orientation prints sideways, with the longer sides of the paper across the top and bottom as with many landscape paintings. Spreadsheets and slides often work better when printed in landscape format.

You could also have a problem with the margin settings. If you reduced the size of the margins to accommodate more text on your page, some of the text might have shifted from the printable area of a page. Because most printers cannot print right to the edge of the paper, some text might be cut off.

How to fix it

To check these settings, you need to view the Page Setup dialog box in your Office program.

1. Open the document you want to print.

2. Click the File menu, and then click Page Setup. The Page Setup dialog box varies slightly in each of the Office products. For example, notice that settings for margins are on the Margins tab in Word and on the Paper tab in Outlook. To do this in Outlook, you click Page Setup, and then choose a style to open the Page Setup dialog box. ▶

3. The printable area varies depending on your printer, but try to make sure your margins allow for at least a half inch of space on the top, bottom, right, and left sides (with PowerPoint, you will work with slide height and width settings). If you need to make changes, use the spinner arrows or type a new value in the margin fields to reset margins to a larger size.

4. Make sure the paper size you're printing to matches the size of the paper in your printer. Close the Page Setup dialog box by clicking OK.

5. You should also view your document in Print Preview to see if any text is out of the printable area. Once again, Print Preview offers slightly different tools in different Office programs; for example, in Word there's a ruler to adjust margins, and in PowerPoint, there's a selection to Scale To Fit Paper.

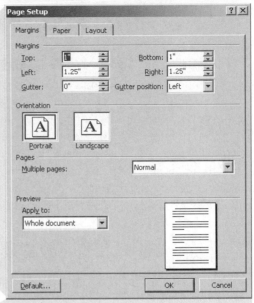

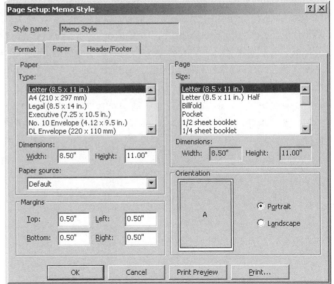

Note

Check the margins you've set manually in your Word documents by dragging the margin icon on the horizontal ruler. This will also cause the margin settings in your Page Setup dialog box to reflect the change.

Printing takes a long time

Source of the problem

Have you noticed that as you get older getting out the door is slower because you have to remember where you put your car keys, where you set down your wallet, and whether you left the bathtub running? Just as our faulty memories might slow us down, when you find that printing documents is slow, there could be a memory glitch at the root of the problem. Your computer uses a certain amount of memory to run applications such as your operating system and the various software programs installed. If you don't have enough memory to access and handle all the processes running, printing can be slow.

If you are using a feature called Background Printing, it could also use up some memory and cause your documents to print as fast as a tortoise running uphill. With Background Printing enabled, you can continue to work on your computer while printing is taking place. The trade-off you face is either having to sit twiddling your thumbs while your document prints, or working and waiting a longer stretch for your printer to finish the document. Even if you're not working with any software or making any demands on your computer while printing is taking place, with Background Printing turned on, you'll experience slower printing than with it turned off.

When it comes to finding your car keys, I can't help you. But when it comes to speeding up your printing, we have a few suggestions. However, keep in mind that all hardware comes with its own capabilities and limitations. If you're using a color inkjet printer, it will take much longer to print a color document than a laser printer because of the way it's designed.

How to fix it

To disable Background Printing in Word or PowerPoint, follow these steps:

1. On the Tools menu, click Options.

2. Click the Print tab (this figure shows the Options dialog box in PowerPoint). ▶

3. Clear the Background Printing check box.

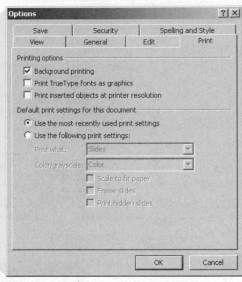

To check the amount of free disk space on your computer (your hard disk should have at least 2 MB of free space), follow these steps:

1. Double-click the My Computer icon on your Windows desktop.

2. Click the drive you want to check (probably Drive C). The amount of free space appears in the status bar along the bottom of the screen. ▶

Tip

You might be able to free up enough memory to print faster by simply closing some programs. If you have a lot of programs open, this uses a great deal of random access memory (RAM), causing processes like printing to be slower.

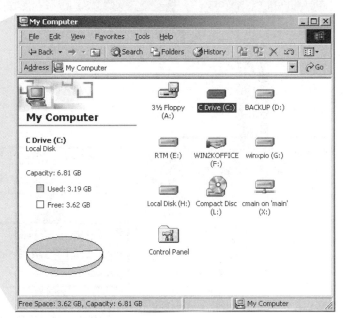

Are you having trouble collaborating on a Team Web Site?

yes

Does your Office program freeze?

yes

no

Are you having trouble e-mailing an Office XP document for review?

yes

Are you having trouble selecting the right e-mail command?

yes

no

Are you having trouble identifying reviewers?

yes

Is the reviewer's name "unknown"?

yes

no

Does the reviewer's name disappear when you save?

yes

no

Do changes seem to be missing from your document?

yes

Are changes missing from your Word document?

yes

no

Are changes missing from your PowerPoint presentation?

yes

no

Are changes missing from your Excel worksheet?

yes

no

Are changes missing from the Excel History worksheet?

yes

Quick fix

I don't see changes in a PowerPoint presentation. Only the creator of a PowerPoint presentation sees marked changes.

Reviewing changes

Go to...
My Office program stops responding when I try to collaborate on a document, page 66.

Go to...
I don't know which command to use to e-mail a document, spreadsheet, or presentation, page 68.

Quick fix
The reviewer's name is "unknown." The reviewer hasn't filled out the User Information tab or the General tab of the Options dialog box.

Quick fix
The reviewer's name disappears when you save. Clear the Remove Personal Information From This File On Save check box on the Security tab of the Options dialog box.

Go to...
Changes made in my Word document are not being tracked, page 70.

Go to...
No changes appear in my Excel workbook, even though I turned on Track Changes, page 72.

Go to...
Changes don't appear on the History worksheet, page 74.

If your solution isn't here, check these related chapters:

- Protecting workbooks, page 184
- Sharing workbooks, page 194

Or see the general trouble-shooting tips on page xix.

My Office program stops responding when I try to collaborate on a document

Source of the problem

Using Office XP, you can share documents using the Web Discussions feature and SharePoint Team Services. All users with discussion permissions can open and attach comments to any Word, PowerPoint, or Excel document. You attach comments using the Web Discussions toolbar, which is available in Word, Excel, PowerPoint, and Internet Explorer. In Word, PowerPoint, and Excel, you display the Web Discussions toolbar by clicking the Tools menu, pointing to Online Collaboration, and clicking Web Discussions. In Internet Explorer, click the Discuss button on the toolbar. ▶

Office programs will stop responding if you attempt to use Secure Sockets Layer (SSL) to connect to a SharePoint Team Services–based Web site when the SharePoint server does not have SSL enabled. For example, your Office programs will hang if you attempt to open a location similar to *https://sharepoint/myserver*.

The Office program stops responding because the server is not expecting you to use SSL. When you use SSL, the server waits for your program to send more information.

How to fix it

Try to connect without using SSL. For example, instead of using a location such as *https://sharepoint/myserver*, use a location such as *http://sharepoint/myserver*.

Reviewing changes

Note

You aren't limited to one Shared Document library; you can create as many as you want.

A little background about collaboration on a Team Web Site

Web Discussions occur on a Team Web Site that is created using SharePoint Team Services, a tool you can install from your Office XP CD. Essentially, SharePoint Team Services lets you create a SharePoint Team Web Site directly from your Office XP programs without writing any HTML code because SharePoint Team Services automatically creates and maintains the site navigation links for you.

The Team Web Site home page contains five lists: Announcements, Events, Tasks, Contacts, and Links—all items that users in the same organization might want to share. It also contains one Shared Document library, where users can upload documents for others to view and edit. Similarly, users with privileges can open and edit documents in shared document libraries.

When a user makes a change to a document in a document library, the owner of the document—the person who uploaded it to the Team Web Site—can receive an e-mail notification that the document has been modified.

If you prefer, you can place restrictions on the document, so that users can view and make comments about a document but not actually edit the document.

To use an established Team Web Site, you need the address of the site, which you can get from your system administrator, and you need Internet Explorer 4 or later, or Netscape Navigator 4 or later.

I don't know which command to use to e-mail a document, spreadsheet, or presentation

Source of the problem

In Excel, PowerPoint, and Word, you'll find several commands on the Send To menu; at first glance, it might be difficult to decide which one to use to get the results you want. The command you choose depends on the actions you want to take.

Be aware that you must be using a MAPI-compliant e-mail program such as Outlook, Outlook Express, or Microsoft Exchange for these commands to function. (MAPI stands for Messaging Application Programming Interface.)

How to fix it

You'll find all the commands you use to e-mail Office documents by following these steps:

1. Click File.

2. Click Send To. ▶

Both the Mail Recipient (For Review) command and the Mail Recipient (As Attachment) command launch your e-mail program and attach the open document to an e-mail message. ▶

There is only one difference between these two commands: you'll see a message in the body of the e-mail if you choose the Mail Recipient (For Review) command. If you choose the Mail Recipient (As Attachment) command, the body of the message will appear blank.

Word and Excel contain an additional command listed as simply Mail Recipient, which you use to send your

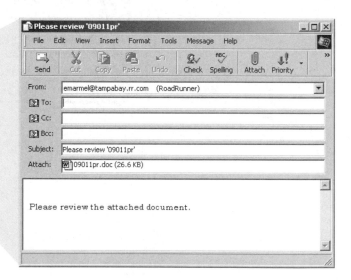

document or spreadsheet as the body of the e-mail message. When you choose this command, the Office XP application adds e-mail header information to the document that you complete. ▶

When you click the Send A Copy button, your e-mail application sends the document; on the screen in the application, the e-mail header information disappears.

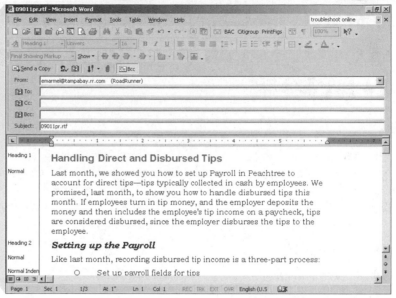

Use the Routing Recipient command on the File menu's Send To menu when you want to send your file to a group of reviewers instead of just one reviewer. When you click the Routing Recipient command, you'll see a Routing Slip box. You use a Routing Slip to provide e-mail addresses for reviewers (when you click the Address button, you'll see the contents of your e-mail address book), give instructions to the reviewers, and decide whether you want to send the file to one reviewer after another or to all reviewers at once. ▶

Changes made in my Word document are not being tracked

Source of the problem

This problem can have several sources. You first need to make sure that Word is tracking changes. Next, you might need to switch to a different view to see the changes that were made to a document. Also, you might have filtering applied. Or, there might be so many balloons on the screen that you can't see all of the tracked changes and comments in the document.

Microsoft Word does not track the following items:

● AutoCaptions

● Background color

● Embedded fonts

● Routing information

● Some types of mail merge information, such as whether a file is a main document or a data file

● Some custom options or commands, such as custom toolbar buttons

Word tracks changes to the formatting and position of pictures and shapes by showing the picture or shape as a deleted and reinserted item.

How to fix it

When the Track Changes feature is enabled, TRK appears black on the status bar at the bottom of your document. When you disable Track Changes, TRK appears dimmed.

To enable Track Changes, follow these steps:

1. Click Tools.

2. Click Track Changes.

To view changes and comments, use either Web Layout view or Print Layout view. Using the buttons that appear at the bottom of your document to the left of the horizontal scroll bar, click the second or third button from the left. (If you turned off the horizontal scroll bar, click the correct view from the View menu.) ▶

> **Tip**
> You can double-click TRK in the status bar to turn tracking on and off.

and folders that reside
offline), not from the

Page 3   Sec 1   3/10

Reviewing changes

To remove any filter-ing that you might have applied and reveal changes, follow these steps:

1. If the Reviewing toolbar is not visible, click the View menu, point to Toolbars, and click Reviewing.

2. On the left side of the Reviewing toolbar, in the Display For Review box, click Original Showing Markup or Final Showing Markup. ▶

3. Click the Show button on the Reviewing toolbar, and then select the items that you want to display. ▶

If you have too many balloons on your screen and you're having trouble seeing everything, click the Reviewing Pane button to open the Reviewing pane at the bottom of the screen, and scroll through all of the changes and comments.

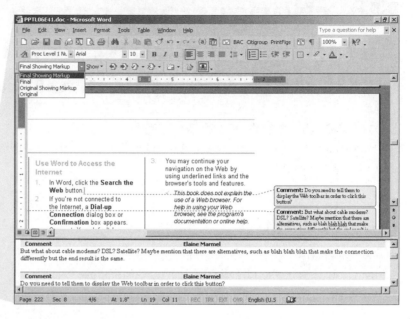

Why doesn't the text in balloons look like the text I changed in my document?

Microsoft Word ignores formatting elements when it displays inserted or deleted text in a balloon to make the text easier to read. Basically all the text you see in a balloon is controlled by the Balloon Text style. If that style is set to use, for example, a 10-point font, any text that you insert or delete will appear in that 10-point font in the balloon regardless of the font you used to make the actual insertion or deletion. You'll also notice that centered or indented text in the body of the document is shown left-aligned in the balloons. To see inserted or deleted text with all of its formatting attributes, view the text in the Reviewing pane at the bottom of the document screen.

No changes appear in my Excel workbook, even though I turned on Track Changes

Source of the problem

You might not see changes in an Excel workbook because of the settings you chose in the Highlight Changes dialog box.

How to fix it

To view all changes made to the workbook, use the following settings in the Highlight Changes box. Follow these steps:

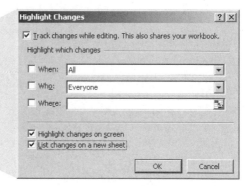

1. Click Tools.

2. Click Track Changes.

3. Click Highlight Changes.

4. Make sure that the Track Changes While Editing check box is selected.

5. Select the When check box and set its option (in the list at the right) to All. The Since I Last Saved option shows only those changes made after you last saved the workbook.

6. Select the Who check box and set its option to Everyone. You won't see your own changes if you choose Everyone But Me.

7. Leave the Where check box cleared. If you want to track changes only for a specific range, select the Where check box, and then select the workbook range to view the changes made to that range.

8. Select the Highlight Changes On Screen check box. Excel places a triangle in the upper-left corner of changed cells. When you move the mouse pointer over the cell, Excel displays information about the change. ▶

Tip

You can find recalculated cells by using the Auditing toolbar.

Excel doesn't track all changes

You might not see certain changes because Excel doesn't track all changes. For example, Excel doesn't track the fact that you inserted a worksheet, but Excel will track subsequent changes to the inserted worksheet. And, although Excel doesn't high-light changes to worksheet names, you'll see the change tracked in the History worksheet. And, because Excel updates the History worksheet only *after* you save changes, you can highlight changes as you make them, but don't expect to see them in the History worksheet until you've saved the work-book. By default, Excel doesn't track rows or columns that you hide or unhide, formatting changes that you make to cells, comments you add or change, or cells that are recalculated by formulas.

Changes don't appear on the History worksheet

Source of the problem

The History worksheet contains the changes Excel tracks when you turn on Track Changes. There are several reasons why you might not see changes on the History worksheet.

How to fix it

If you've turned on Track Changes and don't see the History worksheet, save the workbook. Excel won't create the History worksheet until *after* you save the workbook. To view the History worksheet, follow these steps after turning on Track Changes, making changes, and then saving the workbook:

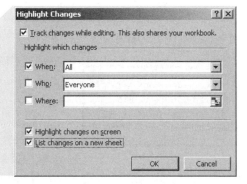

1. Click Tools.

2. Click Track Changes.

3. Click Highlight Changes. ▶

4. Select the List Changes On A New Sheet check box.

5. Click OK to see the History sheet tab.

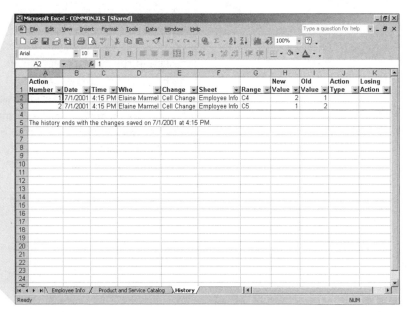

The next time you save the workbook in which you're tracking changes, Excel deletes the History worksheet so that the information won't be out of date. Redisplay it by repeating the preceding steps. ▶

Reviewing changes

If you see the History worksheet, but it doesn't contain all the changes you've made, check the following:

● Review your highlight settings. These settings control the changes that appear on the History worksheet.

● Make sure that other users editing the same workbook have saved their changes.

Excel keeps change history for the last 30 days by default. You can increase or decrease this number by following these steps:

1. Click Tools.

2. Click Share Workbook.

3. Click the Advanced tab. ▶

4. Increase or decrease the number of days in the Keep Change History For box.

I want to format the History worksheet

The History worksheet is only available for viewing; you cannot format or edit it. However, you can copy the history to a new worksheet, and then edit or format the new worksheet.

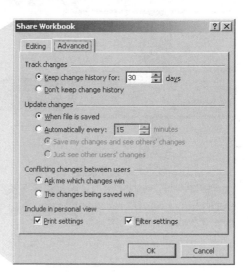

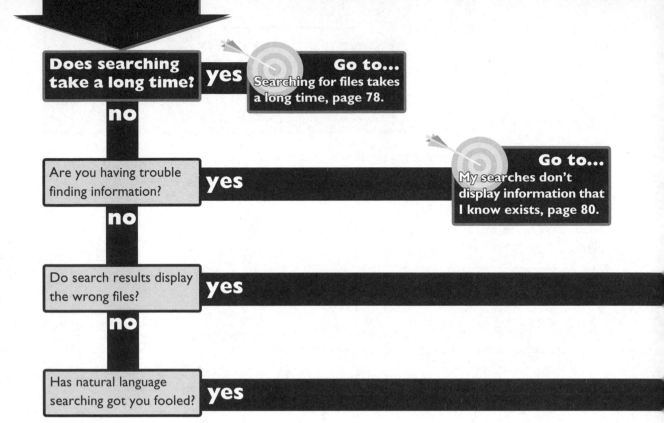

Does searching take a long time? **yes** Go to... Searching for files takes a long time, page 78.

no

Are you having trouble finding information? **yes** Go to... My searches don't display information that I know exists, page 80.

no

Do search results display the wrong files? **yes**

no

Has natural language searching got you fooled? **yes**

Go to...
When I search, I don't find the files I expect to find, page 82.

Go to...
I don't understand how to use natural language searching, page 84.

If your solution isn't here, check this related chapter:

● Text editing, page 482

Or see the general trouble-shooting tips on page xix.

Searching for files takes a long time

Source of the problem

You use the Search command to find files on your computer's hard disk, your local network server, and on any computer available on your network. You can also find specific e-mail messages, meetings, and other information in your Microsoft Outlook mailbox. Your searches might be taking a long time because you're not effectively using the Fast Searching feature that comes with Office XP.

Fast Searching takes information from files and organizes it in a way that makes the files quicker and easier to find—a process called *indexing* files. Once you install and enable Fast Searching, you can specify folders to index, update or delete the index, and view the status of the index.

How to fix it

Fast Searching is an Office XP feature that you must install.

You can tell if Fast Searching is installed by checking its status in the Office XP Basic Search task pane (on the File menu, click Search to display this task pane). If Fast Searching is installed, its status—enabled or disabled—is displayed.

Although Fast Searching is enabled by default when it is installed, it might have been disabled on the computer you are using. To enable Fast Searching, click Search Options in the Basic Search task pane; the Indexing Service Settings dialog box appears; click Yes, Enable Indexing Service And Run When My Computer Is Idle.

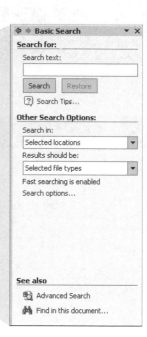

To enable Fast Searching, follow these steps:

1. Click Start.

2. Click Search.

3. Click For Files Or Folders.

4. Click the Search Options link to open the Search Options box.

5. Click the Indexing Service link.

6. Click Yes, Enable Indexing Service And Run When My Computer Is Idle. ▶

7. Click OK.

Once you have installed and enabled Fast Searching, you can set a variety of attributes about the information you want indexed. You can specify the folders to index, update an index, and delete an index.

Open the Search Results window by clicking the Start button, pointing to Search, and clicking For Files Or Folders. In the Search Options box, select the Date, Type, Size, and Advanced Options check boxes to display and set additional parameters for each option. ▶

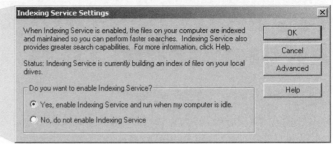

My searches don't display information that I know exists

Source of the problem

You might not find files because of the way you search. Office XP contains two search panes to help you find information, and each has its own use.

The Basic Search task pane provides you with the most comprehensive way to search for text in files, Outlook items, and Web pages. You can search for certain text in the title, contents, or properties of files. You can also specify where to look for files and the types of files for which you want to search. The Advanced Search task pane helps you set up a more specific search to find files based on their properties, using one or more rules that must be true of files found in the search. If searching in one pane doesn't find the information you are looking for, try using the other pane.

How to fix it

When you search for a file or Outlook item containing specific text, use the Basic Search task pane, and type the text for which you want to search into the Search Text box. You can type a question mark (?) to match any single character in your search text, or type an asterisk (*) to match any number of characters. For example, p?t finds "pat," "pet," "pit," "pot," and "put;" s*d finds "sad," "sand," "started," "sound," or "send." To broaden the search, click Everywhere in the Search In box; to limit search locations, click one or more drives, folders, Web sites, or Outlook mailboxes. To find all types of files, Web pages, and Outlook items, click Anything in the Results Should Be box. To limit the types of search results, select the types of items to find in the Results Should Be box. ▶

Using the Advanced Search task pane, you can use conditions and values to search for files based on the files' properties. In the Basic Search task pane, click Advanced Search. Click a property, one or more conditions, and, if appropriate, enter a value for the condition.

Conditions are limitations you set on a file property; setting conditions makes your search more specific. Each type of property has a predefined set of relevant conditions from which you choose. For example, if you click a date property, you'll see, among other condition choices, "today," "tomorrow," and "yesterday."

> **Tip**
>
> When searching for Outlook items, use conversational language, such as "Find all e-mail from Ned Smith."

When you use the Advanced Search task pane, set one or more of the following search criteria: ▶

- Click a property in the Property list or type in a property name.

- Click a condition in the Condition list.

- In the Value box, type the value for the condition. Not all conditions require a value.

- If previous search criteria exist, click And to add a criterion that must be true in addition to previous criteria. Click Or to include a criterion that is independent of any other specified criteria. "And" limits your search, whereas "Or" expands your search.

- Click Add to add the search criterion. If the value is invalid for the condition or property, the Add button is unavailable.

You can open the Search task pane in Office applications other than Outlook and search for files that match the criteria you set up; the search results are available from any application. For example, if you search for files of all types from Microsoft Excel, and you open a Microsoft PowerPoint presentation from the Search Results list, the search results also appear in the PowerPoint Search task pane so that you can continue using them. As soon as you start a search, the Search task pane begins listing the names of files it finds. Files are displayed separately by location: your computer, your mailbox, and your network.

From the results list, you can take any of the following actions on the files you find:

- Open a file

- View a file in a Web browser (if the file type is supported)

- View a file's properties

- Create a new document based on a file

- Copy a hyperlink to a file to the Office Clipboard

When I search, I don't find the files I expect to find

Source of the problem

You might see files you don't expect to see when searching, or you might not see files you do expect to see when you perform a search. The wrong files might appear for any of the following reasons:

- You might have accidentally set criteria that exclude the file, or you might have set criteria that are too general and include too many files

- You might be searching an unsupported type of Web folder

- The Fast Searching index might be out of date

How to fix it

By setting too many criteria, you can miss files when searching. Double-check your search criteria and, if possible, remove some criteria to broaden the search. For example, if you can't find a certain file type, set the Results Should Be field in the Basic Search task pane to Anything.

If you are searching a Web folder, be aware that Office can't support all types of Web folders. You can search for Web folders that are SharePoint Team Web Sites, Web folders on your local network, Web folders on a Microsoft SharePoint Portal Server, or Web folders that point to a shared file where Indexing Service is installed.

Typically, you have no need to manually update the Fast Searching index in Windows 2000 and Windows XP because it updates automatically. However, you might want to update the Fast Searching index manually if you edited an exception word list or added a new language. Follow these steps:

1. Click Start.

2. Click Settings.

3. Click Control Panel.

4. Double-click Administrative Tools.

5. Double-click Computer Management. ▶

6. Click the plus sign next to Services And Applications.

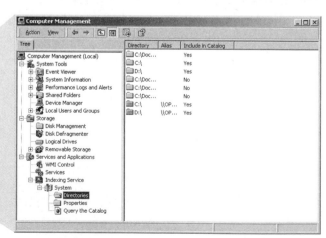

7. Click the plus sign next to Indexing Service, and then the plus sign next to System.

8. Click Directories.

9. In the right pane of the window, click the directory you want to scan.

10. On the Action menu, point to All Tasks.

11. Click Rescan (Full) or Rescan (Incremental).

I don't understand how to use natural language searching

Source of the problem

Natural language searching uses recognizable, common expressions. For example, you can search Microsoft Outlook items from the Basic Search task pane using queries such as "All mail from Nancy" or "All completed tasks." You can use natural language searching to find Outlook e-mail messages, contacts, calendar items, tasks, and notes. You can also search for Word, Excel, and PowerPoint files using natural language phrases—which is particularly useful when you can't remember the name of the document but you do remember what it was about. Natural language searching is only supported in English versions of Microsoft Office XP.

Typically, you can get better results by including more information in your natural language queries. But natural language queries give you more freedom, because you don't need to use full sentences or worry about grammar. For example, "office move" is a perfectly acceptable natural language query.

Natural language queries search the contents of items, such as the bodies of documents, worksheets, presentations, or e-mail messages, along with items' properties, such as the number of pages, the template, and the status of tasks.

How to fix it

You can improve the results you get with natural language searches by ensuring that your natural language search text is clear, not vague. For example, "March" could be a person's last name or a month, and April, May, and June could be a woman's first name or a month. If you're searching for files from the month of April, include enough additional information so that files containing information about women named April are excluded, for example "month of April."

Be careful not to use "and" or "or" in your query in a way that will not work. For example, the query "E-mail from John or Mary" will work, whereas the query "E-mail from Ben or about holidays" won't work. In general, use "and" or "or" to separate possible values for the same field. In the first example, John and Mary are both people from whom you might have received e-mail. In the second example, Ben is a person, but "about holidays" is not a person.

The same caution applies to using "not." Use "not" in a natural language search only as part of a property name, like "All tasks that are not started." But don't try to use "not" in a natural language search to find all tasks except tasks related to a particular project.

Outlook has some particular notes. For example, Outlook does not recognize team roles, so a natural language query of "All mail from the project coordinator" won't return any results. Also, you can't use natural language searching in Outlook public folders.

Natural language search tips

- Don't worry about grammar or try to write sentences when you search. Search using phrases like "messages about sales" or "office move."

- To limit your search and produce fewer search results, you can specify time ranges such as "in the last week" or "in the month of June." You also can specify the folders to search using the Search In list.

- You can control the order of the search results if you specify the order in which you want results returned. In your query, use phrases such as "Show me tasks in progress sorted by oldest date first."

- You can search the properties and other fields of e-mail messages and documents. For example, you can search for recipients of e-mail messages using phrases like "Who received the Office Move message?" Or, you can search file names for phrases like "office move."

- In Outlook, you can search for contacts based on details that you'll find listed on the Details tab when you edit a contact. And, you can search for notes based on properties such as contents, color, or subject and meetings based on who attended.

- Use quotation marks to keep a phrase together. For example, you might enter, "Show me all messages about the "office move" that I sent this week."

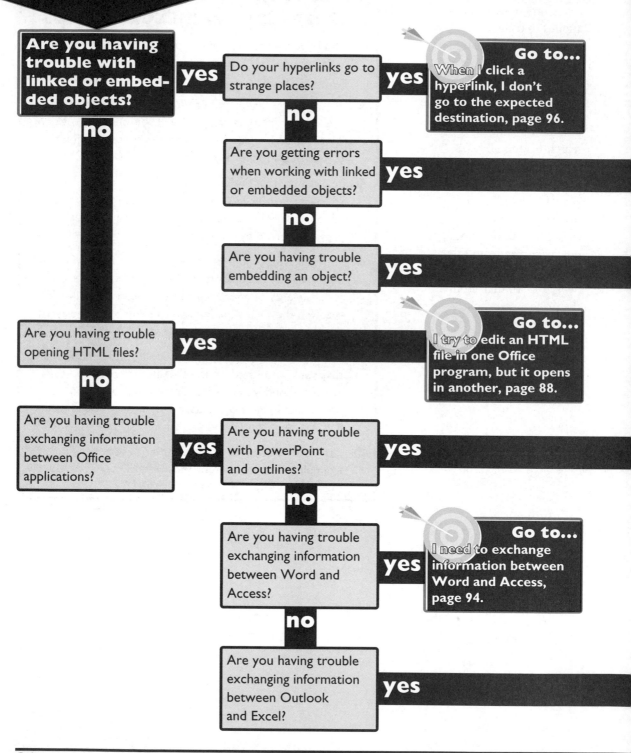

Are you having trouble with linked or embedded objects?

yes → Do your hyperlinks go to strange places?

> **yes** → **Go to...** When I click a hyperlink, I don't go to the expected destination, page 96.

> **no** ↓

Are you getting errors when working with linked or embedded objects? **yes**

no ↓

Are you having trouble embedding an object? **yes**

no ↓ (from main)

Are you having trouble opening HTML files? **yes** →

> **Go to...** I try to edit an HTML file in one Office program, but it opens in another, page 88.

no ↓

Are you having trouble exchanging information between Office applications? **yes** → Are you having trouble with PowerPoint and outlines? **yes**

no ↓

Are you having trouble exchanging information between Word and Access? **yes** →

> **Go to...** I need to exchange information between Word and Access, page 94.

no ↓

Are you having trouble exchanging information between Outlook and Excel? **yes**

Sharing data

Go to...
I get an error message when I double-click a linked or embedded object, page 90.

Quick fix
The type of object I want to embed doesn't appear in the Insert Object dialog box. This situation occurs if the source program for the object you want to embed isn't installed on your computer.

Go to...
I'm having trouble inserting outlines from other programs into PowerPoint, page 97.

If your solution isn't here, check these related chapters:

- Web publishing, page 116
- Importing and exporting, page 174
- Links and embedded objects, page 318
- Trading data with other programs, page 420

Or see the general trouble-shooting tips on page xix.

Go to...
When I try to import information into Outlook from Excel, I get an error message, page 92.

I try to edit an HTML file in one Office program, but it opens in another

Source of the problem

Suppose that while you're in Word you try to open a Hypertext Markup Language (HTML) document to edit it. You click the File menu and click Open; you then navigate to the HTML document that you want to edit. You click the file, click the Open button, and the file opens in Excel!

When you install a program, one function of the installation routine is to associate the types of files the program creates with the program. That's how Windows knows which program to open when you double-click a document.

HTML files are slightly different animals because they can be created by a variety of different programs. So, they open in the program that created them—even if you use the Open dialog box in Office XP, the HTML file will still open in the program that created it.

How to fix it

You will always get better results if you open and edit an HTML or MHTML file in the application that created it. Follow these steps to open an HTML or MHTML document in any Office application or any application that supports HTML editing:

Tip

If the application you want to use doesn't appear on the Open With menu, click Choose Program.

1. Open the Office application you want to use to edit an HTML or MHTML file.

2. On the File menu, click Open.

3. Navigate to the location where the file is stored.

4. Right-click the file.

5. Point to Open With.

6. Click an application to use to open the file. ▶

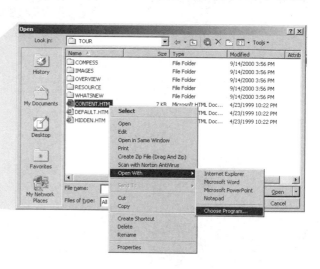

> ## For those interested in jargon: HTML and MHTML
>
> HTML is the standard markup language used for documents on the World Wide Web. HTML uses *tags* to indicate how Web browsers should display page elements, such as text and graphics, and how these elements should respond to user actions. MHTML is a standard method for displaying an HTML document that includes inline graphics, applets, linked documents, and other items referred to in the HTML document.

I get an error message when I double-click a linked or embedded object

Source of the problem

You can edit a linked or embedded object only in the program that created it. You'll receive an error message when Windows can't open the source file or source program related to the embedded or linked object.

How to fix it

Check the following possibilities:

Note

It's possible that you won't see an error message under these conditions; instead, your computer might seem to "hang."

- Sometimes, you can't open a program because you don't have enough memory available—and that situation typically occurs when you have lots of other programs running and you try to open one more program. You can free up memory by closing any open programs you don't need to edit the linked or embedded object (yes, close your e-mail program for a few minutes).

- You can't edit a linked or embedded object if someone else has the object open and is making changes. So make sure someone else isn't using the file.

- The program that created the object might be running but you might not realize it because other windows or dialog boxes might be covering it up on your screen. Check the Windows taskbar to determine if the source program is running (or press Alt+Tab to cycle through open programs) and switch to it.

- You might not be able to edit a linked object if either its name or its location is not the same as when you created the link. To see the name and location of the source file, follow these steps:

  1. Click the linked object.

  2. On the Edit menu, click Links. ▶

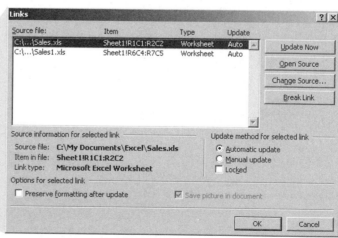

3. If the source file has been renamed or moved, click Change Source in the Links dialog box to reconnect the links.

● If you're trying to edit an embedded object, make sure that the source program (the program that created the file) is installed on your computer and is a version that can edit the object. If the source program isn't installed, install it or edit the object with a program you do have installed by converting the object to another format or to a Microsoft Office drawing object. Follow these steps:

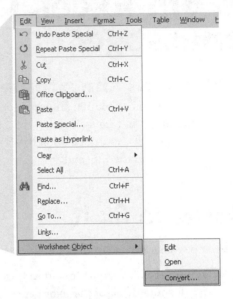

1. Click the embedded object you want to edit.

2. Click Edit.

3. Point to *object name* Object. If you embed an Excel worksheet in a Word document, you'll see Worksheet Object at the bottom of the Edit menu in Word. ▶

4. Click Convert.

5. Do one of the following:

   ● If you want to change the type of the embedded object to the type you specified in the Object Type box, click Convert To.

   ● If you don't want to change the embedded object type but instead want to open the embedded object as the type you specified in the Object Type box, click Activate As. ▶

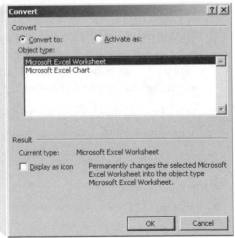

When I try to import information into Outlook from Excel, I get an error message

Source of the problem

Problems that you encounter importing Excel information into Outlook are, in all probability, related to named ranges in Excel.

To import Excel information into Outlook, Outlook expects a named range in the Excel file that follows a specified format.

How to fix it

Check to make sure that your Excel file meets the following requirements:

- All of the information you are trying to import must be contained in a named range in the Excel file. If some or all of the information you are trying to import is not contained within a named range in the Microsoft Excel file, the import will fail.

- Outlook expects the first row of a named range that you plan to import to contain field names. If the range you import does not contain field names, Outlook will try to read the first row of data as if it were field names, and the import process won't work. So, save yourself some trouble and make sure that the first row of the named range contains field names.

- The range name that you use in Excel must be unique—do not name the range using one of the field names—and it cannot contain spaces.

To name a range in Excel, follow these steps:

1. Select the range you want to import into Outlook.

2. Click Insert.

3. Point to Name.

4. Click Define.

5. In the Names In Workbook box, type a name for the range that you selected.

6. Click Add. ▶

7. Click OK.

8. On the File menu, click Save.

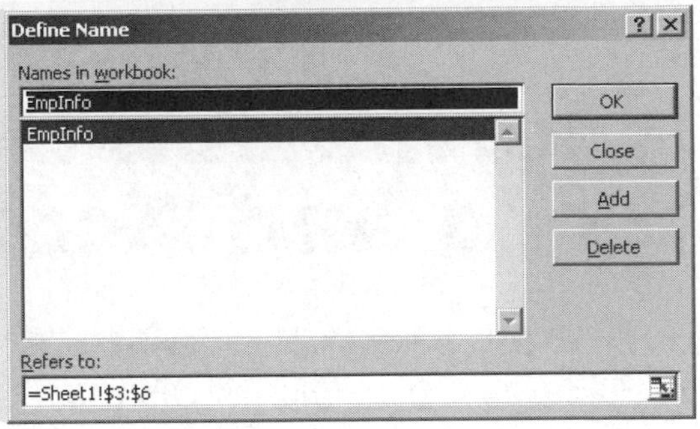

Note

The name cannot contain spaces, and it cannot be the same as the name of a column header.

Define Name

Names in workbook:

EmpInfo

EmpInfo

OK

Close

Add

Delete

Refers to:

=Sheet1!$3:$6

I need to exchange information between Word and Access

Source of the problem

It happens—you start using one Office program and then realize you really want the information in another Office program. You might even want the information in both programs, but you don't want to retype it. You can send a comma-delimited or tab-delimited file from Word to Access. You can convert an Access datasheet to a text file or to a Rich Text Format (RTF) file, and these file types can be read by any Office program including Word.

How to fix it

To send information from Word to Access, save the information as a text file that you can import into Access. The information in Word cannot be in a Word table; if necessary, convert Word tables to text, using the Convert Table To Text command on the Table menu. Make sure that you choose either Commas or Tabs as the separator when you convert. ▶

Follow these steps to save the Word document as a comma-delimited or tab-delimited file:

1. On the File menu, click Save As.

2. In the File Name box, type a new file name.

3. In the Save As Type box, click Plain Text. ▶

4. Click Save.

5. In the File Conversion dialog box, click OK.

6. Switch to Access.

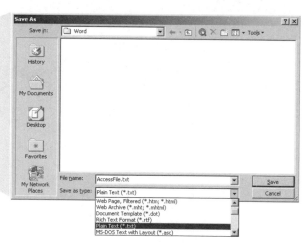

7. In the Database window, click Tables on the Objects bar.

8. On the File menu, point to Get External Data, and then click Import. ▶

9. In the Files Of Type box, click Text Files.

10. In the File Name box, enter the name of the text file to import.

11. Click Import.

12. Follow the directions in the Import Text Wizard dialog boxes. ▶

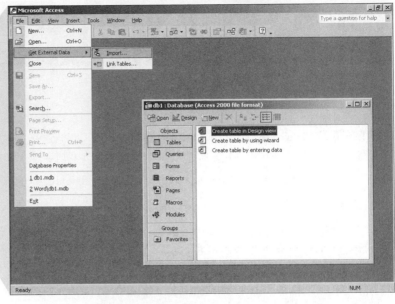

You can export Access information in either text file format or RTF. To send information from Access to Word, reverse the preceding steps:

1. In Access, open the database that contains the information you want to send to Word.

2. In the Database window, click the table containing the information.

3. On the File menu, click Export.

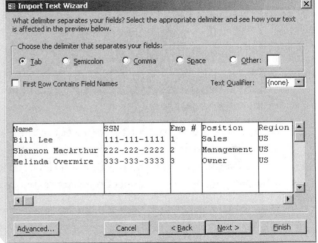

4. In the File Name box within the Export Table box, type a name for the file.

5. In the Save As Type box, click either Text Files (*.txt; *.csv; *.tab; *asc) or Rich Text Format (*.rtf).

6. Use the Save In list to navigate to the folder where you want to store the file.

7. Click Export All.

8. Open Word and open the exported file the same way you open any Word document.

When I click a hyperlink, I don't go to the expected destination

Source of the problem

Clicking a hyperlink and jumping to an unexpected location can happen for several reasons.

- The destination of the hyperlink might have been deleted, moved, or renamed.

- You might not have access to the destination.

- The hyperlink might be one that downloads or opens files, and your browser's security settings might not allow you to download or open files.

- The destination site might be too busy.

How to fix it

To determine why you're jumping to an unexpected location, check the following:

- If you suspect that the destination of the hyperlink might have been deleted, moved, or renamed, and the destination is on an intranet or the Internet, use your Web browser to verify that the destination is valid.

- If you suspect that you don't have access to the destination and the destination is on an intranet, see your network administrator to make sure you have access to the destination. If the destination is on the Internet, you must have Internet access and a Web browser installed. To determine whether your Internet connection is active, try visiting another Web site.

- If the hyperlink opens or downloads files, make sure that the security options in your Web browser permit you to download and open files.

- If you suspect that the destination site is too busy, make sure that you can access other sites; then, try visiting the site again at a later time.

I'm having trouble inserting outlines from other programs into PowerPoint

Source of the problem

You might experience problems inserting an HTML outline or an outline created in Word into a PowerPoint presentation.

When you insert a FrontPage document saved in HTML into PowerPoint, all of the text might appear in a single text box. When you insert a Word outline into PowerPoint, you might not see the correct outline structure on your PowerPoint slides.

Although the problems are different, the ultimate cause of the problem is based on the same factor: heading structure.

How to fix it

When you insert an HTML outline into your presentation, PowerPoint retains the original heading structure of the HTML outline, but all the text from the HTML file appears in a text box on one slide. You can edit the text on the slide but not on the Outline tab. If you're working with an outline, you probably want to create one slide for each heading in the outline—if you're using HTML files, insert one HTML file for each slide you want to create.

Microsoft PowerPoint formats outlines inserted from Microsoft Word using the heading styles in the original Word document. PowerPoint creates a new slide for each Heading 1 in the Word document and includes, on that slide, all the Headings 2–5 (PowerPoint formats up to five levels of text). To appear in PowerPoint correctly, even the lowest level of text on the slide has to be based on a heading in your original Word document. Any information styled as either Normal or Body Text will not appear correctly on your PowerPoint slide.

> **Tip**
>
> When you send an outline from Word to PowerPoint in HTML format, the headings and subheadings are retained, and the outline is structured in the same way as a .doc or .rtf file.

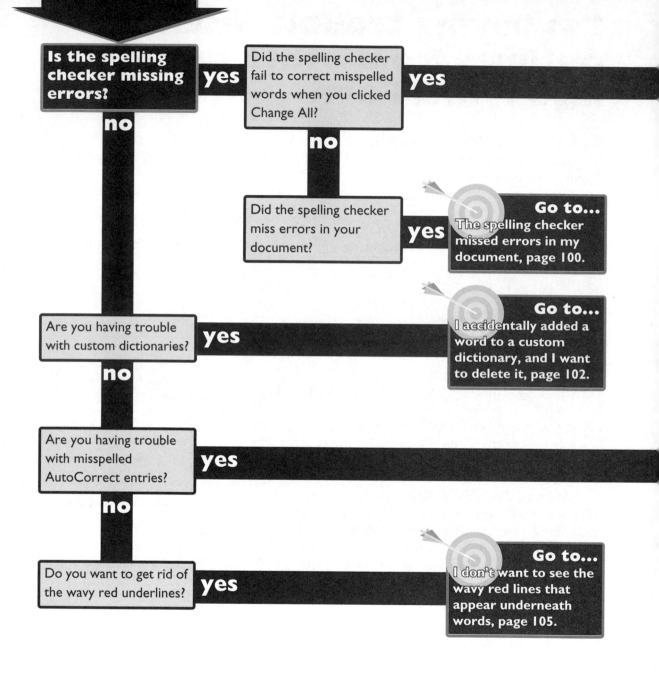

Is the spelling checker missing errors?

yes → Did the spelling checker fail to correct misspelled words when you clicked Change All?

no ↓

Did the spelling checker miss errors in your document?

yes → **Go to...** The spelling checker missed errors in my document, page 100.

Are you having trouble with custom dictionaries?

yes → **Go to...** I accidentally added a word to a custom dictionary, and I want to delete it, page 102.

no ↓

Are you having trouble with misspelled AutoCorrect entries?

yes →

no ↓

Do you want to get rid of the wavy red underlines?

yes → **Go to...** I don't want to see the wavy red lines that appear underneath words, page 105.

Quick fix

Clicking Change All doesn't change all occurrences of a misspelling if you close Spelling And Grammar before checking the entire document. Recheck the entire document before closing the spelling checker.

Go to...

I accidentally added a word as an AutoCorrect entry, and I want to delete it, page 104.

If your solution isn't here, check this related chapter:

● Editing, page 32

Or see the general troubleshooting tips on page xix.

The spelling checker missed errors in my document

Source of the problem

The spelling checker might miss errors in your document for a variety of reasons:

- You might have selected only part of the document.

- You might have closed the Spelling dialog box before an Office program finished checking the entire document.

- You might have used a decorative or symbol font.

- You might have misspelled a word typed in all uppercase letters.

- You might be running into some special cases in Office programs.

How to fix it

If you've selected a range of cells or part of a document or presentation, Office programs check only the selected range. To check the entire document, make sure you have not made a specific selection, and then repeat the spelling check:

1. Click the Tools menu.

2. Click Spelling.

If you close the Spelling dialog box before an Office program finishes checking the entire document, errors in the unchecked portion are not corrected. Follow the preceding steps to recheck spelling.

The spelling checker doesn't check text formatted with a decorative or symbol font. You can apply a different font to such text, and then repeat the spelling check.

> **Note**
>
> If you're working in Word, you might want to reset spelling before you recheck your document. Click the Tools menu and click Options; on the Spelling & Grammar tab, click the Check Document or Recheck Document button.

Spelling

If the spelling checker didn't catch misspelled words typed in uppercase letters, the spelling checker isn't monitoring words typed in uppercase. To make the spelling checker monitor all words regardless of case, follow these steps:

1. Click the Tools menu.

2. Click Options.

3. Click the Spelling tab (Spelling And Style in PowerPoint, and Spelling & Grammar in Word).

4. Clear the Ignore Words In UPPERCASE check box. ▶

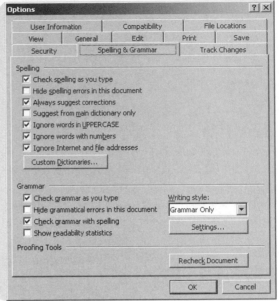

Special cases

- In PowerPoint, the spelling checker does not check the spelling in embedded or inserted objects such as charts, Word documents, or tables, or in special text effects such as WordArt. If the insertion point is in the Notes pane or Slide pane, the spelling checker alternates between the two. If the insertion point is on the Outline tab, all the slides are checked first, and then all the notes are checked.

- In Word, the spelling checker doesn't check spelling in hidden text. To check spelling in hidden text, display the hidden text by clicking the Show All button on the Standard toolbar. Then check spelling. If necessary, reset spelling before you recheck your document. ▶ ¶

- In Excel, the spelling checker checks the entire active worksheet including cell values, cell comments, embedded charts, text boxes, buttons, headers, and footers. However, the spelling checker does not check protected worksheets, formulas, or text that results from a formula. In addition, if the formula bar is active when you check spelling, the spelling checker checks only the contents of the formula bar.

I accidentally added a word to a custom dictionary, and I want to delete it

Source of the problem

As you check spelling in any Office program, the spelling checker compares your spelling to a standard dictionary. You can add words that you use regularly that don't appear in the standard dictionary—such as acronyms, technical terms, and so on—to a custom dictionary that the spelling checker will also consult as you check spelling. Occasionally you might mistakenly press the wrong button and add a misspelled word to the custom dictionary.

How to fix it

You can correct this mistake by editing the custom dictionary. By default, Office programs share a common custom dictionary. If you have Word installed, you can edit the custom dictionary in Word, even if you added the misspelled word from PowerPoint or Excel. Follow these steps:

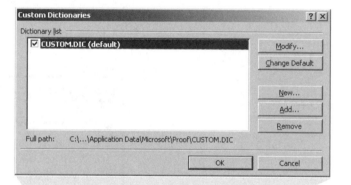

1. Open Word.

2. Click the Tools menu, and click Options.

3. On the Spelling & Grammar tab, click the Custom Dictionaries button to open the Custom Dictionaries window.

4. Under Dictionary List, click the custom dictionary you want to edit.

5. Click the Modify button.

6. Click the word you want to delete.

7. Click the Delete button.

8. Click OK in all three dialog boxes.

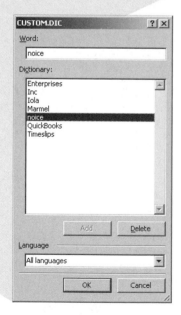

If you don't have Word installed, you can edit the custom dictionary using Notepad. Follow these steps:

1. Open Notepad.

2. Click the File menu, and click Open.

3. Navigate to the Documents and Settings*UserName*\\Application Data\\Microsoft\\Proof folder (where *UserName* is your name).

4. If you can't find the Application Data folder, open Windows Explorer. On the Tools menu, click Folder Options. Click the View tab, point to Advanced Settings, and click the Show Hidden Files And Folders option. Click OK and return to Notepad. The Application Data folder should be visible.

5. In the Files Of Type list, click All Files.

6. Open the Custom.dic file. The entries in your custom dictionary appear in the Notepad, one entry per line. ▶

7. Add or delete entries as necessary.

8. Click the File menu, and click Save. Make sure you save the file with a .dic extension.

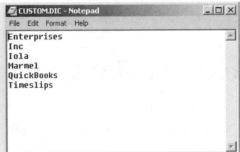

I added a word to the custom dictionary that the spelling checker keeps ignoring

If you've added a word to a custom dictionary but the spelling checker seems to ignore the word, you could be running into several possible problems. You can't add a word that is longer than 64 characters or contains spaces—that is, you can't add phrases. If your word conforms to that requirement, check the size of your custom dictionary—it can't contain any more than 5,000 words, and the file can't be larger than 64 KB. You can circumvent these limitations by cleaning out the current custom dictionary or creating another custom dictionary.

Also, be aware that the spelling checker recognizes various forms of a word. For example, the spelling checker distinguishes between PowerPoint and Powerpoint. To make the spelling checker recognize both forms of a word, store the word in the custom dictionary in both mixed lowercase and capital letters as well as in all lowercase letters.

I accidentally added a word as an AutoCorrect entry, and I want to delete it

Source of the problem

If you accidentally click the AutoCorrect button in any Office program when an incorrect replacement for a misspelled word is selected, you link a word to the incorrect replacement. You also might mistakenly click the AutoCorrect button for a word that is correctly spelled or that you want to ignore, causing that word to be replaced automatically with an unintended word. You can correct these mistakes by editing the AutoCorrect list.

How to fix it

In the AutoCorrect list, you can delete entries. Follow these steps:

1. Click the Tools menu, and click AutoCorrect Options.

2. Click the AutoCorrect tab.

3. In the list of entries, find and click the row containing the entry you want to change. To find the entry quickly, start typing it, and the list will scroll to the word you're looking for.

4. If you don't want to automatically correct the word, click the Delete button, and the word will no longer be replaced.

5. If you do want the word to be replaced, but by a different word, click in the With box, type the new entry, and click Replace.

6. Click OK.

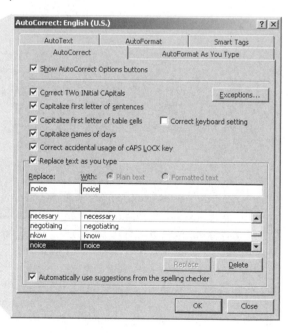

I don't want to see the wavy red lines that appear underneath words

Source of the problem

These red lines indicate that the program doesn't recognize the word you typed. You won't see the red wavy lines in Excel because Excel uses the AutoCorrect feature to help you correct spelling as you type. You can add any words that you regularly misspell to the AutoCorrect list, and Excel will catch the mistakes as you type.

Word, PowerPoint, and certain parts of Outlook (like the bodies of e-mail messages) use the AutoCorrect feature, but in addition, they use another automatic spelling checker that compares what you type to a dictionary as you type. The automatic spelling checker marks any words you type that aren't in the dictionary with a red underline.

How to fix it

You have two choices: You can disable automatic spell checking, or you can modify its behavior to hide the wavy underlines, even though the automatic spell checking continues. Follow these steps:

1. Click the Tools menu, and click Options.

2. Click the Spelling And Style tab (Spelling & Grammar in Word). ▶

3. To disable the feature entirely, clear the Check Spelling As You Type check box.

4. To hide the underlines but continue to check spelling automatically, make sure the Check Spelling As You Type check box is selected, and select Hide All Spelling Errors (in PowerPoint) or Hide Spelling Errors In This Document (in Word and Outlook).

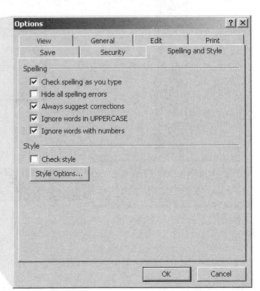

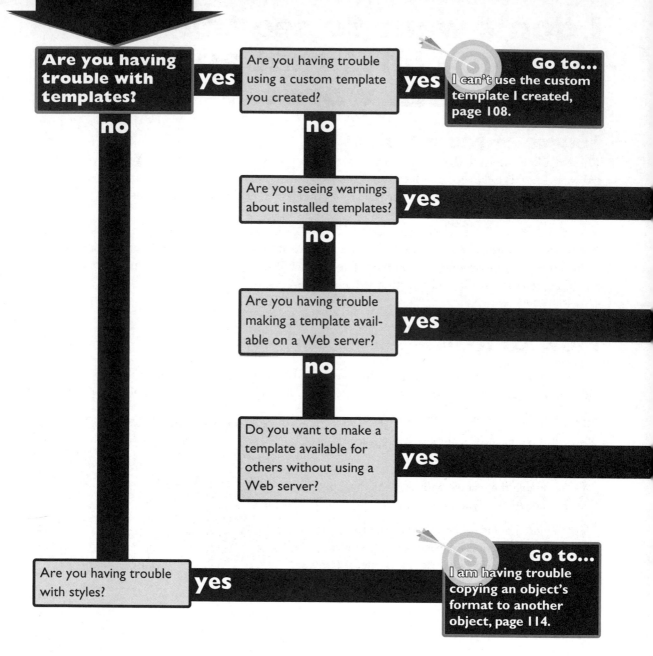

Are you having trouble with templates?

yes → Are you having trouble using a custom template you created?

yes → Go to...
I can't use the custom template I created, page 108.

no

Are you seeing warnings about installed templates? **yes**

no

Are you having trouble making a template available on a Web server? **yes**

no

Do you want to make a template available for others without using a Web server? **yes**

no

Are you having trouble with styles? **yes** → Go to...
I am having trouble copying an object's format to another object, page 114.

Go to...
When I open an Office program, warnings about installed templates and add-ins appear, page 112.

Go to...
I am having trouble making a template available for others to use, page 110.

Quick fix
Share templates using your network. Store the templates in a shared folder on your server. Create a shortcut to the folder and have users place the shortcut in the local Templates folder.

If your solution isn't here, check these related chapters:

- Security and macro warnings, page 472
- Slide design and layout, page 366
- Masters, page 326

Or see the general trouble-shooting tips on page xix.

I can't use the custom template I created

Source of the problem

This can be really frustrating, particularly if you spent a lot of time creating the template, adding custom toolbars and menu commands, macros, and AutoText. You might not be able to use a custom template because it doesn't appear among the templates in the New dialog box or because you meant to but didn't actually save it as a template. Both problems have the same solution.

How to fix it

The location where you save a template determines if it's going to appear in the Templates dialog box. Office programs list templates in the Templates dialog box only if you save the template file in one of the following locations:

- The Templates folder or a subfolder of the Templates folder; the default location is C:\Documents and Settings*UserName*\Application Data\Microsoft\Templates, where *UserName* is your name.

- For Word and Excel templates, the Startup folder. The default location for Excel's startup folder is C:\Program Files\Microsoft Office\Office10\XLStart, and the default location for Word's startup folder is C:\Program Files\Microsoft Office\Office10\Startup.

- In Excel, you'll see templates in the Templates dialog box if you save them to the location you specified in the At Startup, Open All Files In box on the General tab in the Options dialog box (located on the Tools menu).

Assuming that you saved your template to the correct location, you might not see it in the Templates dialog box if you didn't save it as a template. You cannot simply type the template extension (.dot for Word, .pot for PowerPoint, and .xlt for Excel) at the end of the file name. You must click the correct file type for templates and, to make custom templates appear on the General tab of the Templates dialog box, you must save custom templates to the Templates folder. Follow these steps:

1. Click the File menu, and click Save As.

2. In the Save As Type box, click Template (for Excel), Document Template (for Word), Design Template (for PowerPoint), or Outlook Template (for Outlook).

3. If necessary, in the Save In list, navigate to the Templates folder. ▶

4. In the File Name box, enter a file name.

5. Click Save.

I am having trouble making a template available for others to use

Source of the problem

You might have a template that you want to make available for others to use. Sharing a template works particularly well when a group of people are collaborating on a project and individual files need to contain the same formatting specifications. Also, templates can contain macros that will make the work process easier for the collaborating group.

How to fix it

You can make a template available to others by placing the template in a folder on a Web server and then creating a shortcut to the folder. Follow these steps:

1. Open any Office program.

2. In the New Document task pane, click Add Network Place. If you don't see the New Document task pane, open the File menu and click New to display it. ▶

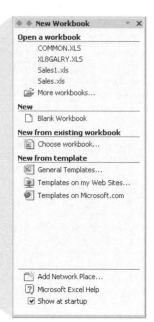

3. Click Create A Shortcut
   To An Existing Network
   Place. ▶

4. Click Next.

5. Type the URL of the Web
   server.

6. Type a name for the shortcut |to
   the Web server.

7. Click Finish. ▼

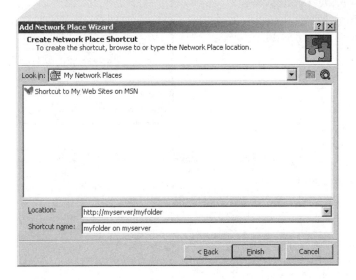

When I open an Office program, warnings about installed templates and add-ins appear

Source of the problem

Templates and add-in programs often contain macros. You'll see warnings about macros if your program security is set to Medium or High and the macros are not digitally signed by a trusted source or the digital signature has expired.

These warnings appear to help you protect your system from the malicious types who'd like nothing better than to melt down your computer by infecting templates or add-in programs with macro viruses.

> **Note**
>
> Add-ins are programs that add additional functionality to Office programs; often they attach custom commands, macros, or toolbars. Digital signatures are files provided by the creator of a macro to guarantee that the macro did, indeed, come from the developer, and that the macro hasn't been altered by anyone except the developer.

How to fix it

If you determine that the macros do not contain malicious programs, you can reenable them by updating your security settings to trust installed macros and templates. Follow these steps:

1. On the Tools menu, click Options.

2. Click the Security tab.

3. Click the Macro Security button to display the Security dialog box. ▶

> **Note**
>
> You can lower your security settings, but this is not recommended because you open your system to virus infiltration.

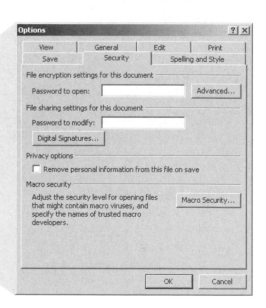

4. Click the Trusted Sources tab.

5. Select the Trust All Installed Add-Ins And Templates check box. ▶

I am having trouble copying an object's format to another object

Source of the problem

A very admirable goal, indeed; why do all that work more than once? When you have several objects and you want them all to look the same, you should definitely copy the formatting from one to the others. And, in Word, Excel, and PowerPoint, you can copy formatting from one object to another using the Format Painter. An object can be text, cells, a chart, an AutoShape, a picture, or WordArt. In Word and Excel, you also can create and use *styles* to apply the same formatting to multiple words, paragraphs, or cells. Styles store combinations of formatting characteristics such as font sizes and italics.

> ### Note
> If you copy an AutoShape with text attached to it, the Format Painter copies the look and style of the text as well as the other characteristics of the AutoShape.

How to fix it

To use the Format Painter to copy formatting, follow these steps:

1. Click the text (words or paragraphs), cells (a single cell or a range), chart, AutoShape, picture, or WordArt, with the attributes you want to copy.

2. On the Standard toolbar, click the Format Painter button. ▶

3. Click the text (words or paragraphs), cells (a single cell or a range), AutoShape, picture, WordArt, or clip art to which you want to copy the attributes.

> ### Tip
> You can copy all attributes of an object to several objects. Click the object you want to copy, double-click Format Painter, and then click several objects in succession. When you finish copying, press Esc or click the Format Painter again.

If you want to create a new style in Word, follow these steps:

1. Apply the formatting you want to include in the style to text or a table cell.

2. Select the text or table cell that you formatted.

3. Open the Styles And Formatting task pane by clicking the Styles And Formatting button on the Formatting toolbar. ▶

---

4. In the Styles And Formatting task pane, click New Style. ▶

5. In the Name box, type a name for the style.

6. In the Style Type box, click Character, Paragraph, Table, or List as appropriate for the style.

7. Make sure that the Style Based On box contains the name of the style you used as the foundation for the new style.

8. Make any other changes you need to make for the new style.

9. Click OK.

Creating a new style in Excel is very similar to creating a new style in Word. Complete the preceding Steps 1 and 2; then click the Format menu and click Style. In the Style Name box, type a new name for the style. To create the new style and apply it to the current selection, click OK. To create the new style without applying it to the current selection, click Add. ▶

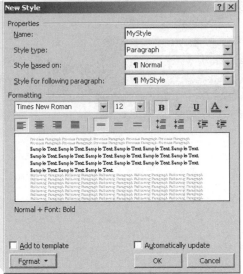

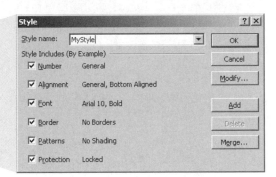

Are you trying to publish documents to the Web?

yes

Are you or others having trouble opening Web files?

yes

Are people having trouble accessing your Web page?

yes

no

no

Are you having trouble working with HTML files?

yes

no

Do you find that your application doesn't create backup files for your Web page?

yes

no

Are text or graphics positioned differently when you save your file as a Web page?

yes

Did your Office application create extra files when you created a Web page?

yes

Go to...
When I saved a Web page, my Office application created a bunch of picture files, page 120.

Web publishing

Go to...
People can't find the Web page I saved on a file server, page 118.

Go to...
I try to open an HTML file, but it opens in another Office application, page 122.

Quick fix

Automatic backing up of Web pages. When you save a Web page, a backup copy is not automatically created. To save a copy of a Web page:

1. On the File menu, click Save As Web Page.

2. In the File Name box, enter a new name for the file, and then click Save.

Quick fix

Obtaining correct positioning of text and graphics on Web pages. When creating documents for the Web, using Web Layout view will ensure that your graphics look the way you want them to when they are viewed as Web pages in a Web browser.

If your solution isn't here, check these related chapters:

- Publishing to the Web, page 392
- Web pages (Word), page 500

Or see the general troubleshooting tips on page xix.

People can't find the Web page I saved on a file server

Source of the problem

There was a time when you were limited to only using eight characters in any file name. This resulted in some very creative file naming techniques, such as NASTI.doc for a Word report on a North Atlantic Sales Trade Initiative or Rpt4Bos.xls for an Excel report on quarterly profits that you prepared for your boss.

Starting with Windows 95, long file names were permitted. The computing world rejoiced and began to name files as if they were tenth generation royalty: John Montgomery Fortesque Langley III Report on Projected Income for His Boss Maria Von Manager. You get the idea.

The use of long file names resulted in a small problem that occasionally frustrates computer users, especially those posting information to the Web, because those accessing the Web use such a broad spectrum of computer software and hardware. When you save a Web page and use a long file name, people who are running computers with Windows 3.1 will not find the Web page. Windows 3.1 doesn't support long file names, but instead is limited to reading short file names with eight characters.

If you run into this problem on a regular basis, you might be forced to revert to shorter file names. But, odds are that it won't take more than a few years before Windows 3.1 users will be upgrading to newer versions of the Windows operating system, and you can go back to making an art of creating lengthy file names!

How to fix it

If you want to be sure that whenever you save a file it is saved with a short file name, follow these steps:

1. On the Tools menu, click Options.

2. Click the General tab, and then click Web Options. ▶

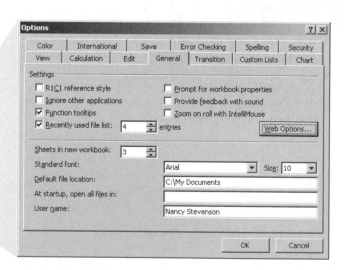

3. Click the Files tab.

4. In the section of the dialog box labeled File Names And Locations, clear the Use Long File Names Whenever Possible check box. ▶

5. Click OK twice to close each dialog box and save the new setting.

6. Be sure to limit yourself to only eight characters plus a three-character file extension when naming files.

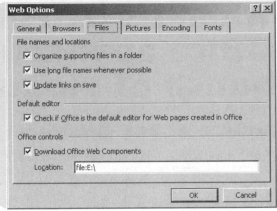

Tip

Short file names are also limited in the use of certain characters; for example, you can't use a space between characters. Instead, you can use an underscore such as Sales_Rpt.doc. It's best to use only letters, numbers, and optionally the underscore or hyphen character.

When I saved a Web page, my Office application created a bunch of picture files

Source of the problem

A Web page typically consists of several files that contain all the text and pictures that make up the Web page. It's like packing a little suitcase full of all the things the Web page needs to take up residence online.

When you save a file as a Web page, and that document contains pictures, copies of picture files are created. These pictures are then available if you want to modify the Web page at any point. Having these files available shouldn't cause any problems, and you can simply leave them where they are.

However, if you would rather link to a picture rather than having a copy of it in your Web page folder, you can, if the picture is in the GIF, JPG, or PNG file format. When you insert a file as a link, you don't insert the entire file into your document. Rather, you insert a link to a file where all the information about that object is stored. This saves space in the destination document, but the source file and the application the source was created in must be available to your document. If the source application isn't available, consider opening the picture file in a graphics editing program such as Paint and saving it with a new format that your Office document can access such as Windows Bitmap.

How to fix it

If you want to change an inserted picture to a linked picture, follow these steps:

1. Click the inserted picture in the original document, and press Delete to remove it.

2. On the Insert menu in Word, click File. In PowerPoint and Excel, click Object on the Insert menu, select Create From File, and enter the file path and name. ▶

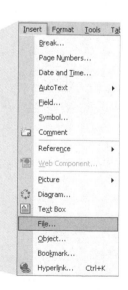

3. Locate the file to insert, and click the file.

4. Click the arrow to the right of the Insert button, and click Insert As Link. In PowerPoint and Excel, click the OK or Insert button, and then select the Link or Link To File check box. ▶

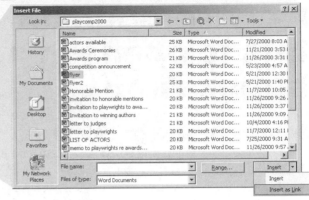

Tip

When you edit a linked picture within an Office application, the picture file is copied to your supporting files folder. If you are short on disk space and therefore want to avoid this, always edit linked pictures in a graphics program.

Working with MHTML

If you want to condense the files that make up your Web page, consider using the Web Archive format. A Web archive saves all the elements of a Web site, including text and graphics, into a single file. This allows you to publish your whole Web site as a single *MIME encapsulated aggregate HTML document* (MHTML) file. What does this mean? Well, in this format, supported by Internet Explorer 4.0 and later, you can send an entire Web site as an e-mail message or attachment. When saving your document, simply save it in the Web Archive format in the Save As dialog box.

I try to open an HTML file, but it opens in another Office application

Source of the problem

The standard markup language used to create documents on the World Wide Web is the Hypertext Markup Language (HTML). HTML uses tags to specify how Web browsers should display the elements of a Web page, such as text and graphics, and how to respond to the actions of the person using the browser. A typical Web page can be made up of several HTML files.

You can create documents in Office programs, and then save them in HTML or Web Archive format (an encapsulated HTML document with all documents saved in a single file). When you open either an HTML or Web Archive file from the Open dialog box on the File menu in any Office program, the file opens in the application in which the file was created. For example, if you try to open an HTML format file in PowerPoint that was created in Word, the file opens in Word. Fortunately, there's a way to open an HTML file with an Office application and control which application it opens in.

How to fix it

To open an HTML file in one Office program that was created in another Office program, follow these steps:

1. Open the Office program in which you want to open the file.

2. On the File menu, click Open to display the Open dialog box.

3. Locate the file name and right-click it.

4. Click Open With in the shortcut menu that appears. ▶

5. Click the appropriate Microsoft program in the Open With menu.

Warning

The Open With option is not available in Windows 98 and earlier versions.

Excel

Part 2

Are you having trouble with chart axes?

yes →

no
↓

Did the chart fail to update when you typed new information?

yes →

Go to...
My chart didn't update when I added new information on the worksheet, page 128.

no
↓

Do font sizes keep changing?

yes →

Go to...
When I resize a chart, the font sizes change, page 133.

no
↓

Are elements missing from a chart based on a user-defined chart type?

yes →

Quick fix
User-defined chart types don't store text boxes, pictures, or floating text. You must add these objects to the chart that you create based on your user-defined chart type.

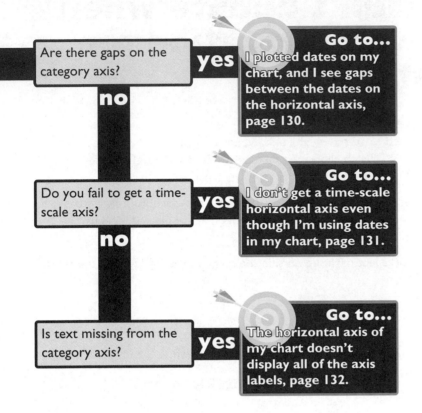

Are there gaps on the category axis?

yes

Go to...
I plotted dates on my chart, and I see gaps between the dates on the horizontal axis, page 130.

no

Do you fail to get a time-scale axis?

yes

Go to...
I don't get a time-scale horizontal axis even though I'm using dates in my chart, page 131.

no

Is text missing from the category axis?

yes

Go to...
The horizontal axis of my chart doesn't display all of the axis labels, page 132.

If your solution isn't here, check these related chapters:

- Drawing objects and pictures, page 310
- Links and embedded objects, page 318

Or see the general trouble-shooting tips on page xix.

My chart didn't update when I added new information on the worksheet

Source of the problem

You thought that Excel was supposed to automatically update a chart when you added information. And, you're right—Excel will update the chart automatically—under the right conditions. Data you add to a worksheet might not update a chart for two reasons:

- Excel breaks the links between the chart and the worksheet data on which the chart is based if you type text or values for the data series (related data points that are plotted in a chart) and categories on the Series tab of the Source Data dialog box.

- The data you added to the worksheet might be outside the range of data included in the chart.

How to fix it

You can reestablish links between the worksheet and a chart sheet or redefine the range of cells used to create the chart. Follow these steps:

1. Click the chart you want to change.

2. On the Chart menu, click Source Data, and then click the Data Range tab.

3. Make sure the entire reference in the Data Range box is selected. ▶

4. On the worksheet, select the cells that contain the data you want to appear in the chart. If you want the column and row labels to appear in the chart, include the cells that contain them in the selection.

If you are working with an embedded chart—a chart that appears directly on a worksheet instead of on a separate chart sheet—

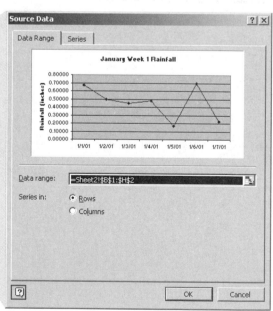

and you've broken the link between the chart and the data, you can reestablish the link if you redefine the cell range. Click the chart to select it, and then, in the data area of the worksheet, drag the color-coded ranges to select the data you want to appear in the chart.

You'll run into a similar problem with charts that appear on their own sheets (called chart sheets). If you add labels and values on the worksheet outside the range of data displayed on the chart, the new data won't automatically appear on the chart. To add information to a chart sheet, select the new information that you want to add to the chart on the worksheet, and click the Copy button. Then, switch to the chart sheet, and click the Paste button. You don't need to try to position the pointer anywhere on the chart sheet; Excel is smart enough to know where to add the information.

To add data to an embedded chart created from adjacent worksheet cells, expand the color-coded ranges that surround the data on the worksheet by dragging the range markers to include the adjacent cells. ▼

Category labels in my chart are positioned differently than when I created the chart

When you view a chart that is linked to data in a workbook that you don't have open on screen, Excel positions multiple-level category labels differently than when you originally created the chart.

For example, you might have originally centered the bottom level of labels, and when you view the linked chart without opening the workbook that contains it, those labels might appear left-aligned instead of centered. To correct the problem, open both the workbook that contains the source data for the chart and the workbook that contains the chart. In the workbook that contains the chart, click Edit, and then click Links. From the list that appears, click the source file that contains the chart data. Then, click Open Source. In the source workbook, the chart's labels should appear in their original positions.

Note

Multiple-level category labels in a chart are automatically displayed on more than one line in a hierarchy. For example, the heading Clothing might appear above a row with headings Shirts, Slacks, and Socks.

You can also add data to an embedded chart by dragging the data from the worksheet to the chart. If your embedded chart is created from nonadjacent selections, use the copy and paste procedure.

Rainfall	1-Jan-01	2-Jan-01	3-Jan-01	4-Jan-01	5-Jan-01	6-Jan-01	7-Jan-01	Week 1
	0.67450	0.49417	0.44611	0.47999	0.16653	0.69647	0.22223	3.18000
	8-Jan-01	9-Jan-01	10-Jan-01	11-Jan-01	12-Jan-01	13-Jan-01	14-Jan-01	
	0.28409	0.23662	0.08707	0.28405	0.91394	0.99760	0.63827	3.44164
	15-Jan-01	16-Jan-01	17-Jan-01	18-Jan-01	19-J			
	0.15435	0.12963	0.30256	0.67394	0.9			
	22-Jan-01	23-Jan-01	24-Jan-01	25-Jan-01	26-J			
	0.34659	0.04460	0.22859	0.20225	0.46523	0.24418	0.32583	1.85726

January Week 1 Rainfall

I plotted dates on my chart, and I see gaps between the dates on the horizontal axis

Source of the problem

Suppose, for example, that you have data for every other week starting March 1—that is, March 1, March 15, March 29, April 12, and April 26—and you have formatted the data in your worksheet using a date number formatting. When you create a chart of the data, placing the dates on the category (X) axis, Excel applies the time-scale axis to the category axis of your chart. A time-scale axis shows a blank category for dates for which you have no data, so you'll see gaps for the missing dates on the category axis.

How to fix it

If you do not want to see these gaps, and you want to plot the days next to each other, you can change the time-scale axis to a standard category axis. Follow these steps:

1. Click the chart.

2. On the Chart menu, click Chart Options.

3. Click the Axes tab.

4. In the Category (X) Axis section, click Category. ▶

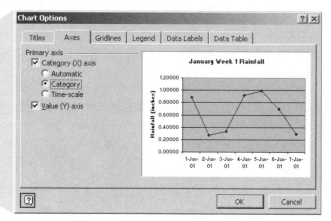

I don't get a time-scale horizontal axis even though I'm using dates in my chart

Source of the problem

When you create a chart from worksheet data that includes dates formatted as dates, Excel auto-matically uses a time-scale axis that displays your dates in chronological order—even if the dates aren't in chronological order in the worksheet data. But, you might not see the time-scale axis if your chart options or axes are set up incorrectly.

How to fix it

Check your chart options and set the category axis to the Time-Scale option. Follow these steps:

1. Click the chart.

2. On the Chart menu, click Chart Options.

3. Click the Axes tab.

4. Click the Time-Scale option.

5. Click OK.

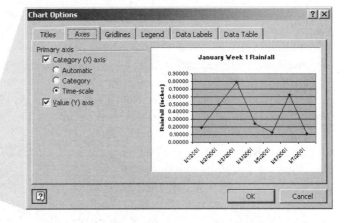

The Time-Scale option is only available on 2-D or 3-D line, column, bar, area, or stock chart types; it isn't available for PivotChart Reports.

Also, make sure that the dates on your chart appear on the category axis (the axis that runs horizontally in your chart; also known as the X-axis), not on the value axis (the axis that runs vertically in your chart; also known as the Y-axis). If necessary, you can swap the two axes. Follow these steps:

By Column

By Row

1. Click the chart. The Chart toolbar appears.

2. Click the By Row button, and then click the By Column button until your dates appear on the category axis.

3. Click OK.

The horizontal axis of my chart doesn't display all of the axis labels

Source of the problem

This is very frustrating—you see the data, but it isn't labeled, so the average viewer will have no clue what he or she is viewing. This problem can occur when there isn't enough room in the chart to display all of the axis labels.

How to fix it

If some of the category names aren't visible along the horizontal axis of the chart, you might need to adjust the way you display the fonts for the labels in the chart. For example, you can enlarge an embedded chart—a chart that is placed on a worksheet rather than on a separate chart sheet—because Excel will scale the fonts proportionally to the size of the chart. Click the chart, and then drag one of the black sizing handles outward.

As an alternative, you can select a smaller font size. Double-click the axis to display the Format Axis dialog box, and then click the Font tab to select a smaller font size.

You have one other alternative: you can change the orientation of the labels so that you don't need as much width for the chart. For example, you can display the labels vertically or on an angle on the horizontal axis. In the Format Axis dialog box, click the Alignment tab, and change the orientation degree. If you choose the values of 0, 90, or –90 degrees, the text will wrap. ▶

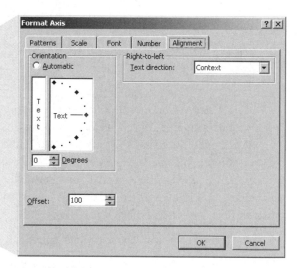

When I resize a chart, the font sizes change

Source of the problem

You might notice the font sizes changing in your chart when you resize it. In particular, when you resize an embedded chart (a chart that is placed on a worksheet rather than on a separate chart sheet) or the chart area (the entire chart and all its elements) of a chart sheet, fonts in a chart scale proportionally.

You can control the way Excel updates font sizes when you resize a chart.

How to fix it

If you want the font sizes in a chart to remain constant when you resize the chart, follow these steps:

1. Select the entire chart area by clicking on or just within its outer border.

2. On the Format menu, click Selected Chart Area.

3. Click the Font tab. ▶

4. Clear the Auto Scale check box.

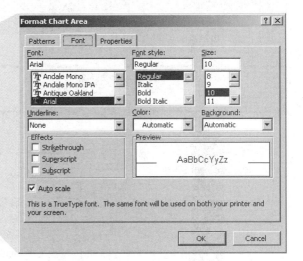

Note

The plot area in a 2-D chart is the area bounded by the axes including all data series. The plot area in a 3-D chart is the area bounded by the axes including the data series, category names, tick-mark labels, and axes titles.

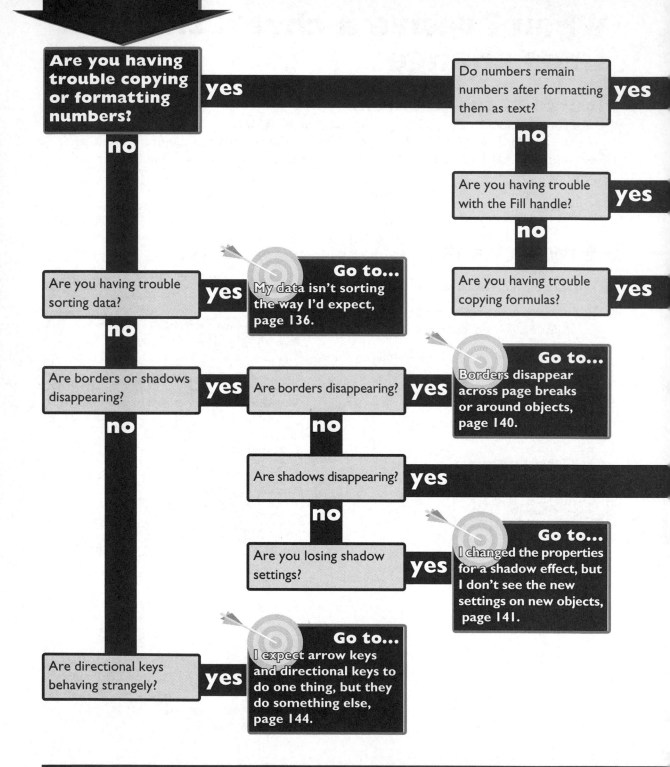

Are you having trouble copying or formatting numbers?

yes → Do numbers remain numbers after formatting them as text? **yes**

no ↓ (from "Do numbers remain numbers...")

Are you having trouble with the Fill handle? **yes**

no ↓

Are you having trouble copying formulas? **yes**

no ↓ (from "Are you having trouble copying or formatting numbers?")

Are you having trouble sorting data? **yes** →

Go to...
My data isn't sorting the way I'd expect, page 136.

no ↓

Are borders or shadows disappearing? **yes** → Are borders disappearing? **yes** →

Go to...
Borders disappear across page breaks or around objects, page 140.

no ↓ (from "Are borders disappearing?")

Are shadows disappearing? **yes**

no ↓

Are you losing shadow settings? **yes** →

Go to...
I changed the properties for a shadow effect, but I don't see the new settings on new objects, page 141.

no ↓ (from "Are borders or shadows disappearing?")

Are directional keys behaving strangely? **yes** →

Go to...
I expect arrow keys and directional keys to do one thing, but they do something else, page 144.

Editing data

Quick fix
If you apply a text formula to a number after you enter the number, you need to edit the cell to apply the format. Select each cell, press F2, and then press Enter.

Go to...
I want to use the Fill handle to copy numbers, but I don't see it, page 138.

Go to...
The results of formulas are wrong after I move or copy cells, page 142.

Quick fix
The shadow disappeared. You can't apply both a shadow and a 3-D effect to the same object.

If your solution isn't here, check this related chapter:

- Entering and selecting data, page 144

Or see the general trouble-shooting tips on page xix.

My data isn't sorting the way I'd expect

Source of the problem

You'd really like to look at your data in a different order than the order you used to enter it. So, you sort it. And then, although the results are close, some of your data appears to be out of order. To get the results you want, you need to understand the defaults Excel uses when sorting. In an ascending sort:

- Excel orders numbers from the smallest negative number to the largest positive number.

- When sorting alphanumeric text, Excel sorts one character at a time, left to right. For example, if you have cells containing "B2," "B21," and "B200," Excel places the cell "B200" after a cell that contains "B2" and before a cell that contains "B21."

- Excel sorts text and text that includes numbers in the following order: 0 1 2 3 4 5 6 7 8 9 (space) ! " # $ % & ( ) * , . / : ; ? @ [\ ] ^ _ ` { | } ~ + < = > A B C D E F G H I J K L M N O P Q R S T U V W X Y Z.

- Excel ignores apostrophes (') and hyphens (-) unless two text strings are the same except for a hyphen. In this case, Excel places the text with the hyphen last in the sorted information.

- In logical values, Excel places FALSE before TRUE.

- Excel sorts all error values equally.

- Excel always places blanks at the end of the list.

In a descending sort, Excel reverses all of the preceding sort orders listed except for blank cells, which always appear at the end of the sorted list.

How to fix it

If you aren't getting the results you expect, check the following:

- If the column you want to sort contains both numbers and numbers containing characters (such as 1, 1a, 2, 2a), you need to format all the cells in the column as text. If you don't, Excel sorts the numbers first, and then sorts the numbers that include text. To format a number as text, follow these steps:

  1. Select the appropriate cells.

  2. On the Format menu, click Cells to display the Format Cells dialog box.

3. Click the Number tab.

4. Click Text in the Category list. ▶

5. Click OK.

6. Select each cell, press F2, and then press Enter.

● If Excel incorrectly sorts a cell that contains a value, the cell might be formatted as text, not as a number. For example, negative numbers from some accounting systems become text when you import the accounting data into Excel.

● Excel treats dates and times as numbers. When you type a date or time that Excel recognizes as such, Excel changes the cell's format from the General number format to a built-in date or time format. For example, if you type 09-01-01, Excel changes the appearance of the date in the cell to 9/1/01; in addition, Excel will change the format of the cell to Date. For Excel to sort correctly, you must format all dates and times in a column using a date or time format because if Excel doesn't recognize a value as a date, time, or number, Excel formats—and then sorts—the value as text. To apply the correct formatting, follow the preceding steps, but in Step 4, click either Date or Time, and then click the appropriate subtype.

Note

To type a number as text when you are entering new data, format the cell as text before you begin typing.

● You might have changed the settings of graphic objects so that the objects don't move with cells. To set objects so that they can be sorted with cells, you first need to select the objects. On the Drawing toolbar, click the Select Objects button and draw a box around the objects to select them or double-click the Select Objects button, and then click each object you want to change while holding down the Ctrl key. On the Format menu, click AutoShape, Picture, TextBox, WordArt, Control, or Object to display the appropriate Format dialog box. On the Properties tab, click Move But Don't Size With Cells. ▶

● If you have any hidden rows or columns in the data you want to sort, unhide the hidden rows and columns.

● Enter column labels in only one row. If you need multiple line labels, wrap the text within the cell.

● Edit your data before you sort to remove leading spaces. Pay particular attention to this tip if you're trying to sort data that you imported from another application.

● Sort orders vary by locale setting. Make sure that you have the proper locale setting in Regional Options in the Control Panel. For information about changing the locale setting, see your Windows documentation.

I want to use the Fill handle to copy numbers, but I don't see it

Source of the problem

The Fill handle is a handy tool that lets you copy information easily in the worksheet. You can use the Fill handle to copy individual cells or a group of cells that contain a series of numbers, dates, or items in a custom fill series that you have defined. By default, the Fill handle extends any series that Excel recognizes. You can, however, copy the series instead of extending it using the Fill handle. If you don't see the Fill handle, you might have your options set so that it doesn't appear.

How to fix it

When you position the mouse pointer in the lower-right corner of any cell, the pointer changes to a black plus sign called the Fill handle. If you don't see the Fill handle when you move the mouse pointer to the lower-right corner of any cell containing information, follow these steps:

1. On the Tools menu, click Options.

2. Click the Edit tab.

3. Select the Allow Cell Drag And Drop check box. ▶

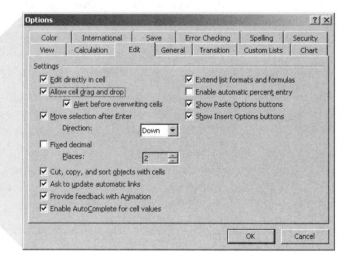

To copy a series of numbers instead of extending the series, press and hold the Ctrl key before you extend the Fill handle. As you drag the Fill handle, the ScreenTip will indicate that Excel plans to copy the numbers in the range instead of extending the range. ▶

    If you forget to press and hold the Ctrl key, click the Auto Fill Options button that appears after you release the Fill handle and click Copy Cells. Excel converts the extended series into a copy of the selected cells. ▶

When you drag the Fill handle, information disappears

When you use the Fill handle, it is possible to delete information accidentally. You'll see this happen if you release the mouse button (while dragging the Fill handle) somewhere inside the selection that you intended to copy. To avoid deleting information, make sure that you drag the Fill handle outside of the selected cells before you release the mouse button.

Borders disappear across page breaks or around objects

Source of the problem

You *know* that you placed a border around certain cells, but you can't *see* the borders. There are a few situations in which you might not see a border.

Borders might not be visible if the border is the same color as the background. You also won't see a border if you apply a 3-D, embossed, or engraved effect to an object. In addition, a border might disappear across a page break.

How to fix it

Excel turns off an object's border when you apply a 3-D, embossed, or engraved effect to an object. If you remove the 3-D effect, the border returns, but it won't return if you remove an embossed or engraved effect; in these cases, you need to reapply the border. To reapply the border, click the object; on the Drawing toolbar, click the arrow next to Line Color, and then click a border color. ▶

Suppose you want to print a border at the bottom of the last row of one page and use the same border at the top of the first row on the next page. Apply an inside border by following these steps:

1. Select the rows on both sides of the page break.

2. On the Format menu, click Cells to display the Format Cells dialog box.

3. Click the Border tab. ▶

4. Click the Inside button under Presets.

5. In the Border section, remove the vertical border by clicking it in the preview diagram.

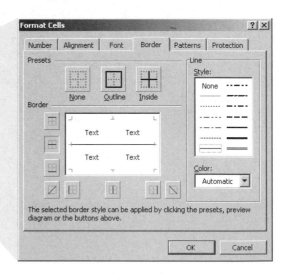

I changed the properties for a shadow effect, but I don't see the new settings on new objects

Source of the problem

You went to some trouble to change the properties of a shadow effect, and you expected to see the changes applied to all objects—but, they aren't. You'll see this kind of behavior in Excel when you change the properties for an object, but you don't change the default style. This behavior not only occurs with shadows, but also with borders, 3-D effects, and fills.

How to fix it

To change the default settings for new objects, follow these steps:

1. Click an object that has the attributes you want to use.

2. On the Drawing toolbar, click Draw.

3. Click Set AutoShape Defaults. ▶

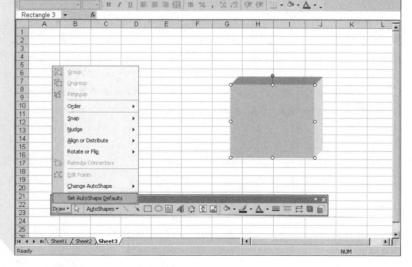

Tip

Changing the fill color of an object only affects its face. To change the color of an object's shadow or 3-D sides, use the Shadow or 3-D tool on the Drawing toolbar.

The results of formulas are wrong after I move or copy cells

Source of the problem

When you copy or move cells containing formulas, the effects on your worksheet depend on the type of cell references used in the formulas you copied or moved: relative or absolute.

How to fix it

Formulas are equations that you create to perform calculations on values in a workbook. A formula starts with an equal sign (=); for example, if you entered the formula =2+3 in cell A1, the contents of cell A1 would be 5, the result of the formula.

Formulas can contain references to other cells in a workbook: if cell A1 contained the number 2, and cell A2 contained the number 3, you could enter the formula =A1+A2 into cell A3, and Excel would display the result of the formula, 5, in cell A3.

The formula in cell A3 in the preceding example contained *relative* cell references. If you copy the formula to cell B3, Excel adjusts the formula so that you'll see =B1+B2 in cell B3. Relative cells references in a formula change as you move or copy the cell containing the formula.

You can, instead, use *absolute* cell references—references that don't change when you copy a formula. Absolute cell references contain dollar signs ($) before one or more components of the cell reference—the column letter, the row number, or both. To restate the original example formula using an absolute cell reference, you would enter the formula in cell A3 as =$A$1+$A$2. If you copied this formula to *any* cell in the workbook, it would *always* return the sum of the numbers found in the cells A1 and A2.

You can also vary the absolute cell reference so that only one portion of the reference remains static. Suppose that, in the preceding example, you entered =$A1+$A2. As you copy this formula into other cells within the worksheet, the column designator, A, would always appear in the formula, but the row numbers would change. If you change the formula to =A$1+A$2 and copy this formula to other cells within the worksheet, the row designators, 1 and 2, would always appear in the formula, but the column designator would change.

You can convert between relative and absolute cell references. Click the cell containing the reference you want to convert, press F2 on your keyboard, move the insertion point to the cell reference you want to change, and then press F4. Each time you press F4, Excel cycles through all four possible combinations. ▶

I expect arrow keys and directional keys to do one thing, but they do something else

Source of the problem

If arrow keys and directional keys, such as Page Up, Home, and Shift+Tab, don't do what you'd expect, be assured that the keys have not taken on a life of their own, and that your keyboard has not been possessed. Instead, the keys might be performing actions associated with Lotus 1-2-3, or you might have engaged Scroll Lock or End mode.

How to fix it

Excel contains a setting that enables Excel to mimic Lotus 1-2-3. If you find that arrow or directional keys are performing unexpectedly, check to see if you have enabled this setting. Follow these steps:

1. On the Tools menu, click **Options**.

2. Click the **Transition** tab. ▶

3. Clear the **Transaction Navigation Keys** check box.

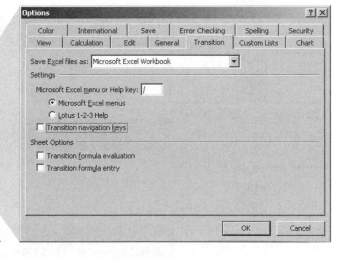

If your arrow and directional keys still behave unexpectedly, make sure you don't have the Scroll Lock key depressed. If you see SCRL on the status bar in the lower-right corner of the Excel window, the Scroll Lock key is engaged. Press it again to disable Scroll Lock. When Scroll Lock is off, the active selection moves as you scroll through a worksheet. If Scroll Lock is on, the navigation keys scroll the screen but don't move the cell pointer.

If neither of the previous solutions fixes your problem, make sure that End mode is off. If END appears on the status bar in the lower-right corner of the Excel window, the End mode is functioning. By default, when you press the End key followed by an arrow key, Excel moves the cell pointer in the direction of the arrow key to the last cell containing an entry.

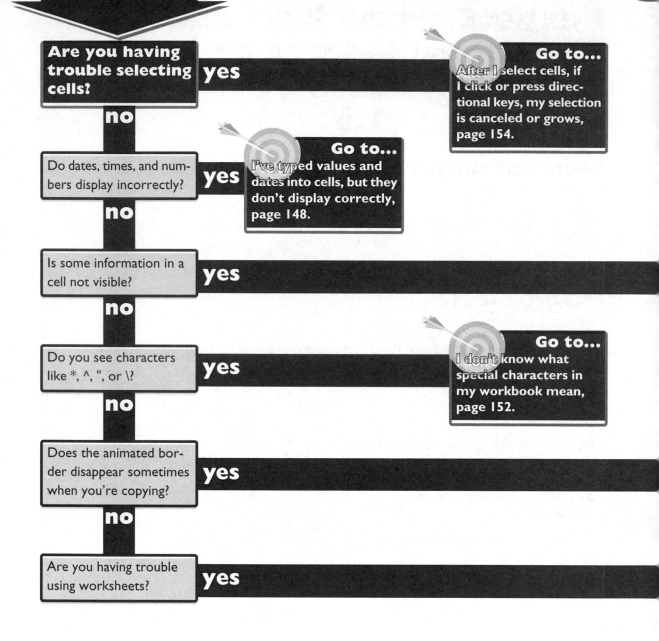

Are you having trouble selecting cells? — **yes**

Go to...
After I select cells, if I click or press directional keys, my selection is canceled or grows, page 154.

no

Do dates, times, and numbers display incorrectly? — **yes**

Go to...
I've typed values and dates into cells, but they don't display correctly, page 148.

no

Is some information in a cell not visible? — **yes**

no

Do you see characters like *, ^, ", or \? — **yes**

Go to...
I don't know what special characters in my workbook mean, page 152.

no

Does the animated border disappear sometimes when you're copying? — **yes**

no

Are you having trouble using worksheets? — **yes**

Go to...
I can't see information in some cells, page 150.

Go to...
Sometimes Excel copies information once and other times repeatedly, page 153.

Go to...
I'm having trouble renaming a worksheet tab, page 146.

If your solution isn't here, check these related chapters:

● Protecting workbooks, page 184

● Formatting worksheets, page 156

Or see the general trouble-shooting tips on page xix.

I'm having trouble renaming a worksheet tab

Source of the problem

You might not be able to rename a worksheet for the following reasons:

- You might not be able to see the worksheet tabs.

- The workbook might be protected.

How to fix it

You might not be able to see the worksheet tabs because they might not be displayed. To display worksheet tabs, follow these steps:

1. On the Tools menu, click Options.

2. In the Options dialog box, click the View tab.

3. In the Window Options section, select the Sheet Tabs check box. ▶

4. Click OK.

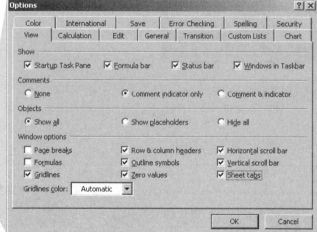

You might not be able to see all the worksheet tabs in the workbook. You can click the tab scrolling buttons to scroll through worksheets, or you can right-click any tab scrolling button and select the worksheet from the menu that appears. ▶

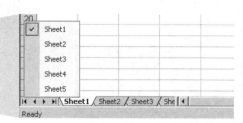

You also can temporarily reduce the size of the horizontal scroll bar. Follow these steps:

1. Point the mouse pointer to the tab split bar.

2. When you see a split pointer, drag the tab split bar to the right. ▶

If the workbook is protected, you cannot rename a worksheet until you turn off protection. Follow these steps:

1. On the Tools menu, point to Protection, and then click Unprotect Workbook. If you instead see Protect Workbook, the workbook is not protected.

2. Type the password to open the workbook.

Selecting multiple worksheets

You might have reason to select more than one worksheet at a time. For example, you might want to enter the same information in the same cells on several worksheets—such as column headings. Or, you might have a formula on Sheet1 that you want to copy to the same location on Sheet2 and Sheet3. You can select and copy the formula on Sheet1, display Sheet2, click in the location where you want the formula to appear, and then select Sheet2 *and* Sheet3. When you click Paste, the formula will appear in the same cell on Sheet2 and Sheet3. If you select more than one worksheet and enter or change data, the changes affect all selected worksheets—and might replace data on the selected worksheets.

- To select only one worksheet, click the worksheet tab. If you don't see the tab you want, click the tab scrolling buttons to display the tab so that you can click it.

- To select two or more adjacent worksheets, click the tab for the first worksheet, and then hold down Shift and click the tab for the last worksheet.

- To select two or more nonadjacent worksheets, click the tab for the first worksheet, and then hold down Ctrl and click the tabs for the other worksheets.

- To select all worksheets in a workbook, right-click a worksheet tab, and then click Select All Sheets on the shortcut menu.

Color-coded worksheet tabs behave a little differently. When you select the worksheet, the worksheet tab name will be underlined in a color you specified. If you see a background color on the worksheet tab, you have not selected the worksheet.

If you have selected multiple worksheets, you can cancel the selection by clicking any worksheet that isn't selected. If you can't see an unselected worksheet, right-click the tab of a selected worksheet, and click Ungroup Worksheets on the shortcut menu. If all the worksheets are selected, clicking one of the worksheet tabs will select that worksheet and cancel the others.

I've typed values and dates into cells, but they don't display correctly

Source of the problem

You typed everything in the same way, but the entries look different. For example, some cells containing numbers show two decimals even if they are both 0, and others show no decimals. You could be having a similar problem with dates and times. Or, maybe you typed a number into a cell and you don't see a number at all—you just see a series of pound (#) signs.

If you have applied one format to some cells and another format to other cells in a workbook, numbers and dates might appear inconsistent. Also, you might see pound signs—which represent error values—when the cell contains a number, date, or time that is wider than the cell.

How to fix it

Check cell formatting for inconsistency. To change the formatting of a cell, follow these steps:

1. Select a cell.

2. On the Format menu, click Cells.

3. On the Number tab, select a category on the left and a format on the right.

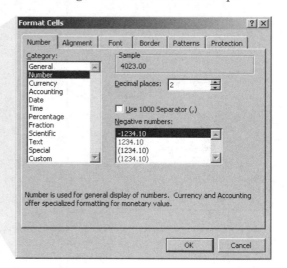

Dates could appear in different formats due to a combination of formatting and lack of formatting. When you apply a date format to a cell, Excel uses that format to display the date. If, however, you type a date into an unformatted cell, Excel uses the format shown in the Regional Options box. To check or change the default format supplied from the Regional Options box, follow these steps:

1. Click the Start button.

2. Point at Settings.

3. Click Control Panel.

4. Double-click Regional Options. ▶

5. Make changes using the list box arrows next to each alternative.

Note

You'll also see an error value in a cell that contains a date or time formula that produces a negative result.

If you see an error value in a cell, you need to widen the column. Move the mouse pointer onto the right boundary of the column heading over the column you want to widen. When the mouse pointer changes to an arrow pointing right and left, drag the column boundary to the right and release it when you think the column is wide enough to display your information. If you still see error values in the column, repeat the process. ▶

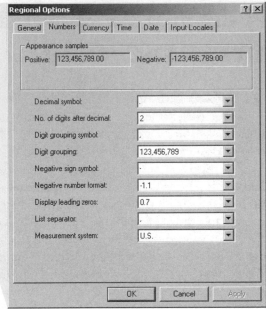

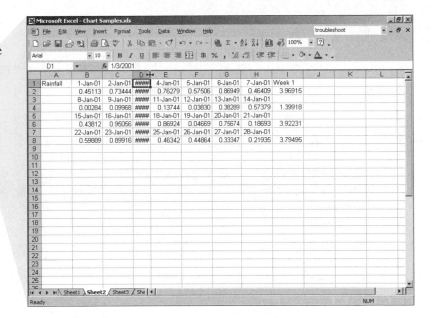

I can't see information in some cells

Source of the problem

This problem can occur if the cells are formatted so that data in the cells is hidden or if text in a cell is the same color as the cell background.

A third situation can also cause this problem: You enter information into A1, and the cell in the adjacent column to the right—B1—also contains information. Column A isn't wide enough to display all the information you entered into A1. Although you can enter up to 255 characters in any cell, Excel displays only as many characters as the column width permits if the adjacent cell to the right contains information. Under these conditions, you won't see all the information in cell A1.

> **Note**
>
> If the adjacent cell to the right is empty, Excel will display all the information you entered; the information will appear to "run over" into the adjacent cell(s).

How to fix it

To remove specific number formats that might be affecting the displayed value, follow these steps:

1. Select the cells.

2. On the Format menu, click Cells.

3. Click the Number tab and, in the Category list, click General.

If you suspect that text and background are the same color, change the color of the background or change the color of the text by selecting the cell(s) and using the Fill Color and Font Color buttons. ▶

In the figure, you can see that cells B1:E1 contain more information than fits within each respective column. Excel displays all the information in cell E1 only because F1 is empty. ▶

	A	B	C	D	E	F
1		Eastern Di	Western D	Northern D	Southern Division	
2	January	4892	4482	4780	4850	
3	February	4673	4119	4388	4046	
4	March	4418	4001	4884	4192	
5	Total	13983	12602	14052	13088	
6						

You can display all the information in any cell using one of two techniques:

- You can widen the column containing information you can't see. To widen a column, move the mouse pointer onto the right boundary of the column heading over the column you want to widen. When the mouse pointer changes to an arrow pointing right and left, drag the column boundary to the right and release it when you think the column is wide enough to display your information. If necessary, repeat the process. ▶

	A	B	C	D	E	F
1		Eastern Di	Western C	Northern C	Southern Division	
2	January	4892	4482	4780	4850	
3	February	4673	4119	4388	4046	
4	March	4418	4001	4884	4192	
5	Total	13983	12602	14052	13088	
6						

- You can wrap the text within the cell so that Excel widens the row instead of the column. Follow these steps:

    1. Select the cells containing information you want to wrap.

    2. On the Format menu, click Cells.

    3. In the Format Cells dialog box, select the Wrap Text check box. ▶

    4. Click OK.

Excel widens the row to accommodate the text. ▼

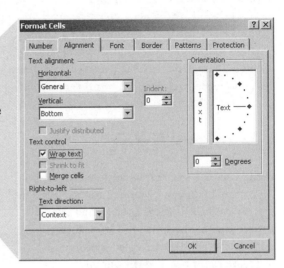

	A	B	C	D	E	F
1		Eastern Division	Western Division	Northern Division	Southern Division	
2	January	4892	4482	4780	4850	
3	February	4673	4119	4388	4046	
4	March	4418	4001	4884	4192	
5	Total	13983	12602	14052	13088	
6						

Tip

You can widen several columns equally and simultaneously. Press the Ctrl key and click each column you want to select. Then drag the right edge of any selected column. When you release the mouse button, Excel resizes all the selected columns equally.

Note

If the text is a single long word, the characters won't wrap. In this case, widen the column or reduce the font size.

I don't know what special characters in my workbook mean

Source of the problem

Wondering where these crazy characters came from or what they mean? You might see special characters such as *, ^, ", or \ in the Formula bar at the beginning of cell information if your workbook was created in Lotus 1-2-3 or if you are working with keys that are used for navigation in Lotus 1-2-3. If the special character appears in the Formula bar but not in the worksheet cells, the character is a Lotus 1-2-3 formatting code.

In Lotus 1-2-3 formats, you include an apostrophe (') to left-align text within a cell. You include a quotation mark (") to right-align text within a cell. Use the caret (^) to center text in a cell, and use a backslash (\) to fill the cell with the character typed in the cell.

How to fix it

If these special characters appear in both the Formula bar and in the cell, they are nothing more than stray characters; you can use the Find and Replace commands to locate and eliminate them.

However, if these special characters appear *only* in the Formula bar, you cannot use the Find and Replace commands to locate them because they are not actual data. Instead, follow these steps:

1. On the Tools menu, click Options.

2. Click the Transition tab.

3. Clear the Transition Navigation Keys check box. ▶

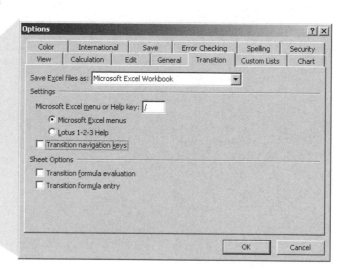

Sometimes Excel copies information once and other times repeatedly

Source of the problem

When you use the Copy commands on the Edit menu or click the Copy buttons, Excel places an animated border of dashed lines around the cell(s) that you copied to identify the information that you're copying. You can paste the information in a variety of ways. The way you paste determines if that animated border disappears—which also determines whether you'll be able to paste the information more than once. ▶

	A	B	C	D	E	F	G	H	I
1	Rainfall	1-Jan-01	2-Jan-01	3-Jan-01	4-Jan-01	5-Jan-01	6-Jan-01	7-Jan-01	Week 1
2		0.45113	0.73444	0.11216	0.76279	0.57506	0.86949	0.46409	3.96915
3		8-Jan-01	9-Jan-01	10-Jan-01	11-Jan-01	12-Jan-01	13-Jan-01	14-Jan-01	
4		0.00284	0.09968	0.16423	0.13744	0.03830	0.38289	0.57379	1.39918
5		15-Jan-01	16-Jan-01	17-Jan-01	18-Jan-01	19-Jan-01	20-Jan-01	21-Jan-01	
6		0.43812	0.95056	0.67403	0.86924	0.04669	0.75674	0.18693	3.92231
7		22-Jan-01	23-Jan-01	24-Jan-01	25-Jan-01	26-Jan-01	27-Jan-01	28-Jan-01	
8		0.59889	0.89916	0.83202	0.46342	0.44864	0.33347	0.21935	3.79495

How to fix it

Completing the copy operation can be a three-step process:

1. Click the cell pointer at the location where you want the information to appear.
2. Paste the information by pressing Ctrl+V or on the Edit menu, click Paste.
3. Press the Esc key.

Pressing Esc removes the animated border that surrounds the cells you selected and copied or cut. If you want to paste the information into more than one location, do *not* press Esc immediately. Instead, repeat Steps 1 and 2 as many times as necessary.

You can also paste information one time (or a final time) by selecting a cell and pressing Enter; if you use this method, the data will be copied, the animated border will disappear, the information you copied will be removed from the Clipboard, and you won't unintentionally paste it again. Or, if you're done copying but the animated border remains (indicating that the Clipboard still contains the copied information), you can clear both while continuing your work in the worksheet by typing in a new cell. The animated border disappears and pasting no longer occurs when you press Enter.

Note

All of this information also applies if you choose Cut instead of Copy. It's the Paste part of the operation that determines when the animated border and the Clipboard contents disappear.

After I select cells, if I click or press directional keys, my selection is canceled or grows

Source of the problem

You might see this type of behavior when you're trying to add to a selection or if Excel is operating in extended selection mode.

How to fix it

If you're trying to include additional adjacent cells in an existing selection, hold down the Shift key and click the last cell you want to include in the selection. The rectangular range between the active cell—the first cell in the selection—and the cell you click becomes the new selection.

You can include additional nonadjacent cells in a selection if you hold down the Ctrl key as you select cells by either clicking or dragging.

If you see EXT in the lower-right corner of the Excel status bar, Excel is operating in extended selection mode. In this mode, your selection will grow as you click or press keys to move around. Effectively, in extended selection mode, you can use your directional keys as if you had also pressed and held the Shift key. Extended selection mode gives you more freedom because it doesn't require that you use both hands.

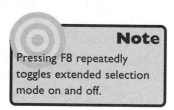

Press F8 to cancel extended selection mode.

> **Note**
> Pressing F8 repeatedly toggles extended selection mode on and off.

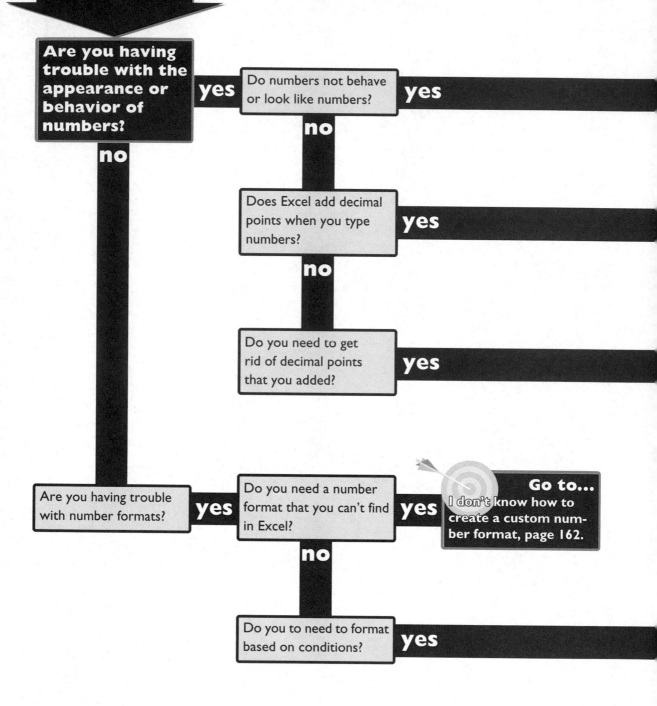

Are you having trouble with the appearance or behavior of numbers?

yes → Do numbers not behave or look like numbers?

yes →

no ↓

Does Excel add decimal points when you type numbers?

yes →

no ↓

Do you need to get rid of decimal points that you added?

yes →

no ↓

Are you having trouble with number formats?

yes → Do you need a number format that you can't find in Excel?

yes → **Go to...** I don't know how to create a custom number format, page 162.

no ↓

Do you to need to format based on conditions?

yes →

Go to...

Numbers don't seem to behave like numbers, page 158.

Quick fix

To stop adding decimal points to numbers as you enter them, follow these steps:

1. On the Tools menu, click Options.

2. Click the Edit tab.

3. Clear the Fixed Decimal check box.

Quick fix

To remove decimal points from numbers you've already entered, type a power of 10 (for example, 10, 100, 1000, etc.) into an empty cell and copy it to the Clipboard. Select the numbers with decimal points, and from the Edit menu, click Paste Special. Then, click Multiply.

Go to...

I want to format based on conditions I specify, page 160.

If your solution isn't here, check these related chapters:

- Editing data, page 134
- Entering and selecting data, page 144

Or see the general trouble-shooting tips on page xix.

Numbers don't seem to behave like numbers

Source of the problem

The number format applied to a cell determines the way Microsoft Excel displays a number in that cell on the worksheet. The number format, which is displayed in the Formula bar when you select the cell, does not affect the cell value Excel uses in calculations.

This problem occurs when the cells containing the numbers are formatted as text, not numbers. The numbers will align to the left of the cell even though you have not changed the default alignment, which is General.

How to fix it

To convert the format to numbers, turn on background error checking by following these steps:

1. On the Tools menu, click Options.

2. Click the Error Checking tab.

3. Make sure the Enable Background Error Checking and Number Stored As Text check boxes are selected. ▶

4. Click OK.

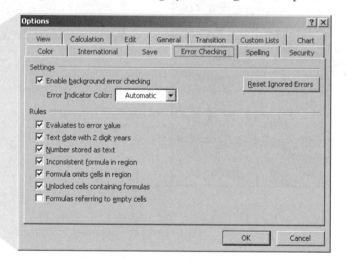

You'll see a green error indicator in any cells formatted as text that contain numbers. To convert the format to numbers, follow these steps:

1. Click the cell(s) you want to convert.

2. Next to the cell, click the button that appears.

3. Click Convert To Number. ▶

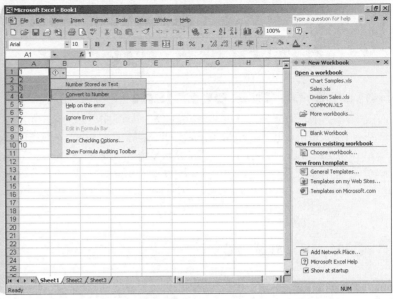

Removing number formats

You can remove number formats that might affect the displayed value. Follow these steps:

1. Click the cells.

2. On the Format menu, click Cells.

3. Click the Number tab.

4. In the Category list, click General. ▶

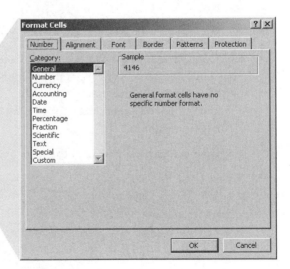

I want to format based on conditions I specify

Source of the problem

When you apply conditional formatting, such as cell shading or font color to a cell, Microsoft Excel applies the formats if the value in the cell meets a condition you stipulate. If the condition is true, conditional formats override formats that you might have applied directly to a cell by using the Cells command on the Format menu or a Formatting toolbar button. You can have Excel evaluate the value in a cell or a formula to determine if the conditional formatting should be applied.

How to fix it

Follow these steps to set up a conditional format that checks values in selected cells:

1. Select the cells to which you want to add conditional formatting.

2. On the Format menu, click Conditional Formatting.

3. Click Cell Value Is in the first list to tell Excel to check the values in selected cells before applying conditional formatting. Click Formula Is to type a formula or select a cell containing a formula that you want to use to specify a formatting condition.

4. Click the comparison phrase in the next box to the right.

5. Type a constant value or a formula. If you enter a formula, precede it by an equal sign (=). ▶

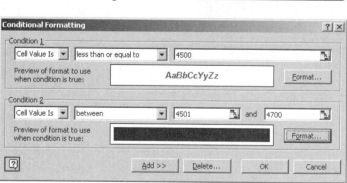

Conditional Formatting

Condition 1
Cell Value Is | less than or equal to | 4500
Preview of format to use when condition is true: AaBbCcYyZz | Format...

Condition 2
Cell Value Is | between | 4501 | and | 4700
Preview of format to use when condition is true: | Format...

Add >> | Delete... | OK | Cancel

When conditional formatting doesn't produce the results you expect

First, check the cell references, particularly if you used a formula as the conditional formatting criteria. It's possible that you included the wrong cell references in the formula. Second, if you've set more than one condition, check to see if conditions overlap. When conditions overlap, Excel applies only the format of the first true condition. For example, if you set up a condition that applies bolding to the fonts of cells with values between 300 and 400, and you add a condition that places a border around cells with values below 340, the cells containing values between 300 and 340 will appear in bold (the first condition) but will not have borders (the second condition). You might be able to switch the order of the conditions or redefine the two conditions to achieve the formatting results you want.

6. Click the Format button in the Conditional Formatting box. The Format Cells box appears.

7. Click the formatting you want Excel to apply when a selected cell contains a value that meets the condition or when the formula you supplied returns the value TRUE. In the figure, the cell contents appears in red, bold, and italic type. You can apply font color, borders, or background color to the cells that meet the condition.

8. Click OK to redisplay the Conditional Formatting box.

9. If you want to include additional conditions, click Add, and then repeat Steps 3 through 7.

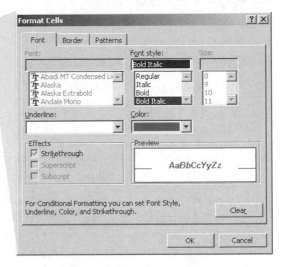

When creating conditions, you can assign a maximum of three conditions. If the selected cells don't meet any of the conditions, the cells retain any existing formatting that you might have applied. If more than one specified condition is true, Excel applies only the formats of the first true condition.

You can use the Format Painter tool to copy conditional formatting.

You also can change or remove formatting from the Conditional Formatting dialog box. Follow these steps:

1. Click the cells that contain conditional formatting.

2. On the Format menu, click Conditional Formatting.

3. To change formats, click the Format button for the condition you want to change. To remove formats on the current tab of the Format Cells dialog box, click the Clear button.

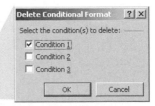

4. To remove one or more conditions, click the Delete button.

5. Select the check boxes for the conditions you want to delete.

I don't know how to create a custom number format

Source of the problem

Although Excel has many number formats available, you might find that you need a format that doesn't exist. You can create your own number format, and then apply it to cells as needed. Custom formats are saved with the workbook.

How to fix it

To create a custom number format, follow these steps:

1. Select the cell(s) to which you want to apply a customized number format.

2. On the Format menu, click Cells.

3. In the Format Cells dialog box, click the Number tab.

4. In the Category list, click a category that is similar to the one you want.

5. To the right of the Category box, under the Sample box, click one of the built-in formats that is similar to the one you want to create. Don't worry about messing up the built-in format, because you'll be creating a copy to customize. ▶

6. In the Category list, click Custom.

7. In the Type box, create the format you want by editing the format codes Excel supplies from the model you chose.

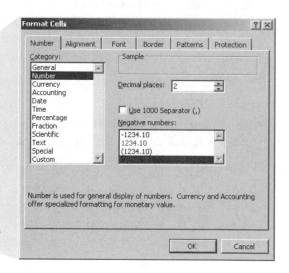

Each custom format code that you create can be composed of up to four sections to describe the appearance of positive numbers, negative numbers, zeros, and text in that order. You separate each section with a semicolon. You don't need to define all four sections: you can, for example, define sections 1, 3, and 4—and skip section 2—by including an extra semicolon after you define section 1. If you don't include an extra semicolon to indicate you're skipping a section and you don't define all four sections, Excel assumes that you are defining sections in the order listed previously. If you define only three sections in your custom format, Excel will format positive numbers, negative numbers, and zeros, but not text. If you define only two sections, Excel will format positive numbers and zeros using the first section and negative numbers using the second section— and again, won't format any text that you enter. If you define only one section, Excel uses it to format all numbers. ▶

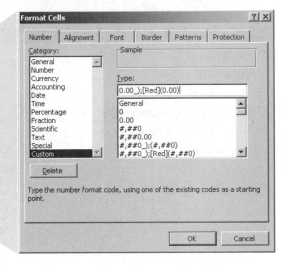

You can display both text and numbers in a cell if you enclose text in quotation marks (""). Suppose, for example, that you want to make sure everyone understands that customer balances are either due to you or are credit balances. You could create a format $0.00 " Due from Customer"; $-0.00 " Credit Balance". Then, a positive amount of $546.32 would appear on the worksheet as $546.32 Due from Customer and a negative amount would appear as $-546.32 Credit Balance. Be sure to include the space character inside the quotation marks before the text to separate the number from the text on screen. You don't need to use quotation marks if you are trying to display any of the following characters: $ - + / ( ) : ! ^ & ' (left single quotation mark) ' (right single quotation mark) ~ { } = < > and the space character.

If you want to set a color for a section of the format, type any of the following eight colors in square brackets in the section, making sure that you place the color code at the beginning of the section: Black, Blue, Cyan, Green, Magenta, Red, White, Yellow.

I don't know how to create a custom number format

(continued from page 163)

Use the following information to create special date and time formats.

To display	Use this code
Months as 1–12	m
Months as 01–12	mm
Months as Jan–Dec	mmm
Months as January–December	mmmm
Months as the first letter of the month	mmmmm
Days as 1–31	d
Days as 01–31	dd
Days as Sun–Sat	ddd
Days as Sunday–Saturday	dddd
Years as 00–99	yy
Years as 1900–9999	yyyy
Hours as 0–23	h
Hours as 00–23	hh
Minutes as 0–59	m
Minutes as 00–59	mm
Seconds as 0–59	s
Seconds as 00–59	ss
Hours as 7 AM	h AM/PM
Time as 7:49 PM	h:mm AM/PM
Time as 7:49:14 P	h:mm:ss A/P
Fractions of a second	h:mm:ss.00

If you use "m" immediately after the "h" or "hh" code or immediately before the "ss" code, Excel displays minutes instead of the month. If you create a format that contains an AM or PM, Excel uses a 12-hour clock to display the time. "AM" or "A" indicates times from midnight until noon and "PM" or "P" indicates times from noon until midnight. If you create a custom format containing a time and you don't include an AM or PM, Excel uses a 24-hour clock to display the time.

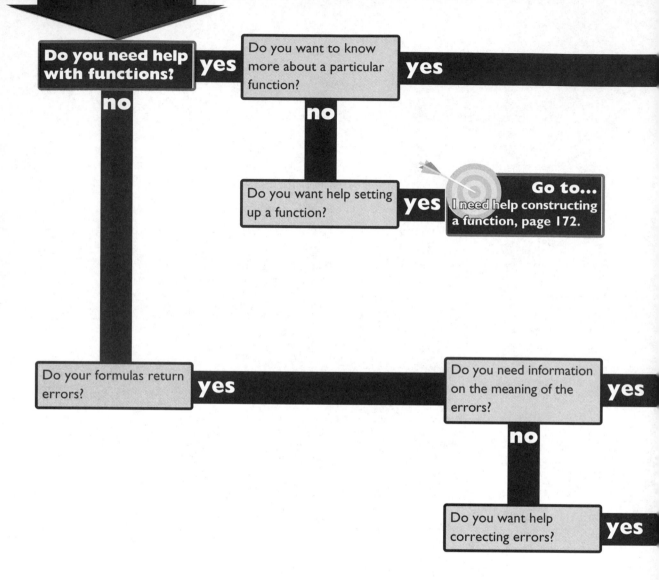

Do you need help with functions?

yes → Do you want to know more about a particular function? **yes**

no

Do you want help setting up a function? **yes**

no

Go to...
I need help constructing a function, page 172.

Do your formulas return errors? **yes**

Do you need information on the meaning of the errors? **yes**

no

Do you want help correcting errors? **yes**

Quick fix

To see details and examples of functions, use Excel's Help system. In the Office Assistant bubble or in the Answer Wizard, type the function's name, and click Search.

Go to...

I see an error message instead of the formula's result, page 170.

Go to...

I need help correcting formulas, page 168.

If your solution isn't here, check this related chapter:

● Help, page 40

Or see the general troubleshooting tips on page xix.

I need help correcting formulas

Source of the problem

Errors in formulas can produce error values or simply "the wrong answer." You can use some tools in Excel to help you find and fix these errors.

How to fix it

Excel contains an error-checking facility for formulas that works very much like a spelling checker. You can let it run as you work in Excel and mark cells that contain errors. You can then examine individual cells to correct them or run the error checker to check the entire worksheet. To enable error checking, follow these steps:

1. On the Tools menu, click Options.

2. Click the Error Checking tab, and make sure that Enable Background Error Checking is selected.

3. Select the appropriate check boxes in the Rules section to enable Excel to follow those rules during error checking. ▶

   To check the entire worksheet, on the Tools menu, click Error Checking. If your worksheet contains errors, you'll see the Error Checking dialog box. Use the buttons on the right to correct the errors. Click Next to continue searching for errors. ▶

   Excel marks errors it finds on your work-sheet with a small triangle in the upper-left corner of the cell. You can check errors one at a time by clicking a cell containing the triangle marker. Excel displays

Note

Once you "ignore" an error, Excel won't find it again unless you reopen the Options dialog box and, on the Error Checking tab, click Reset Ignored Errors.

a button next to the cell that you can click to see a menu of choices to help you fix the error. ▶

For example, if you click Help On This Error, the Help system opens, explaining the error. If you click Show Calculation Steps, you'll see a box like this one that shows you the calculation Excel is actually attempting to make. ▼

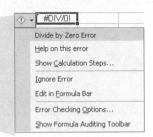

#DIV/0!
Divide by Zero Error
Help on this error
Show Calculation Steps...
Ignore Error
Edit in Formula Bar
Error Checking Options...
Show Formula Auditing Toolbar

Evaluate Formula ? X

Reference:
Sheet4!$B$7

Evaluation:
= 4146/0

The next evaluation will result in an error.

[Evaluate] [Step In] [Step Out] [Close]

If you click Edit In Formula Bar, the formula opens in the Formula bar so that you can change it. If you click Error Checking Options, you'll see the Error Checking tab of the Options dialog box.

You can use another technique to track down errors—you can trace the relationships between formulas and cells. Excel identifies precedent cells and dependent cells and draws arrows on screen to identify relationships. A precedent cell is a cell referred to by a formula. A dependent cell contains formulas that refer to other cells.

To trace relationships, follow these steps:

1. Make sure that you can view objects on the worksheet. On the Tools menu, click Options. Click the View tab. In the Objects section, click Show All or Show Placeholders.

2. Display the Formula Auditing toolbar by right-clicking any toolbar button and clicking Formula Auditing.

3. Click the cell for which you want to see relationships.

4. Click the Trace Precedents or Trace Dependents button. Excel draws arrows to demonstrate the relationship. ▶

> **Tip**
>
> The Evaluate Formula box is particularly useful when you're working with a nested formula. You can use this box to step through the formula. Click the cell containing the nested formula, click the Tools menu, point to Formula Auditing, and click Evaluate Formula.

> **Tip**
>
> To trace precedents, you must click a cell containing a formula. To trace dependents, you must click a cell that is used in a formula (it might contain a value or a formula).

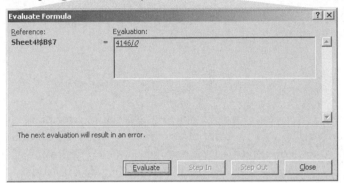

	A	B	C	D	E	F
1		Eastern Division	Western Division	Northern Division	Southern Division	
2	January	4146	4541	4059	4892	
3	February	4402	4545	4942	4026	
4	March	4762	4717	4756	4340	
5	Total	13310	13803	13757	13258	
6						
7		#DIV/0!				
8						
9		0				
10						
11						
12						
13						

Formula Auditing

Trace Dependents

Trace Precedents

I see an error message instead of the formula's result

Source of the problem

Excel displays an error value if it is unable to calculate the result of a formula. Each error type has different causes and different solutions.

How to fix it

Some of the following error values are displayed if Excel cannot evaluate the result of a formula.

You'll see ##### when a formula's result is either a negative date or time or when the column isn't wide enough to display the formula's result. For negative dates or times, double-check your formula; if it's correct, try applying a format that *isn't* a date or time format. Otherwise, try widen-

ing the column, changing the number format of the cell, or shrinking the contents of the cell to fit the available space. You can shrink the font of the selected cell so that the information fits in the cell by following these steps:

1. Click the cell.

2. On the Format menu, click **Cells**.

3. Click the Alignment tab.

4. Select the Shrink To Fit check box in the Text Control section. ▶

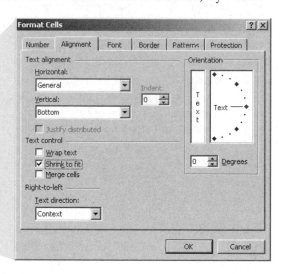

To determine the cause and fix each of the following errors, follow these steps:

1. Click the cell that displays the error.

2. Click the button that appears.

3. Click Trace Error if it appears or click Help On This Error to review the possible causes and solutions. ▶

When your formula contains text that Excel doesn't understand, you'll see the #NAME? error. This error could occur if in the formula you:

● Type a range name that does not exist

● Misspell the range name

● Use a label in a formula that doesn't permit the use of labels

● Enter text in a formula without enclosing the text in quotation marks

● Reference another sheet without enclosing the reference in quotation marks

● Omit a colon (:) in a range reference

You'll see the #VALUE! error value under two conditions. You might have used the wrong type of argument in the formula. An argument is a value in a function that Excel uses to calculate the value of the function. It's also possible that you supplied the wrong kind of item on either side of an operator (+, -, *, and / are examples of operators). You might, for example, have entered text when the formula required a number or a logical value, such as TRUE or FALSE. Or, you might have used a range when the operator or function required a single value.

The #DIV/0! error value appears when you've divided by 0. You might have entered a formula that explicitly divides by zero, such as 3/0, or you might have divided by a blank cell or a cell that contains zero. Click the cell that displays the error, click the button that appears, and then click Trace Error if it appears and review the possible causes and solutions.

You'll see the #N/A error value when a formula is expecting a value that it can't find. For example, the formula might have referred to a cell that was supposed to contain data, but didn't.

The #REF! error value appears when a cell reference isn't valid. You might have a formula that refers to cells you deleted, or you might have pasted over cells referenced in formulas. You'll also see this error value if you are using a link to a program that is not running. (You can solve this problem by starting the program.)

The #NUM! error value appears when you use invalid numeric values in a formula or function. For example, you might have used an invalid number format such as $1,000 as an argument when you should have used 1000. Or, you might have entered a formula that produces a number that is too large or too small to be represented in Excel, which can display values between $-1*10^{307}$ and $1*10^{307}$.

The #NULL! error value appears when you specify an intersection of two areas that do not intersect. You might not have used the colon (:) to separate references in a range such as A1:A5. If your formula operates on two ranges that don't intersect, you need to separate the reference to the ranges with a comma, such as A1:A5,D1:D5.

I need help constructing a function

Source of the problem

You know that Excel contains all these wonderful predefined formulas called functions, and you'd love to use one, but you haven't a clue as to which one to use or how to use it. Excel can actually help you through the process.

How to fix it

To construct a function, follow these steps:

1. Click the cell in which you want to place the function.

2. Click the Insert Function button on the Formula bar.

3. In the Search For A Function box in the Insert Function dialog box, describe the function you want to insert.

4. Click Go. Excel displays suggested functions in the Select A Function list.

5. Click a function to insert. The description of the function appears at the bottom of the box. For more detailed information, click the Help On This Function link to display Help for the function.

6. Click OK. Excel places the function in the Formula bar and displays the Function Arguments dialog box, which contains suggested arguments if Excel can figure them out for you.

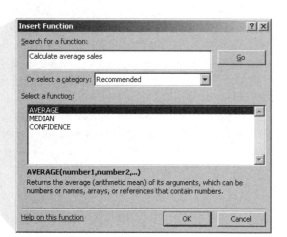

7. If necessary, enter a number, cell address, or range in the first argument box. (You can also move the Function Arguments dialog box and click a cell or range of cells on the worksheet to enter the argument.) At the bottom of the box, Excel displays the result of the formula based on the argument. ▶

8. If necessary, click in the next argument box and enter an argument.

9. When you've supplied all the argument information, click OK.

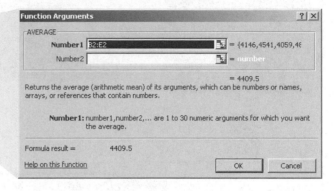

Function Arguments	? X

AVERAGE

Number1 B2:E2 ▦ = {4146,4541,4059,46

Number2 ▦ = number

= 4409.5

Returns the average (arithmetic mean) of its arguments, which can be numbers or names, arrays, or references that contain numbers.

Number1: number1,number2,... are 1 to 30 numeric arguments for which you want the average.

Formula result = 4409.5

Help on this function | OK | Cancel |

Tip

You don't need to fill in the optional argument boxes; the required boxes appear with bold labels.

How Excel searches for functions

Excel matches the words you type to the available functions, looking for common factors. If Excel doesn't suggest a function that does what you want, increase the number of descriptive words that you type. For example, if you want to calculate the mean monthly interest rate of a loan and you type "interest rate" in the Search For A Function box, Excel suggests only five functions—and none of them is appropriate for calculating a mean value. But if you type "mean monthly interest rate" in the search box, Excel returns a much longer list of functions, including the suitable AVERAGE function.

Do you want to exchange information between Excel and FrontPage?

yes → **Go to...** I need to get Excel information into FrontPage, page 176.

no

Do you want to exchange information between Excel and Access?

yes → Do want to use an Access PivotTable in Excel?

yes → **Go to...** I created a PivotTable in Access that I want to include in an Excel worksheet, page 178.

no

Do you want to use other Access information in Excel?

yes →

no

Do you have information in Excel that you want to use in Access?

yes →

Go to...
I want to import Access data into Excel, page 180.

Go to...
I have information in Excel that I want to export to an Access database, page 182.

If your solution isn't here, check these related chapters:

- Trading data with other programs, page 420
- Sharing data, page 86

Or see the general trouble-shooting tips on page xix.

I need to get Excel information into FrontPage

Source of the problem

You have created a table, a chart, or even an entire workbook in Excel and now you need the information in FrontPage.

You can use any of three methods to send Excel information to FrontPage:

- Copy and paste using the Clipboard.

- Save a selection, a worksheet, or a chart as a Web page.

- Save an entire workbook as a set of Web files.

How to fix it

To copy a table or chart from Excel to FrontPage, follow these steps:

1. In Excel, select the table or chart you want to copy.

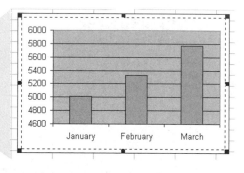

2. Click the Copy button. ▶

> ### Note
> Using the copy and paste method doesn't preserve formatting; you might need to reapply table formatting in FrontPage.

3. Switch to FrontPage and open the Web page where you want the table or chart to appear.

4. Click the Paste button. ▶

To save a table or chart as a Web page, follow these steps:

1. In Excel, select the table or chart you want to copy.

2. On the File menu, click Save As Web Page.

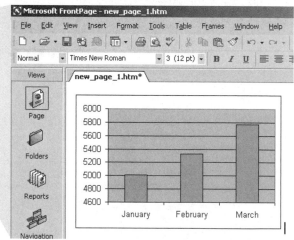

3. In the Save area, click the Selection option. Next to the word *Selection* you'll see the selection type: a cell range, Sheet, or Chart.

4. Click a folder in the Save In list. ▶

5. Type a name for the Web page in the File Name box.

6. Click Save.

7. In FrontPage, import your table or chart.

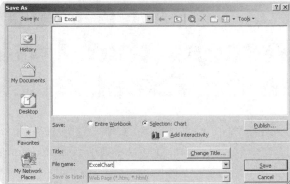

To use a workbook containing two or more sheets as a set of Web files, follow these steps:

1. In Excel, open a workbook containing two or more worksheets or chart sheets.

2. On the File menu, click Save As Web Page.

3. In the Save As dialog box, click the Entire Workbook option.

4. Click a folder in the Save In list.

5. Type a name for the Web page in the File Name box.

6. Click Save.

7. In FrontPage, on the File menu, click Open Web.

8. Navigate to the location where you saved your Excel workbook as a set of Web files.

9. Click Open. FrontPage displays a message asking to add Web-related information to the folder to help manage hyperlinks and other site content.

10. Click Yes.

In FrontPage, click the Folders view to see the Web files created from your workbook. Clicking any .htm file opens the Web version of your workbook in Excel. Files with a .gif extension are charts; if you click a .gif file, the chart opens in the program you typically use when opening .gif files—for many of us, that's Internet Explorer. ▶

Contents of 'C:\My Documents\Excel\Chart Samples_files'					
Name	Title	Size	Type	Modified Date	Modifi
_private					
images					
filelist.xml	filelist.xml	1KB	xml	7/21/2001 4:58 PM	OPTIP
image001.gif	image001.gif	5KB	gif	7/21/2001 4:58 PM	OPTIP
image002.gif	image002.gif	3KB	gif	7/21/2001 4:58 PM	OPTIP
image003.gif	image003.gif	5KB	gif	7/21/2001 4:58 PM	OPTIP
sheet001.htm	sheet001.htm	16KB	htm	7/21/2001 4:58 PM	OPTIP
sheet002.htm	sheet002.htm	16KB	htm	7/21/2001 4:58 PM	OPTIP
sheet003.htm	sheet003.htm	5KB	htm	7/21/2001 4:58 PM	OPTIP
sheet004.htm	sheet004.htm	5KB	htm	7/21/2001 4:58 PM	OPTIP
sheet005.htm	sheet005.htm	13KB	htm	7/21/2001 4:58 PM	OPTIP
stylesheet.css	stylesheet.css	2KB	css	7/21/2001 4:58 PM	OPTIP
tabstrip.htm	tabstrip.htm	2KB	htm	7/21/2001 4:58 PM	OPTIP

I created a PivotTable in Access that I want to include in an Excel worksheet

Source of the problem

The PivotTable exists in Access, but you'd like to include it in an Excel workbook. You can copy the Access PivotTable into Excel so that the Excel copy is not affected by any changes you make in Access. If you prefer, you can export the Access PivotTable. This process creates a link between the Excel and Access PivotTables so that the Excel PivotTable will update if you make changes to the Access PivotTable.

How to fix it

To import a PivotTable that does not update if you make changes in Access, follow these steps:

1. In Acess, open a datasheet or form in PivotTable view.

2. Do one of the following:

   ● To copy the entire PivotTable view, press Ctrl+A.

   ● To copy a part of a PivotTable view, select the elements that you want to copy.

3. On the PivotTable toolbar, click Copy. ▼

4. Switch to Excel and click where you want the data from the PivotTable view to appear.

		Last Name:	Davolio	Dodsworth	Fuller	King	Grand Total
		allahan					
Years	Quarters	SaleAmount:	SaleAmount:	SaleAmount:	SaleAmount:	SaleAmount:	Total Sales
1996	Qtr3	$584.00	$1,614.88	$2,490.50	$1,176.00	$479.40	$33,185.20
		$1,101.20	$1,376.00	$1,873.80	$1,200.80	$1,117.80	
		$420.00	$291.84		$613.20	$88.80	
		$1,488.80	$1,743.36		$121.60		
		$351.00	$1,296.00		$608.00		
		$3,016.00	$848.70		$424.00		
		$819.00	$954.40				
		$2,169.00	$498.50				
		$755.00	$268.80				
		$336.00					
		$11,040.00	$8,892.48	$4,364.30	$4,143.60	$1,686.00	
	Qtr4	$3,741.30	$2,094.30	$5,275.71	$1,614.80	$1,191.20	$77,442.59
		$240.40	$2,835.00	$88.50	$182.40	$112.00	
		$144.80	$1,497.00	$166.00	$1,810.00	$2,036.16	

Note

Because PivotTable reports in Excel cannot display some PivotTable view layouts and calculations, the PivotTable report in Excel might look different from the PivotTable view in Access.

5. Click Paste. The PivotTable appears in Excel. Note that you might need to increase the column width to see all the values. ▶

If you export a copy of the Access PivotTable view to Excel, you can refresh the table in Excel if you make changes to the information in Access. To export an Access PivotTable view, follow these steps:

1. Open a datasheet or form in PivotTable view.

2. Right-click in the body of the PivotTable view and click Hide Details. ▶

3. On the PivotTable toolbar, click Export to Microsoft Excel to run or switch to Excel and display the data in a PivotTable report. ▼

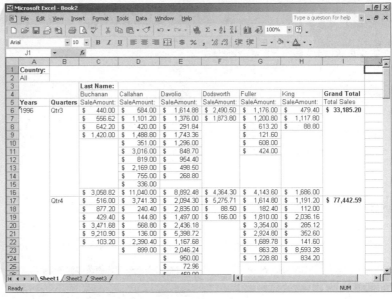

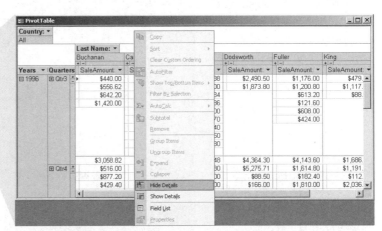

Data is missing after copying from Access to Excel

When you copy data in a PivotTable view to the Clipboard and paste it into Microsoft Excel, only visible rows and columns are copied. Any data that you have hidden or filtered out is not copied.

Before you copy data, turn off filtering to show all data in the PivotTable view and display the detail data that you want copied.

To avoid having to show all the data first, export rather than copy the contents of the Access PivotTable view. When you export instead of copy, all of the data is automatically included with the same filtering in effect. You have the same access to additional fields in the underlying record source that you do in the Access PivotTable view, and you can change the filtering in Excel.

I want to import Access data into Excel

Source of the problem

You've created a great Access database, and you'd like to use information it contains in Excel. From Access, you can save an object's output as an Excel file or load the output of a table, query, form, or report into an Excel workbook.

How to fix it

To save the output of an Access object as a Microsoft Excel file, follow these steps:

1. In the Database window in Access, click the name of the object you want to save. To save part of a datasheet, open the datasheet and select the portion you want to save. ▶

2. On the File menu, click Export.

3. In the Save As Type box, click Microsoft Excel 5-7 (*.xls) or Microsoft Excel 97-2002 (.xls).

4. In the Save In box, click the drive or folder where you want to save the file.

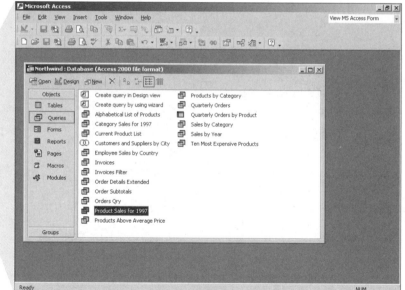

5. In the File Name box, enter a name for the file.

6. Select the Save Formatted check box. Depending on the object you chose to export, the check box might not be available; if the box is unavailable, skip to Step 7. ▶

7. Click Export.

8. In Excel, on the File menu, click Open.

9. Highlight the file you just saved and click Open.

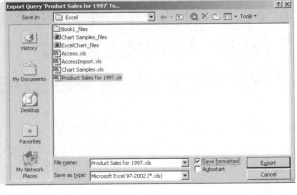

If you prefer, you can load the output of an Access table, query, form, or report into an Excel workbook. This process creates an Excel workbook containing the Access information when you follow these steps:

1. In the Access Database window, click the name of the datasheet, form, or report you want to save and load into Microsoft Excel.

2. On the Tools menu, point to Office Links.

3. Click Analyze It With Microsoft Excel. ▶

The Access table, query, form, or report appears in an Excel workbook.

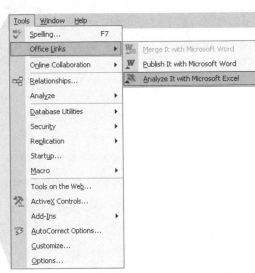

Note

To save a selection of a datasheet, open the datasheet, and then select the portion of the datasheet that you want to use in Excel. Then choose the Analyze It With Microsoft Excel command.

I have information in Excel that I want to export to an Access database

Source of the problem

Suppose that you started entering information into Excel and then realized that it would be better to create an Access database. You don't need to lose the time you've already spent entering information into Excel; you can export the Excel information into a table in an Access database.

How to fix it

Make sure the Excel data is in list format where each column, which represents a field in an Access database, has a label in the first row and contains related information, such as an invoice database or a set of client names and phone numbers. Don't worry if you have more information in the Excel workbook than you want to import into Access; as you complete the import process, Access gives you the opportunity to skip fields. ▶

There should not be any blank rows or columns within the list. Then, follow these steps:

	A	B	C
1	Name	Phone	
2	John	555-1212	
3	Mary	555-1234	
4	Jim	555-3214	
5	Ellen	555-9874	
6	Nancy	555-6547	
7	Harvey	555-4569	
8	Rita	555-3753	

1. Close the Excel workbook that contains the data you want to use in Access.

2. In Access, open the database where you want to store the Excel data.

3. On the File menu, point to Get External Data.

4. Click Import.

5. In the Import dialog box, click Microsoft Excel in the Files Of Type box.

6. In the Look In list, locate the file you want to import, and then double-click the file.

7. Using the Import Spreadsheet Wizard, identify the worksheet or named range you want to mport. ▶

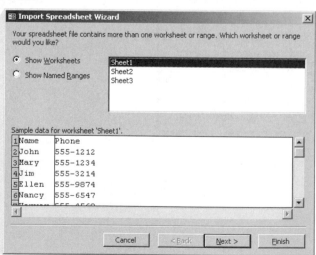

8. Click Next and select the First Row Contains Column Headings check box.

9. Click Next and specify whether to store the Excel information in a new table or add it to an existing table.

10. Click Next and specify information about each of the fields in the worksheet that you want to import. To skip importing a field, click the field, and then select the Do Not Import Field (Skip) check box. To index a field, choose Yes (Duplicates OK) or Yes (No Duplicates) in the Indexed list. ▶

Note

You should index values in your table that you expect to use when searching or sorting; indexing speeds up these processes.

11. Click Next and define primary keys for your table or let Access add the primary key. Access uses the primary key to uniquely identify each record in your table. The primary key also helps you retrieve data more quickly. ▶

12. Click Next to assign a name to your table.

13. Click Finish. The table appears in the Database window in Access.

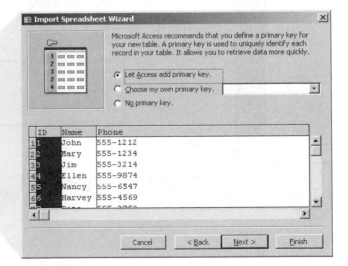

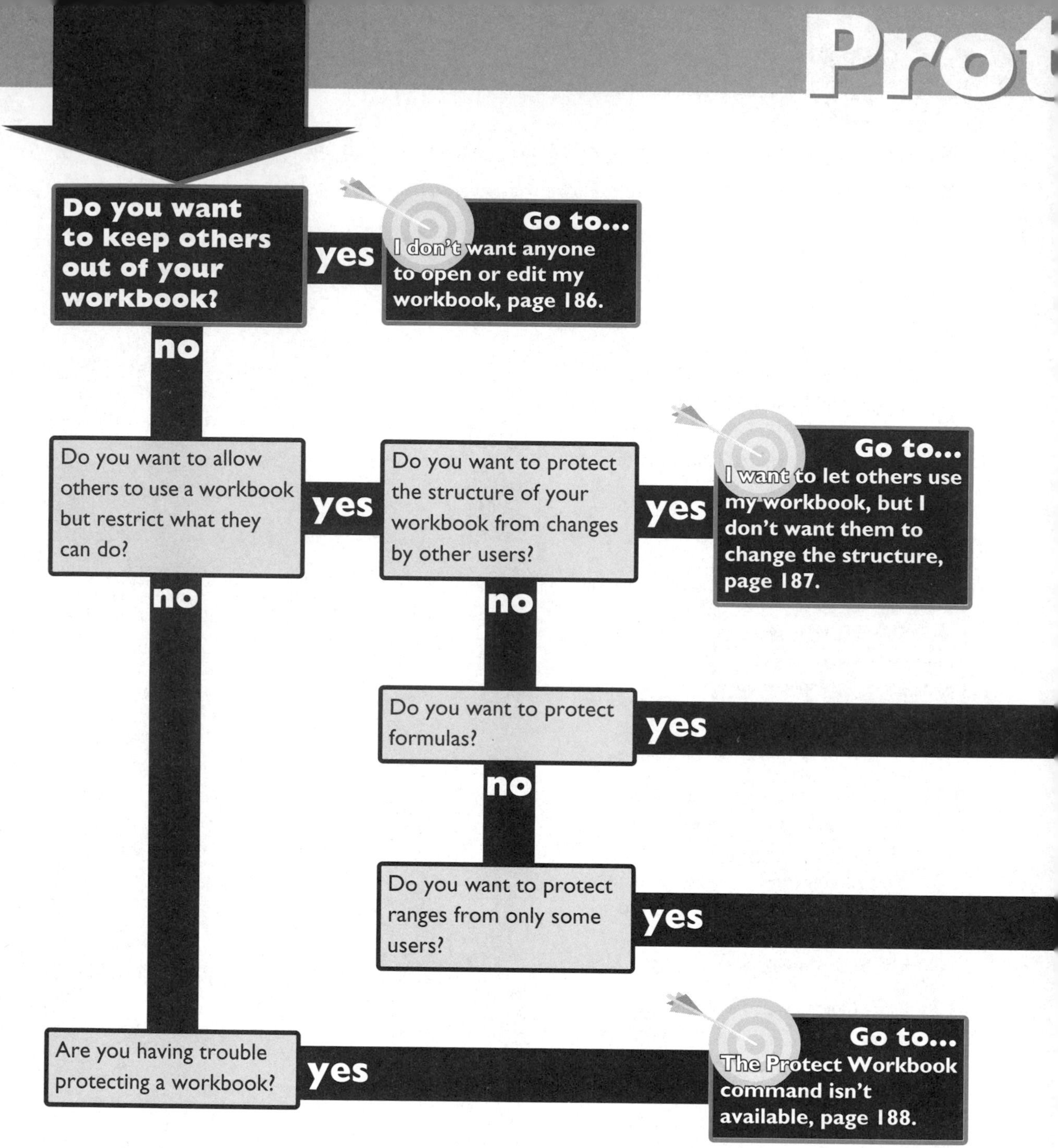

Do you want to keep others out of your workbook?

yes

Go to...
I don't want anyone to open or edit my workbook, page 186.

no

Do you want to allow others to use a workbook but restrict what they can do?

yes

Do you want to protect the structure of your workbook from changes by other users?

yes

Go to...
I want to let others use my workbook, but I don't want them to change the structure, page 187.

no

no

Do you want to protect formulas?

yes

no

Do you want to protect ranges from only some users?

yes

Are you having trouble protecting a workbook?

yes

Go to...
The Protect Workbook command isn't available, page 188.

Go to...
I want to protect parts of my workbook, but allow users to change other parts, page 190.

Go to...
I want to allow users to change protected ranges, page 192.

If your solution isn't here, check this related chapter:

- Sharing workbooks, page 194

Or see the general trouble-shooting tips on page xix.

I don't want anyone to open or edit my workbook

Source of the problem

Feeling the need to keep people out of a workbook? Perhaps it contains private, proprietary information, or perhaps you just want the busybodies to mind their own business. You can protect workbooks in Excel so that only those who know the password to the workbook can open or edit it.

You can set one password that allows people who know it to open and view but not edit the workbook. You can set a separate password that allows people who know it to both view and change the workbook.

How to fix it

1. On the File menu, click Save As.

2. In the Save As dialog box, click the Tools button.

3. Click General Options. ▶

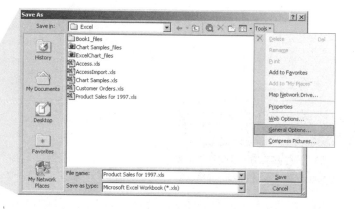

4. To make users type a password to open the file, enter a password in the Password To Open box.

5. If you want to encrypt your password, click the Advanced button.

6. To make users type a password to make changes to the file, enter a password in the Password To Modify box. ▶

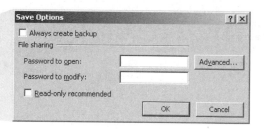

7. When prompted, retype your passwords to confirm them.

8. Click Save.

9. If prompted, click Yes to replace the existing workbook.

Note

Encryption stores the contents of a file in unrecognizable characters. When you supply the password, the contents becomes readable again.

I want to let others use my workbook, but I don't want them to change the structure

Source of the problem

Here's the situation: you've set up a workbook for others to use, and you don't want them to mess with the structure of the workbook—no adding or deleting worksheets, no changing the structure of the workbook in any way. You can protect the structure of your workbook.

How to fix it

1. On the Tools menu, point to Protection.

2. Click Protect Workbook. ▶

3. Select the Structure check box to protect the structure of a workbook. Users won't be able to add, move, delete, hide, unhide, or rename worksheets.

4. Select the Windows check box to preserve the size and position of windows each time the workbook is opened. Users won't be able to move, close, resize, hide, or unhide windows.

5. Type a password to prevent others from removing workbook protection. If you *don't* type a password, the savvy user can disable the other protection you applied.

6. Click OK.

7. Retype the password to confirm it.

> ### Note
> Excel passwords can be up to 255 letters, numbers, spaces, and symbols. You must type uppercase and lowercase letters correctly when you set and enter passwords.

The Protect Workbook command isn't available

Source of the problem

You *want* to protect the workbook, but for seemingly unfathomable reasons, you can't. Actually, the reason is definite, but obscure, and *not* exactly one of those leaps of logic you'd make ordinarily. In all probability, your workbook is shared, and you can't protect a shared workbook. You also can't assign a password to a shared workbook.

Before you start

To solve this problem, you'll be unsharing a workbook. When you unshare a workbook, Excel deletes any change history from the workbook. Change history is information in a shared workbook that is maintained about changes made in past editing sessions. The information includes the name of the person who made each change, when and where the change was made, what data was deleted or replaced, and how conflicts were resolved. Excel stores the information in a separate worksheet called the History worksheet. To save a copy of the change history, you can either copy the History worksheet to another workbook, or you can print the History worksheet. Make sure you take either of these actions *before* you unshare the workbook. See "Printing or copying the History worksheet" on the facing page.

How to fix it

To protect a shared workbook, unshare it, protect it, and then reshare it. Follow these steps:

1. Make sure that no other users are working in the workbook because the following steps will lose any unsaved work.

2. On the Tools menu, click Share Workbook.

3. In the Share Workbook dialog box, click the Editing tab. ▶

Note

To share the workbook again, on the Tools menu, click Share Workbook. Then, on the Editing tab, select the Allow Changes By More Than One User At The Same Time check box.

4. Use the Who Has This Workbook Open Now box to confirm that no other users are working in the workbook.

5. Clear the Allow Changes By More Than One User At The Same Time check box.

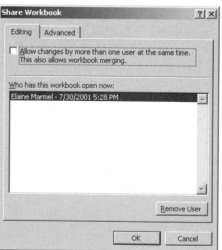

Printing or copying the History worksheet

If you decide that you want to keep a copy of change history before you unshare a workbook, use these steps to create and print or copy a History worksheet:

1. On the Tools menu, point to Track Changes.

2. Click Highlight Changes. If it isn't already selected, select the Track Changes While Editing check box. ▶

3. Select the When check box, and then select All in the When list.

4. Clear the Who and Where check boxes.

5. Select the List Changes On A New Sheet check box.

6. Click OK.

7. Click the History worksheet tab in the workbook.

8. Print the History worksheet by clicking the Print button on the Standard toolbar. Or, copy the history to another workbook using the Copy and Paste tools. Select the cells you want to copy, and click Copy. Then, switch to another workbook, click the cell that you want to be the upper-left corner of the copy, and click Paste.

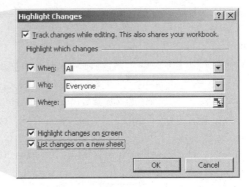

Note

You might also want to print or save the current version of the workbook under a different name to preserve both the workbook and the history at the time you save the history. After all, this history might not apply to later versions of the workbook.

I want to protect parts of my workbook, but allow users to change other parts

Source of the problem

Suppose that you've spent a lot of time creating formulas in a workbook that others are going to use. You *really* don't want to let them use the workbook and overwrite your formulas (and you *know* they will if you can't find some way to stop them).

In this situation, you want to protect worksheets within a workbook and unprotect only the cells and objects that you want to permit users to change.

How to fix it

You unprotect the areas of a worksheet to which you are willing to allow changes before you protect the worksheet. To allow changes to cells or ranges of cells, you unlock the cells. You can also hide formulas that you don't want users to see and unlock objects. To unlock cells or hide formulas, follow these steps:

1. In the worksheet you want to protect, select each cell or range that you want to unlock or hide.

2. On the Format menu, click Cells.

3. Click the Protection tab.

   ● To unlock cells, clear the Locked check box. ▶

   ● To hide formulas, select the Hidden check box.

You can allow users to change graphics (embedded charts, text boxes, pictures, or objects created with drawing tools) by unlocking them. To identify graphic objects on a worksheet, on the Edit menu, click Go To. In the Go To dialog box,

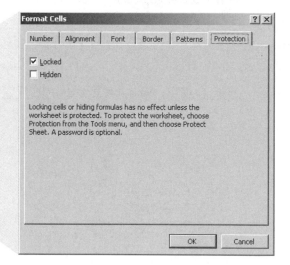

click Special. Then click Objects and click OK. Excel selects all graphic objects on your worksheet. ▶

You can unlock multiple objects simultaneously.

1. Select the objects you want to unlock by holding down Ctrl and clicking each object.

2. On the Format menu, click the command for the object you selected.

3. Click the Protection tab. ▼

4. Clear the Locked check box, and if present, clear the Lock Text check box.

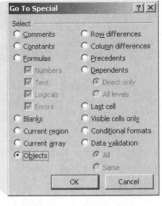

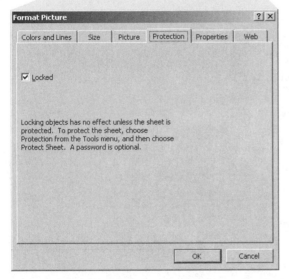

Now you're ready to protect the worksheet. During this process, you'll be prompted for an optional password. We strongly recommend that you set a password; if you don't supply a password, any user will be able to unprotect the sheet and change the protected elements—which really defeats the purpose of protecting them in the first place. Make sure you choose a password you can remember; if you lose the password, you won't be able to make changes to the protected elements on the

> **Note**
>
> The command that you see (AutoShape, Control, Object, Picture, Text Box, or WordArt) changes depending on the type(s) of objects you selected.

worksheet. Follow these steps to protect the worksheet:

1. On the Tools menu, point to Protection.

2. Click Protect Sheet. ▶

> **Note**
>
> Excel passwords can be up to 255 letters, numbers, spaces, and symbols. You must type uppercase and lowercase letters correctly when you set and enter passwords.

3. Type a password for the sheet.

4. In the Allow All Users Of This Worksheet To list, select the worksheet elements that you want users to be able to change.

5. Click OK.

6. If prompted, retype the password.

I want to allow users to change protected ranges

Source of the problem

Okay, so you trust some users. You know that you need to protect the ranges from the ones you don't trust, but you want to permit some people to modify protected ranges. Yes, you can do this by assigning a password to the protected range. You also can select the users who are allowed to edit the range without knowing the password.

Start with a worksheet that is not protected. If you need to remove protection, click Tools, point to Protection, and click Unprotect Sheet.

How to fix it

1. On the Tools menu, point to Protection.

2. Click Allow Users To Edit Ranges. ▶

3. Click the New button to display the New Range dialog box.

4. In the Title box, type a title for the range to which you're allowing changes.

5. Click in the Refers To Cells box, and then select the range to which you're allowing changes.

6. In the Range password box, type a password to access the range. The password is optional, but if you don't supply a password, any user who opens the workbook will be able to edit the cells. Essentially, Excel will treat the range as if it were not protected at all. ▶

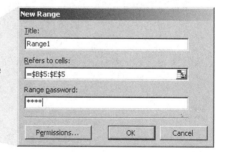

Note

Excel passwords can be up to 255 letters, numbers, spaces, and symbols. You must type uppercase and lowercase letters correctly when you set and enter passwords.

7. Click the Permissions button to specify the users who are allowed to edit the range *without* supplying a password.

8. Click the Add button.

9. Click the users to whom you want to grant access. To select multiple users, hold down Ctrl as you click names. ▶

10. Click the Add button to add the users to the list at the bottom of the box.

11. Click OK three times. If prompted, retype the password.

12. Click OK to close the Allow Users To Edit Ranges box.

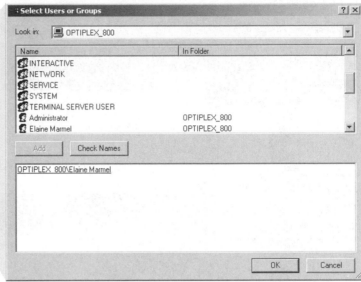

Repeat these steps for each range to which you're willing to allow changes. You can store a record of the users permitted to change ranges without a password and the ranges to which you allowed changes by selecting the Paste Permissions Information Into A New Workbook check box in the Allow Users To Edit Ranges dialog box.

To implement the use of your range passwords, you need to protect the worksheet. On the Tools menu, point to Protection, and click Protect Sheet. Select the Protect Worksheet And Contents Of Locked Cells check box, type a password for the worksheet, click OK, and retype the password when you are prompted. ▶

Although the worksheet password is optional, we suggest you assign one so that nobody can make changes to your range passwords—which would defeat the purpose of setting range passwords in the first place. Make sure you choose a password that you can remember because without the password, you cannot make changes to the protected elements on the worksheet.

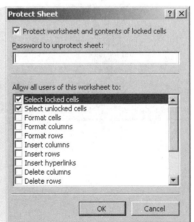

Do you have questions about change tracking and sharing workbooks?

yes → **Go to...** When I turn on change tracking, others can edit my workbook, page 196.

no ↓

Are you unable to save changes to a shared workbook?

yes → **Go to...** I can only get read-only access to a shared file, page 198.

no ↓

Have you lost the connection to a shared workbook?

yes →

no ↓

Did you lose data in a shared workbook?

yes → **Go to...** I made changes and they've disappeared, page 202.

Sharing workbooks

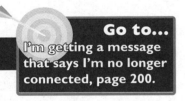

Go to...
I'm getting a message that says I'm no longer connected, page 200.

If your solution isn't here, check this related chapter:

● Protecting workbooks, page 184

Or see the general trouble-shooting tips on page xix.

When I turn on change tracking, others can edit my workbook

Source of the problem

When you turn on change tracking, you also share your workbook—the two features work together. Of course, more than one user can simultaneously edit a shared workbook. This, of course, creates a security risk, because others can change your workbook even if they have no business in your workbook.

How to fix it

Although Excel automatically shares a workbook when you turn on change tracking, there are a couple of ways that you can keep others out of the workbook. For example, in a network environment, don't store the workbook on the server; instead, store it on your local hard disk and do not share the disk (or the folder containing the workbook). That way, somebody must actually sit down and log on (if you've protected your computer by requiring a user name and password) at your computer to use the workbook.

Or, you can assign a password to the workbook before you enable change tracking. If you use password protection, only those who know the password will be able to open and modify the workbook. Excel passwords can be up to 255 letters, numbers, spaces, and symbols, and Excel does distinguish between uppercase and lowercase letters when you set and enter passwords. Follow these steps to password protect a workbook:

1. Click Tools.

2. Click Protection.

3. Click Protect And Share Workbook. ▶

4. Select the Sharing With Track Changes check box.

Note

You cannot assign a password to a shared workbook. You must unshare the workbook first. On the Tools menu, click Share Workbook, and clear the Allow Changes By More Than One User At The Same Time check box.

5. Type a password in the Password box so that only those who know the password can open the workbook.

6. Click OK.

7. Type the password again in the Confirm Password box. ▶

8. Click OK.

Note

If the workbook is shared, you won't see the Protect And Share Workbook command; instead, you'll see the Protect Shared Workbook command.

How Excel tracks changes in a password protected workbook

When you use the Protect And Share Workbook command and apply a password, Excel tracks changes and keeps change history indefinitely. If you don't apply a password, Excel uses the most recent settings when determining how many days of change history to keep. You or other users can increase but not decrease the number of days to keep the change history. To change the number of days of change history, on the Tools menu, click Share Workbook. On the Advanced tab, select Keep Change History For and then specify the number of days.

When you stop sharing a workbook, Microsoft Excel turns off change tracking and permanently erases all change history. When you share the workbook again, Excel tracks changes from that point onward. You can retain a full history of changes if you work in a copy of the workbook and stop sharing only the copy.

I can only get read-only access to a shared file

Source of the problem

You might get a message when you try to open a file that recommends you open the file as a read-only file. *Read-only* is a setting that allows you to view or copy a file, but not save changes—not a terribly practical option when you need to update a workbook, but *really* useful if you don't want anyone to make changes to your workbook. You might see this message for a couple of reasons, and there are a couple of ways to work around the problem.

How to fix it

Another user might have used the Save Options dialog box to make the file read-only when saving the workbook. ▶

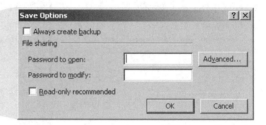

To open the file as read-write—that is, with the ability to save changes—click No in response to the message suggesting that the file should be opened as read-only.

It is also possible that the workbook is a Microsoft Excel 95 shared list. If so, Excel always opens the file as a read-only file. But, don't lose hope—you can convert the file to an Excel shared workbook. Follow these steps:

1. On the File menu, click Save As.

2. Type a new name for the file in the File Name box.

3. In the Save As Type box, click Microsoft Excel Workbook (*.xls).

> **Note**
>
> The user might have required a password to open or modify the file. If you don't know the password, you have no choice but to open the file as read-only. However, you can then make your own copy of the file in which you *can* edit and save changes. Click File, then click Save As and supply a new name for the file.

4. Click Save.

5. Click the Tools menu.

6. Click Share Workbook.

7. On the Editing tab, select the Allow Changes By More Than One User At The Same Time check box. ▼

8. Click OK.

9. Save the shared workbook when prompted.

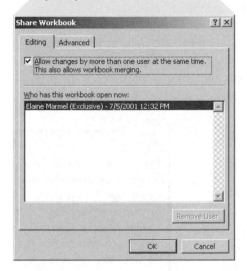

I'm getting a message that says I'm no longer connected

Source of the problem

That's one of those messages that seems to carry a deeper meaning—like somehow, you've entered a time warp. But you're really still in the same dimension as the rest of us. If a message says you're no longer connected, another user might have stopped sharing the workbook you're using, or your connection to the network might have been lost. If your workbook is stored on another computer on the network or on the network server, you will be disconnected from the workbook if you lose your connection to the network.

How to fix it

If another user turned off sharing while you were editing, your goose is cooked. Even if the user shares the workbook again, you'll see the message. Unfortunately, you'll need to reenter changes from your current editing session. Close the workbook and follow up with the owner of the workbook or other users.

    If you lost your network connection, the first thing you need to do is reestablish the connection. Once you're reconnected to the network, you have two choices:

- You can open the shared workbook again. In this case, you'll lose any changes you made but didn't save.

- You can save your work in a different Excel file, and then merge the file of changes into the shared workbook on the network.

> **Tip**
>
> If you can't reestablish the network connection immediately, save the workbook on your local hard disk. After reestablishing the network connection, follow the steps to merge the two workbooks.

To save your changes and merge them into the network file after you've reestablished your network connection, follow these steps:

1. Click OK in response to the message telling you that you are no longer connected.

2. On the File menu, click Save As.

3. In the File Name box, type a new name for the workbook, and then click Save. ▶

4. Close the File.

5. Open the original shared workbook.

6. On the Tools menu, click Compare And Merge Workbooks.

7. Click the file in which you saved your changes when you lost the network connection. Excel will merge the contents of the two workbooks. ▶

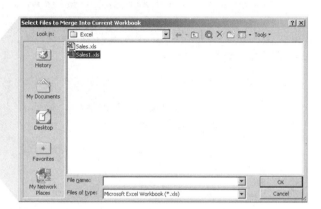

I made changes and they've disappeared

Source of the problem

More than one user can work simultaneously in a shared workbook. And, it is possible that some other user enters information that destroys your data or edits. If this happens, you can use the History worksheet to try to recover your information.

How to fix it

If the change history contains the information you originally entered, you can find the data on the History worksheet and copy it to its original location in the workbook. Follow these steps:

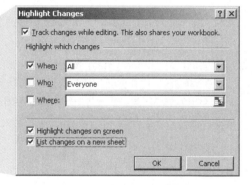

1. On the Tools menu, point to Track Changes.

2. Click Highlight Changes to display the Highlight Changes dialog box. ▶

3. Select the When check box, and from the list, choose All.

4. Clear the Who and Where check boxes.

5. Select the List Changes On A New Sheet check box.

6. Click OK.

7. Click the History worksheet.

Tip

As a safety precaution, you might want to keep a copy of the workbook on your local hard disk to protect against network disconnections. Then, you can password-protect the local copy so that no one but you can open it. On the File menu, click Save As and use the Save In list to save an extra copy of the shared workbook on your local hard disk.

8. For each row of the History worksheet that lists a deleted or changed value you want to recover, select the cell in the Old Value column and click Copy on the Standard toolbar. ▶

9. Noting the location shown in the Range column for the data you've copied, switch to the original worksheet, select the range where the data belongs, and click Paste.

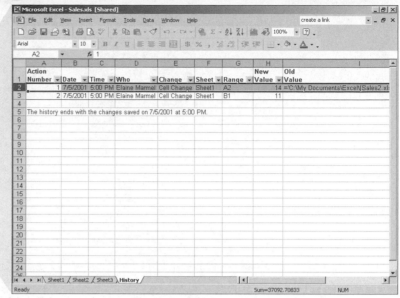

Repeat Steps 8 and 9 for each range of data you need to recover.

Outlook

Part 3

Are you trying to add or use contact information in the Outlook Address Book?

yes

Are you trying to select contact names from an address book?

yes

Are you having trouble finding information in the Address Book dialog box?

yes

no

no

Are you having trouble selecting a contacts folder?

yes

After you address e-mail messages from your address book, are you experiencing delays?

yes

Go to...

When sending e-mail messages, Outlook takes a lot of time to resolve names, page 208.

Are you trying to find a particular address book?

yes

no

Go to...
I try to open a contacts folder in Address Book but Outlook displays a message that the folder can't be found, page 210.

Quick fix

Selecting address books. If you added a contact and can't find it, it may be saved in a different address book. To display the contents of a different address book, do this:

1. Click Address Book on the Tools menu.

2. Open the Show Names From The list.

3. Click the name of the address book you want to view.

Would you like to modify which address book displays by default?

yes

Go to...
The address book I use most often isn't the one that opens first in Address Book, page 213.

If your solution isn't here, check this related chapter:

● Sending and receiving e-mail messages, page 274

Or see the general trouble-shooting tips on page xix.

When sending e-mail messages, Outlook takes a lot of time to resolve names

Source of the problem

You can set up Outlook to check recipient e-mail addresses against directories in your Address Book. Some of those directories are located on your hard disk, others might be on your company network or reside with the e-mail server at your Internet Service Provider. If a recipient's address isn't recognized or there are duplicate addresses for the same person, you will see a dialog box asking you how to proceed. Resolving these e-mail addresses can take seconds, or quite some time, depending on how many directories of contacts you've instructed Outlook to check, how many contacts they contain, and where the directories reside.

One option is to change the way Outlook searches Lightweight Directory Access Protocol (LDAP) directories. LDAP is an e-mail and browser protocol that provides a method for searching online addresses. You might be set up to search a large LDAP directory for your company that seldom contains contacts you correspond with; or, because of traffic on your network, it might be taking a long time to access that directory. Either of these processes will slow you down; luckily, you can easily change these settings.

How to fix it

You can exclude an LDAP directory from the list of directories used to check names by following these steps:

1. On the Tools menu, click Address Book.

2. In Address Book, click Tools, and then click Options.

3. A list labeled When Sending Mail, Check Names Using These Address Lists In The Following Order is displayed. Click the name of the address book you want to exclude. ▶

4. Click Remove.

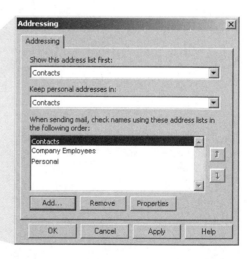

Alternatively, you can reduce the amount of time Microsoft Outlook spends searching LDAP directories:

1. On the Outlook Tools menu, click E-Mail Accounts.

2. In the Directory section, select View Or Change Existing Directories Or Address Books; click Next.

3. Select a directory service, and then click Change.

4. Click More Settings.

5. Click the Search tab.

6. Under Server Settings, set the value for Search Timeout In Seconds to a lower number. ▶

7. Click OK, and then click Finish.

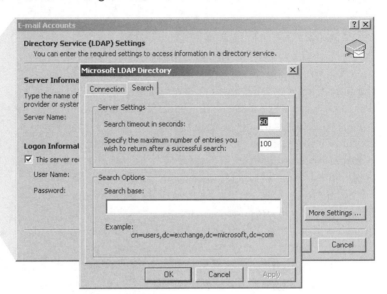

Have you tried this?

If you use a particular address book more often than others, you can have it checked first. This ensures that your most used directory will be searched first and save you time if your mail recipient resides in it.

1. On the Outlook Tools menu, click Address Book.

2. In Address Book, click Tools, and then click Options.

3. In the When Sending Mail list, click the address book that you use most often. Outlook checks address books in this list in order from top to bottom.

4. Click the up arrow to the right of the list to move the address book to the top.

I try to open a contacts folder in Address Book but Outlook displays a message that the folder can't be found

Source of the problem

At some point in your life you've probably moved to a new town or started a new job and lost contact with people from the past. One day a holiday card gets returned or a phone call results in a message that the line is disconnected, and you realize you've lost touch for good. That can be the case with Outlook contacts; you try to open a contacts folder in your Address Book and get a message that it can't be found. This can happen for a few different reasons.

The first cause can relate to other e-mail programs you might use. If you use Microsoft Exchange Client or any e-mail program other than Microsoft Outlook, contacts folders can disappear. These folders can be deleted by these programs when setting up their own folders. If that's the case, there's nothing you can do to retrieve them, but you might consider whether you want to keep another e-mail program active on your system or not.

Another possibility is that your contacts folder is stored on a shared network. If it is and you're having trouble finding or opening it, the problem might be that you don't have permission to use it, perhaps because your administrator made a change in permissions or you've moved to a different department or division and your network setup has changed.

If you think the problem is with access to a shared folder, you'll have to get the person who administers that folder to give you permission. Contact your network administrator to find out about this. Once you're sure you have permission to access the folder, there's no easy way to reinstate your Address Book settings—you just have to set up the folder in your Address Book all over again.

If, on the other hand, you figure the folder just doesn't exist on the network any more or you can't get permission to use it, you might as well just get rid of the folder you've set up in Outlook—and cross those old friends off your Christmas card list while you're at it.

> ### Before you start
>
> Today networks get reworked and people move from office to office and computer to computer. As a result, a contacts folder may disappear or get moved to a place you're unable to access. Being able to change your Address Book setup or remove defunct folders from your Address Book lists helps you keep your Address Book up-to-date.

How to fix it

If you obtain permission to access a folder again, be sure you also get the server name, port number, your user name, and password. You may also have to ask your administrator for the path to reach your Microsoft Exchange server. Then follow these steps to set up the folder in Address Book once more:

1. On the Tools menu, click E-Mail Accounts.

2. Under Directory, click Add A New Directory Or Address Book, and then click Next. ▶

3. In the next dialog box that appears, click Internet Directory Service (LDAP), and then click Next.

4. Enter the server name in the Server Name box.

5. Select the This Server Requires Me To Log On check box if your server is password protected.

6. Type your user name and password.

7. Click More Settings. ▶

8. Under Display Name, type a name for the LDAP address book. Use the name you want to be displayed in the Show Names From list in Address Book.

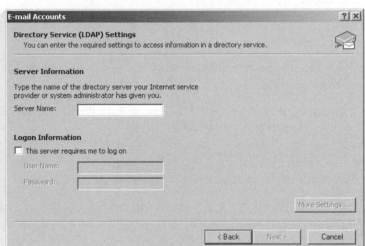

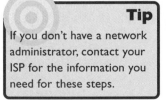

Tip

If you don't have a network administrator, contact your ISP for the information you need for these steps.

I try to open a contacts folder in Address Book but Outlook displays a message that the folder can't be found

(continued from page 211)

9. Under Connection Details, enter the port number.

10. Click the Search tab, and change the server settings to match those given to you by your administrator.

11. Under Search Options, if the Search Base box is not filled in, type in any distinguished names your administrator provided.

12. Click OK, and then click Next.

13. Click Finish to complete and save your changed settings.

If you determine that you can't find or connect to the folder again, remove it from your Address Book lists by using these steps:

1. On the Tools menu, click E-Mail Accounts.

2. In the Directory section, select View Or Change Existing Directories Or Address Books.

3. Click Next.

4. Click the address book or directory that you want to get rid of.

5. Click Remove.

6. Outlook asks you to confirm that you want to delete the folder; click Yes.

7. Click Finish.

The address book I use most often isn't the one that opens first in Address Book

Source of the problem

Today, we have more types of people and contacts to stay in touch with than ever before. You probably have personal contacts (your friends, dentist, and spouse); clients (both the ones you like and the ones you'd like to avoid); company employees (listed by department, division, or branch); vendors (the travel agency, office supply company, and shipping company); a project team (Tom, Dick, and Mary)…well, you get the idea.

Outlook allows you to use several address books to organize your contacts. For example, you might use an Outlook address book called Contacts, a Personal address book, and also access an address book on your network for all company employees. When you open Address Book to address an e-mail message, only one Address Book directory can be open at a time. You can choose to display another address book, but if you're finding that the address book you use most often isn't displayed immediately, you'll save time by changing the Address Book setup to display those contacts first.

Before you start

There's no danger in simply rearranging how address books are displayed in the Address Book, and changing that setting might make it quicker for you to find the address you need.

How to fix it

1. On the Tools menu, click Address Book.

2. In Address Book, click Tools, and then click Options. ▶

3. In the Show This Address List First box, click the address book that you want to open first.

4. Click OK.

Note

If you want your contacts folder to appear first, you must select Contacts, not the Outlook Address Book.

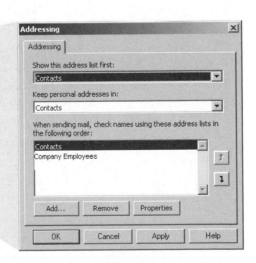

Are you trying to add or view an attachment to an e-mail message?

yes — Have you sent an e-mail message with an attachment?

yes — Is someone having difficulty receiving your attachment?

yes

no

Is someone having difficulty printing your attachment?

yes

no

Are you having trouble working with an attached file?

yes — Have you made changes to an attachment you want to save?

yes

no

Are you trying to include a copy of an e-mail message with another?

yes

Go to...
I don't know how to attach one e-mail message to another, page 220.

Attachments

Go to...

The recipient of my e-mail message can't open the file I attached, page 216.

Quick fix

Printing an attachment. Attachments print to your default printer. Even if you change the printer in the Print dialog box, the attachment will go to the default printer (even though the e-mail message will go to the newly selected printer!). To change your default printer, follow these steps.

1. On the Windows desktop, click Start, Settings, and then Printers.

2. Select the printer you want to make the default, and then click Set As Default Printer on the File menu.

Go to...

I changed an attachment but my changes have disappeared, page 218.

If your solution isn't here, check these related chapters:

- Printing, page 56
- Security, page 266

Or see the general trouble-shooting tips on page xix.

The recipient of my e-mail message can't open the file I attached

Source of the problem

Not being able to open an e-mail attachment is like being given a birthday present only to have somebody take it away before you can see what's inside. It's frustrating and can even be costly if it means you can't get an important file to somebody right away.

Files attached to e-mail messages can cause problems for recipients, and those problems typically relate to the format of the file. There could be a few different things causing these problems.

You might have sent the message in MIME format. MIME (Multipurpose Internet Mail Extensions) is a widely used Internet protocol that enables sending text as well as various binary formats such as graphics and executable programs. If your recipient's e-mail program doesn't support the MIME format, you can use the UUENCODE format to send the attachment. UUENCODE is a UNIX-based program that takes a binary file and switches it into ASCII characters. The recipient's program converts it back to binary format after receiving it.

Another possibility is that you might have sent the message using HTML or Rich Text Format (HTML is Outlook's default format). Although many, many programs today support RTF, there are a few e-mail programs that don't. To solve this problem, you can simply use a different format for e-mail you send to that person, such as plain text.

How to fix it

To change the format of your message to a MIME compatible format, follow these steps, and then resend your message and attachment:

1. On the Tools menu, click Options.

Before you start

Usually when there's a problem with opening an attached file, the problem is the type of file format in which the file was saved. Be aware that if you save a file in a different format so that somebody else can read it, you might run the risk of losing some formatting or data from the file.

Have you tried this?

The person you sent the e-mail to might be using an e-mail application that doesn't support attachments or that stops certain types of attachments from being opened. For example, to protect you from viruses, Outlook won't accept files with an .exe or .bat extension. If you need to distribute files to others, such as .exe files, you can post them to a network folder or file transfer protocol (FTP) site. Use a program such as WS_FTP to work with posting FTP files. Another workaround is to compress such a file as a .zip file, and have the recipient save it to disk before opening it.

2. Click the Mail Format tab to display it.

3. In the Message Format area, click the Internet Format button; the Internet Format dialog box appears. ▶

4. Select the check box labeled Encode Attachments In UUENCODE Format When Sending A Plain Text Message.

5. Click OK twice to close both dialog boxes and save the new setting.

If you sent the message using Rich Text or HTML format and discover the recipient's e-mail program doesn't support those formats, you'll have to specify a different format to use when sending messages. Use this procedure:

1. In the Folder List, click the Contacts folder.

2. Double-click the recipient's contact record to open the contact form.

3. On the General tab, double-click the contact's e-mail address; the E-Mail Properties dialog box opens. ▶

4. Click the Internet Format list and select Send Plain Text Only.

5. Click OK, click Save, and then Close.

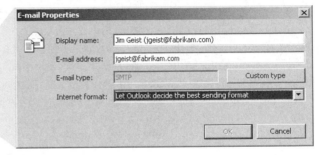

More about text formats

File formats essentially reflect the way files are structured relative to the software program they were created in or a transmission or other standard that was used to encode them. In the past, the only way to open a file was to have the originating software installed on your computer. Over time, programs such as Adobe Acrobat came along, which helped you read files even if the originating software wasn't present. In addition, many software programs are now able to save files in other formats (for example, you can save a Word for Windows document in a Word for Mac format). Some of these formats are accessible using software of a certain type: for example, if you save a Word file as Rich Text Format, you should be able to open that text in many word processing applications, because it is a common format for text files.

I changed an attachment but my changes have disappeared

Source of the problem

Files attached to e-mail messages are like those little nesting dolls where one tucks neatly inside the other. Throw out the big doll and say *sayonara* to all the little dolls inside it as well.

That's the trick to saving changes to e-mail attachments: you have to save the e-mail itself to save changes to an attachment, or you have to save the attachments separately. If you open a file that's attached to an e-mail, such as a Word document, make changes to the document, click the Save button in Word, and then close the e-mail without saving it, none of the changes to the Word file will be saved. You have a few choices in this situation: save the attachment to your hard disk with a new name using the Save As command when you have it open in its originating application, or be sure to save changes to the e-mail item to save any changes you made to its attachment.

How to fix it

To save a separate copy of the attachment after you make changes, follow these steps:

1. Double-click the attached file to open it in its original application.

2. Click the Save As command on the File menu in the program in which you opened the attachment.

Before you start

If you want to save a file that's attached to an e-mail message, be sure that you open it and save it on your hard disk or a floppy disk. Storing files within Outlook can take up a lot of space and make Outlook perform more slowly. If you're on a network, you might find that your e-mail administrator requires that you archive files now and then to save space on the server.

Note

A third option is to use the Save Attachment command on the File menu. By default, this command saves your attachment to your My Documents folder, or anywhere else you specify. By saving the attachment to one of your permanent folders, you can open, edit, and save your changes without a disappearing act.

3. Save the file in your My Documents folder or in another permanent location. ▶

To save all attachment changes along with the e-mail it came with, follow these steps:

1. Double-click the attachment to open it in its original application.

2. Keep the e-mail open while you make changes to the attachment. When you finish your changes to the attachment, save and close the attachment.

3. Now save and close the e-mail.

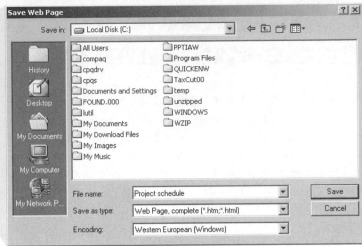

Tip

It's possible that you opened more than one copy of the attachment. If you made changes to both copies (perhaps you switched back and forth from the document to another program and didn't realize you were coming back to a different copy of the document each time), only the changes you saved in the last copy you had open will be saved when you save the e-mail in Outlook.

Warning

If you created the original file, be sure that when you save it with changes you give it a different name; otherwise, it will overwrite your original version of the file.

I don't know how to attach one e-mail message to another

Source of the problem

It is tedious and time-consuming to retype information into e-mail messages if that information already exists elsewhere. If you received an e-mail message about something important, and you want to share that information, don't reinvent the wheel: use Outlook tools to pass the original message on to others.

In many cases, simply being able to forward an e-mail message to somebody else, adding comments above the existing e-mail message content to explain or add information to the original message works fine. However, there are times you might want to actually attach e-mail messages to e-mail messages—for example, to attach a number of e-mail messages about the same subject and convey them in a single message.

You should understand that Outlook consists of various types of items. An e-mail message is one type of item. A contact from your address book is another. Notes and tasks are also items. You can send any of these items along with an e-mail as an attachment. If you send an e-mail within an e-mail, the recipient simply double-clicks the attachment to open it, or he or she can right-click the attachment and save it as a file.

Before you start

You can forward an e-mail message to somebody else and add your own comments, but sometimes you'll want to attach one e-mail to another. This is easy to do, but keep in mind that if the attached e-mail has attachments, your e-mail file could end up being larger than usual.

How to fix it

To insert one e-mail message into another, you can follow this procedure:

1. Create or open the e-mail message in which you want to insert an attachment.

2. Click in the body of the e-mail message.

Tip

You can also select multiple messages in your Inbox and click Forward. The multiple messages will then be forwarded as multiple attachments.

3. Do either of the following:

- If you use Microsoft Word as your e-mail editor, click the arrow next to the Insert File tool (it's the little paper clip icon), and then click the item.

- Click an object in Outlook and drag it into the new e-mail message.

4. On the Insert menu, click File. ▶

5. Click the message that you want to attach, and then click OK.

6. Click Send.

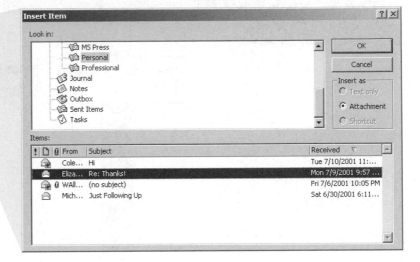

Tip

This process works for inserting any Outlook object into another; for example, if you want to insert an Outlook contact in an e-mail. The last step in this process for other types of items is to click Save, and then click Close rather than Send. The e-mail will be saved in the Drafts folder.

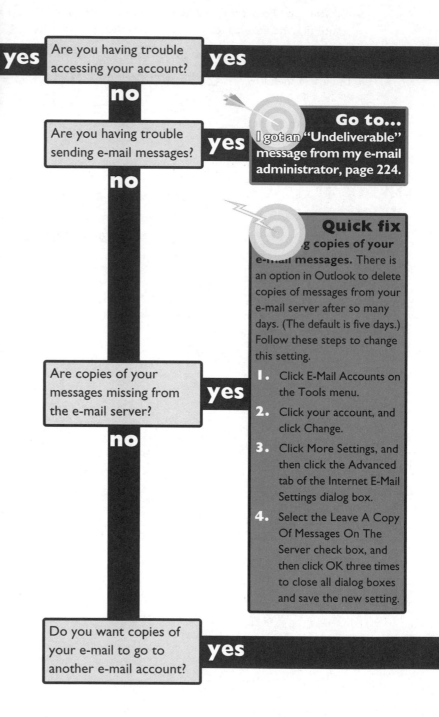

Are you having trouble setting up or accessing your e-mail account?

yes → Are you having trouble accessing your account?

yes →

no

Are you having trouble sending e-mail messages?

yes →

no

Go to...
I got an "Undeliverable" message from my e-mail administrator, page 224.

Quick fix
...g copies of your e-mail messages. There is an option in Outlook to delete copies of messages from your e-mail server after so many days. (The default is five days.) Follow these steps to change this setting.

1. Click E-Mail Accounts on the Tools menu.

2. Click your account, and click Change.

3. Click More Settings, and then click the Advanced tab of the Internet E-Mail Settings dialog box.

4. Select the Leave A Copy Of Messages On The Server check box, and then click OK three times to close all dialog boxes and save the new setting.

Are copies of your messages missing from the e-mail server?

yes →

no

Do you want copies of your e-mail to go to another e-mail account?

yes →

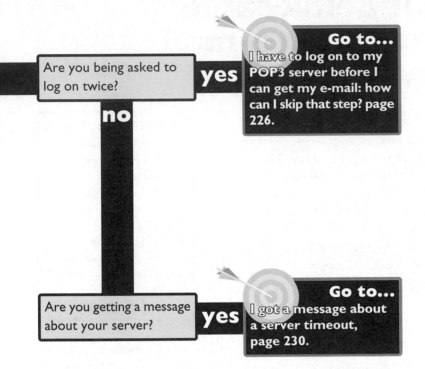

Are you being asked to log on twice?

yes

no

Go to...
I have to log on to my POP3 server before I can get my e-mail: how can I skip that step? page 226.

Are you getting a message about your server?

yes

Go to...
I got a message about a server timeout, page 230.

Go to...
I want to receive the replies to my messages at another e-mail address, page 228.

If your solution isn't here, check these related chapters:

● Sending and receiving e-mail messages, page 274

● Security, page 266

Or see the general trouble-shooting tips on page xix.

I got an "Undeliverable" message from my e-mail administrator

Source of the problem

The Internet, with its convoluted universe of servers and e-mail accounts, can be a very unforgiving place (sort of like the IRS when you forget to report that little $5,000 bonus). If you don't get every tiny setting, address, user name, and password exactly right, your online connections just won't work. If you're having trouble with your Outlook e-mail account and mail is dead lettering to who knows where, there could be a couple of reasons:

● If you are using Microsoft Exchange Server, your name has to exist somewhere on the server.

● When you first created an e-mail account, you might have incorrectly entered something, such as your user name, password, or e-mail server name. If you don't have the right information about your account stored in Outlook, it won't be able to connect to the server.

If you have a problem with "Uundeliverable" e-mail messages, there are some things you can do to check these settings. However, when you do, if you discover your name isn't on the Exchange server, you'll probably have to contact your friendly neighborhood IT person to help you out.

How to fix it

If you are using Microsoft Exchange Server, here's how to check the server to make sure your name is listed on it:

1. On the Tools menu, select E-Mail Accounts.

2. Click View Or Change Existing E-Mail Accounts, and then click Next.

3. Click the Exchange Server e-mail account, and then click Change.

Before you start

When making changes to your e-mail account, be sure you have the correct information from your ISP or IT person. You might also make a note of current settings before making changes, just in case the original information turns out to have been right, and you want to reenter it.

Have you tried this?

If you get an "Undeliverable" message, it's possible the server might be busy or offline temporarily. Wait a little while, and then try sending your message again.

4. Click Check Name. An underline should appear beneath your name and server. If it doesn't, it means your name is not listed on the server, and you need to contact your administrator. ▶

You can take a look at your e-mail account settings to see if they're correct (of course this presupposes you know your correct settings!) by following these steps:

1. On the Tools menu, click E-Mail Accounts.

2. Click View Or Change Existing E-Mail Accounts, and then click Next.

3. Click the e-mail account you want to review to select it, and then click Change. ▶

4. Check to see that the settings entered in this dialog box match the settings provided by your network administrator or ISP.

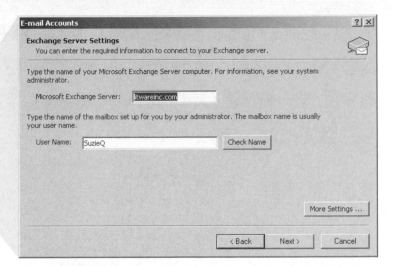

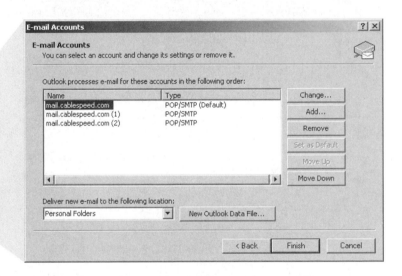

5. If some settings don't match, make any necessary changes. Also, don't forget to click More Settings to view additional settings and make sure they match as well.

6. When you've made necessary changes, click Next.

7. Click Finish to save your new settings.

I have to log on to my POP3 server before I can get my e-mail: how can I skip that step?

Source of the problem

If you have a POP3 server e-mail account, you might have to log on to the server with a user name and password before Outlook can access your e-mail. Post Office Protocol (POP) is a virtual post office. It doesn't sell stamps or rent mailboxes. A protocol is essentially a set of rules or standards. POP3 is one kind of protocol used on Internet e-mail servers to control how e-mail is uploaded and downloaded to the server. It's used by several popular online services such as CompuServe.

Entering your user name and password one extra time isn't really an arduous process, but if you log on or off of e-mail several times a day, it can get tiresome. Luckily, Outlook allows you to automate this step with a simple setting.

How to fix it

You can set up Microsoft Outlook to automatically log on to your POP3 server by following these steps:

1. On the Tools menu, click E-Mail Accounts.

2. Click View Or Change Existing E-Mail Accounts, and then click Next.

3. In the list of e-mail accounts, click the POP3 e-mail account that you want to set up, and then click Change.

4. Click the More Settings button.

5. Click the Outgoing Server tab in the Internet E-Mail Settings dialog box. ▶

6. Select the My Outgoing Server (SMTP) Requires Authentication check box.

7. Select Log On To Incoming Mail Server Before Sending Mail, and then click OK.

8. Click Next, and then click Finish to save the setting.

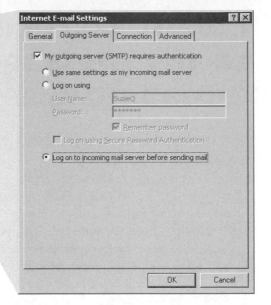

More about e-mail protocols

Two of the other popular protocols used on e-mail servers are Internet Message Access Protocol (IMAP) and Hypertext Transfer Protocol (HTTP). IMAP differs from POP3 in that it allows you to retrieve e-mail from more than one computer. HTTP is a Web protocol that allows requests to be carried from browsers to a Web server using hypertext. HTTP is used to retrieve messages from Internet e-mail providers such as Hotmail.

I want to receive the replies to my messages at another e-mail address

Source of the problem

One thing you can say about the technology-driven age we live in is that people are constantly on the go and have a constant need to stay in touch. Walk through any airport (or even supermarket) and note the number of cell phones, pagers, laptop computers, and PDAs being used or carried.

Consider your own workweek: you might send e-mails from an office e-mail address on Monday and want responses to them sent to your home computer so you can read them on Tuesday—just before you dash to the airport to visit your Hong Kong office with pager, cell phone, and laptop in hand.

In many cases, our e-mail accounts are accessible on line from anywhere. For example, if you use Yahoo! to get your e-mail, all you need is a computer (or even phone) with an Internet connection, and you can access your mail. But sometimes you want responses to your e-mail messages directed to another e-mail address. For example, if you visit a cousin in Alaska on vacation, you might want to have replies to your e-mail go directly to your cousin's e-mail account. Or you might want somebody else, such as an assistant, to get your e-mail messages while you're on the road, so he or she can act on them. Outlook allows you to set this up with an easy-to-make setting.

Before you start

Outlook can be set up to forward replies to messages to another e-mail account. Just make sure your messages go to an account you can access!

Warning

Don't forget to change this setting back when you get back to your computer; otherwise, your cousin in Alaska will continue to get your e-mail replies.

How to fix it

Specify the reply e-mail address for messages by following these steps:

1. On the Tools menu, click E-Mail Accounts.

2. In the E-Mail section of the dialog box, click View Or Change Existing E-Mail Accounts.

3. Click Next.

4. In the list of e-mail accounts, click the one you want to modify, and then click Change.

5. Click the More Settings button.

6. On the General tab, in the Reply E-Mail box, type the e-mail address where you want replies to be sent. ▶

7. Click OK, click Next, and then click Finish to save the setting.

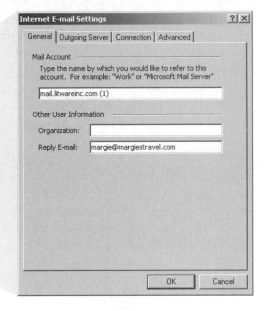

I got a message about a server timeout

Source of the problem

Contrary to popular misconception, a server timeout has no relation to a time out in a football or basketball game. Nobody gets to relax or fill up on Gatorade—in fact, a server timeout could cause the opposite of a relaxed state, because it causes a process you initiated to stop short of completion.

Timeouts in the computer world are settings for a predetermined amount of time that can go by before an event occurs. If the event doesn't occur, for example, if you can't connect to your server within 60 seconds, the process is terminated. This is done in some cases to free up a phone line or to prevent some unscrupulous soul from trying hundreds of password entries until he eventually breaks into your online account.

If you're seeing server timeout messages on a regular basis, you have to adjust your e-mail server timeout setting so it allows more time before aborting the procedure.

Before you start

You can increase the time allowed before a server times out; however, if an event doesn't happen in a minute or two, it's probably not going to happen. Save yourself needless waiting time by choosing a logical amount of time for online events to occur.

How to fix it

To adjust your server timeout, depending on the type of server your e-mail account uses, perform one of the following procedures.

Follow these steps to change the server timeout for a POP3 or IMAP server:

1. On the Tools menu, click E-Mail Accounts.

2. Click View Or Change Existing E-Mail Accounts, and then click Next.

3. Click the e-mail account you want to change, and then click Change.

Note

It's not possible to modify the server timeout setting for an HTTP e-mail account, so don't even try!

4. Click More Settings, and then click the Advanced tab. ▶

5. Under Server Timeouts, move the slider toward Long until the time span shown to the right is the one you want. Click OK.

6. Click Next, and then click Finish to save the new setting.

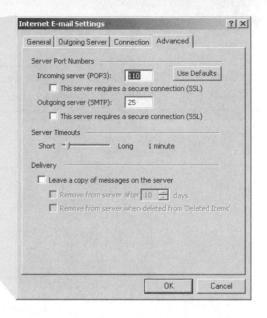

To change the server timeout for a Microsoft Exchange Server account, follow these steps:

1. On the Tools menu, click E-Mail Accounts.

2. Click View Or Change Existing E-Mail Accounts, and then click Next.

3. Click the Exchange Server account you want to change, and then click Change.

4. Click More Settings, and on the General tab, enter a higher number in the Seconds Until Server Connection Timeout box.

5. Click OK, click Next, and then click Finish.

Are you trying to insert a file with Outlook?

yes

Are you working with an embedded object?

yes

no

Are you importing information from another Office program?

yes

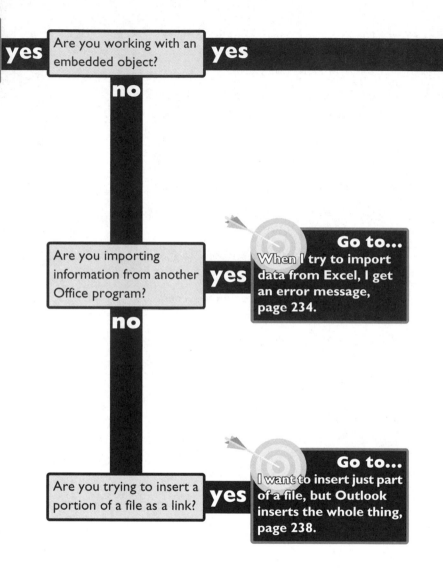

Go to...

When I try to import data from Excel, I get an error message, page 234.

no

Are you trying to insert a portion of a file as a link?

yes

Go to...

I want to insert just part of a file, but Outlook inserts the whole thing, page 238.

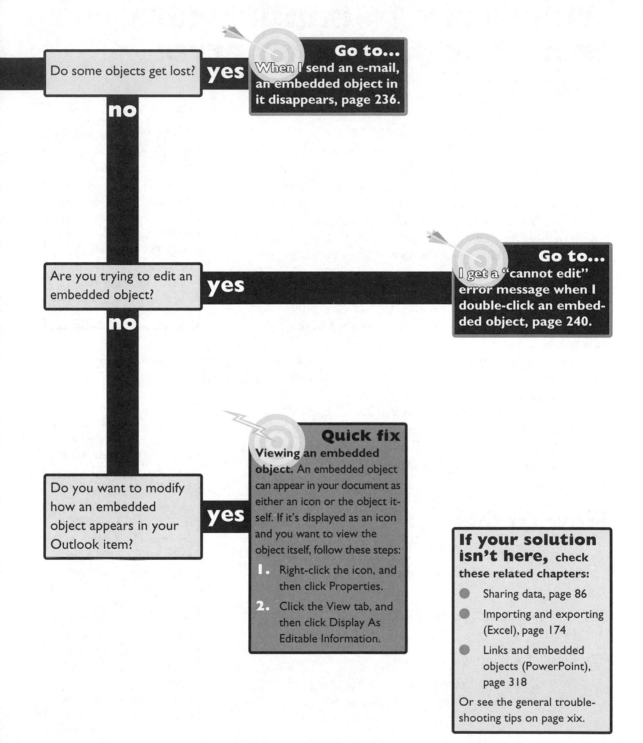

Do some objects get lost? **yes**

Go to...
When I send an e-mail, an embedded object in it disappears, page 236.

no

Are you trying to edit an embedded object? **yes**

Go to...
I get a "cannot edit" error message when I double-click an embedded object, page 240.

no

Do you want to modify how an embedded object appears in your Outlook item? **yes**

Quick fix
Viewing an embedded object. An embedded object can appear in your document as either an icon or the object itself. If it's displayed as an icon and you want to view the object itself, follow these steps:

1. Right-click the icon, and then click Properties.
2. Click the View tab, and then click Display As Editable Information.

If your solution isn't here, check these related chapters:

● Sharing data, page 86
● Importing and exporting (Excel), page 174
● Links and embedded objects (PowerPoint), page 318

Or see the general troubleshooting tips on page xix.

When I try to import data from Excel, I get an error message

Source of the problem

We all make assumptions. A common assumption is that if someone plans a picnic it will rain. Another is that if you retrieve your e-mail, at least 50 percent of the messages will be solicitations from complete strangers for things you neither need nor want.

When you import Excel data, Outlook makes an assumption: it assumes the first row of a named range contains field names. Even if the range you're importing doesn't contain field names at all, Outlook is sure the first row of data contains field names. Because it makes this assumption, it doesn't import that data as data. To ensure that all the data in the named range is imported correctly, you'll have to use the first row for field names.

There could be one other cause of an error message when importing Microsoft Excel data: information you import from Excel has to exist somewhere within a named range in the Microsoft Excel file. If it doesn't, Outlook can't import it.

In addition, even though a piece of data exists in the named range, it could be the case that the range name you used is the same as one of the column header names within the range, and that could cause an error message as well.

How to fix it

If you've used the first row of data in Excel for data rather than headings, insert a new first row and add headings by following these steps:

1. With your Excel file open, click the current first row to select it.

2. On the Insert menu, click Rows.

3. Enter the headings, and redefine the named range to include the new row (see the following steps).

> ### Before you start
>
> To import information from Excel into an Outlook item, you have to be specific about what information you want and be careful not to use a heading name as the named range. You can redefine a named range as often as you like, so use these guidelines to get the named range right before importing.

> ### Have you tried this?
>
> A field is a category of data, such as a name, a street address, or a ZIP code; a record is a complete set of the fields that define a single entry in a list, such as "John Doe," living at "123 Main Street," in ZIP code "10101." Outlook requires that records be placed in rows and fields in columns. If your worksheet is organized the opposite way, try rearranging the data so that each column is a field and each row is a record.

To import the contents of an Excel file, you have to define a named range in your worksheet by following these steps:

1. Click and drag to select the rows and columns that you need to import.

2. On the Insert menu, click Name, and then click Define. ▶

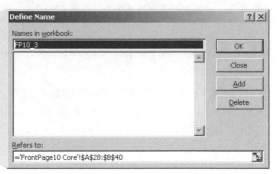

3. In the Names In Workbook box, enter a range name. Remember that you can't include any spaces in the name. Also, don't duplicate a column heading name.

4. Click Add.

5. Click OK.

6. On the File menu, click Save.

7. Close Excel and open Outlook to try the import process again.

When I send an e-mail, an embedded object in it disappears

Source of the problem

Sometimes it seems that the world of computing is one of endless incompatibilities (which makes working with an integrated suite of products such as Microsoft Office XP seem so much easier than working with applications from five different manufacturers). Files saved in various formats can be impossible to open or might open with that funny garbage text floating around like so much binary flotsam and jetsam. Documents saved in one platform, such as the PC or Macintosh, can be incompatible with documents created in another.

Rich Text Format (RTF) is a document architecture that allows you to transfer text documents between applications and even between different platforms. To successfully send and receive e-mail messages that contain embedded objects using Microsoft Outlook, both you and the person you're exchanging e-mail with have to use Rich Text Format. For example, if you embed an Excel spreadsheet or piece of clip art in a message, it could cause problems if you don't use RTF for the message. To be sure you don't encounter problems sending embedded objects, Outlook allows you to configure a global setting to send all messages in RTF or configure a setting so that messages that go to certain contacts use RTF.

Before you start

Sending e-mail in Rich Text Format can ensure that embedded objects can be read. There is little danger that you'll lose any text or formatting by choosing the Rich Text Format for messages.

Note

If your recipient's e-mail program doesn't support Rich Text Format, you might have no choice but to send the embedded object as an attachment. Outlook RTF is supported only by Microsoft Exchange Client versions 5.0 and 4.0, Outlook 97, Outlook 98, Outlook 2000, and Outlook 2002.

How to fix it

To ensure that you send e-mail as RTF, you can make a global change or a change for individual contacts only.

If the people you send e-mail to all use Microsoft Outlook or Microsoft Exchange Client, you can select RTF as your standard setting for e-mail using these steps:

1. On the Tools menu, click Options.

2. Click the Mail Format tab to display it.

---

3. In the Compose In This Message Format list, select Rich Text. ▶

4. Click OK to save the new setting.

Alternatively, you can set up RTF to be used in e-mail you send to specific contacts by following these steps:

1. In the Outlook bar, click Contacts.

2. In the Contacts list, double-click the contact you want to modify.

3. Double-click the contact's e-mail address.

4. In the E-Mail Properties dialog box, in the Internet Format list, click Send Using Outlook Rich Text Format. ▼

5. Click OK, and then click Save And Close to save the new settings.

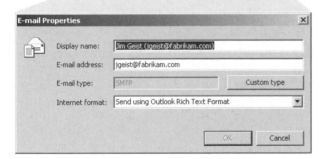

Have you tried this?

If you get an e-mail message that has a linked object in it and have trouble opening it, it might be stored on a server that's not available or one you don't have rights to access. You'll have to contact the administrator for that server to fix this problem.

I want to insert just part of a file, but Outlook inserts the whole thing

Source of the problem

Okay, here's how this works. Let's say you created a chart object in a PowerPoint presentation. Chart objects are created in Microsoft Graph (a shared application that can be used by all Office products). These charts are embedded objects. When you double-click this chart, it opens in Microsoft Graph for editing. So one day you decide that it would be neat to be able to include the chart in an Outlook e-mail message. That's just dandy except that when you insert a link to that object in your message, Outlook plunks the whole dang PowerPoint presentation in your e-mail, not just the chart object.

This happens because when you insert a linked object such as graph from a document into a Microsoft Outlook item such as an e-mail message or contact record, Outlook goes ahead and uses the file the link refers to—the whole file. Not to worry: You can insert part of a file as a linked object as long as the program the file was saved in supports linked objects. Because just about every program in the world today supports linked objects, this should work for you every time.

> ### Before you start
> With a world of shared applications in Office, you'll sometimes find that when working with embedded objects from applications such as Clip Gallery and Microsoft Graph you'll need a little help when exporting or linking them to another file.

How to fix it

Follow these steps to insert part of a file as a linked object:

1. Open the file in the application in which it was created.

2. Click the item you want to insert, and click the Copy button.

3. Go to Outlook, and click in the body of an item such as the body of an e-mail message or the notes section of a contact record.

4. On the Edit menu, click Paste Special.

5. In the Paste Special dialog box, click a format from the As list. ▶

6. Click Paste Link, and then click OK to paste the link.

Paste Special ? ✕

Source: Microsoft Word Document

OK

Cancel

As:

Microsoft Word Document

○ Paste

◉ Paste Link

☐ Display As Icon

Result

Inserts a picture of the clipboard contents into your document. The picture is linked to the source file so that changes to the file will be reflected in your document.

Have you tried this?

If the program the file was created in doesn't support linked objects, you can use the Paste command instead. The object will be pasted into Outlook, but the links to the original version will be broken.

More about Paste Special

The Paste Special feature offers options for pasting the contents of the Windows Clipboard into your document. You can paste the contents as a kind of object, such as plain text, a picture, HTML text, or a Word document. You can also paste the contents as a link, and choose to have the link display as an icon rather than inserting the linked data.

I get a "cannot edit" error message when I double-click an embedded object

Source of the problem

Think of an embedded object as being like an expensive foreign sports car. When you want to get work done on your Ferrari, you take it into the local Ferrari dealership because nobody else in town has the specialized tools to work on this gas guzzler. However, let's say that one day the Ferrari dealership packs up shop and disappears in the middle of the night. You still have to get work done on the car, but how? Well, if your car was a virtual Ferrari, you could try converting it into a Ford format, and then take it to the Ford dealership to be worked on.

If you've followed this analogy (and who could blame you if you got lost in there somewhere), an embedded object is created in one program and then placed in a document created in another program. If you want to edit the embedded object, you have to open it in its original program. But if the original program isn't available to the computer you're using, you can't edit it. The "cannot edit" message appears when the source file or source program can't be opened.

If the source program isn't installed on your computer or available on your network, you can convert the object to the file format of a program you do have installed, and edit it in that program.

Before you start

When you embed an object in a document, you run the risk that the application that object was created in might not be available at some point. Using this work around will help you deal with that eventuality.

Have you tried this?

It could be that you don't have enough memory to run the program in which the embedded object was created. To free up some memory, shut down any programs you aren't using.

How to fix it

To work with an embedded object when its source application is absent, try these steps:

1. Click the embedded object.

2. On the Edit menu, click the bottom command. (The command name will match the type of embedded object you just clicked, such as Worksheet Object, Picture Object, or Document Object.) Then click Convert to display the Convert dialog box. ▶

3. Do one of the following:

- To convert the embedded object, click Convert To, click the file type you want to convert to in the Object Type box, and then click OK.

- To open the file as another file type in a different program but have it revert to the original format when you return to Outlook, click Activate As, click the file format in the Object Type list, and then click OK.

Tip

If you're on a shared network and somebody else has the source file open, that could cause this same error message to appear.

Are you trying to set up an online meeting? **yes**

Are you having trouble with meeting responses? **yes**

Have you received responses you don't want to get? **yes**

no

Did you expect responses but you're not getting any? **yes**

no

Are you having trouble with the Call Using command? **yes**

no

Are you having difficulty changing meeting settings for recurring meetings? **yes**

Go to...
My online NetMeeting settings are unavailable, page 246.

no

Are you trying to join a meeting? **yes**

Go to...
I'm receiving meeting responses, and I don't want to, page 248.

Go to...
I scheduled a meeting but haven't received any responses, page 244.

Quick fix
When Call Using Net-Meeting is unavailable. If you're trying to call contacts with NetMeeting but the Call Using NetMeeting command isn't available, the problem might be that you selected multiple contacts. Try this:

1. Select just one contact.

2. Click the Call Using NetMeeting command.

3. Repeat steps 1 and 2 for each contact in the meeting.

Quick fix
Joining a NetMeeting. If you try to join a NetMeeting through the reminder, you can get an error if the person who called the meeting hasn't started it yet. There are two options:

1. If the current time is before the start time for the meeting, click Snooze and try joining the meeting again later.

2. If the start time for the meeting has passed, contact the meeting organizers and remind them that you're waiting for them to begin the meeting.

If your solution isn't here, check these related chapters:

- Rules, page 258
- Tasks and calendars, page 284

Or see the general troubleshooting tips on page xix.

I scheduled a meeting but haven't received any responses

Source of the problem

There's a reason nobody ever says "as fun as a meeting." Meetings might be necessary and sometimes even productive, but they're not a day at the beach. Even setting up a meeting can be a harrowing experience. You call Joe and leave a message asking if he's available Tuesday at 3. Mary sends you a message that she'll be on a plane at 3. Joe returns your call and leaves a message that 3 is fine. You take an aspirin, and then e-mail Joe to say 3 won't work for Mary. Joe can make 11 on Wednesday; Mary has to meet with her son's teacher. Mary can do Thursday; Joe is having minor surgery. Sound familiar?

Before you start

You can set up Outlook so that messages are either deleted or forwarded automatically. This can be useful, but if you're not aware that those settings are active or you forget to modify them if the situation changes, it can be confusing, or worse—you could lose important messages.

One great feature of Outlook is that it can help you schedule meetings. You can check the schedules of all the attendees online (if they give you access). You can send out a meeting message and track responses automatically. You can have responses forwarded to someone else, perhaps your assistant or office manager, and let them straighten out the conflicts. However, sometimes all the options for managing this process can get confusing.

For example, let's say you only want to get a tally of those who accept or decline a meeting; then, if there are no comments in the messages, you just want to delete them. In that case, you can select the Delete Blank Voting And Meeting Responses After Processing check box in the Tracking Options dialog box. When you do, meeting responses that arrive with no comments are tallied in your original meeting request and are then deleted. Because they never appear in your Inbox, you might think nobody has responded. (Meeting responses that include comments always appear in your Inbox.) Or perhaps you set up Outlook to forward responses to a delegate directly.

If you didn't intend either of these actions and want to receive all responses yourself, it's easy to change the settings.

How to fix it

To see all responses to your meeting request in your Inbox, follow these steps to set e-mail tracking options:

1. On the Tools menu, click Options.

2. On the Preferences tab of the Options dialog box, click E-Mail Options.

3. In the E-Mail Options dialog box, click Tracking Options. ▶

4. Clear the Delete Blank Voting And Meeting Responses After Processing check box.

5. Click OK in all three dialog boxes to save this setting.

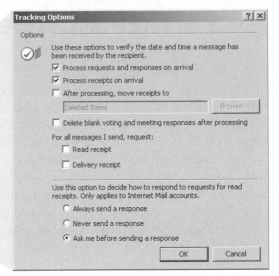

To have meeting request responses sent to you and not only to your delegate, follow these steps:

1. On the Tools menu, click Options.

2. Click the Delegates tab.

3. Clear the Send Meeting Request And Responses Only To My Delegates, Not To Me check box.

4. Click OK to save the setting.

Note

The Delegates option is only available if you are using Microsoft Exchange.

My online NetMeeting settings are unavailable

Source of the problem

In business and in everyday life, many things recur. There are recurring nightmares and meetings that recur at regular intervals (not to be confused with recurring nightmares). Your boss inspects the factory every three months. PTA meetings come up every month on Tuesday nights. Your project team meets once a week on Monday morning. Outlook makes it easy to create recurring meetings; that is, create a single meeting and designate that it recur at a regular interval. Outlook then sends e-mail messages inviting people to those meetings and places all occurrences of that event on your calendar.

The ability to create recurring events can save you time you might otherwise spend having to create essentially the same meeting again and again, but it limits your flexibility in making changes to individual events because it's not possible to change some settings for just one instance of a recurring meeting. You have to open the series and make the changes, which will then apply to all occurrences. Alternately, you can change the recurring meeting to start again after the next event and create a new meeting item for the next event with its own unique settings.

Before you start

The ability to create recurring tasks is helpful when you have a regular weekly or monthly event such as a staff meeting. But using recurring tasks can make it harder to make changes to just one occurrence of the task. What you gain in efficiency you might lose in flexibility.

How to fix it

If you want to make unique settings to the next occurrence of a recurring meeting, open the recurring meeting, modify its start date, and then create a new meeting you can customize for the next event by following these steps:

1. Click the Calendar icon in the Outlook bar to open the Calendar view.

2. Double-click the recurring meeting in the Daily Calendar list.

More about scheduling meetings

If you have scheduled an event and clicked Busy in the Show Time As box, those with access to your schedule see that time as blocked out. This unavailable time is indicated by a line appearing to the left of the appointment times in your calendar. If that's not what you want, click Free in the Show Time As box.

3. In the dialog box that appears, select Open This Occurrence.

4. Click the Recurrence button and under Range Of Recurrence change the start date for the recurring meetings to start one day, week, etc., after the meeting that will have a special meeting time. ▶

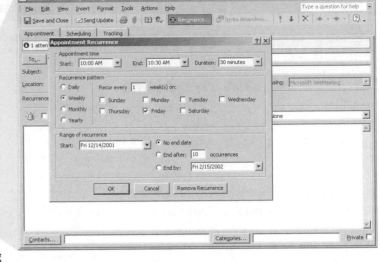

5. Click Save And Close to save the new setting.

6. Select Actions, New Meeting Request.

7. Make new settings for the next occurrence of the meeting that has a different schedule than the recurring series. Click Save And Close and remember to notify attendees of the special meeting time.

I'm receiving meeting responses, and I don't want to

Source of the problem

By default, when you send a meeting request, responses to that request are sent to you. But what if you really don't need to know who's coming or even get a count of how many will show up? For example, let's say you send out an announcement about a company party for a departing employee and attendance is optional. Do you really want to bother with the 50-plus e-mail responses from people telling you why they can or can't come by to wish Harry or Mary a nice life?

Outlook provides a couple of options in this situation, and they are both designed to stop your Inbox from swelling up like some insidious online helium balloon. These options basically fall into two categories. If you haven't sent the meeting request yet, you can avoid having anybody send you responses by not requesting responses. If the meeting request has already been sent, you can create a rule that tells Outlook to move any meeting responses that arrive in your Inbox to your Deleted Items folder.

How to fix it

If you have not yet sent the meeting request, follow these steps to indicate that you do not want people to respond:

1. In the meeting request, select attendees to invite as usual, and then click the Actions menu.

2. Click Request Responses to clear the check box next to it.

3. Click OK to save the setting, and then send the request.

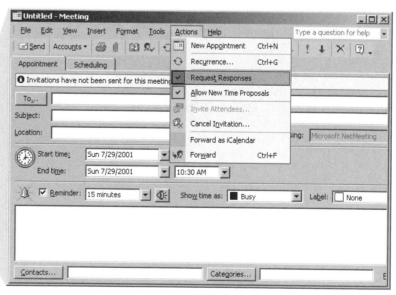

Meetings

If you've already sent the meeting request and did request responses, create a rule to delete the responses by following these steps:

1. Click the Inbox.

2. On the Tools menu, click Rules Wizard.

3. In the Apply Changes To This Folder list, click the Inbox you want to create the rule for, and then click New.

4. Follow the Rules Wizard instructions and apply these settings:

- Start from the template called "Move new messages from someone". ▶

- Designate the messages to be moved. You can do this by specifying words in the subject line, body, or header, for example, to identify the responses you'll be receiving from your meeting request.

- Choose either Move It To The Specified Folder (and specify the Deleted Items folder) or just click Delete It or Permanently Delete It.

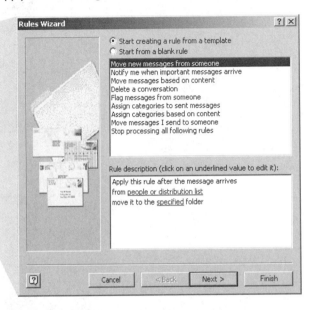

Warning

Be very careful in specifying words in the subject or body of e-mail messages in a rule. If you use the words "staff meeting," for example, every possible message with the phrase staff meeting will be deleted, and that might not be what you want to happen. Get in the habit of using truly unique words or combinations of words in headers if you think you'll use a rule to delete responses to them.

Tip

If you want to run a rule only now and then, create it, and then turn it off. When you want to use it, open the Rules Wizard, click the rule, and then click Run Now.

Are you working with the contents of public folders? yes → Are you having trouble finding information? yes →

no ↓

Are you having trouble making changes to a file in a public folder? yes →

Go to...
Changes I made to a file in a public folder weren't saved, page 254.

no ↓

Do different people in your organization work with the same files in public folders? yes →

Go to...
One of my public folders contains conflict messages, page 256.

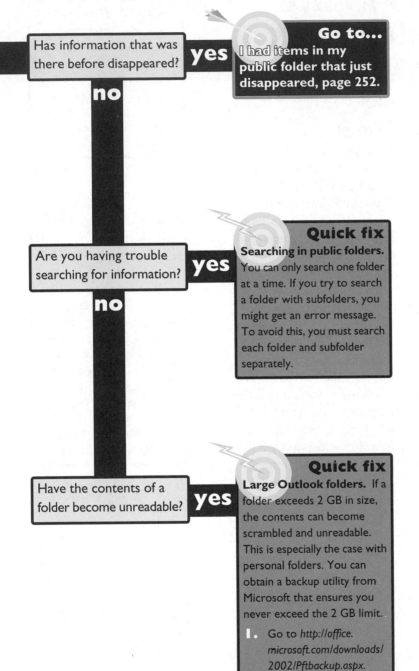

Has information that was there before disappeared?

yes

Go to...

I had items in my public folder that just disappeared, page 252.

no

Are you having trouble searching for information?

yes

Quick fix

Searching in public folders. You can only search one folder at a time. If you try to search a folder with subfolders, you might get an error message. To avoid this, you must search each folder and subfolder separately.

no

Have the contents of a folder become unreadable?

yes

Quick fix

Large Outlook folders. If a folder exceeds 2 GB in size, the contents can become scrambled and unreadable. This is especially the case with personal folders. You can obtain a backup utility from Microsoft that ensures you never exceed the 2 GB limit.

1. Go to *http://office. microsoft.com/downloads/ 2002/Pftbackup.aspx.*

2. Download and run the free utility.

If your solution isn't here, check this related chapter:

● Security, page 266

Or see the general trouble-shooting tips on page xix.

I had items in my public folder that just disappeared

Source of the problem

We might wish that taxes, telemarketing calls, and excess pounds would disappear, but when things start disappearing from our Outlook folders, that's seldom a good thing. This problem could occur for a couple of reasons. Folders can get hidden if you've applied a filter to a view. Or, if you're working offline, you might not have the shortcuts in place to access subfolders within your public folder.

Filters are used to limit what displays on your screen. You might use a filter to view only e-mail messages from a certain person or e-mail messages that haven't yet been read, for example. Filters are applied by customizing a view. If you think you're not seeing some items you expected to see, you can clear all filters from your view and see if that solves the problem.

If the information you want within Public Folders is in an offline folder, Outlook is essentially using a shortcut to it from the public folder. If a public folder contains subfolders, the shortcut to the offline folder won't show the subfolders. You have to create shortcuts in the Favorites folder under Public Folders for every subfolder you want to work with offline.

How to fix it

To remove any filters and view all of the items in a folder, follow these steps:

1. Click the View menu, and then click Current View.

Before you start

One cause of this problem could be that you've applied filters to an Outlook view. Filters are great for zeroing in on specific sets of items, but don't forget to remove them if you want to be able to see all the items again.

Have you tried this?

Outlook allows you to organize items in tables, such as the tasks in your task list, by groups. You can group tasks by start date, for example. You can collapse groups, and when you do, you won't be able to see every item in the group. You can identify a collapsed group by the plus sign to the left of the group. Click the plus sign (the Expand button) to display every item in that group.

Warning

Be aware that filters can use more than one criterion. If you clear a filter, several types of filtering might be removed.

2. Click Customize Current View.

3. Click Filter, and then click Clear All. ▶

To create a shortcut to a public folder, you must be using Microsoft Exchange. Follow these steps:

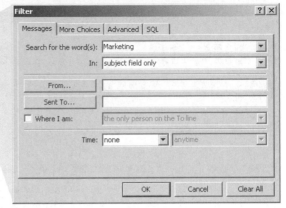

1. In the Folder List, right-click the public folder for which you want to add a shortcut for offline viewing.

2. Click Add To Favorites on the shortcut menu.

3. To change the name of the folder as it displays in your Favorites folder, click the public folder name.

4. Type a new name in the Favorite Folder Name box.

5. Click Options to add shortcuts to subfolders of this folder.

6. Click the options you need, and then click Add.

Changes I made to a file in a public folder weren't saved

Source of the problem

Object linking and embedding, affectionately known as OLE, is a technology that enables the transfer and sharing of information among different computer applications. Linked objects essentially contain a reference to an object that was created in another program.

When you open a file in Outlook, if it was created in a program that supports linked objects, your document will open in that application. Any changes you make will be saved to the file and be reflected in the file in the Outlook public folder. If, however, the file originated in an application that doesn't support linked objects, you could have a problem. Microsoft Outlook might open the file as read-only, and in that case, any changes you make won't be saved.

How to fix it

To make changes to a file created in a program that doesn't support linking, follow these steps:

1. Open the file and click File, Save As.

2. Save a copy of the file on your hard disk.

Before you start

Though most programs today support object linking and embedding, if you are working with a program that doesn't, you might find that you can't save changes to an item. In this case, your only choice is to work with a copy of the file on your computer, and then save the copy back to the public folder when you're done.

Have you tried this?

If the file is created in a program that supports linked objects and embedded objects and changes you made weren't saved, there could be another explanation. You and another person might have been working on the file at the same time. In this scenario, only the first changes saved will be kept. If you want several people to make changes to an item, consider attaching the file to an e-mail to let recipients make changes one at a time.

3. Open the copy of the file in the application in which it was created, and make your changes.

4. Save the copy in the public folder. ▶

One of my public folders contains conflict messages

Source of the problem

Most organizations have pretty sophisticated networks these days. Your company might have several network servers in place, and those servers might be connected in ways that make the human central nervous system seem simplistic. Here's one scenario you might encounter because of such a multilayered setup: if your company places Microsoft Exchange Server public folders on more than one computer, and an item is modified by you or your coworkers on different servers, when those computers are synchronized, you might get a message that there's a conflict.

Outlook provides a method for resolving these conflicts. However, it might involve deleting some versions of an item. Because other versions might belong to other people, be careful when using this procedure. You might know who else is working with copies of this item, or you might not.

Before you start

Outlook items, such as a contact record or e-mail message, might end up on more than one server in your company network. Resolving conflicts among versions of an item can involve deleting all but one version. Be cautious about this step unless you're sure that the version you save is acceptable to everybody accessing it.

How to fix it

To resolve conflict messages by combining all versions of an item into one version, follow these steps:

1. When the conflict message appears, open it. The message actually contains every one of the conflicting versions.

2. Open one of the items listed in the conflict message.

3. Open each of the other versions in turn and copy and paste any information you want into the open document.

4. Click Keep This Item. The other conflicting documents are deleted.

Tip

To save all of the documents with a conflict as separate documents in the public folder, you can click Keep All.

More about servers

On a network, a server is a computer with server software installed that responds to commands from a client, such as a user at a workstation. File servers often contain data or program files. When a request comes in, the server sends a copy of the requested file to the client or user. Multiple users can request a copy of the same file and make different changes to each copy. This is why things can get complicated when the servers attempt to synchronize the changes and need "human help" to decide how to combine the changes.

Public folders

Are you encountering problems with rules?

yes

Are you trying to get rules to apply to different items or areas of Outlook?

yes

no

Are you trying to import rules?

yes

Go to...
I don't know how to import a copy of all my rules into Outlook, page 264.

no

Are you trying to work with Rules Wizard?

yes

Are you having trouble getting Rules Wizard to complete?

yes

Would you like a rule to apply to only one e-mail account?

yes

no

Go to...
I want to create a rule that applies to only one e-mail account, not all of them, page 260.

Are you having trouble finding a rule you created in all inboxes?

yes

Go to...
I can't find a rule I created in the Organize pane in one of my inboxes, page 262.

Quick fix

Working with Rules Wizard In several of its steps, Rules Wizard requires that you enter a specific condition, exception, or action. Some steps require that you enter a value, and you will get a message that stops you from moving forward until you do. To specify a value, click any underlined text in the Rule Description box. In the dialog box that appears, set an initial value (for example, enter a name or select a folder). You can change these values in subsequent steps in the wizard.

If your solution isn't here, check these related chapters:

- E-mail accounts, page 222
- Sending and receiving e-mail messages, page 274

Or see the general trouble-shooting tips on page xix.

I want to create a rule that applies to only one e-mail account, not all of them

Source of the problem

Rules are a tool Outlook provides to manage e-mail messages. They're like little online traffic cops that can route your messages for maximum efficiency. Rules can be used for a variety of actions. They can move messages to different folders, delete messages, flag messages for action, and assign messages to categories. You can apply rules in a specified order and even designate to which e-mail account a rule will apply.

You can set up Outlook to work with more than one e-mail account, for example, a personal e-mail account and a work e-mail account. When you create a new rule, Outlook applies it to all the e-mail accounts in the Inbox that is active at the time you run Rules Wizard. But what if you decide you want a rule, such as one that moves messages from your boss into a priority folder, to only apply to your work e-mail account? To apply a rule to just one account, you have to change the rule by specifying the account to which it should apply.

Before you start

Outlook allows you to create different e-mail accounts, but sometimes it can get a little confusing trying to understand which actions you perform relate to which accounts. You can use a setting in the Rules Wizard to apply a rule to specific accounts.

How to fix it

To modify a rule to apply it to only selected accounts, follow these steps:

1. Click an Inbox in the Folder List.

2. On the Tools menu, click Rules Wizard. ▶

3. Click the Inbox you want to apply the rule to in the Apply Changes To This Folder list.

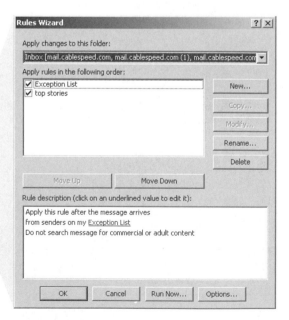

Tip

Use the Organize pane to quickly apply some common rules to manage e-mail. Click the Organize button on the toolbar to display the pane, and then make selections such as applying color to the text of junk mail.

4. Click the rule you want to make changes to in the Apply Rules In The Following Order list.

5. Click Modify.

6. Proceed through the wizard to the second screen. In the Which Condition(s) Do You Want To Check list, select the check box for the condition Through The Specified Account. ▶

7. Click the link Specified in the Rule Description area to open a dialog box that allows you to specify which e-mail account to apply the rule to.

8. Click Finish to complete the wizard and save your changes.

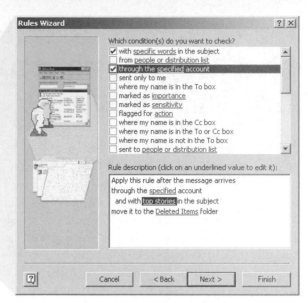

I can't find a rule I created in the Organize pane in one of my inboxes

Source of the problem

If Rules Wizard is the complete salad bar of Outlook rules, Organize is the fast-food drive-through. It's faster, but has less to offer. The Organize pane is a useful place to manage how messages are stored in folders and what elements are shown in views by making simple selections. You can also use this pane to apply preset rules to e-mail using colors; for example, you can make a setting to apply a color, such as red, to the text of all messages from a certain person or blue to all junk mail. You can also access Rules Wizard from this pane.

However, you should be aware that when you create rules in the Organize pane, they are only applied to the Inbox you are currently working in. To use the rule in your other inboxes, you'll need to copy the rule, and then apply it to a different Inbox using Rules Wizard.

Before you start

Rules are applied to inboxes. If you create a rule with Rules Wizard, you can choose the Inbox. If you create a rule in the Organize pane, it's quicker, but applies to the active Inbox by default. You must make a copy of the rule using Rules Wizard if you want to apply it to another Inbox.

How to fix it

To copy an existing rule and apply it to a different Inbox, follow theses steps:

1. Click an Inbox in the Folder List.

2. On the Tools menu, click Rules Wizard.

3. In the Apply Changes To This Folder list, click the Inbox that contains the rule you want to copy to another Inbox.

4. Click the rule you want to copy in the Apply Rules In The Following Order list.

Warning

If you put a copy of a rule into an Inbox it's already in, the first rule stays active, and the copy of the rule is turned off.

5. Click Copy. ▶

6. In the Copy Rule To dialog box that appears, click the Inbox into which you want to copy the rule from the Folder List.

7. Click OK.

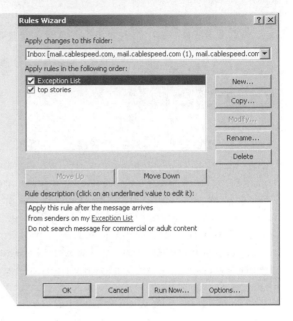

I don't know how to import a copy of all my rules into Outlook

Source of the problem

Software is built on a business model of upgrading, which frankly has its pros and cons. Instead of just starting from scratch with something brand new, when you upgrade software, a lot of things happen. Many little files are installed and uninstalled, new features are added, new problems are introduced, and sometimes, items you worked hard to create in a previous version just don't make the transition the way you thought they would.

Luckily, the software industry has come a long way. Upgrading used to be a hair-raising experience, but most upgrading today is done seamlessly by clever wizards and technical thingamabobs. However, when you move from one version of Outlook to another, some things might be left behind, such as all the rules you created over time. But don't despair: all you have to perform is a simple import procedure.

Before you start

When you upgrade to a new version of Outlook, you have to import any rules you've created in the previous version or re-create the rules. Importing is simple but a bit tedious because you can only import one set of rules at a time.

How to fix it

While still using your old version of Outlook, export your rules to a file on your hard disk. Do this by opening Rules Wizard and clicking the Options button; then click Export Rules. (Rules files use the .rwz file extension.)

You can then import the rules into Rules Wizard of Outlook 2002. Follow this procedure to do so:

1. Click the Inbox. On the Tools menu, click Rules Wizard.

2. Click the Inbox you want to import the rules to from the Apply Changes To This Folder list.

Tip

When you import rules, they wind up at the end of any existing list of rules. You can use the Move Up and Move Down buttons in Rules Wizard to rearrange the order in which your rules are applied.

3. Click Options.

4. Click Import Rules. ▶

5. Locate the file of rules you want to import in the File Name box. The Files Of Type list allows you to click Outlook 2000 Compatible Rules Wizard Rules or Outlook 98 Compatible Rules Wizard Rules in addition to the default Rules Wizard Rules selection.

6. Click Open, and then click OK. The imported rules will be listed in the Rules Wizard dialog box.

Warning

If the word "failed" appears in the name of a rule, it means that Outlook wasn't able to import the entire rule. Typically, the problem is that the rule is just too complex and specifies too many conditions. Take a look at such rules and modify them to make them simpler.

Are you concerned about sending or receiving secure messages?

yes →

Are you having trouble opening a secure message you received?

yes →

Go to...

I received a secure message, but I can't open it, page 270.

no

Are you trying to send a secure message?

yes

no

Are your security label settings not working?

yes

no

Quick fix

Security label settings. If the default security setting is changed from S/MIME to Exchange Server security, security labels, secure receipt requests, and clear text signed messages won't work. Do this to make S/MIME the default format:

1. Click Options on the Tools menu, and then click the Security tab.

2. Click the Settings button.

3. Click S/MIME in the Secure Message Format list.

Does your message format change when working with secure messages?

yes

Security

Are you getting an error message about security policy?

yes

Go to... When I try to send secure e-mail, I get a message about my security policy, page 272.

no

Are you trying to send an encrypted message?

yes

Go to... Outlook won't send an encrypted message page 268.

Quick fix

Working with message formats. When you send a secure message using an S/MIME digital ID and you use Microsoft Exchange Rich Text format, the message gets changed to HTML format. This ensures that the ID is processed correctly. However, some formatting can be lost when this happens. To avoid this, compose the message in HTML format by using these steps:

1. Open a new message.
2. Click HTML on the Format menu.

If your solution isn't here, check these related chapters:

- Web publishing, page 116
- Sending and receiving e-mail messages, page 274

Or see the general trouble-shooting tips on page xix.

Outlook won't send an encrypted message

Source of the problem

When you think about it, we spend a lot of time trying to prove who we are these days. We have drivers' licenses we flash to write a check, passports to cross borders, and passwords galore to do everything from getting cash at ATMs to entering our own houses without alarms going off. Well, the Internet is no different. Your ID for secure e-mails is called a digital ID or digital certificate. Essentially, it authenticates that you are really the sender of a message. Authentication is done with something called public key encryption. With this process, you work with a service that issues a digital certificate along with two keys: you use one key to sign your message, and a public key is used by your recipient to unlock your message.

If you're trying to send an encrypted message, but you're having trouble, it's possible that you don't have a copy of the intended recipient's digital ID. To successfully send an encrypted message to others over the Internet, you have to add a copy of their digital ID to their address in your Address Book or Contacts folder.

Before you start

Digital IDs provide some protection when sending sensitive information or payments on line. They allow the recipient to verify your identity. However, if you don't have information about a recipient's digital ID, you won't be able to send the encrypted message.

How to fix it

The contact must send you an e-mail with the "public" part of his or her digital ID attached. To update your Address Book or Contacts folder to include the digital ID, follow these steps:

1. Open the message sent to you that has the digital ID attached.

2. In the From field, right-click the sender's name.

Note

To obtain a digital certificate, click Tools, Options. Display the Security tab, and click Get A Digital ID. This will connect you to a Microsoft Web site with links to providers of digital certificates.

3. On the shortcut menu that appears, click Add To Contacts. ▶

4. If it's not already displayed, click the Certificate tab of the Contact form.

5. The digital ID should appear in the Certificates list, or you can click the Import button to add a certificate from a file.

6. Click Save And Close. If your Address Book or Contacts list already has an entry for this person, you'll see the Duplicate Contact Detected dialog box. You can choose to add the new information as a separate, duplicate entry for this person, or click Update New Information From This Contact To The Existing One to merge the digital ID information into the existing record.

The digital ID is now stored with your contact entry for this recipient. You can send encrypted e-mail messages to this person by selecting this record in the To field of an e-mail. Click Options on the message's View menu, click Security Settings, and then click Encrypt Message Contents And Attachments.

I received a secure message, but I can't open it

Source of the problem

The most obvious explanation for this problem is that the sender's digital certificate might have expired. Outlook allows you to easily check the status of the certificate. If it has expired, you'll have to contact the sender and have him or her resend an e-mail with a current certificate or resend the e-mail without encryption so you can read it.

On the other hand, you might have problems with trust. Don't worry—it's not as serious as it sounds. You can still have healthy emotional relationships. However, you need to understand how Outlook looks at secure communications. Outlook allows you to set trust levels for a contact or specifically instruct it to trust or not trust a particular secure communication. If your settings are set to not trust the source, the message won't open. Trust settings exist to protect you from sources that might transmit viruses to your computer via e-mail messages.

How to fix it

If you have to change trust settings, follow these steps:

1. Click the Certificate symbol on the right side of the message.

2. In the Message Security Properties dialog box, click Edit Trust.

3. Click Explicitly Trust This Certificate. ▶

4. Click OK, and then click Close.

5. If prompted, click Yes to add the certificate to the Root Store.

If you think the sender's certificate might have expired, follow this procedure to check:

1. Click the Certificate symbol on the right side of the message.

2. In the Message Security Properties dialog box, click View Details.

3. Click View Certificate in the Signature dialog box.

4. Click the Details tab in the View Certificate dialog box, and check the date listed for the Valid To field. ▶

If the certificate is no longer valid, you'll need to request a new one from the sender of the message.

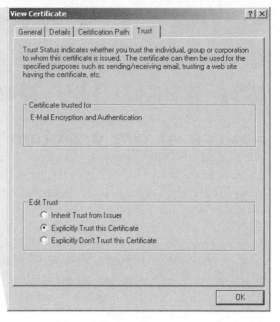

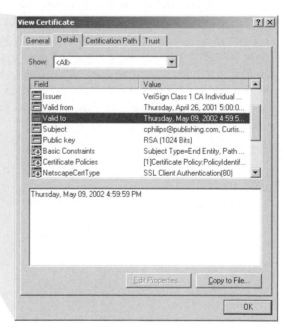

When I try to send secure e-mail, I get a message about my security policy

Source of the problem

The person administrating your network is likely to create certain security policies in Outlook. Security policies are attached to security labels. Security labels are little messages that you can set to appear in a message header; for example, "Internal Use Only." If you see the message—The Security Policy You Selected Does Not Allow One Of The Certificates In This Security Profile To Be Used—it means you have a security policy in place that doesn't accept certificates. You can change the security label for that message or confer with your administrator about security policies.

However, there is a setting you can control that can cause a glitch in the way Outlook notifies you about invalid digital certificates. If you have a setting for security options to use labels on every message, Outlook won't notify you if your digital certificate becomes invalid. As the saying goes, don't shoot the messenger—it won't help. But you could try to reconfigure Outlook to not send labels, so that it will notify you if a certificate has problems.

> **Before you start**
>
> Removing security labels from all messages might allow Outlook's automatic configuration to alert you to invalid certificates, but it also means you have to add security labels manually to messages.

> **Have you tried this?**
>
> If you have difficulty sending a secure message it could be because the certificate wasn't attached to it. If you have more than one contact record for the recipient, you might not have used the contact that contains the certificate. Locate that contact, and send the e-mail message again.

How to fix it

To set up Outlook to notify you of problems with your default certificates, follow these steps:

1. On the Tools menu, click Options.

2. Click the Security tab, and then click Settings.

3. Click Security Labels.

4. Click None in the Policy Module list. ▶

5. If you can't specify None, contact your administrator to obtain the correct certificates.

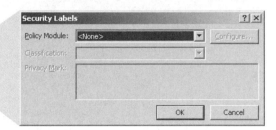

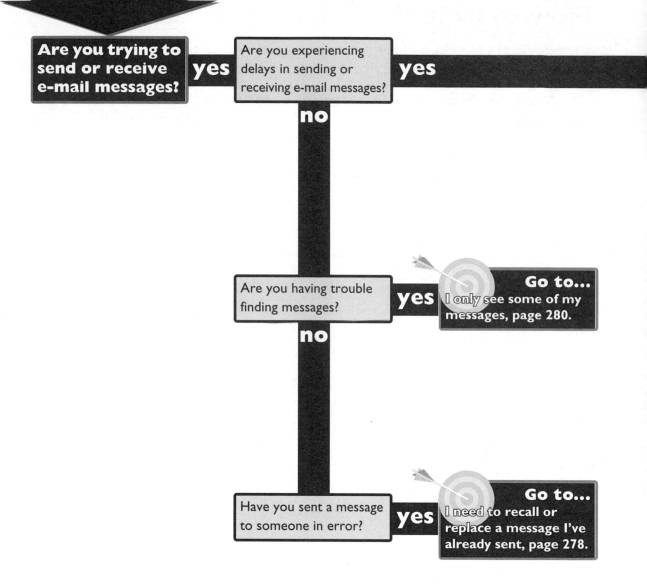

Are you trying to send or receive e-mail messages? **yes** Are you experiencing delays in sending or receiving e-mail messages? **yes**

no

Are you having trouble finding messages? **yes**

Go to... I only see some of my messages, page 280.

no

Have you sent a message to someone in error? **yes**

Go to... I need to recall or replace a message I've already sent, page 278.

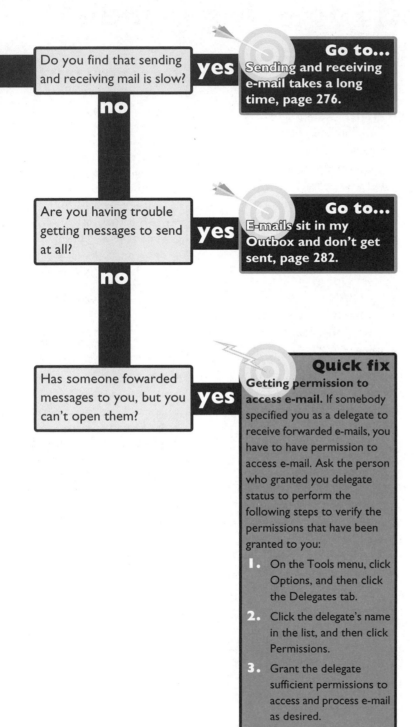

Do you find that sending and receiving mail is slow?

yes

Go to...
Sending and receiving e-mail takes a long time, page 276.

no

Are you having trouble getting messages to send at all?

yes

Go to...
E-mails sit in my Outbox and don't get sent, page 282.

no

Has someone fowarded messages to you, but you can't open them?

yes

Quick fix

Getting permission to access e-mail. If somebody specified you as a delegate to receive forwarded e-mails, you have to have permission to access e-mail. Ask the person who granted you delegate status to perform the following steps to verify the permissions that have been granted to you:

1. On the Tools menu, click Options, and then click the Delegates tab.

2. Click the delegate's name in the list, and then click Permissions.

3. Grant the delegate sufficient permissions to access and process e-mail as desired.

If your solution isn't here, check these related chapters:

- Security, page 266
- Rules, page 258

Or see the general trouble-shooting tips on page xix.

Sending and receiving e-mail takes a long time

Source of the problem

If processes are moving pretty slowly in your computing world, there could be several reasons, but essentially the reasons fall into two categories. You might not have enough available memory, or processes might be occurring in the background that you might not be aware of and might not even need. If you're experiencing snail-like e-mail functions, here are three likely culprits:

- Microsoft Word should have at least 16 MB of memory available for optimum performance. If you use Word as your e-mail editor, check your System settings in the Windows Control Panel for the total RAM on your computer, or open Task Manager (press Ctrl+Alt+Delete, click Task Manager, and click the Performance tab) to see how much memory you have available.

- Checking more than one e-mail account can take a chunk of your resources. If you use more than one account, try changing your settings to check mail with only selected accounts.

- Some programs work in the background—that is, they allow you to work in other programs while they are active. Any program that automatically backs up files is a good example of such a program. If you have such programs on your computer, they could be slowing it down. Although some are absolutely necessary, such as antivirus software, others might not be necessary or could be set to run less frequently. Use the Processes tab of the Task Manager to see whether you're running programs that have an impact on your computer's performance. This program also tells you which applications use the highest percentage of processor (CPU) time.

Before you start

Speed can be a trade-off. You might have to free up memory or disable background processes that are useful, but that cause your e-mail send/receive to go slowly. In some cases, you might find there are processes occurring that you don't need. Turning them off costs you nothing and might help to increase your e-mail speed.

Have you tried this?

If you're using Microsoft Word to write your e-mail, make sure there aren't any stray Word dialog boxes open; this could slow down sending your e-mail.

How to fix it

Using Word as your e-mail editor requires extra memory. To select Outlook's built-in e-mail editor instead, follow these steps:

1. On the Tools menu, click Options.

2. Click the Mail Format tab, and clear the Use Microsoft Word To Edit E-Mail Messages check box. ▶

To modify send/receive activity when working offline, follow these steps:

1. On the Tools menu, point to Send/Receive Settings, and click Define Send/Receive Groups. ▼

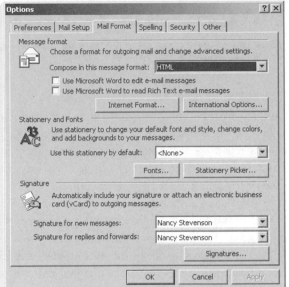

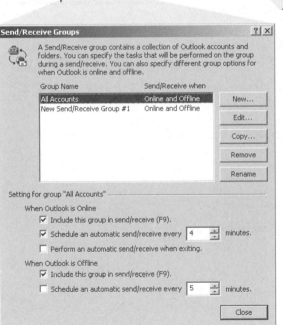

2. Click each group whose e-mail doesn't need to be checked when you're working offline. Under When Outlook Is Offline, clear the check box labeled Include This Group In Send/Receive (F9).

3. Click Close to save the setting.

More about Send/Receive Groups

A new feature in Outlook 2002 helps you control how different e-mail accounts deal with sending and receiving. This feature, called Send/Receive Groups, allows you to group accounts and configure them separately. In one account, you might choose to preview messages before downloading, and in another group, you might download without previewing, for example.

I need to recall or replace a message I've already sent

Source of the problem

Outlook offers something you seldom get in life: a chance to take it all back when you've said the wrong thing. You can do this by recalling or replacing an e-mail message, for example, if you sent it to the wrong person by mistake or put the wrong date or time in a meeting announcement.

Because this feature only works if the recipients are logged on and using Microsoft Outlook and have not read the message or moved it from their inboxes, it's best if you use it within minutes of sending the original message. Even with these limitations, this feature might just save you from cluttering peoples' inboxes with useless, incorrect, or even embarrassing communications.

To use this feature, you have to use Microsoft Exchange.

> **Before you start**
>
> Don't count on being able to recall a message because it might be too late. Always compose messages with a professional, calm tone so you don't risk sending out something that could prove embarrassing!

How to fix it

If you want to recall or replace a message you've sent out to one or more recipients, follow this procedure:

1. On the View menu, click Folder List.
2. Click the Sent Items folder to display its contents.
3. Double-click the message you want to recall or replace to open it.
4. On the Actions menu, click Recall This Message.
5. Do one of the following.

To recall the message, do this:

1. Click Delete Unread Copies Of This Message.

2. If you want Outlook to let you know whether the recall for each recipient worked, select the Tell Me If Recall Succeeds Or Fails For Each Recipient check box. ▶

To replace the message, do this:

1. Click Delete Unread Copies And Replace With A New Message.

2. Click OK, and then enter a new message.

3. If you want Outlook to let you know whether the replacement for each recipient worked, select the Tell Me If Recall Succeeds Or Fails For Each Recipient check box.

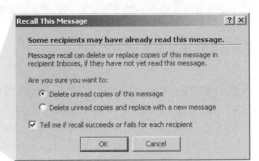

Note

If you want to replace a message, you have to create a new one, but you don't have to send it. Whether you send it or not, the first message is recalled.

I only see some of my messages

Source of the problem

There are several features of Outlook that can be used to take actions on e-mail messages, for example, hiding them or actually deleting them. Most of these actions require that you proactively modify a setting, but it's possible that somebody else used your computer and changed some settings, or you did something to change one of these settings in the past and have forgotten about it. So take a quick look at three of the settings that would cause messages to disappear.

Filters can be set up to display only the messages that meet certain conditions. You might have turned a filter on to hide some or all of the items in a folder. If there is a filter applied to a folder you have open, "Filter Applied" is displayed in the status bar.

AutoArchive is a feature that is turned on by default without you making any changes. AutoArchive archives or even deletes older items from your folders. Any message with a time frame that has expired—for example, a meeting notice for a certain date—would be deleted. Other messages would be saved in a special data file for a period of time (which you can adjust). You do get a message stating that Outlook is going to AutoArchive items, which also asks you to confirm or to hold off, but it's easy to just click Yes in this message box without realizing that it's moving messages out of your folders.

In addition, if you have created rules that specify that certain messages should be moved or deleted, you might be losing track of some e-mail. For example, you might have created a rule to delete any messages from a certain contact after you read them.

How to fix it

To remove any applied filters, follow these steps:

1. On the View menu, point to Current View, and then click Customize Current View.

2. Click Filter.

3. Click Clear All. ▶

To turn off automatic archiving, do this:

1. On the Tools menu, click Options.

2. Click the Other tab.

3. Click AutoArchive.

4. If the Run AutoArchive Every check box is selected, click to clear it.

5. Click OK.

To see what rules you have active, follow these steps:

1. On the Tools menu, click Rules Wizard. ▶

2. Click each rule in turn, and read the rule description.

3. To remove a rule, click it, and then click Delete.

4. To modify a rule, click it, and then click Modify.

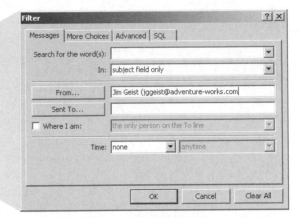

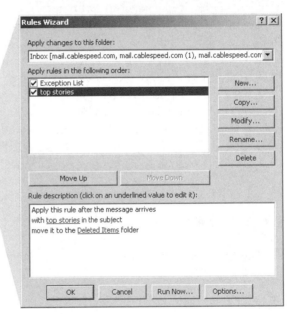

E-mails sit in my Outbox and don't get sent

Source of the problem

Mail that you can't send is about as pointless as a car without an engine. If your e-mail is sitting in your Outbox not going anywhere, you need to understand how Outlook deals with sending mail.

When you compose a message and click Send, your message first goes into your Outbox. In most cases, it almost instantaneously leaves your Outbox, but in certain situations— for example, if you're working offline or the message is very large—it might sit in your Outbox for several seconds or until you go online again. During that time, you can go to the Outbox and open your e-mail message. If you open a message

Before you start

You can make settings that control when Outlook sends mail. If you aren't aware of those settings, it can seem like mail isn't being sent at all. However, sending mail at one time rather than message by message might make better use of your online time.

in the Outbox, modify it, and save the e-mail message, the message isn't sent, it's just saved as a draft. You have to open it and click Send again to move it along.

Another cause of e-mail that won't budge from your Outbox is that you might have set up Outlook so that messages aren't sent until the next time you click Tools, Send/Receive. If you use dial-up networking to connect to the Internet and you set up Outlook to send messages immediately, Microsoft Outlook connects to the server after you click the Send button in a message. If you don't have this setting, your message will eventually be sent when you next click Send/Receive.

How to fix it

Messages that have been saved are located in the Drafts folder. To send a draft message:

1. Double-click the message to open it.

2. Click Send.

Tip

To send all messages in the Outbox you can also simply click Tools, Send/Receive, Send/Receive All.

To modify settings for when messages are sent, follow these steps:

1. On the Tools menu, click Options.

2. Click the Mail Setup tab. ▶

3. Select the Send Immediately When Connected check box. With this setting, an e-mail message is sent when you click Send.

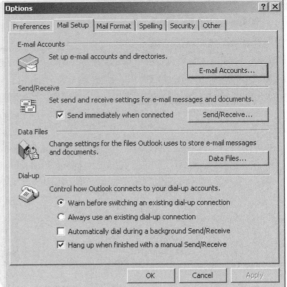

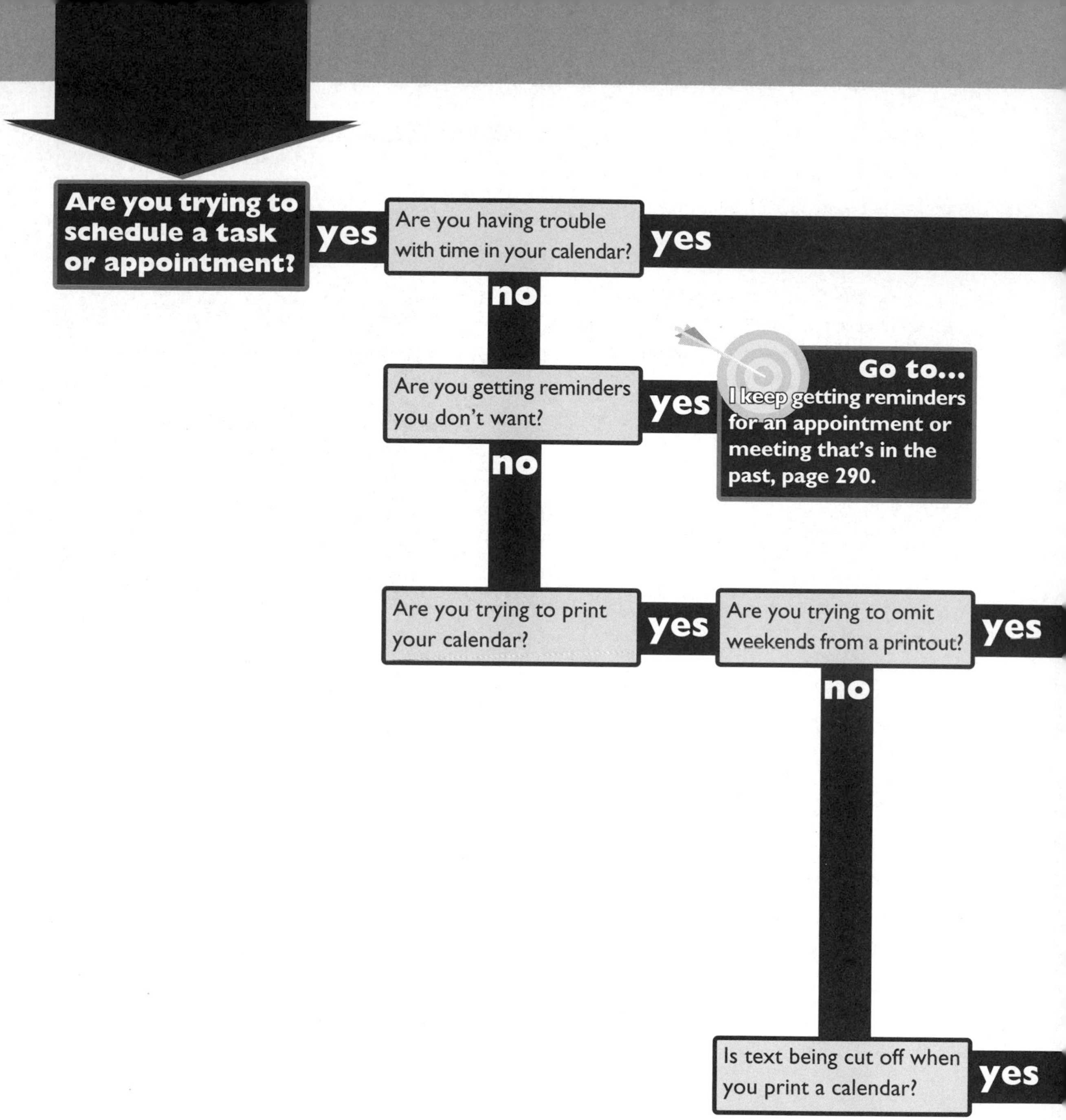

Are you trying to schedule a task or appointment? yes → **Are you having trouble with time in your calendar?** yes →

no ↓

Are you getting reminders you don't want? yes →

Go to...
I keep getting reminders for an appointment or meeting that's in the past, page 290.

no ↓

Are you trying to print your calendar? yes → **Are you trying to omit weekends from a printout?** yes →

no ↓

Is text being cut off when you print a calendar? yes

Tasks and calendars

Are you having problems with time units?

yes → **Go to...** I entered a task in hours, but it's not converting to days and weeks correctly, page 288.

no

Are tasks showing at incorrect times?

yes → **Go to...** My appointments and meetings show at wrong times, page 286.

Quick fix

Printing weekdays only. If you only want weekdays to print when you print your monthly calendar, follow these steps:

1. Click Print on the File menu.
2. Select Monthly Style in the Print Style box.
3. Click Page Setup.
4. Select the Don't Print Weekends check box.

Quick fix

Fitting a calendar into a printout. Outlook only prints the text that fits in a calendar view. Try these steps to fit more on your screen:

1. Select File, Page Setup.
2. In the Page Setup dialog box, choose smaller font sizes for headings and appointments.

If your solution isn't here, check these related chapters:

- Printing, page 56
- Meetings, page 242

Or see the general trouble-shooting tips on page xix.

My appointments and meetings show at wrong times

Source of the problem

If you've ever flown across country and found your internal clock so out of whack that you meet yourself coming and going (although your luggage never made it at all), you understand about time zones. Appointments and meetings that you create in Outlook are scheduled based on the time zone you have set on your computer. Although you can set your time zone in Windows, many people don't realize you can also make changes to your time zone from Outlook. If events you schedule in Outlook are popping up at odd times, you or somebody else might have changed your time zone.

Outlook also offers a feature that allows you to swap time zones. Essentially, Outlook allows you to create more than one time zone and to switch between them. This is very handy, for example, if you have a laptop computer and frequently travel among time zones or you live in a part of the country where daylight saving time is not used (this places those locales in two different time zones during the year). When you swap time zones in Outlook, it affects the time settings in all your Microsoft Windows–based programs and has the same effect as modifying the current time zone in the Windows Control Panel. If you swapped the time zones by mistake or forgot to swap them back after a trip, this could be the source of your problem.

How to fix it

To determine whether you've swapped time zones in Outlook and whether Outlook is set to the wrong one, follow these steps:

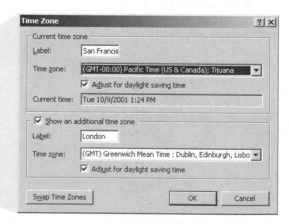

1. On the Tools menu, click **Options**.

2. Click **Calendar Options**, and then click **Time Zone**. ▶

3. If the Show An Additional Time Zone check box is selected, compare that location with the location shown in the Current Time Zone section.

4. If your physical location corresponds to the additional time zone setting, click the Swap Time Zones button to make it the current time zone.

If swapping time zones isn't the source of your problem, you can directly change the current time zone by following these steps:

1. On the Tools menu, click Options.

2. Click Calendar Options, and then click Time Zone.

3. Click the correct time zone for your location in the Time Zone list.

4. See whether the Adjust For Daylight Saving Time check box is selected; if it is and you don't want this setting, clear it.

I entered a task in hours, but it's not converting to days and weeks correctly

Source of the problem

When you tell your boss it will take five days to accomplish something, you don't mean 5 × 24 hours. You're talking about five typical, eight-hour workdays. By default, Outlook also bases tasks on an eight-hour workday and a five-day week. If you enter 10 hours of actual work, Outlook converts that to 1.25 days.

However, you can change the number of hours Outlook uses to calculate a day or a week. For example, if you always work a 10-hour day and 30 hours a week total, you might want to change your calculation for a workday to 10 and a workweek to 30. Be aware, however, that making this universal change will affect all tasks you create. If this is a one-time need, you might want to try a workaround: in a 12-hour task scenario, create two tasks on a particular day—one eight-hours long and one four-hours long, and track actual work on each.

How to fix it

To make changes to how Outlook calculates your typical workday and workweek hours, follow these steps:

1. On the Tools menu, click Options.

2. Click the Other tab, and then click Advanced Options. ▶

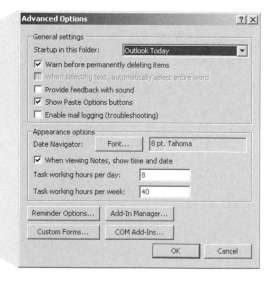

3. Enter a number in the Task Working Hours Per Day box that matches your typical workday.

4. Enter a number in the Task Working Hours Per Week box that matches your typical workweek.

5. Click OK to save your new settings.

Tip

You can set which days of the week you work by clicking the Preferences tab of the Options dialog box, and then clicking Calendar Options. Click to place a check mark next to the days of the week you work.

I keep getting reminders for an appointment or meeting that's in the past

Source of the problem

Our lives are pretty darn hectic these days. We have appointments with doctors, lawyers, clients, and psychiatrists (who help us deal with all the stress caused by all these appointments). In fact, we have so many appointments and meetings to deal with, most of us need help keeping them straight.

One of the points of setting up appointments or meetings in Outlook is to be reminded of an impending event so you don't miss it. When you set up an appointment or meeting in Outlook, you are also setting up how Outlook will remind you of it. Outlook will remind you of recurring appointments or meetings at the interval you've set. With one-time appointments, you'll be reminded of them until you tell Outlook to stop. Even if an appointment's scheduled time has passed, until you dismiss the task, Outlook will keep reminding you about it. The theory here is that not all meetings happen when they are scheduled, and you might want to be nudged now and then about it so you remember to reschedule or attend at a later time. But if you want to get rid of those reminders, you can do so easily.

Before you start

Deleting reminders you no longer need is easy; just be sure you don't delete an item that you need and miss an important appointment!

How to fix it

To dismiss an appointment when its reminder appears, click Dismiss or Dismiss All.

To change a recurring appointment or meeting to a one-time meeting, follow this procedure:

1. Click Calendar in the Outlook bar to display appointments.

2. Double-click a recurring appointment.

Have you tried this?

You might have created an appointment or meeting twice, and even though you thought you dismissed it, it keeps reappearing. To remove a duplicate, right-click it in the Calendar, and then click Delete.

3. Click Open The Series, and click OK.

4. Click the Recurrence button. ▶

5. Click Remove Recurrence.

6. Click Save And Close to close the dialog box.

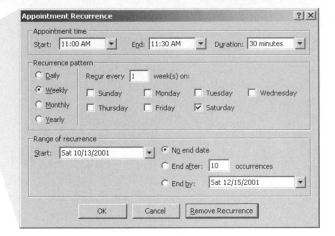

PowerPoint

Part 4

Aligning and

Are you having difficulty with the way objects are lining up on your slide?

yes → Are you trying to use the Align or Distribute feature? **yes** →

no

Do you want to change an object's rotation angle? **yes** →

Go to...
An object on my slide is upside down!, page 300.

no

Are you trying to move an object just a little bit on the slide? **yes** →

Quick fix

Nudging objects. Sometimes all you want to do is move an object just a smidgen in one direction or another. Try these steps:

1. Click the object.
2. Hold down the Ctrl key, and press an Arrow key to nudge the object one pixel at a time in the direction of the arrow.

no

Are objects on your slide overlapping each other? **yes** →

Go to...
I inserted several objects, but they overlap each other, page 296.

Are you having trouble getting objects to move when you try to align or distribute them?

yes

Go to...
Objects aren't moving where I want them when I try to align or distribute them, page 298.

no

Are items on the Align Or Distribute menu dimmed so that you can't select them?

yes

Quick fix
Using Align Or Distribute. Unless the Relative To Slide option is active, you have to have at least two objects selected to use alignment and three to use distribution. To select multiple objects:

1. Click the first object.
2. Hold down the Shift key, and click additional objects.

If your solution isn't here, check these related chapters:

- Slide design and layout, page 366
- Text boxes and text in objects, page 376

Or see the general trouble-shooting tips on page xix.

Aligning

I inserted several objects, but they overlap each other

Source of the problem

Objects such as drawings, clip art, and PowerPoint placeholders can all be moved around on a slide, which gives you great control over your slide's overall design. You can stack objects on top of each other to create a design effect or build a drawing. But just as layering your clothes must be done with taste (orange plaid on pink paisley—I think not!), layering objects on a slide has to be done judiciously.

On the simplest level, if you find objects stacked on top of each other and you don't want them to be, you can simply click each item in turn and move it to separate areas of your slide. However, if you want objects layered because of space limitations or to create a design effect, but want to control how those layers behave, you can use PowerPoint's Order feature. This feature enables you to place objects within the stack, just as you might place a one-eyed Jack at any position in a deck of cards.

In addition to the Order feature, you can work with transparent effects that allow objects in your stack to show through other objects that overlap them.

How to fix it

To change the order of objects on your slide, follow these steps:

1. Click an object.

2. Display the Drawing toolbar, and click the Draw button to display its menu.

3. Point to Order to display its submenu.

4. Click one of the commands to order your object. If you think of your objects as a stack of playing cards, here's what each command does:

- **Bring To Front** brings the object to the top of the deck.

- **Send To Back** places the object at the bottom of the deck.

- **Bring Forward** brings the object forward as if it were moving one card closer to the top of the deck.

- **Send Backward** moves the object one slot lower in the deck.

Repeat Steps 1 through 4 until all the objects in your stack are in the correct order.

You can also make objects partially transparent; when you do, any object underneath shows through. It's just another way to control the appearance of objects stacked on top of each other. You make an object transparent this way:

1. Click the object.

2. On the Format menu, click AutoShape.

3. In the Format AutoShape dialog box, adjust the Transparency slider control to make an object totally opaque (0%), completely transparent (100%), or anything in between. ▶

4. Click Preview to see the results, adjust as necessary, and then click OK to save the setting.

More about moving objects

If you have stacked objects and just want to unstack them, you only have to click each object and drag it away. But if you only want to move, say, the third item down, it might be hard to click it if it's completely covered by another object. One method you can use to click a stacked object is to click the top object and keep sending each top object backward until the object you want is on top. It's easy to then simply click the object and drag it away.

Note

An alternate approach to letting objects underneath show through is to set the top object format to have no fill color applied. Then the object is simply a line drawing with nothing in the middle, and objects under it can be seen. However, if you want to use some sort of fill color and still be able to see objects underneath, use the transparency setting.

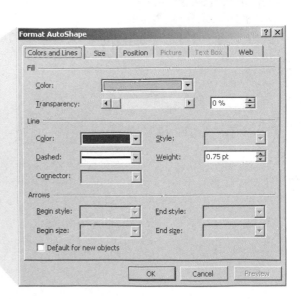

Aligning

Objects aren't moving where I want them when I try to align or distribute them

Source of the problem

Each slide in a PowerPoint presentation is like a miniature work of art, and the way you arrange various elements on the PowerPoint canvas can mean the difference between a masterpiece and graffiti. PowerPoint offers you the ability to move objects around by simply clicking and dragging them. But the program also provides tools to align and distribute objects on a slide. This allows you to position objects relative to each other precisely on a slide with a single step.

Align options include aligning an object to the left, center, or right of your slide; or the top, bottom, or middle of your slide. Distribute options are used to arrange several objects horizontally or vertically on a slide. If you use one of the Align Or Distribute choices on the Draw menu and objects don't move as you expected them to, the Relative To Slide option might be selected. When this option is selected, objects move relative to the outer edges of the slide as well as to other objects on the slide. With this setting active, if you align three objects to, say, the top, they align to the top of the slide. If you turn the setting off and align three objects to the top, they align so that their tops are all aligned with each other, but they won't actually move to the top of the slide.

Alternatively, there is a setting in the Grid And Guidelines dialog box that might be affecting the way your objects are placed. The Snap Object To Grid option, which is selected by default, aligns objects to the nearest intersection of lines in the grid when you draw objects or move them around your slide.

How to fix it

The Relative To Slide setting can be turned on or off. When on, it will have an impact on any alignment you make, but will not cause changes to alignments you've already set. To turn off the Relative To Slide setting, do this:

1. Display the Drawing toolbar, and click the Draw button.

2. Point to Align Or Distribute, and then click Relative To Slide.

3. Point to Align Or Distribute again, and click any align or distribute setting you want for the selected objects. ▶

The Snap Objects To Grid option can be toggled on or off. When it's on, it controls how things behave when you move them on your slide. When turned off, there are no restrictions on how objects move around a slide. Again, if you turn this on, it will not have an effect on the current position of existing objects. To turn off the Snap Objects To Grid option, follow these steps:

1. On the View menu, click Grid And Guides.

2. Clear the Snap Objects To Grid check box.

3. Click OK to save the setting. ▶

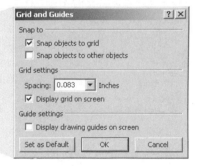

Tip

You can also display the Grid And Guides dialog box by clicking Grid And Guides on the Draw menu.

An object on my slide is upside down!

Source of the problem

Maybe you opened somebody else's PowerPoint presentation, or perhaps you were just playing around with objects in your own presentation. However it happened, you find that an object on a slide has flipped upside down or rotated at an odd angle. Short of standing on your head, how can you get the object to appear right side up again?

By using the Rotate Or Flip command on the Draw menu or by using the rotation handles on selected objects, PowerPoint allows you to spin objects around at various angles to your heart's content or flip objects to become mirror images of themselves. For example, you might insert a clip of an airplane, and then rotate it at an angle so that it looks like it's taking off into the sky. Or, you might want a text object containing a word like "FREE" to sit at a jaunty angle across the top corner of your slide, creating what's called a banner effect. But if you end up with an object at an awkward angle, you should know how to set things right.

Before you start

If you rotate or flip an object on a slide, remember that it might need to be moved so as not to obscure another object or for better slide design. But don't worry about doing any damage using rotate or flip: with PowerPoint tools, it's easy to reverse a flip or control the rotation of an object on a page.

Have you tried this?

If you rotate an object and want to set it back to its original orientation, on the Format menu, click AutoShape or Object. Click the Size tab, and change the Rotation setting back to zero degrees.

How to fix it

If you want to take an object that's upside down and turn it right side up, follow this procedure:

1. Click the object.

2. With the Drawing toolbar displayed, click the Draw button, and then point to Rotate Or Flip to display its submenu. ▶

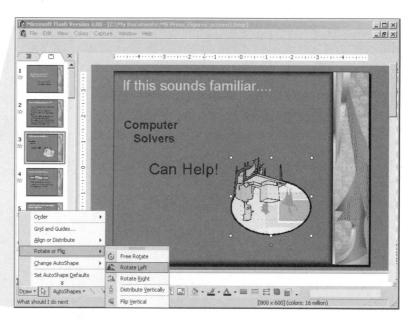

3. Click either Rotate Left or Rotate Right to move the object a quarter turn in the selected direction.

4. Repeat Steps 2 and 3 to turn the object a full 180 degrees, so that the side that was on top is now on the bottom. (Or just press F4 to repeat your last action.) ▶

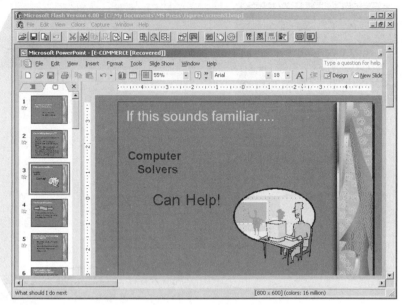

Tip

You can also use the green rotation handle that appears when you click an object to rotate it in a freehand style. PowerPoint maintains the outline of the original shape, making it easy to rotate the object and align its sides with the original position to get an accurate mirror image of the original position.

Are you trying to copy, move, or paste a PowerPoint object?

yes → Are you trying to paste an object?

yes → Are you having difficulty retaining formatting when you paste?

yes →

no ↓

Are you trying to paste data from another program into PowerPoint?

yes →

no ↓ (from "Are you trying to paste an object?")

Are you trying to move an object on a slide?

yes →

Go to...
There's an object on my slide that I can't move, page 306.

no ↓

Are you trying to copy more than one object at a time?

yes →

Quick fix

Copying several objects at once. You can copy more than one object at a time by either grouping them and working on them as a single object, or by using this method:

1. Press Shift, then click each object to select it.
2. Click the Copy button.
3. Display the slide where you want to paste the objects.
4. Click the Paste button.

Go to...
When I copied a slide, all the formatting disappeared, page 304.

Are you trying to embed an object from another program so it updates automatically?

yes

Go to...
I pasted data from Excel in my slide, and it doesn't update when I make a change in Excel, page 308.

no

Are you trying to create a PowerPoint presentation from an outline created in Word?

yes

Quick fix
Copying a Word outline into PowerPoint. The simplest way to get the contents of a Word outline into PowerPoint is to use the Send To feature from Word.

1. Display the destination PowerPoint presentation, and open the Word outline.

2. On the File menu in Word, point to Send To, and click Microsoft PowerPoint.

The outline is copied into your PowerPoint presentation.

If your solution isn't here, check these related chapters:

- Links and embedded objects, page 318
- Masters, page 326
- Notes and handouts, page 342

Or see the general trouble-shooting tips on page xix.

When I copied a slide, all the formatting disappeared

Source of the problem

Slides that you cut and paste in PowerPoint have a Jekyll and Hyde thing going on: they change personality and take on the formatting of the slide they're inserted after in a presentation. This is good when you want slides you place in your presentation to conform to the formatting you've applied to the rest of the presentation. But it's bad if you want pasted slides to retain their original formatting.

How to tame the Hyde beast? Easy. Just use the Paste Options feature in PowerPoint 2002. This little button shows up right after you paste something with formatting into your presentation. Here's how it works:

- If you paste a slide with different formatting into another presentation or to another location in its own presentation, you can use the Paste Options button to keep the formatting of the source. The button appears under the slide you paste in Normal view on both the Outline and Slides tabs, and in Slide Sorter view.

- The Paste Options button also appears when you copy text, various shapes, and tables if the destination you paste to has different styles applied. You can use the Paste Options button to choose the formatting you want to use. (The Paste Options button is enabled by clicking Options on the Tools menu and selecting Show Paste Options Buttons on the Edit tab.)

Before you start

When you paste an item, it typically takes on the formatting of the document you are pasting it into. Office's new Paste Options feature helps you avoid that. But don't worry: if you make the wrong choice in Paste Options, you can simply undo the paste and try it again.

Warning

If you copy and paste a slide using the Slide Finder dialog box and want to retain the original formatting, you must select the Keep Source Formatting option in the Slide Finder dialog box before you perform the copy operation.

How to fix it

To go through the cut or copy and paste process to copy slides or objects from one presentation to another and keep the original formatting of your slide or object, follow these steps:

1. Click a slide or object.

2. Click the Copy or Cut tool button or press Ctrl+C or Ctrl+X.

3. Locate the slide where you want to paste the object, or place your cursor at the end of the slide after which you want to paste another slide in either Normal or Slide Sorter view.

4. Click the Paste tool button or press Ctrl+V to paste the object or slide.

5. Click the Paste Options button. ▶

6. Click Keep Source Formatting on the menu that appears.

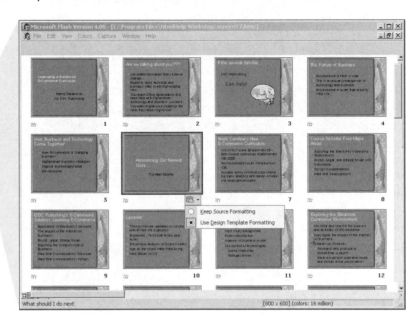

Note

If you use the Paste Special command to paste a link to an object or text in another application, you are essentially pasting a picture of the item in your PowerPoint slide. That linked content will take its formatting from the original document in the other application.

There's an object on my slide that I can't move

Source of the problem

If you try to move an object on a slide but it doesn't go any-where, odds are the object was inserted not on the individual slide, but on the Slide Master.

Why would somebody put an object on the Slide Master rather than on individual slides? Well, let's say you are creating a presentation about a hotel promotion for romantic weekends and you want to put a picture of Cupid in the right corner of every slide except one, what would you rather do—paste that picture of the winged cherub 49 times or paste it once and have it magically appear on all the slides (knowing that you can omit the graphic from the one slide that doesn't need it)? If you have a life, you'd probably choose the second option.

PowerPoint's masters help you place and format objects that will appear on most, if not all, of your slides, such as page numbers or a company logo. In addition to objects you place on it, the Slide Master stores information about the design template you've applied to a presentation including font styles, placeholder sizes and positions, any background design, and color schemes.

But here's the rub: if you want to do anything to that object, you can't do it on individual slides. You have to go back to the Slide Master and move or change the object. If you want the object on all the slides but want to change it in some way on one of the slides, omit the master graphic on the one slide, and then insert that same graphic on the individual slide and change away!

Before you start

There are pros and cons to placing objects on master slides rather than individual slides. If you put them on the master, you can't move or change them on individual slides. If you paste something on individual slides, and you want to use it on many slides in the presentation and make global changes to position or formatting, you can't. Determine the trade-off of having to make slide-by-slide changes before you make a choice of where to place objects.

How to fix it

If you decide the change you want to make to an object should be universal, you can work with it in the Slide Master. To move an object on the master, follow these steps:

1. On the View menu, point to Master, and click Slide Master.

2. On the Slide Master, click the object to select it, and then drag it to the position where you want it to appear on all your slides. ▶

3. Click Close Master View on the Slide Master View toolbar.

To omit a master graphic from your slide and insert the same object on an individual slide so that you are able to move it, follow this procedure:

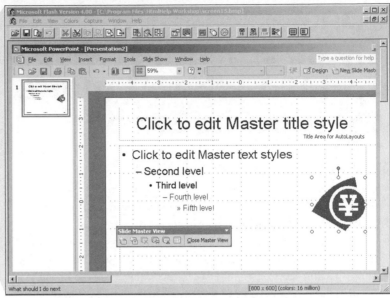

1. Display the slide from which you want to omit the graphic.

2. Click the Format menu, and then click Background.

3. In the Background dialog box, select the Omit Background Graphics From Master check box, and then click Apply. ▶

4. Either change the layout of the slide to include a graphic placeholder, or click the Insert menu, click the type of object you want to insert (for example, Picture, Clip Art to insert a clip), and make any choices specific to the object to insert it.

Warning

If you choose Apply To All in the Background dialog box, you'll omit the master graphic from all your slides. You should never take this approach—if you don't want the object to appear on slides anymore, it's better to remove it from the Slide Master.

More about masters

There are actually three kinds of masters: Slide, Handout, and Notes. The Slide Master consists of sets of masters—one for the title slide and one for nontitled slides. You will see one set of slides for each slide design you have applied to your presentation. Masters contain preset footer areas across the bottom that you can use to include date and time, page number, or any text common to your entire presentation, such as a company or presenter name.

I pasted data from Excel in my slide, and it doesn't update when I make changes in Excel

Source of the problem

We've all become used to the way technology allows software products to interact with each other. For example, with linking and embedding technology, you can insert data from one application into another and have it update seamlessly. But, you have to understand when and how this linking happens, because it doesn't happen without making certain choices.

When you copy cell ranges from Microsoft Excel and paste them into PowerPoint, the Paste Options button appears. This button contains different choices than it does when you paste PowerPoint objects. You can select Table to paste the Excel data in a PowerPoint table format. You can select Excel Table to place the data in PowerPoint as an Excel object (this is the default setting). Another option is to choose Keep Text Only, which loses all table or Excel worksheet formatting. In addition, you can select Picture Of Table to embed the Excel table as a picture, which has a smaller file size.

If you paste Excel data and you make changes in the Excel file, you'll have to paste the information in again, using either the Excel Table or Picture Of Table paste option. If you want to link Excel data in a PowerPoint slide so it updates automatically when the Excel file changes, use the Paste Special command, and click Paste Link to create a link to the data.

> ### Before you start
>
> When you paste an object from Excel into your presentation, you can choose to insert it as a PowerPoint table or a linked object, which essentially places a picture of the selection in Excel. If you paste it as a PowerPoint table, there is no link to the original material; if the Excel data changes, you'll have to update it in PowerPoint manually.

How to fix it

To have data from Excel update automatically, you can paste it as a link. If you pasted Excel data in as a table, you'll have to first delete the table, then repaste the Excel material as a linked object.

1. Click the table, and then press Delete.

2. Open the Excel file, select the material you want to insert into PowerPoint, and then click Copy.

3. Display the PowerPoint slide and click Paste Special on the Edit menu.

4. In the Paste Special dialog box, click Paste Link, click Microsoft Excel Worksheet Object in the As box, clear the Display As Icon check box, and click OK. ▶

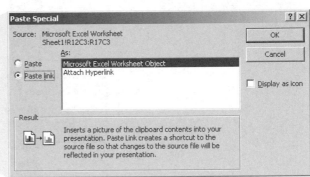

5. If you double-click the embedded object, Excel opens and displays the worksheet or segment of the worksheet in Excel so you can edit it.

6. When you're done, save your changes in Excel, and the new values will appear in PowerPoint.

Are you trying to edit a drawing or picture? — **yes** — Can you access the object for editing? — **yes** — Are you trying to crop a picture or object? — **yes**

no

no

Are you working with drawing object attributes such as 3-D or shadow? — **yes**

Did you insert an object created in another program? — **yes**

Go to...
I want to edit an embedded object, but the program it was created in isn't available, page 316.

no

Are you having trouble editing because there are too many pieces to edit? — **yes**

Quick fix
Grouping objects. If you ungrouped a drawing or picture, you can't work with it as a single object, for example, to resize or move it. You should group the pieces and try to edit it again.

1. Click at one corner near the edge of the objects and drag to form a box around them. This selects all the objects.

2. Click the Draw menu, and then click Group.

Go to...

I'm having trouble cropping a picture, page 314.

Are you working with a shadow but find it difficult to see?

yes

Go to...

I can't see the shadow I applied to my drawing object, page 312.

no

Are you having difficulty applying a color to a 3-D object?

yes

Quick fix

Adding color to a 3-D object. If a 3-D object has the Wire Frame style applied to it, it will look like a line drawing of a frame. You won't be able to add any fill color to it.

1. Click the object, click the 3-D Style button on the Drawing toolbar, and then click 3-D Settings.

2. On the 3-D Settings toolbar, click the Surface button, and then click to select a surface other than Wire Frame.

3. Click the 3-D Color button, and click a color to fill the object.

If your solution isn't here, check these related chapters:

● Links and embedded objects, page 318

● Text boxes and text in objects, page 376

● Drawing, page 24

Or see the general trouble-shooting tips on page xix.

I can't see the shadow I applied to my drawing object

Source of the problem

Shadows help add depth and visual appeal to objects. You can apply a shadow effect to any object in PowerPoint. PowerPoint also allows you to apply a shadow style that controls the direction and angle of the shadow, and to set the color of the shadow.

When you apply a shadow effect, PowerPoint applies a default color that complements the current color scheme of your slide. However, you can change this, and choose any color you like for your shadow. Shadow is a result of the combination of light and dark, and on a PowerPoint slide, shadow is affected by the contrast between dark and light colors. In other words, if you have a gray shadow on a gray background, don't waste your time trying to find the shadow!

To fix shadow issues, you have a few choices: you can manually apply new shadow colors until you find one that works; you can go back to the automatically applied default color; or you can choose another color from the color scheme that should work with the background color.

Before you start

If you've assigned a color to your shadow that blends in with your slide's background color, it might be hard to see. If you change the shadow to a color that doesn't work, you can easily return to the default shadow color.

How to fix it

Follow these steps to change the color of a shadow:

1. Click the picture, drawing object, WordArt, or text box you want to change.

2. On the Drawing toolbar, click the Shadow Style button, and then click Shadow Settings.

Have you tried this?

By making a shadow semi-transparent, you let the background color come through; this could be another cause of a less distinct shadow. You can toggle this setting on and off in the Shadow Settings dialog box.

3. Click the arrow on the Shadow Color button on the Shadow Settings toolbar. ▶

4. Do one of the following:

● To change to a color in the color scheme, click one of the colors displayed underneath Automatic.

● To change to a color that isn't in the color scheme, click More Shadow Colors. Click the color you want on the Standard tab, or click the Custom tab to mix your own color, and then click OK. ▶

● To change the shadow color back to its default, click Automatic.

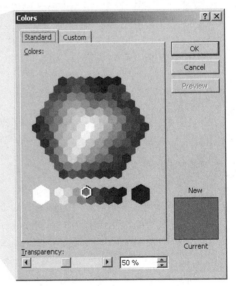

Note

For objects with 3-D settings, you can use the 3-D Settings toolbar to modify the colors on the 3-D portion of an object. However, you cannot apply a shadow and 3-D setting to the same object.

I'm having trouble cropping a picture

Source of the problem

Have you ever wondered what a map of the United States would look like without Florida hanging down there? In PowerPoint, you can make it happen. All you need is a map of the U.S. you can insert on a slide and the PowerPoint cropping tool.

Cropping is a handy feature, because when you work with PowerPoint, you often use predesigned pictures and images such as clip art. Although you have no control over the design of the image, you might need to modify it in several ways to get it to fit into your presentation perfectly. For example, you might trim a picture of a crowd of people to just include two for space limitation reasons. One tool at your disposal is cropping: the cropping tool lets you trim off little bits from the edge of a picture until you're left with just what you want. However, you need to know some cropping tricks of the trade to use this tool efficiently.

You can use the cropping tool on any picture format except an animated GIF file. If you're having difficulty with cropping, check to see if your picture is an animated GIF. If it is, you'll have to use an animated GIF editing program. Edit the picture in that program, and then insert it into PowerPoint again. If you're having a problem controlling the cropping feature, use some of the following techniques.

> **Before you start**
>
> If you crop a picture and decide you don't like what you've done, you can simply reinsert the original picture or undo one or more cropping actions.

How to fix it

1. Check to see if the image is in animated GIF format. Do that by looking at the properties of the original file you inserted. Or, from the image preview in the Insert Clip Art task pane, click the arrow to the right of the image, click Preview/Properties, and then check the Type field of the file. ▶

2. If the image isn't in animated GIF format, proceed with the following steps to crop it.

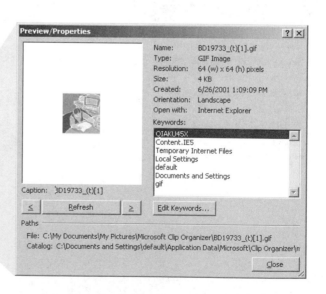

3. Click the picture you want to crop.

4. Click Crop on the Picture toolbar.

5. Place the cropping tool cursor over a cropping handle, and then use one or more of these cropping techniques:

- Drag the center handle on one side inward to crop only that side.

- Hold down Ctrl as you drag the center handle on either side inward. This will crop equally on two sides at once.

- Hold down Ctrl as you drag a corner handle inward to crop equally on all four sides at the same time. ▶

6. To turn off the Crop feature, click Crop again on the Picture toolbar.

Tip

The Picture toolbar should appear when you click an image. If it doesn't, right-click the image and click Show Picture Toolbar on the short-cut menu that appears.

Warning

You can undo a crop up until the point where you next save the file. Once the file's been saved, you'll have to reinsert the picture and crop again from the original image.

I want to edit an embedded object, but the program it was created in isn't available

Source of the problem

You can think of an embedded object as if it were a rental car. The rental car might be in your possession for a few days, but if it breaks down, the rental company will frown on you taking your own tools and having a go at the engine. You have to take it back to the company to have the car fixed. But what if you buy that rental car second hand someday? Then you can tinker to your heart's content. The trade-off is that you can't look to the rental car company to take care of it for you anymore.

When you embed a picture in a PowerPoint presentation that was created in another program, you can't do much to edit it from within PowerPoint besides resizing it and moving it from place to place. If you want to modify the image, you have to take it back to the program it was created with and use the tools available in that program. If an embedded object's source program isn't available, however, you can convert it to a Microsoft Office drawing object to work with it. But just as with the rental car, after you convert an embedded object to an Office drawing object, it is no longer associated with the original program, and you'll have to use PowerPoint's tools to work with it.

> **Before you start**
>
> If you convert an object to a drawing object so that you can edit it in PowerPoint, you won't be able to open it in its source program and use the features of that program to work with the image in the future.

How to fix it

To convert an embedded object to a drawing object, follow these steps:

1. Click the embedded object you want to convert to an Office drawing object.

2. Click the Edit menu, and then click the type of object (typically Picture Object) command.

3. In the alert message that appears, click Yes to convert the picture into a drawing object. ▶

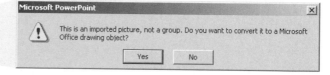

4. On the Drawing toolbar, click Draw, and then click Ungroup.

5. Make any changes to individual pieces of the image. ▶

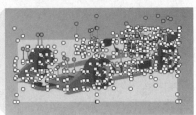

Warning

You cannot ungroup a bitmap so don't even try!

6. Click on your slide to the side of the objects you want to group and drag your cursor forming a border around all the objects to select them, then click Draw, Regroup to group the pieces of the object again to form a single object.

Have you tried this?

You can often open picture files saved in several formats in the Windows Paint program and work with them there if the original application is unavailable. To locate Paint, click the Windows Start menu, and then click Programs, Accessories, Paint.

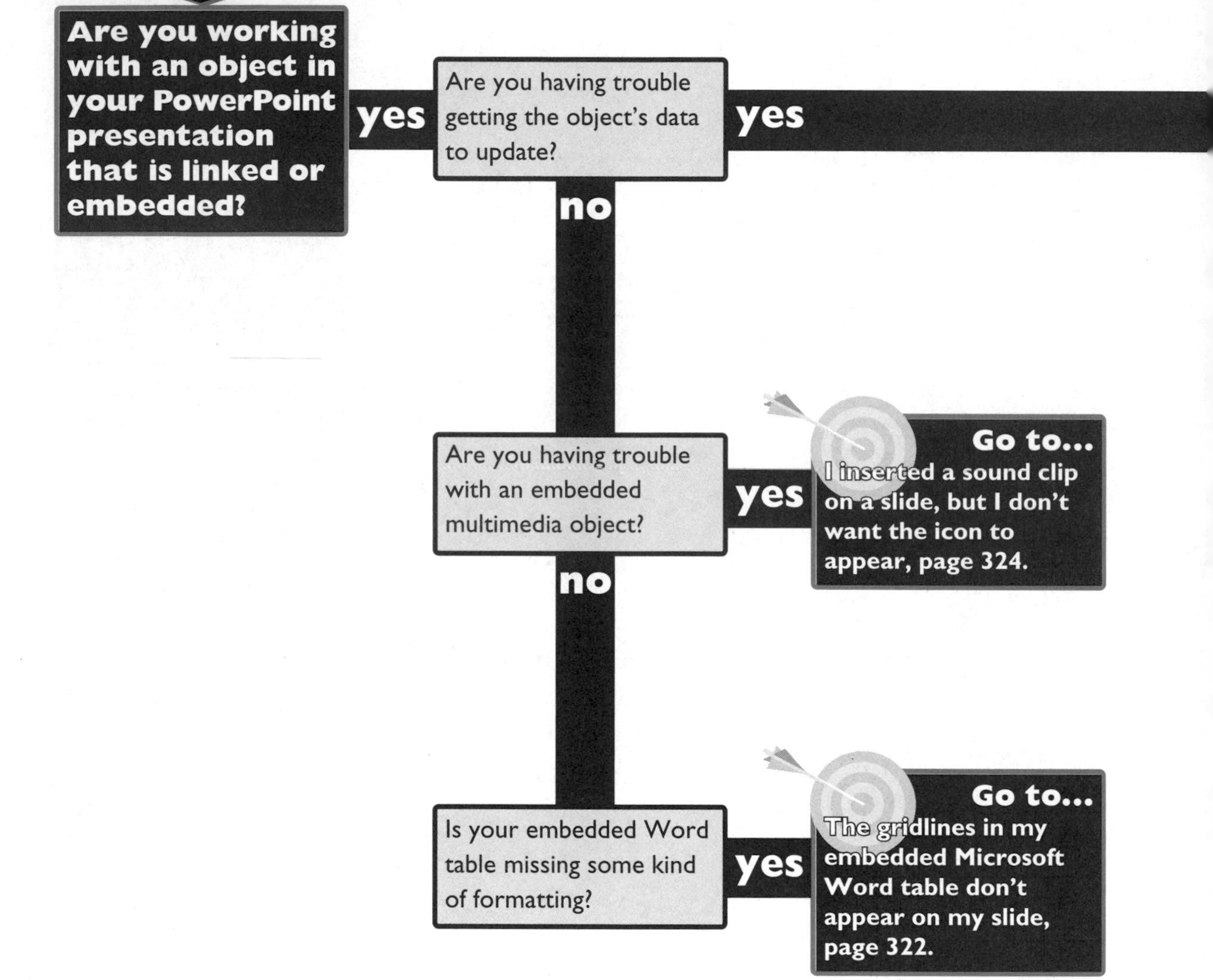

Are you working with an object in your PowerPoint presentation that is linked or embedded?

yes → Are you having trouble getting the object's data to update?

yes →

no

Are you having trouble with an embedded multimedia object?

yes →

Go to...
I inserted a sound clip on a slide, but I don't want the icon to appear, page 324.

no

Is your embedded Word table missing some kind of formatting?

yes →

Go to...
The gridlines in my embedded Microsoft Word table don't appear on my slide, page 322.

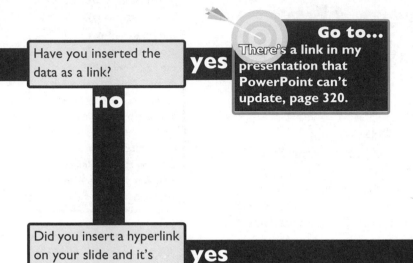

Go to...

There's a link in my presentation that PowerPoint can't update, page 320.

Have you inserted the data as a link?

yes

no

Did you insert a hyperlink on your slide and it's not working?

yes

Quick fix

Working with hyperlinks. Hyperlinks only function when you're running a slide show. They don't work when you're working in Normal or Slide Sorter view. To run your show to see if hyperlinks are working, do this:

1. On the View menu, click Slide Show.

2. When you come to a hyperlink, click it, and the linked document should open.

If your solution isn't here, check these related chapters:

● Sharing data, page 86

● Importing and exporting, page 174

Or see the general trouble-shooting tips on page xix.

There's a link in my presentation that PowerPoint can't update

Source of the problem

When you place a link to a file in a PowerPoint presentation, it's like writing yourself a note about where you left your home insurance policy. If your significant other reorganizes the den and moves the policy to the bedroom, your note to yourself will lead to a dead end. If you insert a link to a file in PowerPoint, it points to a specific location for a file. All data is updated from the application where that file was originally created. If the file gets moved or its name is changed, PowerPoint won't be able to find it and the link will fail to update. The object you linked to—say an Excel table—will still be in your presentation with the last version of data available before the link was severed, but you can no longer update it with the link feature. To edit this object you would have to remove the link and convert it to an object, such as an Excel table.

You can deal with this problem by editing the link so it once again points to the correct location. You should also take some precautionary measures to prevent the problem in the future. You might, for example, consider putting any files you've linked to within a single folder on your hard disk or network and don't let others access the files in that folder. And remember, if you go on the road with a PowerPoint presentation and you are going to make any changes to the source files, you should take the files that you've linked to and their source programs with you and let PowerPoint know where to find those files on your laptop.

Before you start

If you move or rename a file and there's a link to it from a program such as PowerPoint, the link won't work anymore. Relinking the object should solve the problem, but take precautions when you're on the road with a presentation and make sure that you take the linked files with you so PowerPoint can locate them.

Note

Don't confuse a linked file with a hyperlink. If you click a hyperlink, you go to a document, typically on the Internet in HTML format, but you can also place a hyperlink to another slide in your own presentation. A linked file, on the other hand, places information from another file within your presentation and updates that information if it changes in the source file.

Tip

Objects created in Office shared applets, such as Microsoft Graph, can't be updated outside of your presentation. To update a Microsoft Graph object, double-click it from within PowerPoint to open it and make changes.

How to fix it

If a source file has been moved or given a different name, you can relink to it using this procedure:

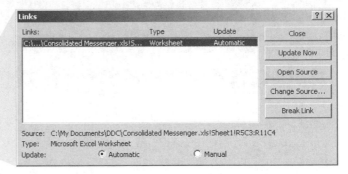

1. On the Edit menu, click Links, and then click Change Source in the Links dialog box. ▶

2. Click the source file, and then click Open. ▼

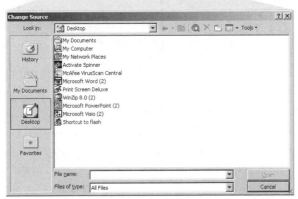

3. Click the Update Now button to update PowerPoint to the current data in the source file.

4. You can reset the way the link updates, either automatically or manually, by selecting Automatic or Manual in this dialog box. The Automatic option checks the source file to see if there are any changes every time you open your PowerPoint presentation and updates the data in PowerPoint as you make changes in the source application (if PowerPoint is open at the time). With the Manual option, your PowerPoint data is only updated when you click the Update Now button in the Links dialog box.

5. Click Close to save your settings and return to your presentation.

The gridlines in my embedded Microsoft Word table don't appear on my slide

Source of the problem

Tables are useful tools for organizing information. In a PowerPoint presentation, where space can be at a premium, they offer a great way to provide a concise snapshot of data. Microsoft Word offers a somewhat more robust table feature than PowerPoint, so you might sometimes create tables in Word, and then insert them in your presentation. If you have embedded a Microsoft Word table in your PowerPoint presentation that has gridlines turned off, gridlines will show on the screen, but they won't print. To print vertical and horizontal lines between cells, you need to apply borders to the table.

The simplest way to edit the table is to double-click it and use Word's Table AutoFormat tool to apply formatting. Table formatting can include not only borders around the table and gridlines between cells, but also shading and color to create visual interest. AutoFormat can apply all this formatting with a single click. Alternatively, you can set only borders and gridlines with the tools Word offers for formatting the border.

Once you've changed the format and decide you like it, click outside the table to return to PowerPoint, and then save your changes.

How to fix it

The easiest way to apply borders in Word is to use the Table AutoFormat command on the Table menu in Word, which automatically applies predefined borders and shading. Follow these steps:

1. Double-click the table object in PowerPoint to open the table in Word for editing.

2. Click the table, and then click the Table AutoFormat command on the Table menu. ▶

3. Click a table style, and then click Apply.

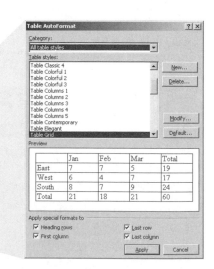

If you'd rather, you can apply a border style instead of using AutoFormat. Follow these steps to apply a border:

1. Click anywhere within the table, and then click Format, Borders And Shading. ▶

2. Click a Setting for the border, for example, use Box for an outside border, Grid for a heavier outside border and lighter inner lines, or All for heavy outside and inside lines. Your choice will be reflected in the Preview area of the dialog box.

3. Click selections for Style, Color, and Width to refine the settings.

4. In the Apply To list, click Table to apply the settings to the entire table.

5. Click OK to apply the settings, and then click anywhere outside the table to return to PowerPoint.

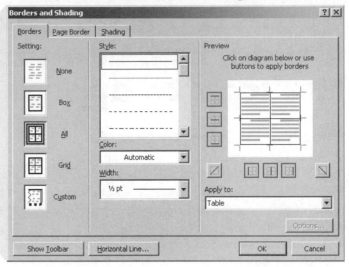

More about tables in PowerPoint

You can also create a table directly in Microsoft PowerPoint. To insert a table, click the Tables And Borders button and draw your table, or click Table on the Insert menu, and specify the number of rows and columns. Gridlines are displayed and will print.

I inserted a sound clip on a slide, but I don't want the icon to appear

Source of the problem

When you place a media clip on a PowerPoint slide, a cute little icon appears: you can activate the clip manually by clicking that icon during your presentation. However, you have the trade-off of having this little media clip icon sitting there distracting you and your listeners as you speak.

Naturally, you're wondering if you can hide that little icon. Unfortunately, there's no handy "hide this darn icon" command in PowerPoint. You can click and drag the icon off your slide, but before you do, you have to allow for some method of playing the sound because the icon won't be there to click when you run your show. If you set the icon to play automatically along with another action, you can then drag the icon off the slide so it doesn't show in the presentation, and it will play without your having to click it. You can alternatively set the sound file to play automatically at a certain timing interval following the last action in the slide show, such as a slide transition.

How to fix it

To create the automatic setting for an existing sound clip:

1. Right-click the sound file to select it.

2. On the shortcut menu, click Custom Animation. ▶

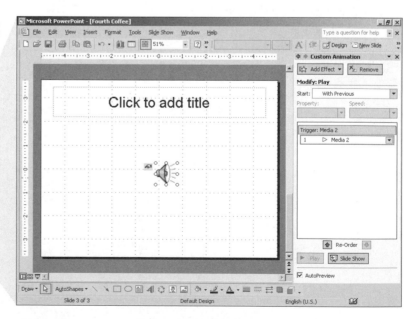

3. In the Custom Animation task pane, do either of the following:

● Click the arrow next to the Start box, and click With Previous.

● Click the arrow next to the Start box, and click After Previous. Then select the media object in the list, click the arrow next to the object to open its menu, and click Timing. In the Delay box, enter a time delay in seconds; the sound will play that many seconds after the previous action. Click OK to close the Play Sound dialog box. ▶

4. Click the sound icon, and drag it to the edge of the slide until it's no longer visible.

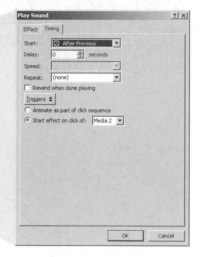

Note

If there is a custom animation sequence or animation scheme for the slide, the With Previous command works in the context of the animations. After Previous can also be used to automate the sound if it is part of an animation sequence.

Are you trying to make changes to your slides with Slide Master?

yes →

Are you having difficulties with placeholders?

yes →

no ↓

Have you applied font styles in the Slide Master but you don't get the results you expected?

yes →

Go to...
I applied a different font on a Slide Master, but fonts on a few of my slides didn't change, page 332.

no ↓

Have you inserted a picture in Slide Master that doesn't show up?

yes →

Go to...
I added a picture to a Slide Master, but it doesn't appear on some of my slides, page 330.

no ↓

Are you unable to find the Title Master?

yes →

Quick fix
Working with Title Master. If the Title Master part of the Slide Master duo has been deleted, try this:

1. Click View, Master, Slide Master.

2. Click Insert New Title Master on the Slide Master View toolbar.

A new Title Master appears. Click it to make your edits.

Have some placeholders disappeared?

yes

Go to...
I deleted a placeholder on a Master slide and don't know how to get it back, page 328.

no

Did you delete the <date/time> or <#> text in the footer placeholders?

yes

Quick fix
Working with footers in Slide Master. Some of the footers have text that automatically places the date and time or slide number on slides in your presentation. If you accidentally delete this text, you can:

1. Just retype it, or

2. On the Insert menu, click Slide Number or Date And Time.

If your solution isn't here, check these related chapters:

● Slide design and layout, page 366

● Page formatting, page 450

Or see the general trouble-shooting tips on page xix.

I deleted a placeholder on a Master slide and don't know how to get it back

Source of the problem

Placeholders are a fact of life with PowerPoint. The more you can work with placeholders rather than dropping text and objects onto your slides willy-nilly, the more control PowerPoint gives you over your presentation's content. For example, if you place all your slide titles in title placeholders, you can then use the Master feature to change the font for all titles in one go. If you've placed text outside of placeholders on your individual slides, you can't make global changes to that text.

Just as various slide layouts contain placeholders for objects such as titles, bullet list content, and media objects, Masters contain placeholders. The Slide Master layout contains placeholders for a title, bulleted text, and three types of footers: date, footer (a kind of catchall footer placeholder for whatever text you like, such as your company name), and page number. Handout Master contains placeholders for various arrangements of slides on a printed page as well as several header and footer placeholders. Notes Master contains a slide placeholder, notes area placeholder, and headers and footers.

You can delete Master layout placeholders just as you can change slide layouts, but the placeholders aren't actually deleted: they're simply removed from view. You can redisplay any placeholder by modifying the Master layout.

How to fix it

If you delete a placeholder on the Master and you want to reinsert it, do the following:

1. On the View menu, point to Master, and then click Slide Master. ▶

2. On the Format menu, click Master Layout.

3. Under Placeholders, select the check box for the type of placeholder you want to restore.

4. Click OK. ▶

This same procedure works to restore placeholders on the Notes Master or Handout Master.

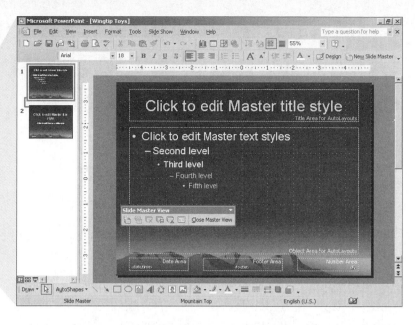

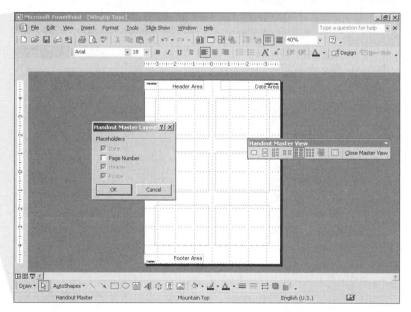

Tip

If you want to restore a placeholder that you have moved or resized to its original state, click the placeholder and delete it. Then follow the steps in this section to restore it to its original settings.

I added a picture to a Slide Master, but it doesn't appear on some of my slides

Source of the problem

The PowerPoint Master is actually a library for slide design settings. When you apply a design template to your presentation, a pair of Masters is created that reflect all the settings of that design. These are the Title Master and Slide Master.

If you apply a second design to your presentation, a second set of Masters is created. If you want to make a change to every slide in your presentation, you have to make that change in each Master set you've added. For that reason, and because consistency of look and feel is desirable in presentations, you shouldn't go running through your slides applying different designs like a kid in a design candy shop.

If you have added a picture to the Slide Master but don't see it on every slide, you might have to insert the picture on other Master sets.

Before you start

The beauty of Masters is that you can make global changes easily, yet you can override Master settings on individual slides. However, if you create too many Masters by applying several design templates to your presentation, you necessitate having to change each and every Master to make any kind of global setting, which can become cumbersome.

Warning

Don't get confused here: there's a Slide Master that contains two types of Masters: a Title Master and a Slide Master. The duplication of the name "Slide Master" for both the Slide Master feature and one of the Master objects it contains can be confusing!

Have you tried this?

If an object from the Slide Master is missing from a slide, you might also have selected the setting to omit Master graphics from that slide's background. Check that setting by displaying the slide, clicking Background on the Format menu, and then making sure that the Omit Graphics From Master check box isn't selected.

How to fix it

To check to see which Masters you've placed a graphic on and add an object to additional Masters, follow these steps:

1. On the View menu, point to Master, and then click Slide Master. ▶

2. Click the master object where you inserted the picture to display it.

3. Click the picture and use the Copy button or command to copy it.

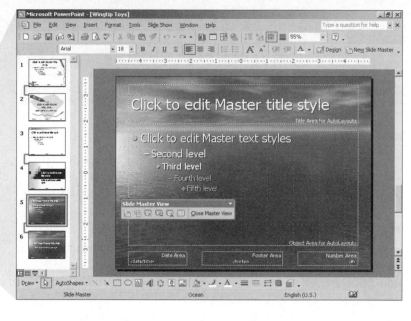

4. Display each Title Master and Slide Master from each design template in the presentation and paste the picture.

5. Move picture objects around the Masters as you want them to appear in either a consistent location throughout the presentation or in locations that match each design template's layout so as not to overlap text placeholders.

6. Click Close Master View. The picture should appear on all slides. ▶

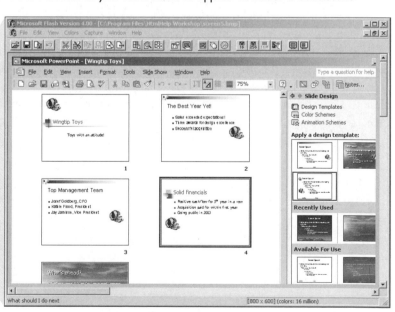

I applied a different font on a Slide Master, but fonts on a few of my slides didn't change

Source of the problem

One of the most confusing things for people working with PowerPoint is how changes to text on individual slides work with the slide design template and the corresponding Master objects that contain the design template settings in Slide Master. At some point, it can start to feel like gremlins have entered your presentation and are shifting formatting around on some mad whim. That's because, just as Congress is made up of a House and Senate and it's hard to figure out who's doing what, there are two sources of control over formatting of your text. You have to know which one is in control at any point in time or you'll go nuts.

Remember this simple rule and life will be a lot easier: Microsoft PowerPoint always preserves changes you make to specific slides, no matter what you do in the Slide Master. It might be that you changed some font styles on your slides before you made a change to the font styles on the Slide Master.

If you follow the design guideline that the best presentations are ones that use only a few fonts with consistent colors and font effects across slides, you shouldn't have too many problems. But if, for some reason, you have to use many different fonts or font effects and they differ from slide to slide, be aware that design template settings just plain won't work wherever you've done so. However, be assured that you can reapply design template settings to bring uniformity back to your presentation.

How to fix it

To make the formatting of text on individual slides conform to the design template style, you can reapply the slide layout:

1. Display the slide on which you've made changes in Normal view.

2. On the Format menu, click Slide Layout.

3. In the Slide Layout task pane, right-click the slide icon representing the format you want to reapply (you can identify it by its heavy border). ▶

4. Click Reapply Layout.

5. Repeat Steps 1 through 4 for each slide you want to reapply default formatting to.

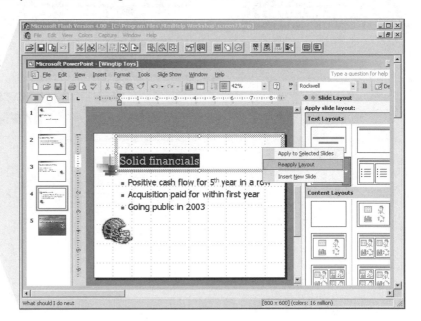

Tip

Besides text formatting, you can also modify placeholder position and size in the Slide Master. If you change a placeholder position or size on individual slides, just as with text formatting, those changes take precedence over master settings. You can use the same method presented in this section for reinstating master place-holder settings.

Are you having trouble getting sounds or movies to play correctly?

yes → Are you trying to add a sound to a slide?

yes →

Go to...

I want to add a sound to a slide, but I don't know how, page 340.

no ↓

Are you trying to add a movie to your presentation?

yes → Are you having difficulty playing a movie file?

yes →

no ↓

Is the quality of the movie playback poor?

yes →

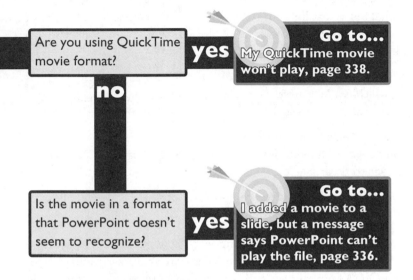

Are you using QuickTime movie format? **yes**

Go to...
My QuickTime movie won't play, page 338.

no

Is the movie in a format that PowerPoint doesn't seem to recognize? **yes**

Go to...
I added a movie to a slide, but a message says PowerPoint can't play the file, page 336.

Quick fix

Improving movie playback. You might have to make a movie smaller to scale it for your presentation. Follow these steps to do this:

1. Click the movie to select it.

2. Click the Format menu, and then click Picture.

3. Click the Size tab, and select the check box for Best Scale For Slide Show.

4. Click Reset.

If your solution isn't here, check these related chapters:

- Running a show, page 358
- Transitions and animations, page 384

Or see the general trouble-shooting tips on page xix.

I added a movie to a slide, but a message says PowerPoint can't play the file

Source of the problem

Playing movies in PowerPoint might not be as complex as producing a Cecil B. DeMille spectacular, but you still might run into a problem or two in the process. One potential problem area occurs because movies are video files that come in a variety of formats. Some of the most common are:

Before you start

If PowerPoint doesn't recognize a movie file format, you can try to use Windows Media Player to play it. However, certain animation and timing settings will not work with this method.

- Audio Video Interleaved (AVI), which is a Microsoft Windows multimedia format for sound and movie files.

- QuickTime, a product developed by Apple Computer that you can use to create, edit, and publish multimedia files. Windows programs can use QuickTime files, but they need a special player to do so.

- Moving Pictures Experts Group (MPEG), a standard for compression of sound and video files. MPEG comes in several types, such as MPEG-1 through MPEG-4.

If the file is a format that Microsoft PowerPoint doesn't support, you'll get a message saying PowerPoint can't play the file. If this happens, you can try to use Microsoft Windows Media Player to run your movie. (If the movie is a QuickTime file, see the next section in this solution for advice.) You should be aware, however, that movies you play with Windows Media Player won't be able to use any animation settings or timings you've assigned. You have to play the movie by using the buttons in Media Player itself.

How to fix it

To play a movie using Microsoft Windows Media Player, follow these steps:

1. In Microsoft Windows, click Start, Programs, Accessories, Entertainment, Windows Media Player.

2. On the File menu in Windows Media Player, click Open, and then type the path or browse for the file you want to insert, and click OK. ▶

The movie should play. If it does, close the file and proceed to the next step. If the movie can't play in Windows Media Player, don't continue past this step. Your best option is to consult Windows Media Player Help to try to troubleshoot the problem.

3. Display the slide you want to place the movie on.

4. On the Insert menu, click Object.

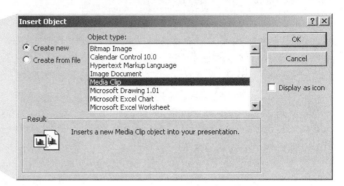

5. Click Media Clip as the Object Type; click Create New if it's not already selected.

6. Select the Display As Icon check box if you want an icon for the movie to appear on your slide.

7. Click OK.

My QuickTime movie won't play

Source of the problem

Movies can be very useful in many types of presentations. For example, you might use a movie clip of your CEO offering a motivational message to the troops in a human resources presentation. Or, you might use a short movie to demonstrate a technical process or new product feature in a sales training presentation.

One movie format, QuickTime, was created by Apple Computer for creating, editing, and viewing multimedia content. QuickTime supports animation, graphics, video, and various sound and music formats. QuickTime files require a QuickTime player to play them back. The QuickTime player is available from Apple's Web site for free download and from many Web sites that use it to play back multimedia on their Web pages.

If you have a QuickTime movie or a movie in another format not supported by PowerPoint or Windows Media Player that you want to insert in a PowerPoint presentation, you can try to play the movie in Microsoft PowerPoint by creating a link to the source application.

> ### Before you start
> If you can't use PowerPoint's built-in features to play a QuickTime movie, you can try to create a link from PowerPoint to QuickTime, if it's installed on your computer.

> ### More about playing movies
> If you try to use your DVD to add a digital video movie to a presentation, you'll have problems because this isn't possible with PowerPoint 2002. However, several companies have created programs that enable playback of DVD in PowerPoint. Check Microsoft's Web site to learn more about these programs.

How to fix it

To create a link from PowerPoint to QuickTime to play a movie, follow these steps:

1. Open the movie file by double-clicking the file name in the My Computer folder on your computer's hard disk.

2. If you have an application installed that will play the file, the movie will play, and you can proceed. If you don't have a program that will play the movie, you'll get a message indicating that there is no application available. Download the QuickTime program from Apple Computer's Web site (*http://www.apple.com*) and continue.

3. Display the slide on which you want to place the movie in PowerPoint.

4. On the Slide Show menu, point to Action Buttons, and click the Movie action button (the one with a video camera icon).

5. Click the slide, and drag to draw the button. The Action Settings dialog box appears.

6. Click Run Program, and then click Browse. ▶

7. Change the Files Of Type setting to All Files.

8. Locate and click your movie file, and then click OK.

9. In the Action Settings dialog box, click OK.

10. To play a movie while showing a presentation, click the movie object to launch QuickTime.

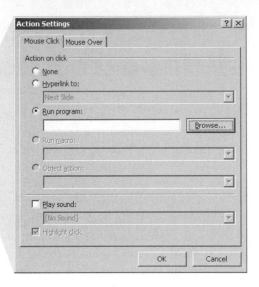

Tip

If QuickTime doesn't play the movie right away, you might have to click Play to start the movie.

I want to add a sound to a slide, but I don't know how

Source of the problem

Music is a universal language, and using it in a PowerPoint presentation can help get your message across in an exciting way. You can use music and sounds from audio files stored on your computer or a network. You can download sound clips from the Internet, use music from your favorite CD, or use sound files available in Microsoft Clip Organizer. You can even record your own sounds to add to a presentation with programs such as RealAudio or Sound Recorder in Windows Accessories.

You can insert sound files on slides in your presentation. When you do, a sound icon is displayed. You can also add sounds by associating them with an existing animation. You can configure settings that control how you play the music or sound. For example, you can have the music start during a slide transition, start when you click its icon, start at a preset time, or play along with an animation sequence.

To add a sound to an element of a slide, you first apply an animation effect to the element, such as a graphic or title placeholder, and configure settings to play a sound along with the animation.

How to fix it

Use the following process with an existing animation to add a sound effect to it:

1. Display the slide that contains the text or object you want to associate a sound with.

2. On the Slide Show menu, click Custom Animation.

3. The Custom Animation task pane appears with all animations for the slide listed. Click the arrow next to the item you want to modify in the Custom Animation list, and then click Effect Options on the menu. ▶

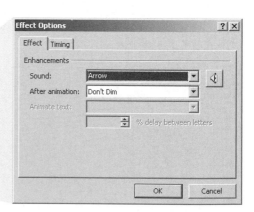

4. On the Effect tab, in the Enhancements section, click a sound from the Sound list. If you don't see the sound you want to add, click Other Sound, and then locate the sound file.

5. Click OK to apply the sound and close the dialog box.

Have you tried this?

If you have problems playing sound, be sure to check that the audio and Musicial Instrument Digital Interface (MIDI) settings are correct. Do this in the Sounds And Multimedia area of the Control Panel.

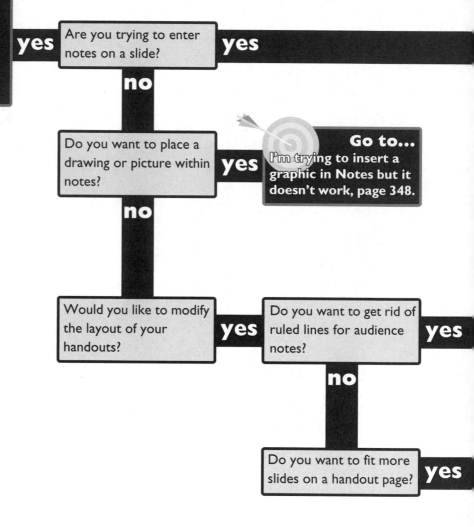

Are you having difficulty entering or printing notes or handouts for your presentation?

yes → Are you trying to enter notes on a slide?

yes →

no ↓

Do you want to place a drawing or picture within notes?

yes → **Go to...** I'm trying to insert a graphic in Notes but it doesn't work, page 348.

no ↓

Would you like to modify the layout of your handouts?

yes → Do you want to get rid of ruled lines for audience notes?

yes →

no ↓

Do you want to fit more slides on a handout page?

yes →

Notes and handouts

Are you having trouble fitting information you want in your notes?

yes

Go to...
I want to use more than one Notes Page for a slide, page 344.

no

Are you having trouble formatting notes?

yes

Quick fix
Formatting notes. If you format notes text and display the Notes pane, the formatting might not appear. Click the Show Formatting button on the Standard toolbar to turn this feature on.

Go to...
I want to print a three-slides-per-page handout, but I don't want those ruled lines, page 346.

Quick fix
Printing more slides on handouts. The largest number of slides you can print on a single handout page in PowerPoint is nine. If you have a PostScript printer, you might have the ability to print more than one page on one piece of paper. This way you could print two 6-slides-per-page handouts on one page, resulting in 12 slides on a page. Check your printer documentation to see if this is an option for you.

If your solution isn't here, check these related chapters:

- Printing, page 350
- Copying, pasting, and moving, page 302

Or see the general troubleshooting tips on page xix.

I want to use more than one Notes Page for a slide

Source of the problem

Just as the love songs would have you believe there's only one gal for every guy, there's only one Notes Page per slide in a PowerPoint presentation. So how do you cheat and squeeze more notes on a single slide? There are a few tricks you can try.

The AutoFit feature fits more text in the notes place-holder by reducing the font size if there's a lot of text. You can also adjust the text size manually. In addition, you can resize the slide area on the Notes Page to be smaller and resize the notes area to be larger, thereby fitting more text in it.

Another idea is to create a second slide after the current one that gives you another Notes Page with a blank slide on top. If you prefer, you can duplicate the slide and add notes to the second copy. But with either of these methods, you should remember to hide the slide during slide show playback. Keep in mind that if you have that much to say about one topic, you might consider breaking up the information on the slide into multiple slides; the instant benefit of doing this is that you get more Notes Pages as well.

How to fix it

To verify that AutoFit is turned on, follow these steps:

1. On the Tools menu, click AutoCorrect Options.

2. Click the AutoFormat As You Type tab.

3. Check to see that the AutoFit Body Text To Placeholder check box is selected. ▶

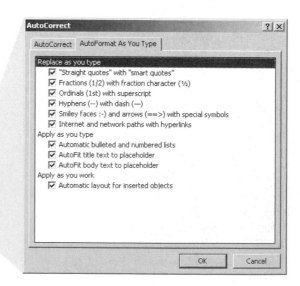

To make the slide area smaller and provide for more room for notes on the page, follow these steps:

1. On the View menu, click Notes Page.

2. Click the slide placeholder, and drag a sizing handle to make it smaller.

3. Click the notes placeholder, and drag a sizing handle to enlarge it.

Tip

If you use this procedure to adjust placeholder sizes in the Notes Master, the change will apply to all your slides, which might save you time if you need more space for notes throughout your presentation.

I want to print a three-slides-per-page handout, but I don't want those ruled lines

Source of the problem

Audience handouts aren't just great places for your audience to doodle pictures of their cats or calculate their trip expenses as you talk. Handouts help those viewing your presentation to follow along and even take notes as you move through your slides. They offer a take-away record of the facts you've covered in your bulleted content, so your audience can better retain the information presented.

Handouts are essentially a printing option in Microsoft PowerPoint. You can choose to print out 1, 2, 4, 6, or 9 slides to a page or 3 slides to a page with ruled lines for your audience to take notes. If you don't want the ruled lines, consider whether using a two- or four-slide-per-handout page layout might work for you.

If you absolutely have to have three slides to a page and you don't want the ruled lines included, you can send the handout to Microsoft Word and delete the ruled lines there.

> ### Before you start
>
> Sending a presentation to Microsoft Word gives you some flexibility in deleting or adding elements to a handout page. However, don't forget to export the updated slides to Word if you make changes to your presentation so the handouts match your on-screen presentation.

How to fix it

If you decide another handout layout might do, follow these steps to print that layout:

1. On the File menu, click Print.

2. In the Print dialog box, in the Print What list, click Handouts.

3. In the Handouts section, choose a layout with more or less than three slides per page.

4. Click OK to print the handouts.

To send a PowerPoint presentation to Microsoft Word, follow this procedure:

1. On the File menu, click Send To, and then click Microsoft Word.

2. In the Send To Microsoft Word dialog box, click a layout option with blank lines. The Blank Lines Next To Slides option will result in three slides per page.

3. When your slides appear in Word, there will be a column for notes containing ruled lines.

4. On the first page, click the column of ruled lines at the top of the column. The pointer will appear as a downward pointing arrow and clicking will select the entire column.

5. Right-click the column, and click Delete Columns from the menu. After a moment or two, the entire column of ruled lines will disappear.

6. If you like, you can expand the column containing each slide, and then click and drag the slides' images to enlarge them. ▶

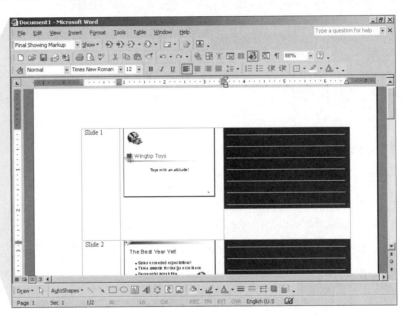

I'm trying to insert a graphic in Notes but it doesn't work

Source of the problem

If you're having trouble inserting a graphic object into Notes, you're probably trying to do it in Normal view. No matter how hard you try, you won't be able to insert a graphic in the Notes pane of the Normal view. Don't ask why, just head for the Notes Page because that's the place in Microsoft PowerPoint where you can add these types of objects.

However, keep in mind that once you've drawn an object or inserted a picture in the Notes Page view, although they will appear in printed output, they still will never show in the Notes pane in Normal view.

How to fix it

To place a drawn object or picture in your notes, follow these steps:

1. Display the slide that you want to add a graphic element to.

2. On the View menu, click Notes Page.

3. Do one of the following:

   - On the Insert menu, point to Picture, and click Clip Art or From File to insert a graphics file.

   - On the View menu, point to Toolbars, and click Drawing to display the Drawing toolbar. Click a drawing tool, and click in the notes area to draw an object.

Before you start

You can use graphics in Notes, but you can only do it in the Notes Page view. Remember, if you add graphics to notes as well as to slides, you might end up with a very large PowerPoint file.

More about Notes Page view

There are also a few things you should know about what you can and can't do in Notes Page view: although you can insert a graphic and apply a design template or color scheme while in Notes Page view, you can't apply any animations or transitions, or set the layout for a slide. For those tasks, you have to return to Normal view!

4. A drawn object appears where you draw it in the notes area; however, an inserted graphic will appear in the middle of the page straddling the slide and notes area. Click the graphic and drag it to move it into the notes area. ▶

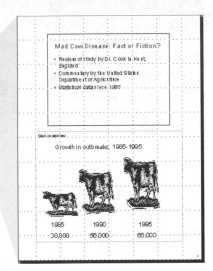

Warning

Because you can only have one page of notes per slide, consider resizing graphics you include in notes to be smaller to allow enough room for notes text.

Are you having trouble printing slides, handouts, or notes?

yes

Are you trying to print in black and white?

yes

no

Are some of your slides not printing at all?

yes

no

Are you having trouble with the format of your printed output?

yes

Does PowerPoint say you have too many fonts?

yes

no

Do you want to modify a border around printed text?

yes

Go to...
I printed my presentation in black and white, but it looks odd, page 352.

Go to...
I want to print my entire presentation, but I get a message that some of my slides are hidden, page 354.

Quick fix
Managing presentation fonts. If you get a "too many fonts" message when trying to print, it could be that you're using fonts not installed on your printer or that can't be downloaded to your printer. Try using fewer fonts in your presentation, or check your printer documentation for information about how to download additional fonts.

If your solution isn't here, check these related chapters:

- Masters, page 326
- Slide design and layout, page 366

Or see the general trouble-shooting tips on page xix.

Go to...
When I print a Notes Page, I get a border I don't want, page 356.

I printed my presentation in black and white, but it looks odd

Source of the problem

There's a reason motion pictures went from black and white to color: black and white doesn't offer the nuances or provide the depth and resolution to objects that color does. Pure black and white printing in PowerPoint is even worse: it removes all shades of gray including any color fills you've added to objects. PowerPoint does allow you to modify black and white settings for objects on your slides so that you can improve the look of your black and white printout. However, even with these modified settings, perhaps the only good reason to use pure black and white is if you have an ancient printer that can't handle grayscale, or to print working drafts of your presentation that use the very least amount of ink and time in the printing process.

If you don't want to (or can't) print in color, consider the option of using grayscale. Grayscale uses many shades between white and black to mimic the shading of colors. This saves your color ink cartridge or expensive color copying charges and produces a pleasing and readable page.

How to fix it

To modify grayscale or black and white settings in your presentation, follow this procedure:

1. On the View menu, point to Color/Grayscale, and click Pure Black And White or Grayscale.

Before you start

Printing in grayscale instead of black and white does use a little more ink from your printer and a tad more time. However, the difference in quality is often dramatic.

Have you tried this?

If you really only want to review your presentation's text and not its graphic elements, consider printing just the outline rather than the slides.

Tip

You can apply different grayscale or black and white settings to different objects on the same slide.

2. Right-click an object, and then click a color option from the menu (for example, Light Grayscale or Inverse Grayscale). Whichever setting you choose will be used when you print. ▶

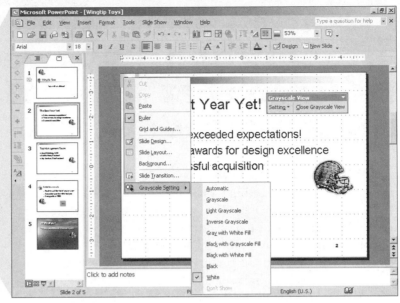

To set up your presentation to print in grayscale, follow these steps:

1. On the File menu, click Print.

2. In the Color/Grayscale list, click Grayscale. ▼

3. Make any other print settings you want, and then click OK to print or click Preview to see how your document will look before printing.

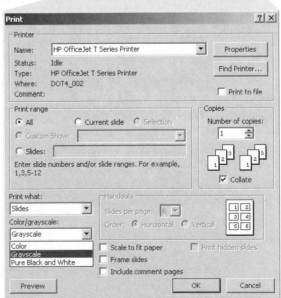

I want to print my entire presentation, but I get a message that some of my slides are hidden

Source of the problem

In this world where everything is not always as it appears, there can be hidden costs, hidden agendas, and in PowerPoint, hidden slides. You might hide slides to show a subset of your presentation that's more appropriate to a certain audience. Or, you might want to print out your presentation for some people to review, but decide to hide some slides that aren't relevant to them. When you hide slides, they are still visible in Slide Sorter and Normal view, but there is a line drawn through the slide icon. Hidden slides do not appear when you present a slide show or when you print.

If you've hidden slides and want to print all of the slides in your presentation, you can do one of the following:

- Reveal hidden slides so that they show.

- Keep the slides hidden, but select the Print Hidden Slides check box in the Print dialog box. With this setting, any hidden slides will print.

How to fix it

To change hidden slides so that they are no longer hidden, do this:

1. In Normal view, click the hidden slides on the Slides tab or click the slides in Slide Sorter view.

2. On the Slide Show menu, click Hide Slide to clear the hidden setting. ▶

You can also keep the hidden slides hidden, but mark them to be printed. To do this, follow these steps:

1. On the File menu, click Print.

2. Select the Print Hidden Slides check box in the Print dialog box.

3. Click OK to print, or click Preview to see what your printed document will look like. ▶

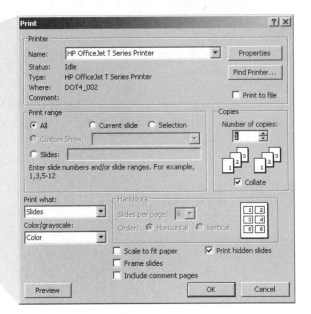

When I print a Notes Page, I get a border I don't want

Source of the problem

Borders are useful for setting things apart on a printed page. Borders are simply lines surrounding an object: they act as a frame that can help create order on your page. But if you don't want a border, removing it is as easy as making a simple formatting change.

You can apply formatting to placeholders just as you can apply formatting to drawn objects or text. A border around the notes area of your Notes Page is actually a line format applied to the notes placeholder. When you apply a line to the notes placeholder, it creates a border around the notes on your printed Notes Pages. If you apply a fill color to a notes placeholder, it creates a colored or shaded box in the background of your notes text. Changing either is done through the Format Placeholder dialog box.

Before you start

If you don't want a border around your notes, it's easy to get rid of it; if you want it back at some point, just reformat the notes placeholder.

Warning

If you select a dark font color for text and a dark fill color for a placeholder containing that text, you might not be able to read your text.

How to fix it

1. Click a slide and, on the View menu, click Notes Page. Or, to remove borders from all the notes in your presentation, point to Master on the View menu, and click Notes Master.

2. Click within the notes placeholder to select it.

3. On the Format menu, click Placeholder.

4. On the Colors And Lines tab of the Format Placeholder dialog box, in the Line section, set the Color box to No Line.

5. In the Fill section, set the Color box to No Fill.

6. Click OK to save your changes. ▶

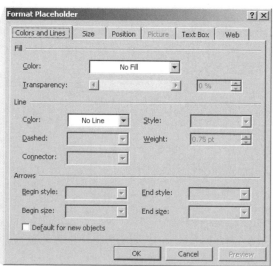

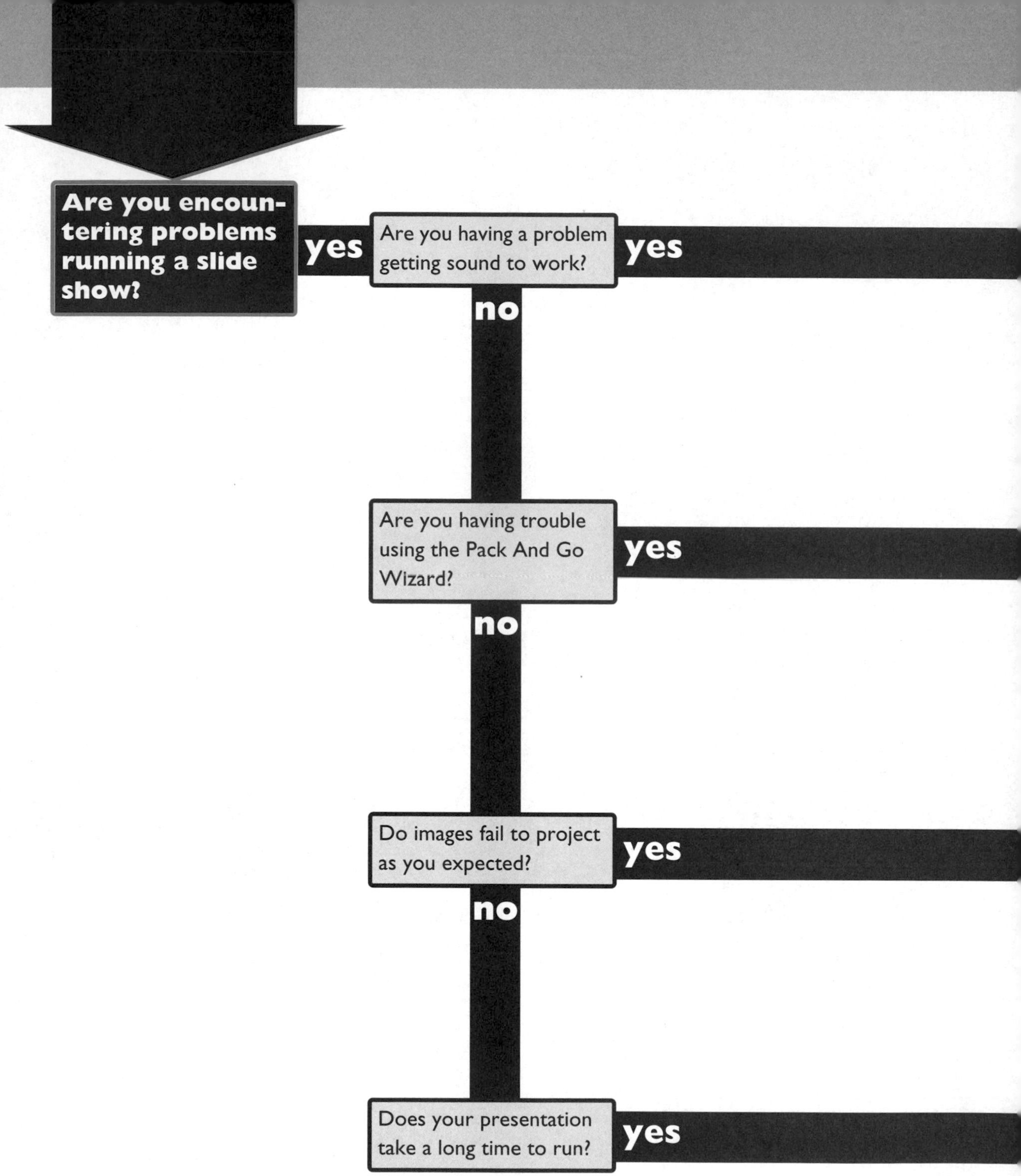

Are you encoun-tering problems running a slide show? **yes** Are you having a problem getting sound to work? **yes**

no

Are you having trouble using the Pack And Go Wizard? **yes**

no

Do images fail to project as you expected? **yes**

no

Does your presentation take a long time to run? **yes**

Go to...
I'm not getting any sound, page 360.

Quick fix
Pack And Go Wizard. You can't run the Pack And Go Wizard in PowerPoint 2002 to save a presentation if you're working on a computer that uses Windows 3.1 or Windows 95. However, you can unpackage and run a presentation on a computer running Windows 95. Also, remember that you must open a presentation in PowerPoint to make the Pack And Go command available on the File menu.

Go to...
Nothing's projected on the screen, page 364.

Go to...
My slide show is running very slowly, page 362.

If your solution isn't here, check this related chapter:

● Multimedia, page 334

Or see the general trouble-shooting tips on page xix.

I'm not getting any sound

Source of the problem

There could be several sources of problems with audio during a presentation. Assuming all your sounds worked when you created your presentation and ran it on your own computer, you'll need to look at some possibilities outside of PowerPoint to pinpoint the cause of this problem.

Look for sound controls on both your computer and projector. Many people don't realize that projectors have their own controls on the projector itself and often on the remote control device for the projector. Laptop computers also have sound controls, such as a mute button on the hardware or by using function keys, to moderate the volume. You can also look to Windows sound controls: you might have had your laptop mute setting turned on so you didn't disturb your fellow airplane passengers. Make sure it's set correctly before you try to give that next presentation!

There's also the old "make sure it's plugged in" advice. You might not have inserted the input connector completely into the input outlet. Or, perhaps your sound cable is faulty. In addition, manufacturers aren't known for standardizing accessories such as power adapters. If your audio cable wasn't made for your computer or projector, it might not work. Make sure you're using the correct cables for all equipment: they are usually stamped with the projector or computer manufacturer's name.

Before you start

Sound for a PowerPoint presentation is the result of the coordination of a sound card, your speakers and sound cables, and the sound settings in your computer and the projector you're using. You might have to check several of these settings and components before you find the culprit.

How to fix it

To adjust the audio source on your laptop, follow these steps:

1. On the Windows Start menu, point to Settings, and click Control Panel.

Tip

If you're having trouble getting sound to work on a computer, double-click System in the Windows Control Panel, and click Device Manager on the Hardware tab to see whether a current sound driver is installed.

2. Double-click the Sounds And Multimedia icon in Control Panel. ▶

3. Click and drag the slider in the Sound Volume area to adjust audio volume.

4. Click OK to close the dialog box and save the new setting.

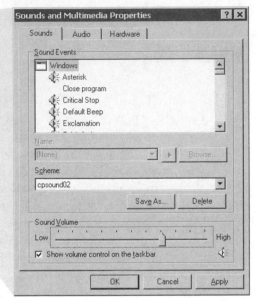

My slide show is running very slowly

Source of the problem

Perhaps you made resolutions for the New Year: if one of them was to make your presentations run more quickly, you have to look to the resolution on your computer. In the world of computers, resolution is the amount of detail used in a monitor or projection system to reproduce images. Resolution is measured in dots per inch (dpi) and is used to refer to both printed output and monitor images. Resolution ranges from 125 dpi for the quality of output you get from an inexpensive dot matrix printer to resolutions of over 1,000 dpi with higher quality printers, monitors, or presentation display systems.

Higher resolutions might cause your slides to slowly appear on the screen. Reducing the resolution for your slide show presentation display can help speed up performance. For the best performance, set the color depth to 16 bit and the resolution to 640×480. But realize that there will be a trade-off in the crispness of the images on screen.

How to fix it

Follow these steps to adjust resolution for your slide show:

1. On the Slide Show menu, click Set Up Show.

2. Click 640×480 in the Slide Show Resolution list. ▶

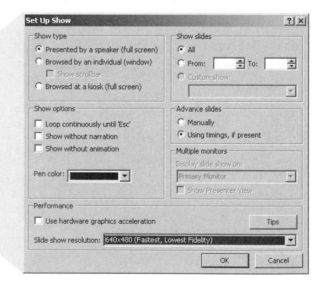

To set the color depth to 16 bits follow these steps:

1. On the Windows Start menu, point to Settings, and click Control Panel.

2. Double-click Display to open the Display dialog box.

3. Click the Settings tab.

4. Click High Color (16 Bit) in the Colors list, and then click OK. ▶

5. On the Slide Show menu, click Set Up Show.

6. Select the Use Hardware Graphics Acceleration check box. Not all computers have this capability, but if yours does, PowerPoint 2002 will attempt to take advantage of it.

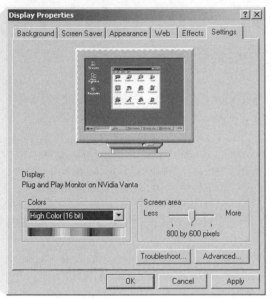

Warning

Some people experience problems with computer performance after changing the hardware graphics acceleration setting. If you do, turn off this option.

Nothing's projected on the screen

Source of the problem

A Microsoft PowerPoint presentation with no light from a projector is like a diamond in a vault: nobody can see it and nobody is impressed. As with sound, images in a presentation might fail for a variety of reasons, most of which have to do with hardware, not with PowerPoint.

First, both the computer and the projector have to have a working power source. The problem could lie with the electrical outlet in the room where you're presenting or with a loose power cable connection or faulty cable. Second, projectors use lamps as light sources, and lamps burn out. Third, determine whether the video connection cable between the computer and the projector is functional. Any of these problems could be causing your problem, so get to work jiggling cables, crawling under tables to check power connections, and probing your projector!

Before you start

You'll have to work through various hardware functions to find the problem if your presentation isn't projecting an image.

How to fix it

If images aren't projecting properly, perform any one of these steps to isolate the problem:

1. Check the room's electrical outlet with another piece of equipment to make sure it's working properly.

2. Check to make sure the power cord is connected to the projector.

3. If you're using a power strip, check to see that the strip is turned on.

4. Determine whether the projector is in standby mode or whether your computer has been inactive and is displaying a screen saver.

5. Make sure the projector has a working bulb.

6. Check the video connection cable for any damage, such as broken pins.

Tip

It might seem obvious, but it's easy to forget: make sure you take the lens cap off the projector!

Running a show

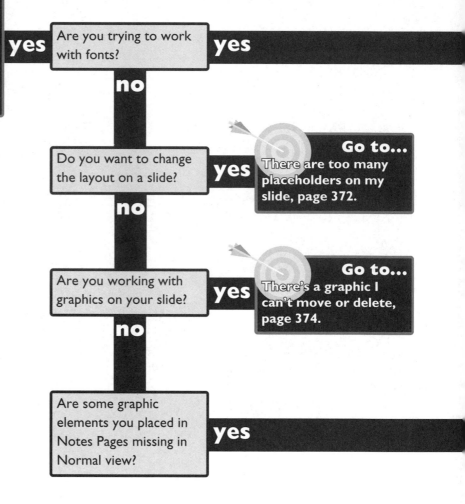

Are you working with design elements such as fonts, layout, and graphics and encountering problems?

yes

Are you trying to work with fonts?

yes

no

Do you want to change the layout on a slide?

yes

Go to...
There are too many placeholders on my slide, page 372.

no

Are you working with graphics on your slide?

yes

Go to...
There's a graphic I can't move or delete, page 374.

no

Are some graphic elements you placed in Notes Pages missing in Normal view?

yes

Are you running a show on another computer and not getting the fonts you expected?

yes

Go to...
Font styles that were on my computer disappear when I show my presentation on another computer, page 370.

no

Would you like to change the fonts in your presentation?

yes

Go to...
I don't know how to replace all occurrences of one font with another, page 368.

Quick fix

Adding graphics to notes. If you placed graphic elements in your notes, they will not show in Normal view because it only shows text in the Notes area. If you need to reference these graphics while presenting a show, do this to view Notes Pages with a slide show running:

1. Display Notes Page view.
2. Click the Slide Show icon to run a slide show.
3. Click Alt+Tab to switch to Notes Page view.

If your solution isn't here, check these related chapters:

● Masters, page 326
● Text boxes and text in objects, page 376

Or see the general trouble-shooting tips on page xix.

I don't know how to replace all occurrences of one font with another

Source of the problem

When new fashions come out every year, people rush to replace last year's tight-fitting tailored suits with flowing chenille caftans. Well, fonts are like fashions for your text. They create a look and feel that can range from fun and wacky to corporate and conservative. When you decide it's time for a change, you don't have to search through your presentation substituting fonts word by word or phrase by phrase. If you want to replace one font throughout your presentation with another, you can simply use the Replace Fonts command.

There are options available if you're not sure you want to replace every instance of a font, or you want to replace several fonts with another. You can select the entire outline or a portion of the outline in the Outline pane in Normal view and apply a new font. Or, if you want to change the font for all title placeholders or all content placeholders, you can change the Slide Master.

How to fix it

Follow these steps to replace all instances of a font with another in PowerPoint:

1. On the Format menu, click Replace Fonts.

2. Click the font style you want to change in the Replace box.

3. Click the font you want to use in your presentation in the With box.

4. Click Replace.

5. Repeat Steps 2 through 4 for all the fonts you want to replace.

To change the fonts globally for a text placeholder, perform these steps on the Slide Master:

1. On the View menu, point to Master, and click Slide Master. ▶

2. Select the placeholder or click and drag to select any text in a placeholder (title or content), click the Font list on the toolbar, and click the font you want to use for the text in that placeholder.

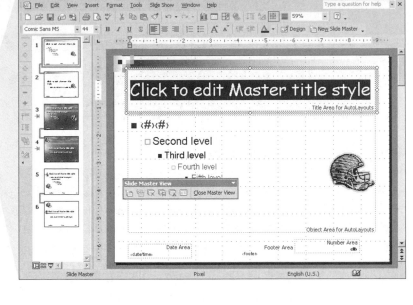

Warning

Any formatting changes you have made on individual slides will take precedence over Master slide settings.

Font styles that were on my computer disappear when I show my presentation on another computer

Source of the problem

Electronic fonts, such as Arial and Times Roman, are probably available in all of your software programs for you to apply to text in your documents. However, if you move a document to a different computer that doesn't have some of these fonts available, you might get error messages indicating that a font is missing.

Many different companies have created electronic fonts. One font type, TrueType, was introduced by both Apple Computer and Microsoft in the early 1990s. TrueType fonts offer WYSIWYG technology, which means that what you see on the screen is identical to what you get when you print a document.

When you show a PowerPoint presentation on a different computer than it was created on, some TrueType fonts might not be installed on that computer. When that happens, PowerPoint might replace the font you used with one that's present on that system. You might, or might not, like those replacements, which could cause lines to break in odd places or cause elements on the slides to shift in ways you don't intend. To prevent this kind of potentially nasty surprise when showing a presentation, you can embed TrueType fonts at the time that you save your PowerPoint file.

Before you start

You can embed TrueType fonts with your presentation file, which makes them available on any computer you're using to run your slide show. However, embedded fonts will make your file larger.

Warning

Some fonts can't be embedded. This is because they have certain restrictions regarding how they're licensed to certain software manufacturers.

How to fix it

1. On the File menu, click Save As.

2. On the Save As toolbar, click Tools, and then click Save Options.

3. Select the Embed TrueType Fonts check box.

4. To embed just the characters that you used in the presentation, select Embed Characters In Use Only. To embed every character in the entire font set, select Embed All Characters. ▶

Save Options

Save

Save options

☑ Allow fast saves
☐ Prompt for file properties
☑ Save AutoRecover info every `10` minutes
☑ Convert charts when saving as previous version

Save PowerPoint files as:
`PowerPoint Presentation`

Default file location:
`C:\My Documents\`

Font options for current document only
☑ Embed TrueType fonts
  ⦿ Embed characters in use only (best for reducing file size)
  ○ Embed all characters (best for editing by others)

[OK]   [Cancel]

Tip

If you intend to allow others to edit your presentation, the best option to choose is Embed All Characters. Then, whoever works on the presentation will have all characters in your fonts available. If you need to keep your file size small, and you don't think anybody else will need to make changes, select Embed Characters In Use Only.

There are too many placeholders on my slide

Source of the problem

Placeholders in PowerPoint are wonderful things. They make editing easier—for example, click in a placeholder and all text is selected, making it quick to replace or format the text. Placeholders make it possible to make global settings to titles and text (bullet list) material by using the Master feature. Placeholders also make it easy to move blocks of text around a slide as well as automate the process of inserting objects, such as clip art or a chart.

Layouts are the organizers of placeholders. All layouts except the blank one contain at least one placeholder. The main placeholder types are title, text, and content (for inserting a variety of objects such as charts or clip art). Many new users of PowerPoint simply choose the blank slide layout and add text boxes or other objects to each slide, but that's a big mistake. It undermines many editing and other features of PowerPoint and often creates presentation content that isn't reflected in the Outline pane.

If there are too many placeholders on your slide, your best bet is to change layouts, not to delete a placeholder. There are many layouts available, using vertical or horizontal arrangements, one or two columns, and various combinations of placeholder types.

How to fix it

To select a different layout for your slide, follow these steps:

1. On the Format menu, click Slide Layout.

2. In the Slide Layout task pane, scroll through the list as needed to locate the layout you want to use.

3. Click the arrow on the right side of the layout and click Apply To Selected Slides. ▶

If you chose to delete one or more placeholders on a layout, you can reinstate them by following these steps:

1. Click Format, Slide Layout.

2. Move your cursor over the preview of the previously applied layout, and then click the arrow along the right side of the layout.

3. Click Reapply Layout.

There's a graphic I can't move or delete

Source of the problem

When you run up against an immovable object, whether it's a person with a rigid political stance or a graphic on a PowerPoint slide, it can be frustrating. If you run across something on a PowerPoint slide that you just can't budge no matter what you do, odds are it's not really on the slide, it's on the Slide Master.

The Slide Master feature allows you to place objects on one Master slide and have them appear on all the slides in the presentation. This is a timesaving feature, but it doesn't allow you to move or delete these objects on individual slides. You can easily go to the Slide Master view and move or delete a graphic, or if you don't want that kind of global change, you can choose to omit a graphic from individual slides. If you want a graphic but want it in a different position on a particular slide, omit the graphic from the Master slide, insert the graphic as an object on each slide where you want it to appear, and position it where you like on each slide.

How to fix it

To move a graphic on the Master, follow these steps:

1. On the View menu, point to Master, and click Slide Master.

2. Click either the Title Master or Slide Master where your object is located.

3. Click the object and drag it to a new position.

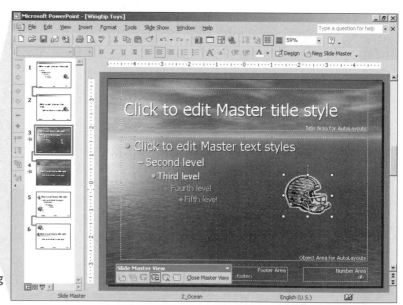

To prevent a graphic contained on a Master slide from appearing on a single slide, use Background settings by following these steps:

1. Display the slide that contains the graphic.

2. On the Format menu, click Background. ▶

3. Select the Omit Background Graphics From Master check box.

4. Click Apply to omit the graphic from the selected slide or Apply To All to omit Master graphics from all slides in the presentation.

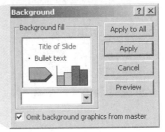

Tip

You might use the Apply To All feature to omit all Master graphics in one saved version of the file from which you can print slide content, but not a global graphic.

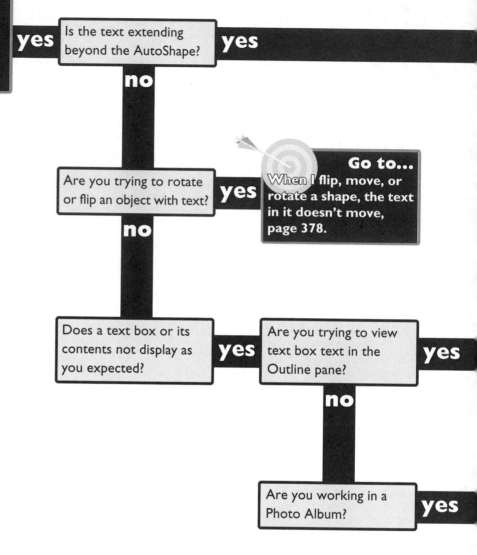

Are text boxes or text in AutoShapes not performing as you expected?

yes → Is the text extending beyond the AutoShape?

no ↓

Are you trying to rotate or flip an object with text?

yes → **Go to...**
When I flip, move, or rotate a shape, the text in it doesn't move, page 378.

no ↓

Does a text box or its contents not display as you expected?

yes → Are you trying to view text box text in the Outline pane?

yes →

no ↓

Are you working in a Photo Album?

yes →

Go to...
I have trouble getting shapes and text to fit together, page 380.

Go to...
I created a text box, but its contents don't appear in the outline, page 382.

Quick fix

Text boxes in Photo Albums. If you're working with a Photo Album and you select Fit To Slide as your picture layout, text boxes will be inserted as blank slides. To add a text box:

1. On the Format menu, click Photo Album.

2. In the Photo Album dialog box, click the New Text Box button.

If your solution isn't here, check these related chapters:

● Editing, page 32

● Drawing objects and pictures, page 310

Or see the general trouble-shooting tips on page xix.

When I flip, move, or rotate a shape, the text in it doesn't move

Source of the problem

Being able to move or rotate text can be handy if you want to create a design effect or emphasize certain information. You can, for example, take the text "Soaring to New Heights!" and rotate it to have the text seem to scale a graphic of a mountain. There are two common problems you could encounter when manipulating text. First, PowerPoint text cannot be flipped; if you're trying to flip text so it appears as a mirror image of itself, you need to create a WordArt object. Second, if you're having trouble moving or rotating text along with a shape, the text was probably created in a text box that you've placed within an AutoShape. When you do this, the two objects aren't connected in any way, so moving one doesn't move the other.

Before you start

If you use the Text Box tool to place text on an AutoShape, remember that the two aren't attached; if you move the AutoShape, that won't have any effect on the text unless you group the two objects.

To solve this second problem, you have to attach your text box to your AutoShape by grouping the two objects. Then, when you move or rotate the AutoShape, your text will move along with it. Another option is to delete the text box, click the AutoShape, and type the text directly in it. Text typed on an AutoShape rather than being created with the Text Box tool is part of the AutoShape object and will move with it.

How to fix it

To group the text box and object so they move as a single unit, follow these steps:

1. If necessary, use the Order command on the Draw menu to make both objects selectable.

2. Press the Shift key as you click the text first and then the object.

3. Click the Draw button on the Drawing toolbar, and click Group. ▶

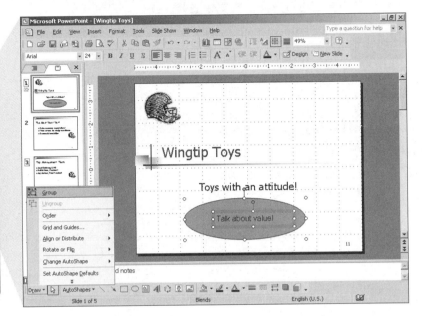

> **Tip**
>
> You can also cut and paste the text in the text box into the AutoShape itself. Select the text box text, and click Cut. Click in the AutoShape, and then click Paste.

To flip a WordArt object, do this:

1. Click the object.

2. Click the Draw button on the Drawing toolbar, and then click Rotate Or Flip.

3. Click Flip Horizontal or Flip Vertical on the submenu.

I have trouble getting shapes and text to fit together

Source of the problem

Sometimes entering text in a shape feels like you're standing in front of a fun-house mirror. Things distort oddly, and it's hard to make sense of it all. There is a logic to how this works, though. Essentially, you can make settings that control how text wraps around to the next line within an AutoShape, and you can control how a shape expands to accommodate text. Here's the lowdown on how this works:

- To make text wrap to the next line to fit the shape, you have to make sure the word wrap option is selected. With this option, as you type, the text wraps to fit the width of the AutoShape, but might extend above or below the top and bottom of the AutoShape.

- To make the shape resize to fit the text, the Resize AutoShape To Fit Text option must be selected. With this option, the AutoShape shrinks or expands to accommodate the text as you type. However, if the word wrap option isn't also enabled, the object will just stretch out side to side and distort for longer strings of text.

- With both options selected, the text will wrap and the AutoShape will expand to accommodate the text within it.

How to fix it

To enable the Resize AutoShape To Fit Text or Word Wrap Text In AutoShape options, follow these steps:

1. Click the object.

2. Double-click the selection rectangle of the AutoShape or text box to display its Format dialog box.

3. Click the Text Box tab and select one or both of these two options:

- Select the Word Wrap Text In AutoShape check box to have text wrap as you type.

- Select the Resize AutoShape To Fit Text check box to have the AutoShape expand to accommodate text. ▶

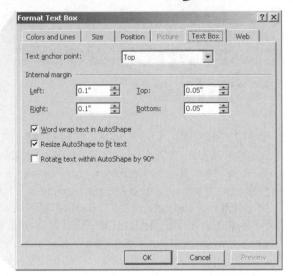

I created a text box, but its contents don't appear in the outline

Source of the problem

You can add text to PowerPoint slides in several ways. You can create a text box, insert WordArt, or enter text in placeholders, for example. However, text created outside of a layout placeholder will not appear and isn't editable in the Outline pane. This includes text added with the Text Box tool, text attached to an AutoShape, WordArt text, and text in embedded objects. Your only option is to move the text from this type of object and place it in a placeholder.

One other possibility for why you're not seeing some text in your outline exists: if Expand All on the Standard toolbar is toggled so that only slide titles appear in the Outline pane, you won't see all of your text. In this case, the text exists, it's just temporarily hidden, so this is an easy fix.

How to fix it

If you want to move text from a text box into a placeholder so that it will appear in your outline, follow these steps:

1. Click and drag to select the text in the text box.

2. Click the Cut button.

3. On the Format menu, click Slide Layout to display the Slide Layout task pane.

4. Click a layout with the placeholder you want to move the text to.

5. Click the placeholder, and then click the Paste button.

6. Click the text box object again, and press Delete.

Before you start

When you insert text in anything other than a layout placeholder, it won't appear in your outline. Moving that text into a placeholder is a solution, but it might deprive you of some features of the other object, such as the design possibilities offered by WordArt.

Tip

Embedded objects, such as Word tables or Microsoft Graph charts, won't appear in your outline. They will appear on individual slides so if you need to print them print slides rather than the outline.

If you think text is hidden because your outline isn't completely expanded, do this:

1. Display the Outline tab in Normal view.

2. On the View menu, point to Toolbars, and click Outlining.

3. Click Expand All on the toolbar to display all the text.

If you don't need the Outlining toolbar, you can use the Expand All button located on the Standard toolbar. ▶

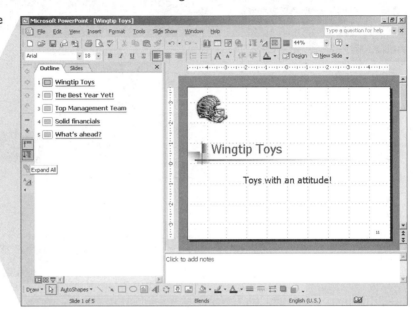

Is an animation or transition not working correctly?

yes →

Are effects playing when you don't expect them to, or not playing when you do?

yes →

no ↓

Are you trying to view a presentation with a browser?

yes →

Go to...
I don't see animations when I run my Web presentation, page 390.

no ↓

Is the animation playback slow or glitchy?

yes →

Have you animated large pictures on your slides?

yes →

no ↓

Have you used many letter-by-letter or word-by-word animation effects?

yes →

Are effects playing out of order?

yes

Go to...
An item I animated on my slide is labeled with a "1", but it doesn't play first, page 386.

no

Are you trying to change what action causes an effect to play?

yes

Go to...
The option to play an animation effect with a mouse click isn't available, page 388.

Quick fix

Improving animation performance. If you reduce the size of pictures and text that have animations associated with them, it will smooth the playback. To resize these objects, follow these steps:

1. Click the object to select it.

2. Drag the sizing handles to reduce the size of the object, using corner handles to retain the object's original proportions.

Quick fix

Choosing the best animations. Using many letter-by-letter or word-by-word animations will slow down the performance of your show. Try changing several of these to nonsequential animations by following these steps:

1. Click the object.

2. Click the Slide Show menu, and then click Slide Transition, Animation Schemes, or Custom Animation.

3. In the appropriate task pane, click another animation effect for the object.

If your solution isn't here, check these related chapters:

- Multimedia, page 334
- Running a show, page 358

Or see the general trouble-shooting tips on page xix.

An item I animated in my slide is labeled with a "1", but it doesn't play first

Source of the problem

If you're having trouble controlling or playing an animation in the animation list from an individual slide, odds are this animation was probably created on the Master slide. When an animation effect is applied to an item such as a graphic or placeholder on the Master, it will play on all slides in the presentation where that object appears.

To see what's going on, take a look at the list in the Custom Animation task pane. This is the list of animation sequences for a slide, which includes icons that indicate timing in relation to other animation events. If an animation was created in the Master, it will be listed in the Custom Animation task pane as Master: *item name*. You can break the link to a Master animation effect from an individual slide, just as you can omit a Master graphic.

If you don't recall adding these animations to the Master, they are probably the result of applying an animation scheme. Animation schemes add preset visual effects to text on slides. Every scheme usually includes an effect for the slide title and an effect that is applied to bullets or paragraphs on a slide. These effects can be applied on both the individual slides and the Master.

> **Before you start**
>
> If you break a link to a Master animation, don't forget to either reinstate the effect on the individual slide or take the shift in animation effect into account when you make your presentation.

How to fix it

To make a custom animation effect play before a Master effect, you first have to break the link to the Master for that particular slide. This will not affect any other slides in your presentation. To do this, follow these steps:

1. On the Slide Show menu, click Custom Animation to display the Custom Animation task pane.

2. In the custom animation list, click a Master animation.

> **Warning**
>
> Be sure that you really want to sever ties between the animation and the Master slide animation. The process of breaking a link to the Master cannot be reversed.

3. Click the arrow on the animation item, and click Copy Effects To Slide. The Master animation is applied on the slide. ▶

4. In the custom animation list, click and drag the animations into any order you prefer.

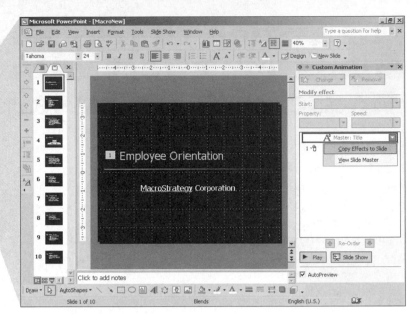

The option to play an animation effect with a mouse click isn't available

Source of the problem

In Microsoft PowerPoint, you can set up animations and transitions to be triggered manually by the presenter or be triggered by a preset timing or sequence. If you want an effect to run when you click an item, you need to set it to use a manual trigger from the presenter. This is called an interactive trigger because it requires interaction between the presenter and the presentation.

You can set up interactive triggers to advance to the next slide and invoke the next slide animation effect with a mouse click, by clicking an arrow key on your keyboard, or by using a shortcut menu on screen. However, animations must have a trigger set—they don't work on mouse clicks until you tell them they're supposed to.

How to fix it

To set a trigger for an animation, follow these steps:

1. On the Slide Show menu, click Custom Animation.

2. In the Custom Animation task pane, click the arrow next to the item, and then click Timing.

3. Select the Timing tab if it's not already displayed. ▶

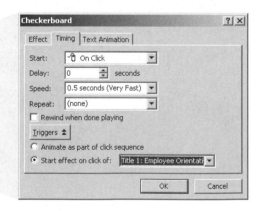

4. Make sure the Start box is set to On Click.

5. Click Triggers, and then click the Start Effect On Click Of option.

6. Click an item in the list (the list includes the items on the slide), and click OK.

Tip

If you add clip art on a slide, the reference to it in the Start Effect On Click Of list will be the file name (without the file extension) of the clip art, such as J0195284. If you have more than one clip art object on the slide, you might have to experiment to figure out which one you're selecting. You can note the file name when you insert the clip art by clicking the arrow next to its preview in the Insert Clip Art task pane, and then clicking Preview/ Properties and checking the Name field.

I don't see animations when I run my Web presentation

Source of the problem

Did you know that with PowerPoint and a Web server, you can become your own Internet publisher? The world becomes your audience, your message becomes virtual, and you might just get your 15 minutes of fame. But there are things you have to understand about how PowerPoint publishes a presentation to the Web to help the Web audience view it successfully.

Publishing a PowerPoint presentation to the Web involves saving a copy of the file in Hypertext Markup Language (HTML) format to a Web server. HTML is the standard markup language used for documents on the World Wide Web. HTML uses tags to specify how Web browsers should display page elements, such as text and graphics, and what a browser should do in response to user actions. When you publish a presentation to the Web, how animations and transitions play is affected. You have to set it up to run these properly by using the Web Options feature.

> **Before you start**
>
> When you publish a presentation to the Web, you have to be aware of how browsers will interact with the presentation or which functions might not work as you expect.

How to fix it

To have animation and transition effects run properly when viewed on line, do the following:

> **Warning**
>
> Some animation effects won't work when you publish to the Web. For example, Animate Text By Word and Animate Text By Letter won't work; neither will any effects applied to charts, linked objects, or embedded objects. Paragraph effects including Spiral, Spin, and Zoom won't work either. Review your Web presentation with your browser to see if an effect you used isn't working, and consider replacing it with one that does.

1. Open the presentation.

2. On the Tools menu, click Options.

3. Click the General tab.

4. Click Web Options.

5. On the General tab of the Web Options dialog box, select the Show Slide Animation While Browsing check box. ▶

6. Click OK to save the new setting.

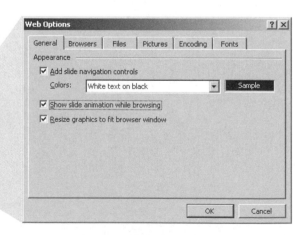

Are you having difficulty working with presentations you published to the Web?

yes → Have you already published a presentation to the Web?

yes →

no ↓

Are you about to make a presentation broadcast and you want to record your online presentation?

yes →

no ↓

Quick fix

Saving broadcasts. You might want to save a broadcast presentation so that you can replay it and work at improving your presentation style. To do this, follow these steps:

1. On the Slide Show menu, point to Online Broadcast, and click Record And Save A Broadcast.

2. Click Settings.

3. Type the file location in the Save Broadcast Files In field.

4. Click OK.

This change will apply to all broadcasts made from your computer.

Are you trying to update a scheduled broadcast? **yes** →

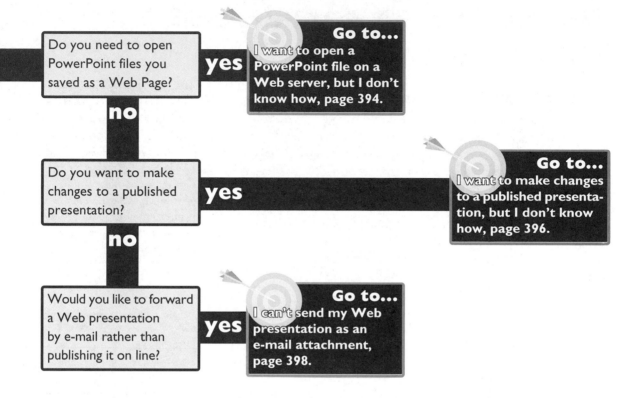

Do you need to open PowerPoint files you saved as a Web Page?

yes → Go to...
I want to open a PowerPoint file on a Web server, but I don't know how, page 394.

no

Do you want to make changes to a published presentation?

yes → Go to...
I want to make changes to a published presentation, but I don't know how, page 396.

no

Would you like to forward a Web presentation by e-mail rather than publishing it on line?

yes → Go to...
I can't send my Web presentation as an e-mail attachment, page 398.

Quick fix

Working with presentation broadcasts. If you want to update a broadcast you've already scheduled, you have to reschedule it by following these steps:

1. Open the presentation, make your changes, and save it.

2. On the Slide Show menu, point to Online Broadcast, and click Reschedule A Live Broadcast.

3. Click Reschedule.

4. When your e-mail program opens, click Save And Close or click Send Update to renotify attendees.

If your solution isn't here, check these related chapters:

- Running a show, page 358
- Web publishing (Common elements), page 106

Or see the general troubleshooting tips on page xix.

I want to open a PowerPoint file on a Web server, but I don't know how

Source of the problem

Once you publish a PowerPoint presentation to the Web, you might want to access it to make some changes or view information in a file. You can create, copy, save, or manage folders and files that are located on a company network, a Web server, or an FTP server. To do so, you should create a shortcut. Once you've created a shortcut, you can access these folders and files from a couple of places: the Open and Save dialog boxes in Office programs and My Network Places. You can then work with the files just as though they were on your computer hard disk.

     To create a shortcut to a PowerPoint presentation on a Web server, you'll need its Web Universal Resource Locator (URL). If you don't know the URL, you might have to talk to your system administrator or Internet service provider to get it.

Before you start

Creating a network shortcut simply allows you to go to that server and open files, assuming they are not protected and that you have permission to open them. If you're not sure about either, speak with your network administrator.

Note

This procedure also works the same way in Microsoft Windows Me.

How to fix it

To create a shortcut to a Web server in Windows 2000, follow these steps:

1. On the File menu, click New to open the New Presentation task pane.

2. At the bottom of the New Presentation task pane, click Add Network Place.

3. Click Create A Shortcut To An Existing Network Place. ▶

4. Click Next.

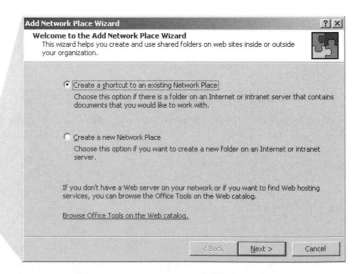

5. Click or enter the URL of the Web server, and type a name for your shortcut in the Shortcut Name box. ▶

6. Click Finish.

7. You should now find the icon for the server in My Network Places. Double-click it to see a list of files.

8. Double-click the file you want to open.

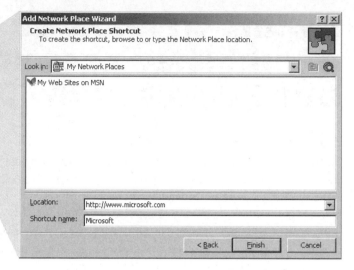

I want to make changes to a published presentation, but I don't know how

Source of the problem

In this age of information, where statistics change hourly and facts become fiction in a short amount of time, you are likely to have to update presentations you publish to the Web to keep them accurate. Once you've published a presentation to the Web, you can make changes to it to update, delete, or add information. But to do this, you have to go back to the original file, make changes, and then publish it to the Web again.

One tip might save you from having to edit after publishing to the Web: if you want to be sure you'll be happy with a presentation before you publish it, you can see how your published Web presentation will look by selecting Web Page Preview from the File menu before publishing the presentation.

Before you start

If you edit a presentation and publish it again to exactly the same server with exactly the same name, it will overwrite the presentation you previously published. If you want two versions of the presentation online, save the edited version with a new name.

How to fix it

To edit a presentation you've already published to the Web, follow these steps:

1. Open the original file of the presentation you want to edit (don't open the file you published to the Web).

2. Make your edits.

3. On the File menu, click Save As Web Page.

4. In the File Name box, enter the Web presentation name.

5. In the Save As Type box, click to save the file as a Web page (this creates a folder that includes all supporting files, such as graphics, used in the presentation).

6. Click a location for the Web page in the Folder List.

7. If you want to change the title that appears in the browser's title bar, click Change Title, and then type the title in the Page Title box.

8. Click OK.

9. Click Publish.

10. At this point, you can make any changes to settings for which slides to publish, optimize the presentation for various browsers, use speaker notes, or modify any other page formatting and display options. ▶

11. Click Publish.

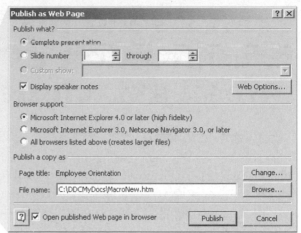

I can't send my Web presentation as an e-mail attachment

Source of the problem

You can't send a Web page presentation as an e-mail attachment because it is made up of so many associated files. The best way to send a PowerPoint presentation by e-mail is to convert it back to a .ppt file or save it as a Web archive.

A Web archive allows you to save all the elements of a Web site, including text and graphics, in a single file. This format enables you to publish your whole Web site as a single MHTML (which is a MIME encapsulated aggregate HTML document) file. What does this acronym mean to you? It means that you can send an entire Web site in one file as an e-mail message or attachment that can be opened and viewed as a complete presentation using Internet Explorer 4.0 or later.

Before you start

You can save a PowerPoint file in as many formats as you like. When you save in a new format, you don't overwrite the original file, you simply create an additional file.

How to fix it

To save the presentation as a Web archive, follow these steps:

1. On the File menu, click Save As.

2. In the Save As Type list, click Web Archive.

3. Click Save. ▶

To save a Web page format presentation as a .ppt file, do this:

1. Open the Web presentation.

2. On the File menu, click Save As.

3. In the Save As Type box, click Presentation, and then click Save.

Tip

You could also consider publishing a PowerPoint file to a shared location, such as an FTP site, instead of e-mailing it.

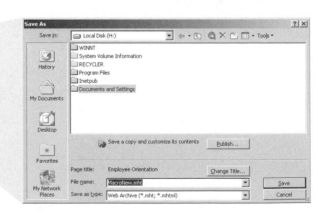

Word

Part 5

Are you having trouble with borders or shading?

yes

no

Are you having trouble with bullets or numbering?

yes

Are bullet characters unusual?

yes

no

Go to...
I see strange bullet characters, page 408.

Are you having trouble changing bullets or numbers in a list?

yes

no

Go to...
I changed the bullets in a list, but only some bullets changed, page 410.

Do you want to add a new line of text without adding bullets or numbers?

yes

no

Quick fix
To add text without adding bullets or numbers, place the insertion point at the end of the list item and press Shift+Enter. The new line indents to align with the text from the previous line, with no new bullet or number.

Are your headings missing numbers?

yes

Go to...
My headings aren't numbered even though I'm using Outline Numbering, page 404.

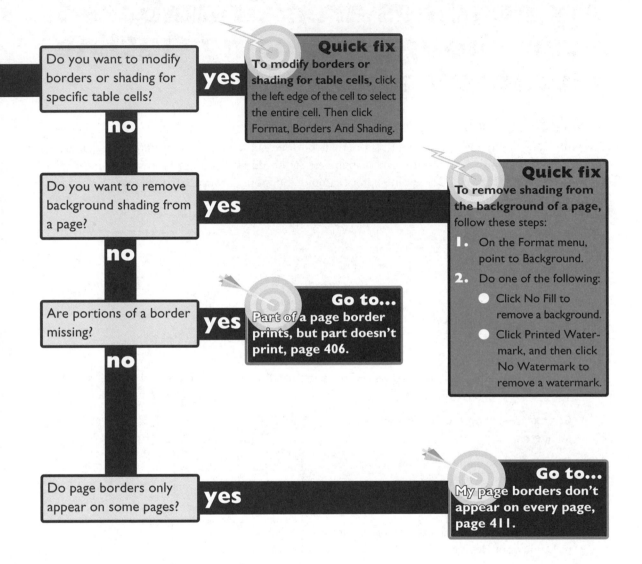

Do you want to modify borders or shading for specific table cells?

yes

Quick fix

To modify borders or shading for table cells, click the left edge of the cell to select the entire cell. Then click Format, Borders And Shading.

no

Do you want to remove background shading from a page?

yes

Quick fix

To remove shading from the background of a page, follow these steps:

1. On the Format menu, point to Background.
2. Do one of the following:
   - Click No Fill to remove a background.
   - Click Printed Watermark, and then click No Watermark to remove a watermark.

no

Are portions of a border missing?

yes

Go to...

Part of a page border prints, but part doesn't print, page 406.

no

Do page borders only appear on some pages?

yes

Go to...

My page borders don't appear on every page, page 411.

If your solution isn't here, check this related chapter:

- Drawing, page 24

Or see the general troubleshooting tips on page xix.

My headings aren't numbered even though I'm using Outline Numbering

Source of the problem

If Outline Numbering is enabled, you'd think that you'd see numbers next to headings. By default, Word's Outline Numbering feature displays numbers for headings if you use Word's built-in heading styles (Heading 1, Heading 2, Heading 3, for example). Suppose, however, that you have a document using styles like the one shown in the figure. You can use your own styles for headings and still get Word to display heading numbers. ▶

Chapter Title	AUTORECOVER¶
Task	• → When·I·saved·a·document·in·Rich·Text·Format·(RTF),·my·bitmap·icon· disappeared.¶
Task	• → I·turned·on·the·AutoRecover·feature·before·I·lost·my·document,·but·I·can't· save·or·open·the·recovery·file.¶
Task	• → The·recovery·file·doesn't·contain·my·changes.¶
Task	• → I·used·the·AutoRecover·feature,·but·I·can't·find·my·recovery·file.¶
Chapter Title	CLIPART¶
Task	• → I·don't·see·the·pictures·I·added·to·Microsoft·Clip·Organizer.¶
Task	• → I·can't·select·all·the·pieces·in·my·clip.¶
Task	• → There·are·way·too·many·clips·in·the·Results·box,·and·they·didn't·match·the· search·criteria.¶
Task	• → The·Clip·I·want·isn't·in·the·Gallery¶
Chapter Title	DRAWING¶
Task	• → I·can't·see·the·border·around·an·object.¶
Task	• → I·changed·the·fill,·border,·shadow,·or·3-D·effect,·but·when·I·draw·an·object,·I· get·the·old·settings.¶
Task	• → I·can't·resize·an·object.¶

How to fix it

To display heading numbers when you are not using built-in heading styles, assign heading level numbers to the styles you are using as headings. Follow these steps:

1. Click anywhere on the first line you want numbered.

2. On the Format menu, click Bullets And Numbering.

3. Click the Outline Numbered tab.

4. Click the numbering format that you want to use in your document. ▶

5. Click Customize.

6. If the dialog box is not fully expanded, click the More button immediately below the Cancel button. (The More button changes to the Less button.)

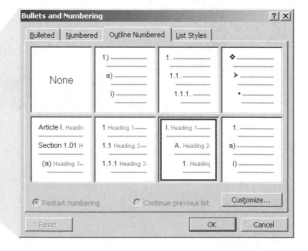

7. In the Level box, click the heading level you want to number. For example, suppose that you've set up styles named Chapter Title, First Subhead, Second Subhead, and so on. The Chapter Title is the top-level heading, First Sub-head is the next level down, and Second Subhead follows First Sub-head. To number Chapter Title in your document as a first-level head, click 1 in the Level box. To number First Subhead as a second-level head, click 2.

8. In the Link Level To Style box, click the style that corresponds to the level you selected in Step 7. For example, if you clicked 2 in Step 7, click First Subhead. ▶

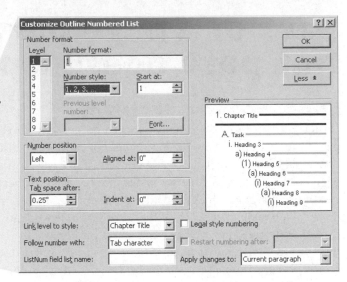

9. Repeat Steps 7 and 8 for each heading style in the document you want to number.

10. Click OK to close both dialog boxes. Word adds numbers to the styles you designated. ▼

You can move head-ings to different numbering levels using buttons on the Formatting toolbar. Place the insertion point any-where on the heading line you want to move to a dif-ferent level. Then, click the Increase Indent button to move the heading to a lower number level (demote it) or the Decrease Indent to move the heading to a higher number level (promote it). ▼

Part of a page border prints, but part doesn't print

Source of the problem

It's just as frustrating to see only part of a border as it is to see all of a border, but not on every page. Typically, page borders don't appear or print if the distance between the border and the edge of the page is too small. Two different sets of margins, working together, control that distance: the page border margins, which is the distance between the border and the edge of the page, and the document margins, which is the distance between the text and the edge of the page.

It's possible to set each of these borders independently and accidentally force the border to disappear on screen as well as when you print because the border might end up being too close to the edge of a page for the printer to be able to print it. (You also won't see it when you preview on screen because Print Preview mimics the printed appearance of your document.)

Although it might seem strange, most printers cannot print to the top, bottom, left, or right edge of a page. Printers automatically establish a minimum margin around all edges of the paper—and these minimum margins vary with the model of the printer. As a rule of thumb, most laser printers won't print in the outer half inch of the page. For example, when I set the page border margins to 29 points measured from the text and the page margins to .6-inch all around, my page border doesn't appear when I print to my laser printer; only the top appears when I print to my inkjet printer. You might find that different combinations of these two margin settings will make your page borders disappear.

How to fix it

To adjust the page border margin, follow these steps:

1. On the Format menu, click Borders And Shading.

2. Click the Page Border tab.

3. Click the Options button.

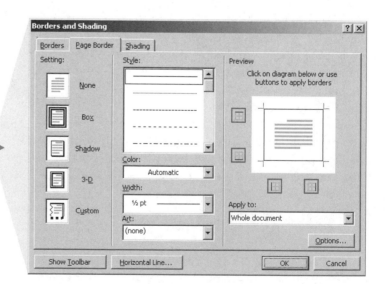

4. In the Measure From list, click Text. ▶

5. In the Margin section, adjust the settings to specify the distance between the text and the page border.

You can adjust page margins in the Page Setup dialog box. On the File menu, click Page Setup. Page margins appear on the Margins tab. ▼

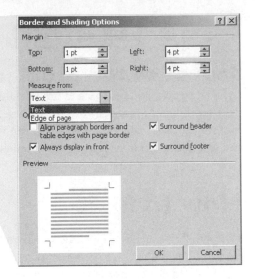

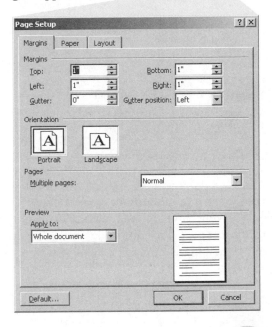

When my paragraph splits across two pages, my paragraph border looks strange

A paragraph border is designed to surround a paragraph. If the paragraph flows from the bottom of one page to the top of the next page, the border splits to surround the paragraph. To keep the paragraph border in one piece, you need to keep the paragraph on a single page. Place the insertion point in the paragraph that's flowing onto another page. On the Format menu, click Paragraph. Then, on the Line And Page Breaks tab, select the Keep Lines Together check box. Word will then move the entire paragraph to "the next page," and your paragraph border will be intact.

I see strange bullet characters

Source of the problem

Typically, you'll see strange and unusual bullet characters when you don't use the Symbol font for your bullets. Because Word tries to use the Symbol font by default for bullets, the Symbol font might be damaged or you might not have it installed. Or, you might have gotten creative and selected a different font for your bullets.

How to fix it

When bullets appear as clock faces, Word is using the Wingdings font for bullets instead of the Symbol font. When you create a bulleted list using the Marlett font, instead of inserting a single bullet, Word either inserts at least one box or inserts a bullet and a box.

⏱ AUTORECOVER	▯ HELP
⏱ CLIPART	▯ MENUS AND TOOLBARS
⏱ DRAWING	▯ PRINTING
⏱ EDITING	▯ REVIEWING CHANGES

If you didn't deliberately select the Wingdings font—that is, if you thought you were using the Symbol font—try reinstalling the Symbol font, selecting a different font, or selecting a different bullet character from the Wingdings font. If you're having trouble with bullets and you're using the Marlett font, select a different font. To select a different font, click any bullet in the list to select all the bullets in the list. On the Format menu, click the Font command. Click a new font.

To select a different character but continue to use the same font, follow these steps:

1. Click a bullet to select all the bullets in the list.

2. On the Format menu, click Bullets And Numbering.

3. On the Bulleted tab, click the Customize button.

4. If it's not already selected, click the bullet character you want to change. ▶

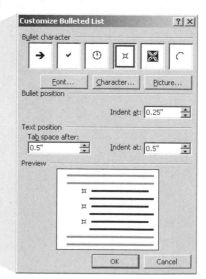

5. Click the Character button. You see the Symbol dialog box.

6. Optionally, click a new font. ▶

7. Click a symbol.

8. Click OK in both dialog boxes.

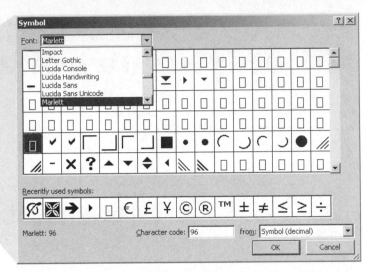

I want bold bullets and plain text

You can format bullets or numbers separately from text by selecting just the bullets or numbers and then applying the formatting. Clicking one bullet or number at any level in a list selects all bullets or numbers at that level in the list.

I changed the bullets in a list, but only some bullets changed

Source of the problem

You'll see this kind of behavior when a bullet or number isn't actually part of the list of bullets or numbers that you selected to change. Or, at least, Word doesn't consider it part of the list. So, of course, you're wondering just how Word makes such decisions. Well, it uses your modem to call a psychic hot line—okay, no, it doesn't, even though it might seem like that's what happens.

When you click a bullet or number in a list, Word selects all the items on that level of the list. The bullet or number that you clicked looks dark gray on screen, whereas the rest of the bullets or numbers in the list at that level look light gray. ▶

If you see a bullet or number on the same level that is not dark or light gray, that bullet or number is not part of the list (yes, we know it *looks* like it is part of the list, but it really isn't). If you change the selected bullets or numbers, the changes

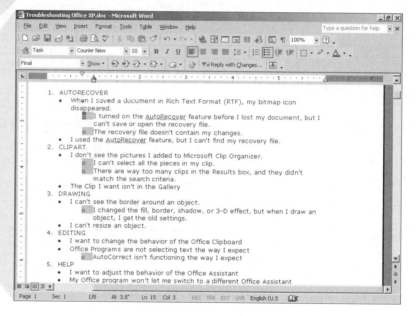

will affect only those bullets and numbers that are part of the list. It's a group thing, and those bullets or numbers that aren't dark or light gray just aren't part of the group.

How to fix it

You need to include in the list the bullet or number that isn't part of the list. Place the insertion point into the text beside the bullet or number that is not light or dark gray, and then click the appropriate button (Bullets or Numbering) on the Formatting toolbar. The bullet or number will then appear either light or dark gray. If you think it might be easier, you can select the entire list (including that item that isn't light or dark gray) and remove and reapply the formatting by clicking the appropriate toolbar button twice.

My page borders don't appear on every page

Source of the problem

Foolish consistency might be the hobgoblin of small minds (is that Emerson or Thoreau?), but when you're using page borders, they need to appear on every page or their effect is diminished. One source of the problem could be a document with sections; another source of the problem could be the view you're using. Page borders will appear in Print Layout view or in Print Preview, but not in Normal, Outline, or Web Layout view. Normal view and Outline view don't display graphic items (and page borders are a graphic item). Web Layout view ignores page breaks—and if you don't have any page breaks, you're not going to have any page borders.

How to fix it

If you apply a border to a document that contains sections, Microsoft Word by default applies the border to the current section only. But, you can change that and apply borders to the entire document. Follow these steps:

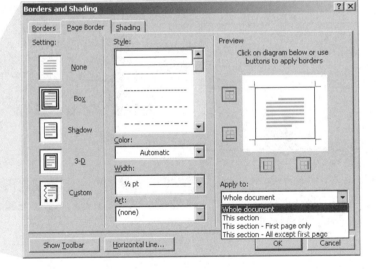

1. On the Format menu, click Borders And Shading.

2. Click the Page Border tab.

3. In the Apply To list, click Whole Document. ▶

One last little quirk—you won't see top or bottom borders if you are viewing your document in Print Layout view and white space is hidden. To change this setting in Print Layout view, move the mouse pointer to the top of the page just below the horizontal ruler (if you aren't displaying rulers, move the pointer to just below the toolbars). When you see the Show White Space indicator, click. ▶

Do you want to add a delivery point barcode or courtesy reply mark to envelopes or labels?

yes

Go to...
I want to use the POSTNET barcode, but I don't know how, page 418.

no

Are you having problems printing envelopes?

yes

no

Do you want to permanently change envelope formatting?

yes

Go to...
I want to permanently use a different font for addresses than the one that appears in my document, page 416.

no

Is the address in your letter missing when you open the Envelopes And Labels dialog box?

yes

Go to...

I put envelopes in the printer tray, but Word still prompts me to feed envelopes manually, page 414.

Quick fix

If Word doesn't display the address in your letter when you open the Envelopes And Labels dialog box, try any of the following:

- Make sure that a paragraph mark appears at the end of each line.

- Make sure addresses in your document are left-aligned.

- Don't add formatting between paragraph marks in the address lines.

If your solution isn't here, check this related chapter:

- Printing, page 462

Or see the general troubleshooting tips on page xix.

I put envelopes in the printer tray, but Word still prompts me to feed envelopes manually

Source of the problem

You bought that particular printer specifically so that you could store envelopes in one tray and not be bothered with loading envelopes whenever you need to print one. Very annoying, indeed!

You might experience this problem if you haven't selected the correct printer tray, envelope feed method (face up or face down), or envelope feed direction (clockwise or counterclockwise). Or, it's possible that you are using an out-of-date printer driver (the software needed by Windows to run the printer correctly).

How to fix it

To check the selected printer tray, follow these steps:

1. On the File menu, click Print.

2. Click the Options button.

3. Click the correct tray in the Default Tray list. ▶

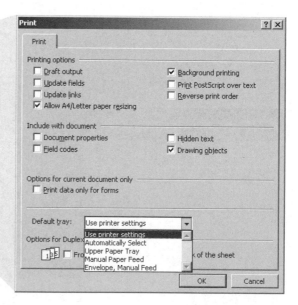

Next, check the documentation that came with your printer to find out whether you should feed envelopes through the printer face up or face down. Then, follow these steps to select the correct setting for envelopes in Word:

1. On the Tools menu, point to Letters And Mailings, and then click Envelopes And Labels.

2. On the Envelopes tab, click Options.

3. Click the Printing Options tab.

4. Click the correct Feed Method.

5. In the Feed From list, click the correct source for the envelopes. ▶

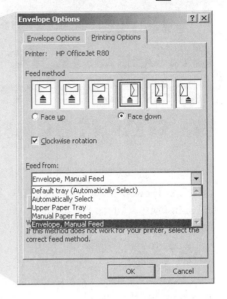

If the envelope feed method is still incorrect, return to the Envelope Options dialog box and, on the Printing Options tab, select the Clockwise Rotation check box. This box controls the direction in which an envelope feeds when you insert it in the printer—clockwise or counterclockwise.

If these solutions don't solve the problem, check with the printer's manufacturer for an updated printer driver. You might be able to download a driver from the manufacturer's Web site.

Note

Be aware that you can't control the feed direction on some printers.

I want to permanently use a different font for addresses than the one that appears in my document

Source of the problem

When you open the Envelopes And Labels dialog box, you notice that the font that appears is the same one that you're using in your document. And, you come to the logical conclusion that Word included the font for the address when it included the address in the dialog box. But you want to use a different font for envelopes. So, being the creative and intelligent person that you are, you select the address in the Envelopes And Labels dialog box, right-click, and then click Font. You then click a new font in the Font dialog box, and things seem fine until the *next* time you use the Envelopes And Labels dialog box, and the old font reappears. This is annoying and mystifying.

The secret is that Word stores the formatting for envelopes and labels in the Envelope Address style and the Envelope Return style. To permanently change envelope formatting, you must change those styles—and you can't change them from the Envelopes And Labels dialog box.

How to fix it

1. If you don't see the Styles And Formatting task pane on the side of your screen, click the Styles And Formatting button on the Formatting toolbar.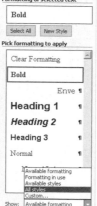

2. In the Show box, click All Styles.

3. Right-click the Envelope Address style, and then click Modify Style.

4. Change the font and any other options that you want to change.

5. To permanently change the style in all documents based on the current template, select the Add To Template check box.

6. To change the Envelope Return style, repeat Steps 3 through 5, but click the Envelope Return style in Step 3.

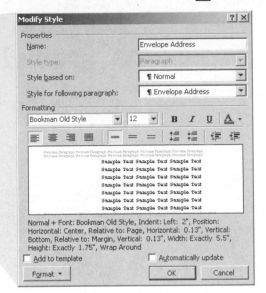

Tip

You can see more options if you click the Format button, and then click the attribute that you want to change.

I want to use the POSTNET barcode, but I don't know how

Source of the problem

You should be able to add the delivery point barcode to envelopes and labels.

How to fix it

You add a delivery point barcode to labels or envelopes in the same manner; let's look at the steps to add the delivery point barcode to labels.

Tip

You also can add the FIM-A courtesy reply mail option to envelopes, but it isn't available for mailing labels.

1. On the Tools menu, point to Letters And Mailings.

2. Click Envelopes And Labels.

3. Click the Labels tab. ▶

4. Select the Delivery Point Barcode check box.

Note

If the box is not available, the label you're using is too small to support adding the barcode. We recommend that you use a larger label if you want to use a delivery point barcode.

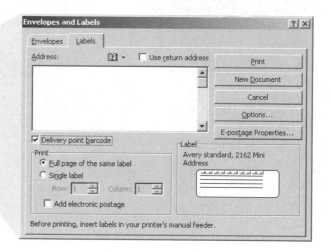

To add the delivery point barcode (and a FIM-A courtesy reply mail) to envelopes, follow these steps:

1. On the Tools menu, point to Letters And Mailings, and click Envelopes And Labels.

2. Click the Envelopes tab.

3. Click Options, and then click the Envelope Options tab.

4. Select the Delivery Point Barcode and FIM-A Courtesy Reply Mail check boxes.

The delivery point barcode and FIM-A code options are available in the U.S. English version of Word for U.S. addresses. You might find both options are unavailable if you typed an address in a language other than English. Under these conditions, Word is smart enough to recognize an address that is outside the United States.

Note

The FIM-A Courtesy Reply Mail check box becomes available only after you check the Delivery Point Barcode box.

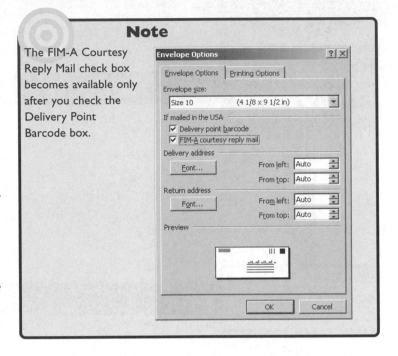

Do you want to exchange information between Word and Excel?

yes

no

Do you want to exchange information between Word and Access?

yes

Go to...

I have a table in Word that contains information I need in Access, page 422.

no

Do you want to exchange information between FrontPage and Word?

yes

Go to...
The information for my Word mail merge data source is in an Excel file, page 426.

Go to...
I need to get information from FrontPage into a Word mail merge document, page 424.

If your solution isn't here, check these related chapters:

- Sharing data, page 86
- Importing and exporting, page 174
- Importing and embedding, page 232
- Links and embedded objects, page 318

Or see the general troubleshooting tips on page xix.

I have a table in Word that contains information I need in Access

Source of the problem

There you were minding your own business, creating a terrific table in Word, and somebody had the gall to tell you they need the information in Access. No, you do *not* need to do it all over again. You can use the information in your Word file to create a file that Access can read. No problem.

How to fix it

Access can read and import a "comma-separated file," and Word can create a comma-separated file. What's a comma-separated file? It's a file where each piece of information is separated by commas. It's no more mysterious than that.

You'll need to convert your Word table to text. Follow these steps:

Company Name	Address	City	Zip
A. Datum Corporation	14021 Wolcott Drive	St. Mary	95624
Adventure Works	3908 Venetian Way	St. Mary	95695
Alpine Ski House	1205 12th Street North	Oak Hill	95705
Baldwin Museum of Science	1508 W. Palm Circle	Valhalla	95594
Blue Yonder Airlines	513 Sandridge Drive	Valhalla	95594
City Power & Light	125 Tidy Island	Seneca	95210
Coho Vineyard	4770 Devonshire Boulevard	South Harbor	95685
Coho Winery	2904 Barret Avenue	Winter Isle	95567
Coho Vineyard & Winery	5630 35th Court E.	Seneca	95203
Contoso, Ltd	6963 4th Street S.	Oak Hill	95705
Contoso Pharmaceuticals	4712 George Road	St. Mary	95695
Consolidated Messenger	10105 Kingshyre Way	St. Mary	95647
Fabrikam, Inc.	10802 W. Hillsborough Ave. #1806	St. Mary	95615
Fourth Coffee	4800 S. Westshore Boulevard #1017	St. Mary	95611
Graphic Design Institute	2261 Westbury Avenue	Backwater	95764

1. Select the rows of the table (or the entire table) that you want to convert. ▶

2. On the Table menu, point to Convert, and click Table To Text.

3. Click Commas under Separate Text With. ▼

4. Click OK. Word replaces the column boundaries with commas, and each row of the former table appears on a separate line. ▶

Convert Table To Text ? ✕

Separate text with
- ○ Paragraph marks
- ○ Tabs
- ● Commas
- ○ Other: -

☑ Convert nested tables

OK   Cancel

Company Name, Address, City, Zip¶
A. Datum Corporation, 14021 Wolcott Drive, St. Mary, 95624¶
Adventure Works, 3908 Venetian Way, St. Mary, 95695¶
Alpine Ski House, 1205 12th Street North, Oak Hill, 95705¶
Baldwin Museum of Science, 1508 W. Palm Circle, Valhalla, 95594¶
Blue Yonder Airlines, 513 Sandridge Drive, Valhalla, 95594¶
City Power & Light, 125 Tidy Island, Seneca, 95210¶
Coho Vineyard, 4770 Devonshire Boulevard, South Harbor, 95685¶
Coho Winery, 2904 Barret Avenue, Winter Isle, 95567¶
Coho Vineyard & Winery, 5630 35th Court E., Seneca, 95203¶
Contoso, Ltd, 6963 4th Street S., Oak Hill, 95705¶
Contoso Pharmaceuticals, 4712 George Road, St. Mary, 95695¶
Consolidated Messenger, 10105 Kingshyre Way, St. Mary, 95647¶
Fabrikam, Inc., 10802 W. Hillsborough Ave. #1806, St. Mary, 95615¶
Fourth Coffee, 4800 S. Westshore Boulevard #1017, St. Mary, 95611¶
Graphic Design Institute, 2261 Westbury Avenue, Backwater, 95764¶
¶

---

5. On the File menu, click Save As, and enter a new file name in the File Name box.

6. In the Save As Type list, click Plain Text, and then click Save. ▶

7. In the File Conversion dialog box that appears, click Windows (Default), and then click OK.

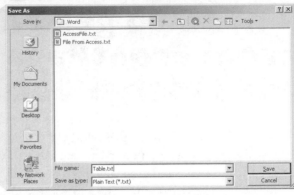

To import the file into an Access database, close the file in Word, open Access, and follow these steps:

1. Open the database into which you want to import the Word file.

2. In the Database window under Objects, click Tables.

3. On the File menu, point to Get External Data, and click Import. ▶

4. Navigate to the folder containing the comma-separated file you created in Word.

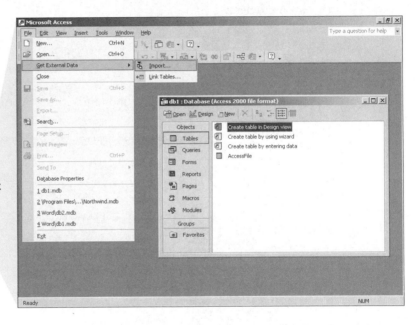

5. In the Files Of Type box, click Text Files.

6. Click the Word file you created, and click Import. ▶

7. Follow the directions in the Import Text Wizard dialog boxes.

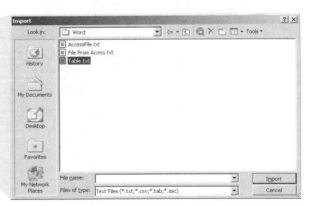

I need to get information from FrontPage into a Word mail merge document

Source of the problem

Here's the situation: you want to create a form for visitors to your Web site to use, and you'd like to use the information they supply in a Word mail merge. For example, users might come to your Web site to register a product, and you want to put them on your mailing list to contact them about updates. Not a problem.

How to fix it

To create a Web page that collects information and sends it to a Word file, follow these steps:

1. In FrontPage, open the page you want to use as an input form on the Web. You might create an input form based on the Feedback Form template or the User Registration template. ▶

2. Right-click anywhere on the form, and click Form Properties.

3. Click Send To.

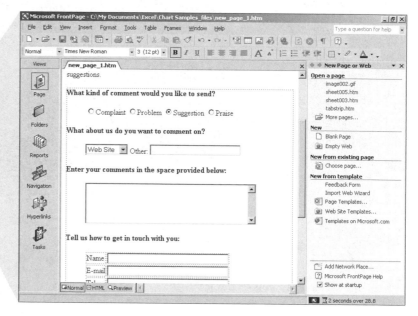

4. In the File Name box, type the name of the Word document you'd like to use to save the information. Be sure to include the .doc extension. ▶

5. Click the Options button.

6. In the File Format box, click Text Database Using Tab As A Separator. ▼

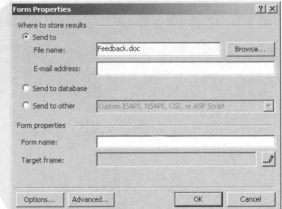

7. Click OK in both dialog boxes.

8. Save the Web page. ▶

To test the page, click the Preview In Browser button in FrontPage.

Type some information, and then click the Submit button. In FrontPage, switch to Folder view, and you'll see your Word .doc file. Double-click the file to open it in Word. Because the information in the file is separated by tabs, you can use it in a Word mail merge.

The information for my Word mail merge data source is in an Excel file

Source of the problem

You have a name and address list in Excel, and you want to use it in a Word mail merge operation. This is not at all unreasonable, and it is doable. You need to make sure that your Excel file is set up correctly to use it in a Word mail merge. Once you've done that, you can use the Excel file the same way you would use a data source you created in Word.

> **Before you start**
>
> If you set up a mail merge with Excel data in earlier versions of Word, you can still use those mail merges, but you need to install Microsoft Query to open and use them in Word 2002. If you are creating a new mail merge using Excel data in Word 2002, keep reading.

How to fix it

Your Excel data file should resemble the file shown in the figure. Check the file for the following requirements: ▶

- Make sure that the Excel data that you plan to use in the mail merge is contiguous. This means the Excel data should not contain any blank rows or columns.

- Make sure that the Excel data contains a separate column for each element that

you want to include in the mail merge. For example, if you're creating form letters that you plan to bulk mail—and therefore need to sort by ZIP code—include a separate Zip Code field in the data. Don't combine the ZIP code with any other part of the address information.

- Make sure each column has a label that clearly identifies the type of information in the column because those labels will come in handy when you are trying to identify the location for fields such as First Name or City in the mail merge.

- If you use Excel's Name feature, you'll be able to easily identify the range of cells that contain the information that you want to merge. When you name a range, you assign it a word or string of characters as an alternate way to refer to that range, which is particularly useful if you can't remember the cell address of the range. For example, if your data appears in cells A1:F100, you can assign a name such as "Address_List" to that range, and then you can refer to the range using its cell address (A1:F100) or its name (Address_List). To create the name in Excel, follow these steps:

1. Select the range of cells that contain the data you want to name.

2. On the Insert menu, point to Name.

3. Click Define. ▶

4. Type a name for the list. The range name cannot include any blanks.

5. Click Add, and then click Close.

6. Save and close the Excel workbook.

To use the list in the Word mail merge, follow these steps in Word:

1. On the Tools menu, point to Letters And Mailings, and click Mail Merge Wizard.

2. In the Mail Merge task pane, select the document type (Letters, E-Mail Messages, Envelopes, Labels, or Directory) and click Next: Starting Document.

3. Click a starting document (the current document, a template, or an existing document), and then click Next: Select Recipients.

4. Click Use An Existing List, and then click Browse. ▶

The information for my Word mail merge data source is in an Excel file

(continued from page 427)

5. In the Select Data Source box, navigate to the folder in which you saved the workbook with your data, click it, and then click Open.

6. In the Select Table dialog box, click the name you created. Select the First Row Of Data Contains Column Headers check box, and then click OK. ▶

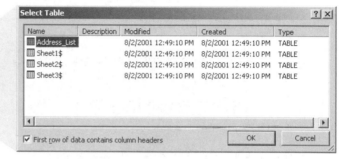

Note

While Word has your workbook open to create the mail merge, you can't open the workbook in Excel.

7. In the Mail Merge Recipients dialog box, click a column heading to sort the data by that column.

8. Click OK. ▶

9. Complete the wizard to write, preview, and conclude the mail merge.

Tip

If you want to exclude recipients from the mail merge, remove the check marks next to their names.

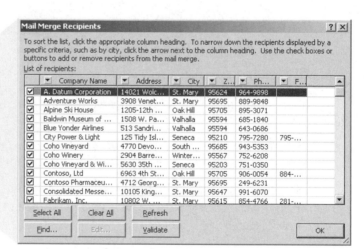

Does your merge document contain unwanted information? — **yes**

no

Do you get security warnings when you merge e-mail from Outlook? — **yes**

no

Is some recipient information missing in merged documents? — **yes**

no

Do you need to restore a merge document to a regular Word document? — **yes**

no

Does your merge document contain fields instead of data? — **yes**

Quick fix

To merge e-mail from Outlook after receiving a security warning, follow these steps:

1. Select the Allow Access For check box.
2. Select the amount of time you need to complete the merge.

Go to...

Some address information is missing for some recipients, page 436.

Quick fix

To print data instead of merge fields, follow these steps:

1. On the Tools menu, click Options.
2. Click the Print tab.
3. Clear the Field Codes check box.

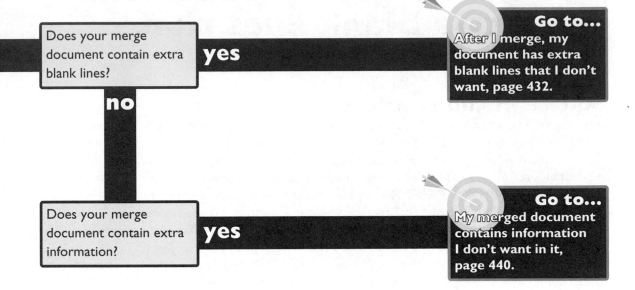

Does your merge document contain extra blank lines?

yes

Go to...
After I merge, my document has extra blank lines that I don't want, page 432.

no

Does your merge document contain extra information?

yes

Go to...
My merged document contains information I don't want in it, page 440.

Quick fix

To restore a main merge document to a Normal document:

1. Open the main merge document.
2. Display the Mail Merge Toolbar.
3. Click the Main Document Setup button.
4. Click Normal Word Document.

If your solution isn't here, check this related chapter:

- Trading data with other programs, page 420

Or see the general trouble-shooting tips on page xix.

After I merge, my document has extra blank lines that I don't want

Source of the problem

You could tear your hair out trying to figure out how to make blank lines disappear in a mail merge. You might even get so frustrated that you manually fix each merged document. But please don't do that. Instead, check to see if you are using the IF, SET, or ASK fields in your mail merge. These fields are most often the culprits that create spare blank lines.

Fields are codes that direct Word to automatically insert text, graphics, page numbers, or other information into a document. You might use the IF field to have Word insert information in a mail merge if certain conditions exist—for example, if the customer's outstanding balance is over 90 days past due, insert "Our collection agent, Broken Legs, Inc., will be contacting you." You might use the SET field to establish a value for a condition that you want Word to check in a statement using the IF field. For example, you could "set" a SpecialOffer value to "Yes" or "No" to determine which customers receive a special offer, and then have Word check the value before including the special offer information in a mail merge letter. You might use the ASK field to have Word prompt you for information during a mail merge. For example, you might have Word "ask" you for a discount rate to offer a customer and then insert your response in that customer's letter.

How to fix it

If you provide a response to an ASK or SET field sometimes, but don't provide a response other times, you can insert the field within a paragraph of the mail merge letter—not on a separate line (placing the field on a separate line creates an extra blank line when you don't provide a response to an ASK or SET field). If, however, you must place the field in a separate paragraph, but you *don't* want a blank line to appear, format the paragraph mark (¶) as hidden text.

To format the paragraph mark as hidden text, follow these steps:

1. If you don't see paragraph marks on screen, click the Show/Hide ¶ button on the Standard toolbar. ▶ ¶

2. Select the paragraph mark on the line of the SET or ASK field.

3. On the Format menu, click Font.

4. Select the Hidden check box. ▶

If you need to print text inserted by an IF field in a separate paragraph, include the paragraph mark inside the field. Insert the statement containing the IF field in the main document at the location where you want the text to appear

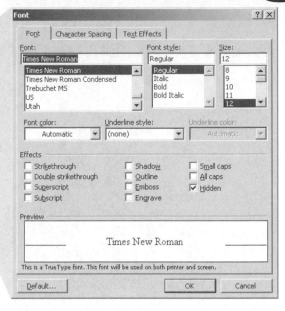

when you merge. Then, with field codes displayed, insert the paragraph mark inside the IF field code within the appropriate set of quotation marks. In the first figure, you see the statement containing the

> **Note**
>
> Before you merge, click Tools, and then click Options. On the Print tab, make sure the Hidden Text check box is cleared.

IF field set up to print the two sentences that follow "City" *and the two paragraph marks* only if the letter's recipient resides in the city of St. Mary. The third sentence, "We look forward to hearing from you," will print in a separate paragraph regardless of the recipient's city. ▶

In the next figure, you see a merged letter to a recipient in St. Mary. ▼

Let·our·highly·qualified·staff·help·you·better·understand·and·use·the·principles·of·
accounting·and·finance.·Who·needs·this·training?·Anyone·who·prepares,·interprets,·or·
approves·budgets,·financial·reports,·or·business·plans.·Our·training·class·is·specifically·
designed·for·those·individuals·who·are·not·formally·trained·in·finance·and·accounting·but·
whose·responsibilities·require·them·to·deal·with·financial·data.¶

{·IF·{·MERGEFIELD·City·}·=·"St·Mary"·"We·have·other·classes·available·in·St.·Mary.·
Please·call·our·office·for·a·complete·list·of·class·dates·and·times.¶
¶
"·"·}¶We·look·forward·to·hearing·from·you.¶
¶
Sincerely,¶

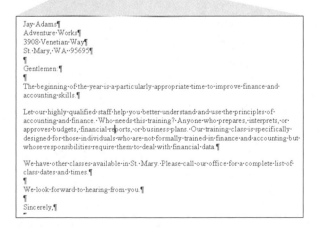

Jay·Adams¶
Adventure·Works¶
3908·Venetian·Way¶
St.·Mary,·WA··95695¶
¶
Gentlemen:¶
¶
The·beginning·of·the·year·is·a·particularly·appropriate·time·to·improve·finance·and·
accounting·skills.¶

Let·our·highly·qualified·staff·help·you·better·understand·and·use·the·principles·of·
accounting·and·finance.·Who·needs·this·training?·Anyone·who·prepares,·interprets,·or·
approves·budgets,·financial·reports,·or·business·plans.·Our·training·class·is·specifically·
designed·for·those·individuals·who·are·not·formally·trained·in·finance·and·accounting·but·
whose·responsibilities·require·them·to·deal·with·financial·data.¶

We·have·other·classes·available·in·St.·Mary.·Please·call·our·office·for·a·complete·list·of·
class·dates·and·times.¶
¶
We·look·forward·to·hearing·from·you.¶
¶
Sincerely,¶

After I merge, my document has extra blank lines that I don't want

(continued from page 433)

And in the following figure, you see a letter to a recipient who doesn't reside in St. Mary. ▶

To display field codes so that you can correctly place paragraph marks, click Tools, and then click Options. On the View tab, select the Field Codes check box and click OK. ▼

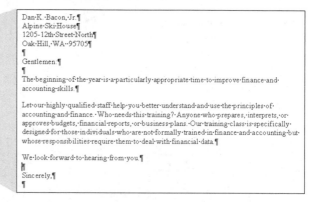

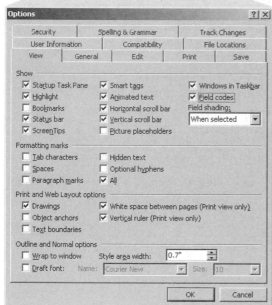

Mail merge

Some address information is missing for some recipients

Source of the problem

Do you feel like you're playing hide and seek with the recipients of your mail merge letter? When you preview the mail merge, you see complete information for some but incomplete information for others. This can be very frustrating.

The problem most likely lies in the data source file—the file that contains the recipients' information. But, it could also be a problem in the main merge document itself.

How to fix it

In the data source, you could be running into one of two problems. First, the information might not be in the data source file. In Step 3 of the Mail Merge task pane, Select Recipients, click Edit Recipient List.

In the Mail Merge Recipients dialog box, find the record that is missing information. If you don't see the information in the Mail Merge Recipients dialog box, you won't see it in your merged document because the information is missing from your data source file.

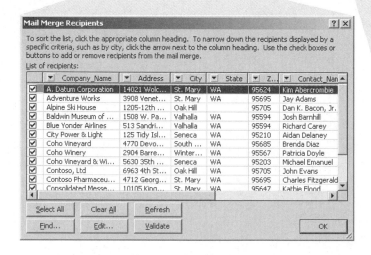

You can exclude that recipient from this merge by clearing the check box next to the recipient's name. Or, you can correct the record by clicking the Edit button and then using the buttons at the bottom of the Data Form dialog box to display the record so that you can correct it. ▶

The other possible problem in the data source is associated with the column headings. If the Mail Merge Wizard doesn't recognize a column heading in the data source file, Word won't be able to assign the information in the column to a merge field. You can correct this by using the Match Fields dialog box. You can open the Match Fields dialog box from Step 4 of the Mail Merge Wizard; click Address Block, Greeting Line, or More Items in the Mail Merge task pane. In the resulting dialog box, click the Match Fields button. In the Match Fields dialog box, click the arrow next to (Not Available), and then click the field from your data source that corresponds to the field required for the mail merge. ▶

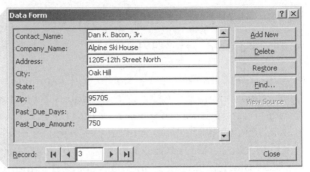

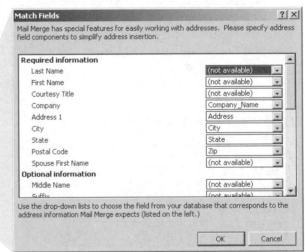

Some address information is missing for some recipients

(continued from page 437)

In the main mail merge document, you might have information missing from the Address Block field or the Greeting Line. To make sure that the Address Block includes all the information you want, right-click the field, click Edit Address Block to display the Insert Address Block dialog box, and then check the information included in the Address Block field. ▶

To make sure that the Greeting Line field includes all the information you want, right-click the field, and then click Edit Greeting Line to display the Greeting Line dialog box. ▼

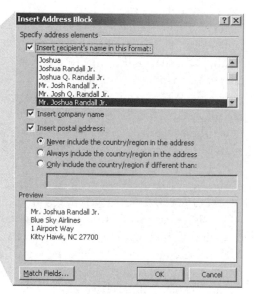

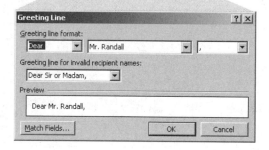

Note

The Insert Address Block and Greeting Line dialog boxes provide sample information for preview purposes. The sample recipient you see in these dialog boxes will not appear anywhere in your merged document.

Mail merge

My merged document contains information I don't want in it

Source of the problem

What? You don't think the recipient will want to see this stuff? Okay, okay, let's see what we can do to get rid of it.

One source of unwanted information is an extraneous field in the main document. You might also get extra information if you include information in the greeting block that Word includes automatically. In addition, you might see character formatting in merged letters that didn't appear in the main document.

How to fix it

Check the main document for fields you didn't mean to insert. To help you find fields easily, enable Field Shading. Follow these steps:

1. On the Tools menu, click Options.

2. Click the View tab.

3. In the Field Shading list below the Field Codes check box, click Always. ▶

4. Click OK.

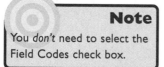

Note

You *don't* need to select the Field Codes check box.

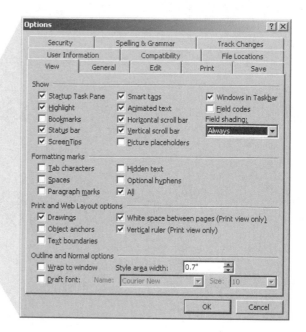

Word will redisplay the main document and all merge fields will appear shaded in gray. ▶

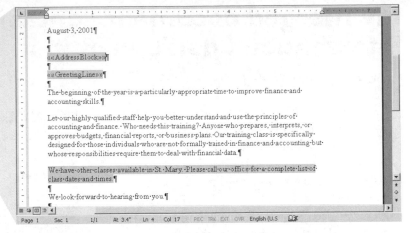

Do you see a double greeting, like Dear Dear Mr. Jones? ▶

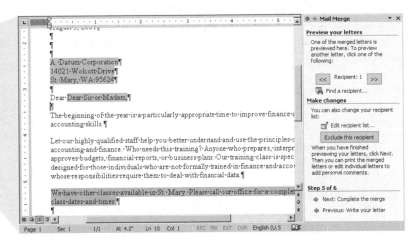

If so, you probably typed the word "Dear" immediately before the Greeting Line. ▶

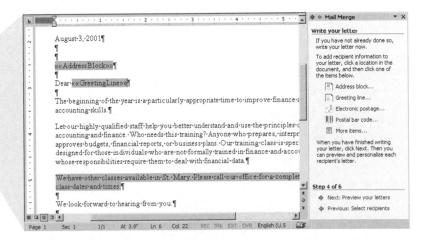

My merged document contains information I don't want in it

(continued from page 441)

By default, the Greeting Line includes a saluta-tion. It's easier to simply delete the text you typed, but you also can suppress the salutation in the Greeting Line dialog box. In Step 4 of the Mail Merge Wizard, click Greeting Line. Then, in the first list click (None). ▶

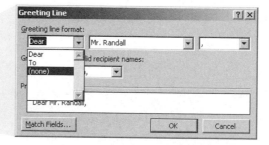

If you see character formatting in merged documents that doesn't appear in the main merge document, open the data source and look for character formatting. Word will include character formatting in the merged document if the data source contains the formatting or if you format the merge fields in the main merge document.

Mail merge

Are you having trouble opening a converted document?

yes

Go to...
I'm trying to convert text and graphics, but I'm having trouble with the graphics, page 446.

no

Are you having trouble saving?

yes

Are you getting two extensions on the file name?

yes

no

Are you getting error messages when you save?

yes

no

Does information disappear after you save?

yes

Do changes disappear?

yes

no

no

Are characters replaced when you save in a different format?

yes

Do you need to save in a format that doesn't appear in the Save As dialog box?

yes

Quick fix

You'll get two extensions on your file name if you include an extension other than .doc when you save the file. By default, Word adds ".doc" to any other extensions. Enclose the entire file name in quotes to avoid appending the .doc extension.

Go to...

I get an error message when I try to save a document, page 448.

Go to...

I know I saved my document, but my changes don't appear in it, page 449.

Quick fix

Word replaces right-aligned tabs in tables with spaces when you save a document as Text With Layout or MS-DOS Text With Layout. Avoid using right-aligned tabs if you plan to save using one of these formats.

Quick fix

If the file format you need doesn't appear in the Save As box, it might not be installed. Check your Office XP CD for converters. Also, check the Microsoft Office Web site. In Word, click the Help menu, and click Office On The Web.

If your solution isn't here, check this related chapter:

- Trading data with other programs, page 420

Or see the general troubleshooting tips on page xix.

I'm trying to convert text and graphics, but I'm having trouble with the graphics

Source of the problem

If it isn't one thing, it's another. Converting text and graphics isn't fun, so when *part* of your document converts but another part doesn't, the frustration level can reach new heights. When you convert text and graphics, graphics might disappear or fonts might change.

How to fix it

If graphics have disappeared, make sure that you're not looking for graphics in Normal or Outline view—neither view displays graphics. If you're using Print Layout, Print Preview, or Web Layout view and you don't see graphics that you know should be there, check your settings. Follow these steps:

1. On the Tools menu, click Options.

2. Click the View tab.

3. In the Show section, clear the Picture Placeholders check box. ▶

Next, make sure that you have installed the filter needed to display the graphic.

1. On the Insert menu, point to Picture, and then click From File.

2. In the Files Of Type list, check the list of filters. If the filter you need is not listed, install it using your Office XP CD. ▶

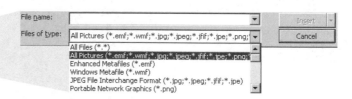

Suppose that you convert a document created in another word processing program and find that the converted document contains different fonts than the original. The original document might have been created using fonts that you don't have installed on your computer. When you open the converted version, you'll find that Word has substituted fonts that you do have installed on your computer.

However, you can control the fonts that Word substitutes by following these steps:

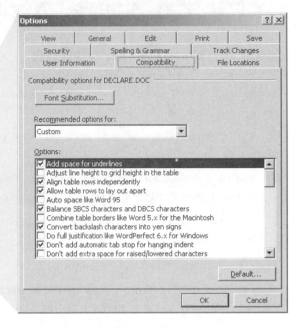

1. Open the converted document that contains fonts not installed on your computer.

2. On the Tools menu, click Options.

3. Click the Compatibility tab. ▶

4. Click the Font Substitution button.

5. Click each font listed in the upper box under Missing Document Font, and then click a substitute font in the lower-right Substituted Font list. ▶

6. To convert all missing fonts in the document to their currently substituted fonts, click the Convert Permanently button.

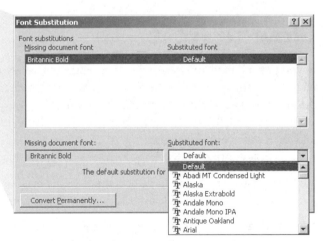

I get an error message when I try to save a document

Source of the problem

There you are, working diligently, and then you try to save your work and get an error message. You might get a *read-only* error message, a *file too large* error message, or a *same name* error message. This is *not* an ideal situation, but there are ways around each of these problems.

- You'll see the read-only error message when you try to save changes you made to a document you've opened in read-only mode.

- You'll get the file too large error message when Word can't find enough disk space or memory to save the entire file.

- You'll see the same name error message under the following conditions:

  - You enabled background saving.

  - You tried to save your document at the same time Word is trying to perform the background save.

> **Note**
>
> If you enable background saving, you don't need to wait until Word finishes saving your document (using the same name you assigned to the document) to continue working in it.
>
> You enable (and disable) background saves from the Save tab of the Options dialog box. On the Tools menu, click Options, and then click the Save tab.

How to fix it

If you get the read-only error message, you can't save your changes to the open file—but you *can* save the document to a different location or use a different file name.

If you get the same name error message, just wait until Word finishes the background save and then save your document.

If you get the file too large error message, you have two choices:

- You can convert the large document into a master document and save portions of it as individual subdocuments.

- You can divide the large document into smaller documents by cutting part of the document and pasting it into a new document. You can then save each smaller document individually.

> **Tip**
>
> If you connect the documents with INCLUDETEXT fields, you can print the files in sequence.

I know I saved my document, but my changes don't appear in it

Source of the problem

This problem will make you gray before your time. And it will add a lot of stress to your life. You *know* you saved the changes—but where are they?

There are two situations in which you'll see this problem. In one situation—saving on a network (the more common situation, actually)—your changes are saved, so you can start breathing again. In the other situation, changes saved using AutoRecover, *some* of your changes are saved; others are not.

How to fix it

Here's the network scenario:

Suppose that you opened a document that is stored on a network server. When you saved it, you clicked the File menu, and then clicked Exit. You saw a message asking if you want to save the changes, and you clicked yes.

You just saved the document on your local hard disk. So, when you reopen the document on the network server, you won't see your changes because they appear only in the copy on your local hard disk. You can avoid saving changes to a network-based document in a separate copy of the document on your hard disk if you click File, and then click the Save command before you quit Word. Don't rely on that "Do you want to save" message.

On to the AutoRecover scenario:

Suppose you are working along very nicely, thank you very much, when Word unexpectedly shuts down. Your heart rate accelerates thinking of all the work you just lost, and then you remember that you're using the AutoRecover feature in Word—so you're "safe," right?

Well, almost. The AutoRecover feature saves your document every X number of minutes—and you get to select X on the Save tab of the Options dialog box (click Tools, Options, and then click the Save tab). If you made changes *after* the AutoRecover feature last saved your document, those changes won't appear when AutoRecover displays your document.

So, what's a good number for X? Don't get nuts, because having the AutoRecover feature saving every minute will slow down Word's ability to function. Ask yourself this question: how much work do I think I can remember if I have to re-create it? The default setting for the AutoRecover feature is 10 minutes—and most people can remember most of the information they created in the last 10 minutes.

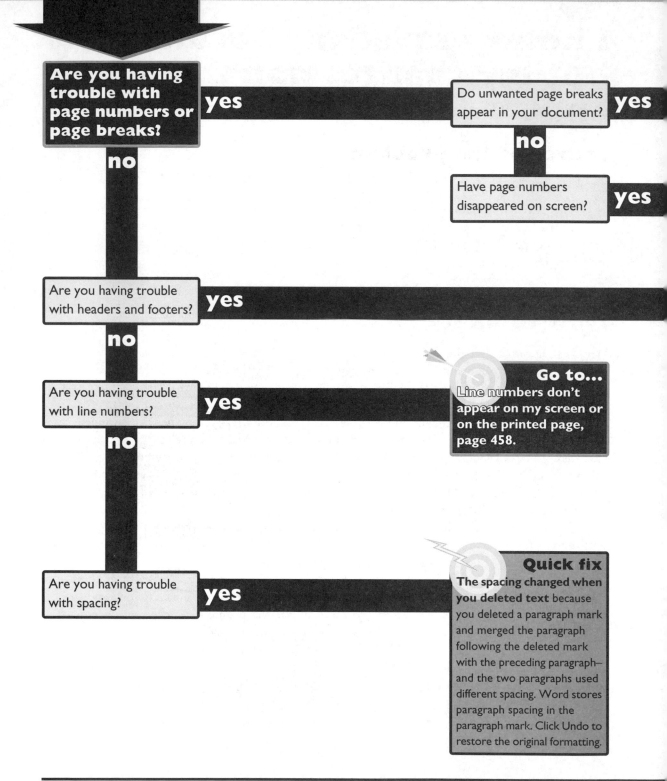

Are you having trouble with page numbers or page breaks?

yes

Do unwanted page breaks appear in your document?

yes

no

Have page numbers disappeared on screen?

yes

no

Are you having trouble with headers and footers?

yes

no

Are you having trouble with line numbers?

yes

Go to...
Line numbers don't appear on my screen or on the printed page, page 458.

no

Are you having trouble with spacing?

yes

Quick fix
The spacing changed when you deleted text because you deleted a paragraph mark and merged the paragraph following the deleted mark with the preceding paragraph—and the two paragraphs used different spacing. Word stores paragraph spacing in the paragraph mark. Click Undo to restore the original formatting.

Page formatting

Go to...
I have page breaks in my document that I don't want, page 452.

Go to...
My page numbers are missing on screen, or I see {PAGE} instead of my page number, page 456.

Go to...
The headers and footers have disappeared or contain inaccurate information, page 454.

Have headers and footers disappeared on screen?

yes →

no

Did changes to headers and footers in one section affect the whole document?

yes →

Go to...
I changed the header in one section, and all headers in the document changed, page 460.

no

Do you need odd and even headers in a one-page template?

yes →

Quick fix
To set up different odd and even headers or footers for a one-page template, insert a manual page break in the template, create the headers or footers you want, and then delete the page break. The unique headers and footers will appear in multipage documents based on the template.

If your solution isn't here, check this related chapter:

● Printing, page 462

Or see the general troubleshooting tips on page xix.

I have page breaks in my document that I don't want

Source of the problem

Mysteriously appearing page breaks create a tricky situation. Word automatically inserts page breaks in your document based on page settings, such as margins. However, you can force page breaks—on purpose or by accident. To solve this problem, check for manual page breaks, section breaks, and column breaks. Manual page breaks work like automatic page breaks except that the manual page break ignores other page settings, like margins. There are four kinds of section breaks, and some of them force a page break. Also, if you insert a column break in the last column of a page, the column break will act as a page break.

If you still haven't found the reason for the mysterious page breaks, check pagination options because you might have set a pagination option that causes page breaks to appear.

How to fix it

If you have accidentally inserted a manual page break, section break, or column break, you can delete the break to eliminate the unwanted page break. To delete a break, place the insertion point on the break, and press the Delete key on your keyboard.

If you work in Normal view, you can easily see and delete the markers for manual page breaks, section breaks, and column breaks. Click the Normal View button at the left edge of the horizontal scroll bar to switch to Normal view. Then, follow these steps to use Word's Find feature to search for manual page breaks, section breaks, or column breaks. ▶

1. On the Edit menu, click Find.

2. In the Find And Replace dialog box, click the More button—which then changes to the Less button.

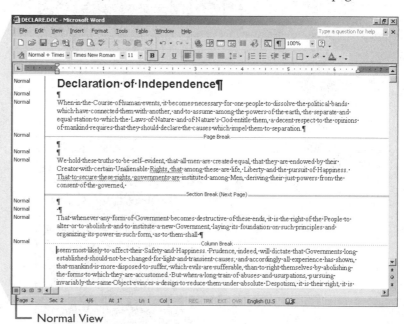

Normal View

3. Click the Special button.

4. Click a page formatting element for which you want to search, such as Manual Page Break. ▶

5. Click Find Next.

6. When Word displays a page formatting element (in our example, a manual page break) that you want to delete, select it in the document, and press the Delete key.

7. Repeat Steps 5 and 6 until you have deleted all extraneous page formatting elements of the type you selected—in our example, manual page breaks.

8. Delete the characters that appear in the Find What box.

9. Repeat Steps 3 through 8 until you have deleted all extraneous page formatting elements of all types.

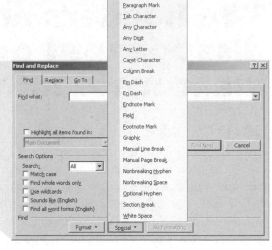

If a break isn't the source of your mysterious page break, one of three pagination options might be the culprit: Keep Lines Together, Keep With Next, or Page Break Before. Select the paragraph that appears immediately after the unwanted page break; on the Format menu, click Paragraph. Then, click the Line And Page Breaks tab. Clear the Keep Lines Together, Keep With Next, and Page Break Before check boxes. ▶

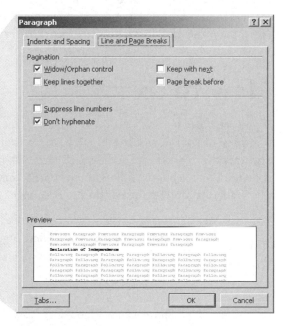

The headers and footers have disappeared or contain inaccurate information

Source of the problem

Are you feeling like a magician except you have no clue what magic words you uttered to make your headers or footers disappear? Or, even better, they appear, but the dates in them are inaccurate. You can trace these problems back to a few possible sources.

First, you need to make sure that you're in Print Layout view or Print Preview when you try viewing headers and footers. Headers and footers only appear in Print Layout view and in printed documents. You won't see them in Normal or Outline view because neither view displays graphic elements. Nor will you see them in Web Layout view, which ignores pagination elements such as headers and footers.

Second, check to see if you are working in a Web page version (.htm) of your document. If so, you won't see the headers and footers and they won't print, but you'll see them when you reopen the .doc format of the document.

> **Tip**
>
> You can add a header or footer to a Web page using a header frame or a footer frame.

How to fix it

If you see a header or footer on all pages except the first page of your document, check to see if your document is divided into sections. If your document is divided into sections, follow these steps to make the header or footer reappear on the first page.

1. Click in the section in which you want the header or footer to appear on the first page.

2. On the File menu, click Page Setup.

3. Click the Layout tab.

4. Clear the Different First Page check box.

You can insert the date and time into a header or footer in a couple of ways; the method you choose can affect automatic updating. Word can update

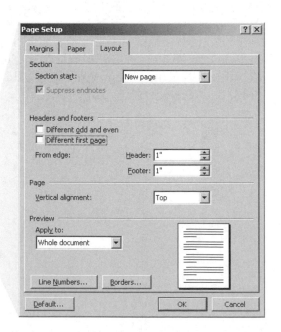

information in your document that appears as the result of fields that you insert. If you simply type in the header or footer, Word will not update your information.

Word inserts fields when you use the Header And Footer toolbar to add dates, times, titles, and other elements to a header or footer, and Word will automatically update these fields each time you open the document. You can manually update them by selecting the entire document (press Ctrl+A) and then pressing F9. ▶

If you insert the date and time in a header or footer by clicking the Insert menu and then clicking Date And Time, you control whether the date and time automatically update. To make these fields update automatically, select the Update Automatically check box. ▶

If you don't select the Update Automatically check box, you can manually update the field at any time by clicking the field in the header or footer or selecting the entire document and pressing F9.

Only part of the header or footer prints

The header or footer might be located too close to the edge of the paper—in the area that your printer can't print. Consult your printer's documentation to find out the minimum margin setting for your printer. For example, most laser printers have a minimum margin setting of one-half inch; that is, most laser printers cannot print in the first half inch around the page. Then, on the File menu, click Page Setup. On the Layout tab, in the From Edge boxes for Header and Footer, enter values that are equal to or greater than your printer's minimum margin setting.

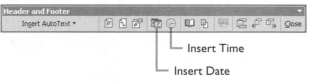

Insert Time

Insert Date

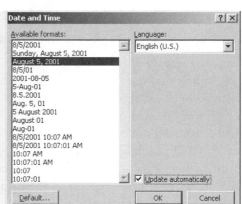

Tip

Do you want to convert a field to information that doesn't update anymore? Select the field and press Ctrl+Shift+F9.

My page numbers are missing on screen, or I see {PAGE} instead of my page number

Source of the problem

You know you had page numbers—they printed, for goodness sake! Why can't you see them on screen? These problems relate to your on-screen settings.

How to fix it

As part of a header or footer, page numbers, like the rest of header or footer information, appear only in Print Layout view, Print Preview, and in printed documents. You won't see them in Normal or Outline view because neither view displays graphics. Nor will you see them in Web Layout view, which ignores pagination settings like headers and footers. And, if you're viewing them in Print Layout view, they'll appear dim compared to the rest of your text.

Once you switch to Print Layout view, you might find that page numbers partly cover other text or graphics in the header or footer area. This situation

can occur if you inserted a page number into a header or footer by clicking the Insert menu and then clicking Page Numbers. When you use this method, Word inserts the page number enclosed in a frame, and the frame containing a page number might cover up other text or graphics in the header or footer area. Try repositioning the frame by clicking the box that appears around the number and dragging when the mouse pointer contains a four-headed arrow. Or, you can delete the page number you inserted using the Page Numbers command on the Insert menu and replace it with a page number that you insert using the Header And Footer toolbar.

Page formatting

If you see {PAGE} instead of a page number, then you're viewing field codes instead of field results. ▶

Word inserts fields when you use the Header And Footer toolbar to add dates, times, titles, and other

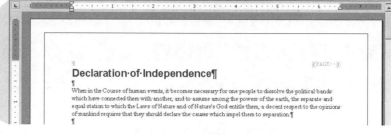

elements to a header or footer, and Word will automatically update these fields each time you open the document. If you see field codes such as {PAGE} instead of the actual page numbers, press Alt+F9, and Word will switch from displaying field codes to displaying field results.

I'm trying to change or remove some page numbers, but I can't

Typically, when you change or delete page numbers, Word automatically changes or removes the page numbers throughout the document. However, if your document contains odd and even headers or footers or a different first-page header or footer, Word won't delete or change page numbers throughout the document; instead, you need to change or remove the page numbers in each different header or footer. Also, if you have divided the document into sections and broken the connection between the sections by clicking the Same As Previous button on the Header And Footer toolbar, Word changes or deletes page numbers only in the section containing the insertion point. You need to place the insertion point in each section of the document and remove or change the page number.

Line numbers don't appear on my screen or on the printed page

Source of the problem

You can trace this problem back to "settings"—either screen or page.

Check the view; line numbers appear only in Print Layout view, Print Preview, and in printed documents. You won't see them in Normal or Outline view because neither view displays graphics. Nor will you see them in Web Layout view, which ignores pagination settings like line numbers.

If you're using Print Layout view or Print Preview or printing and you don't see line numbers, you need to check page settings.

How to fix it

Line numbers won't appear on screen or in print if your margins are too small because Word displays line numbers in the left margin or to the left of each newspaper style column. If the margins are too small and force the line numbers into the area of the page that your printer can't print, Word won't have room to display or print line numbers. Try increasing the margins in the Page Setup box. On the File menu, click Page Setup. ▶

Word also won't have room to display or print line numbers if the distance between the line numbers and the text is greater than or equal to the left margin. Think about that. If the left margin is one inch *and* you set the distance between the text and the line number to one inch *and* Word displays or prints line numbers in the left margin, you haven't allowed any place for Word to display or print the line number.

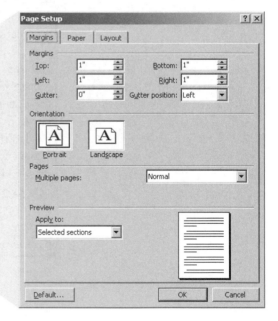

To adjust the distance between text and line numbers, follow these steps:

1. On the File menu, click Page Setup.

2. Click the Layout tab.

3. Click the Line Numbers button.

4. In the From Text box, enter the number you want. Use the Auto setting to allow Word to select the distance between text and line numbers. ▶

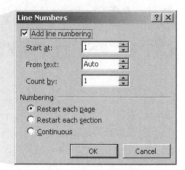

I changed the header in one section, and all headers in the document changed

Source of the problem

Oops...didn't want to change headers and footers for the entire document, huh? Thought you had that problem licked by dividing the document into sections? Well, almost. You forgot one thing— you need to break the connection between the headers or footers across sections.

How to fix it

To break the connection between the sections, on the View menu, click Header And Footer. On the Header And Footer toolbar, click the Show Next button until you are viewing the section you want to disconnect. Then, click the Same As Previous button to break the connection. ▶

> **Note**
> The section number appears in the title of the header or footer.

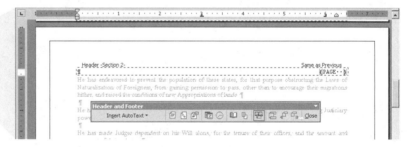

Certain buttons on the Header And Footer toolbar don't work

The Show Previous and Show Next buttons function only if the document is divided into sections whose headers and footers are not identical across the sections, if a section has different odd and even page headers or footers, or if a section contains a unique first page header or footer. If you click these buttons under any other conditions, nothing happens.

The Same As Previous button isn't available unless the document is divided into sections and you're viewing a header or footer for any section except Section 1. You can follow the logic here— if you're viewing the header or footer for Section 1, there *is* no previous section.

Page formatting

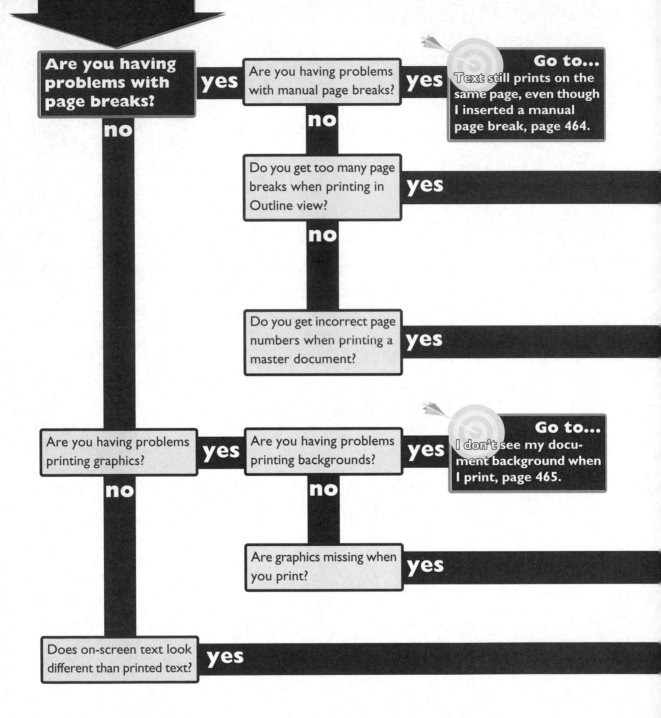

Are you having problems with page breaks?

yes → **Are you having problems with manual page breaks?**

    yes → **Go to...** Text still prints on the same page, even though I inserted a manual page break, page 464.

    no → **Do you get too many page breaks when printing in Outline view?**

        yes

    no → **Do you get incorrect page numbers when printing a master document?**

        yes

no → **Are you having problems printing graphics?**

    yes → **Are you having problems printing backgrounds?**

        yes → **Go to...** I don't see my document background when I print, page 465.

        no → **Are graphics missing when you print?**

            yes

    no → **Does on-screen text look different than printed text?**

        yes

Quick fix
If only a few headings print per page in Outline view, you have manual page breaks in the document. To temporarily remove them, save the document, delete the page breaks, and then print. Close without saving.

Quick fix
To avoid different page numbers and headers appearing at the beginning of each section when you print a master document, set these formatting elements in the master document, not the subdocument.

Go to...
My document contains graphics that don't print, page 466.

Go to...
The appearance of printed text and on-screen text isn't the same, page 468.

If your solution isn't here, check this related chapter:

● Page formatting, page 450

Or see the general trouble-shooting tips on page xix.

Text still prints on the same page, even though I inserted a manual page break

Source of the problem

It seems totally unreasonable—when you insert a page break, you should get a page break. And, in most cases, you will. There's one combination of circumstances that will result in this problem, though. Typically, most people don't print hidden text, so you can assume that you're not printing hidden text. If you then format your manual page break as hidden text, Word pays no attention to the manual page break. You won't see the new page in Print Preview nor when you print the document.

How to fix it

To remove the hidden text format, follow these steps:

1. Switch to Normal view so that you can see the manual page break.

2. If you still don't see the manual page break, click the Show/Hide ¶ button on the Standard toolbar to view hidden text. ▶

3. Click the page break to select it.

4. On the Format menu, click Font.

5. In the Font dialog box, clear the Hidden check box. ▶

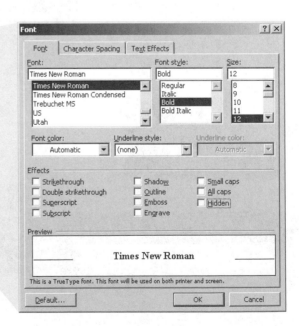

I don't see my document background when I print

Source of the problem

This problem doesn't have a satisfying answer. You see, document backgrounds are designed to appear only on your screen. They don't print. As a workaround, though, you can add a border or shading to your document, or you can create a printed watermark. These elements *will* print.

How to fix it

To add borders and shading, use the Borders And Shading dialog box. On the Format menu, click Borders And Shading. ▶

    To create a printed watermark, follow these steps:

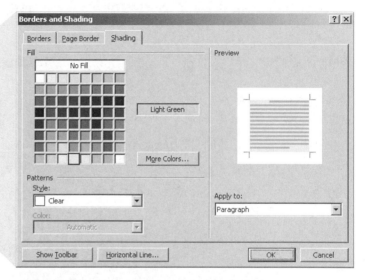

1. On the Format menu, point to Background.

2. Click Printed Watermark.

3. Click the type of watermark you want— a picture or text. ▶

4. Click OK.

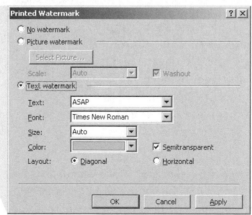

    If watermarks don't print on every page, your document is probably divided into different sections that contain different headers and footers. For example, you might have established a unique first page header, or you might have set up odd and even headers or footers. Simply insert the watermark again on the pages where you don't see it.

My document contains graphics that don't print

Source of the problem

You managed to get all those neat graphics into the document, and now they won't print! The only place you can see them is on screen, in Print Layout view, Print Preview, or Web Layout view (that's how you know they're there). The most common source of this problem lies with Word settings. However, you also can trace this problem to insufficient operating system resources (memory).

How to fix it

Before you start messing with system resources, check your settings. Follow these steps:

1. On the Tools menu, click **Options**.

2. Click the Print tab. ▶

3. Make sure that the Drawing Objects check box is selected.

4. If necessary, clear the Field Codes check box.

5. Click OK.

    If graphics still don't print, your printer might not have sufficient memory to print the selected graphics. If the document contains many graphics, select one, and copy it to a new document. If it prints, then you might have too many graphics in the original document. Break the document into smaller chunks for printing.
You can either:

- Divide the large document into smaller documents by cutting and pasting portions of the large document into new, smaller documents. You can print the individual files in order using only one Print command if you use INCLUDETEXT fields to connect the documents.

- Convert the large document into a master document and create individual subdocuments.

Note

When the Field Codes check box is selected and you're trying to print a graphic from a linked file, the graphic won't print.

If graphics *still* don't print, your system might not have sufficient resources to print graphics. Follow these steps:

1. Close and reopen Word and the document, and then try to print.

2. Close other programs that are running to free up the memory they're using. Then reopen the document, and try to print. If this doesn't help, then restart your computer, reopen Word and the document, and try to print.

3. Temporarily hide on-screen elements that you don't need while printing (these elements use memory). You'll need to switch to different views to hide all of these elements. From Print Layout view, you can hide picture placeholders, the status bar, and the horizontal and vertical scroll bars. From Normal view, you can hide the Style area. From any view, you can hide all toolbars.

- To hide Print Layout elements, switch to that view. On the Tools menu, click Options, and then click the View tab. Clear the check boxes for Picture Placeholders, Status Bar, Vertical Ruler, Horizontal Scroll Bar, and Vertical Scroll Bar.

- To hide the Style area, switch to Normal view. Reopen the Options dialog box, and in the Style Area Width box, type 0.

- To hide toolbars, right-click any toolbar. From the list that appears, click any toolbar that is selected to hide it (repeat this process until you've hidden all toolbars).

4. Disconnect any network connections, and then close programs that run behind the scenes. You'll find these listed in Windows Task Manager. Press Ctrl+Alt+Delete, click the Task Manager button, and select the Applications tab.

Before you start

Before you try the last item, be aware that ending programs can have unexpected results. Your system could become unstable. If this occurs, reboot your computer.

The appearance of printed text and on-screen text isn't the same

Source of the problem

There are several reasons why the on-screen appearance of your document might not match its printed appearance. For example, you might be trying to print animation effects. Or, Word could be displaying or printing your document with draft fonts. Or, the on-screen font you're using might not be the same as the font that prints—or vice versa. It's also possible that margins are being ignored when you print, and text is running off the edge of the page. Last, your document might not paginate as you expect; for example, too little material might print on an 8.5" × 11" page, even though you don't have manual page breaks in your document that would force material onto a new page.

How to fix it

Let's start by talking about animated effects. They don't print, so you're out of luck. Word will print the actual text, but the animation part is designed for screen viewing only.

Whenever you're dealing with appearance problems, use Print Layout view or Print Preview before you print. In Print Layout view, you can see the position of page specific elements like headers, footers, or graphics on screen and when you print. In Print Preview, you also can magnify and reduce the size of pages and see multiple pages at one time.

If things look squirrelly in Print Layout view or Print Preview, try the following suggestions to clear up the problems:

● To check for draft font issues, on the Tools menu, click Options. To make sure that Word isn't displaying draft fonts, click the View tab and clear the Draft Font check box in the Outline And Normal Options section. To make sure that Word isn't printing draft fonts, click the Print tab and clear the Draft Output check box. ▼

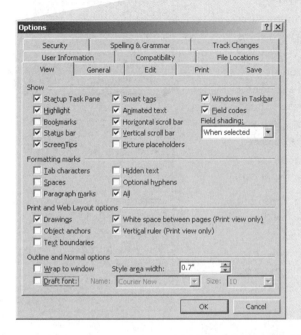

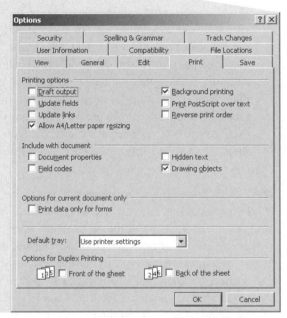

● It's possible that the on-screen font you're using might not be the same as the font that prints—or vice versa. If the font you're using is available on your printer but not on screen, Windows, which controls printing, substitutes a TrueType font. You can try switching to a different TrueType font that more closely matches the printer font. If the font you're using on screen is *not* available on your printer, change the on-screen font to a different TrueType font that more closely matches a printer font, or select a font that is available on your printer. In the figure, the symbol next to Brougham indicates a printer font, while the symbol next to Calisto MT below it represents a TrueType font. You can change fonts by selecting your text and clicking the Font list on the Formatting toolbar. ▶

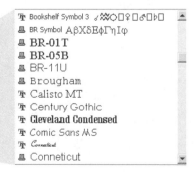

The appearance of printed text and on-screen text isn't the same

(continued from page 469)

- If Word seems to be ignoring your margins and text is running off the page, check to make sure that you and Word agree on the printer to which you're printing. Along with the text and graphics in your document, Word saves the name of the printer that was active when you saved the document. You'll see this problem a lot if you share documents with other people who use a different printer than you use. On the File menu, click Print. In the Name box, click the name of the printer you want to use. If you're using the correct printer, make sure that you've selected the correct paper size in the Page Setup dialog box. On the File menu, click Page Setup, and then select the Paper tab.

- If your document doesn't paginate as you expect, you might be printing a document that was formatted for a different paper size—again, a common problem when you share documents with others. You can format the document to your printer's paper size by clicking File, Print. In the Zoom section, click the Scale To Paper Size list, and then click the paper size you want to use. The Scale To Paper Size feature enlarges or reduces the output in the same way that a photocopy machine can enlarge or reduce a copy. ▶

Note

It's a common misconception that each program controls printing. In MS-DOS, programs did control printing. But, with the advent of Windows, the operating system began controlling printing.

Tip

If you plan to return the document to the originator, save before you change printer and page settings. Don't save *after* changing printer and page settings. That way, you won't mess up the settings for the originator, who might not own a copy of this book.

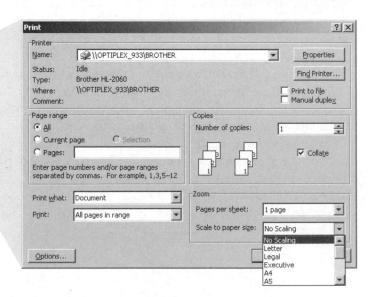

Have custom commands or macros quit working? **yes**

no

Are you getting macro warnings? **yes** → Are you getting warnings about digital signatures? **yes**

no **no**

Are macros disabled that used to work? **yes**

Go to...
I get warnings about macros being disabled for the current template, page 478.

no

Did you give someone a file containing macros that work on your computer, but they get warnings? **yes**

Do you want to add a certificate to the list of trusted sources? **yes**

Go to...
I want to update the list of trusted sources with a new certificate, page 480.

no

Are you having trouble changing macro security levels? **yes**

Go to...
Wizards, custom commands, and macros that used to work don't work, page 474.

Go to...
When I open Word, I see warnings about expiring digital signatures, page 476.

Quick fix
If you signed macros using the **SelfCert tool,** others can run them only if they set macro security to Medium or Low.

1. On the Tools menu, click Options.

2. Click the Security tab, and then click the Macro Security button.

3. On the Security Level tab, click Medium or Low.

Quick fix
If you can't change the macro security level, check with your network administrator, who might have enforced a security level for your workgroup to help you avoid viruses.

If your solution isn't here, check this related chapter:

● Templates and styles, page 106

Or see the general trouble-shooting tips on page xix.

Wizards, custom commands, and macros that used to work don't work

Source of the problem

That's right—certain features that worked fine in other versions of Word just don't work in Word 2002. The probable source of this problem lies with Visual Basic for Applications (VBA)—or should we say the lack of VBA. If wizards, templates, custom commands, and macros don't work, VBA might not be installed.

How to fix it

To reenable VBA, follow these steps:

1. Quit all programs.

2. Click Start, and point to Settings.

3. Click Control Panel.

4. Double-click Add/Remove Programs.

5. Click Microsoft Office XP or the name of your program.

6. Click the Change button.

7. Click Add Or Remove Features, and click Next.

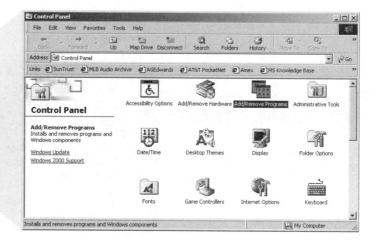

8. Click the plus sign (+) next to Office Shared Features.

9. Click the icon next to Visual Basic For Applications.

10. Click Run From My Computer, and click Update. ▶

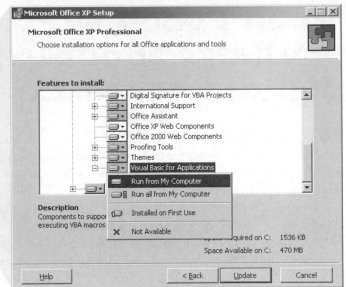

When I open Word, I see warnings about expiring digital signatures

Source of the problem

And Word doesn't even bother to tell you *what* a digital signature is. At this point, all you know is that you get an annoying message that allows you to use the macros, but you have to enable them every time you open Word.

If you understand what a digital signature is, you might still be annoyed by the warning, but at least you can take steps to resolve the issue.

A digital signature is a stamp of authentication on a macro that confirms that the macro came from the signer and has not been altered. Digital signatures help to ensure that macros you allow to run on your computer came from a known source that you can trust. Digital signatures are electronic, as their name implies, and they are encrypted to make sure that nobody can steal the signature. In this day and age of malicious people who seem to have nothing better to do than wipe out your computer with a virus, digital signatures can become your best friends. Digital signatures are valid for a specified period of time; when that time has passed, you start seeing messages about digital signatures expiring.

How to fix it

Temporarily, you can do what you've been doing. If you need to use the macros and you know they won't harm your computer, enable them every time the message pops up by clicking the Enable Macros button. ▶

For the long term, you can contact the source of the macro and obtain an updated certificate. Once you install the updated certificate, you'll no longer see the message. You can click the Details button to see who signed the macro.

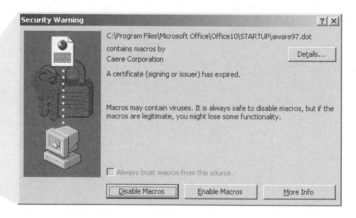

When you receive the certificate—which is actually a file—you can install it from the warning message. Follow these steps:

1. Click the Details button.

2. Click the View Certificate button. ▶

3. Click the Install Certificate button. The Certificate Import Wizard starts.

4. Click Next.

5. Click Automatically Select The Certificate Store Based On The Type Of Certificate. ▼

6. Click Next.

7. Click Finish.

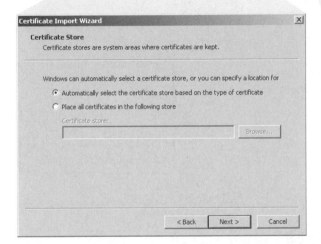

When you can't find the macro source

If you can't contact the macro source for some reason, decide whether you still need the macros. Typically, they load as an add-in that you'll find in the Startup folder. If you don't need the macros anymore, remove the add-ins from the Startup folder. Follow these steps:

1. In the Security Warning dialog box, note the name of the add-in containing the expired certificate.

2. Close Word.

3. In either Windows Explorer or My Computer, find the Office Startup folder. The default location is C:\Program Files\Microsoft Office\Office10\Startup.

4. Rename the add-in containing the expired certificate or drag it to a different folder.

5. Repeat Steps 3 through 4 for the items in the Word Startup folder: C:\Documents and Settings*User Name*\Application Data\Microsoft\Word\Startup.

I get warnings about macros being disabled for the current template

Source of the problem

You'll see this message— which is designed to protect you from the crazies of the world who seem to enjoy destroying hard disks—if you've set macro security to either Medium or High, and Word tries to run a digitally signed macro that is not from a known source.

How to fix it

Okay, it isn't tough to solve this problem. Check to see if the Trust All Installed Add-Ins And Templates check box is selected. It should be. Follow these steps:

1. On the Tools menu, click Options.

2. Click the Security tab.

3. Click the Macro Security button.

4. Click the Trusted Sources tab.

5. Select the Trust All Installed Add-Ins And Templates check box. ▶

> **Note**
>
> Microsoft digitally signs all templates, add-ins, and macros shipped with Microsoft Office XP. You only need to add Microsoft to your list of trusted sources once; all subsequent use of these files will not generate messages.

The template is "missing in action"

If you upgraded to Word 2002 or Office XP from Office 97 or earlier and you open a document you originally created in the earlier version of Word, you might see a message about macros that used to work being disabled. In this case, Word is looking for the template in the wrong location. If the template location is incorrect, Word "disables" the macro because it can't find the macro.

In Office 97 and earlier, templates were stored in C:\Program Files\MS Office\Templates. In Office 2000 and later, templates are stored in C:\Windows\Application Data\Microsoft\Templates.

Suppose that you moved your personally created templates to the new location where Office XP stores templates. You then tried to open an existing document based on one of your personally created templates—and the template contained macros. Word will disable the macros because it will be looking for the template in the old location.

Follow these steps to check the template location:

- On the Tools menu, click Templates And Add-Ins.

- Check the path listed in the Document Template box.

- Change the path to the correct location for the template. Word will then reenable the macros.

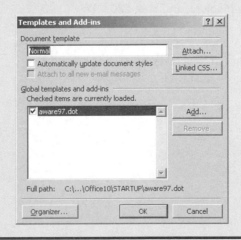

I want to update the list of trusted sources with a new certificate

Source of the problem

A "trusted source" is a person or company that wrote a macro or add-in that you have designated as "okay"—that is, you've told Word it's okay to run macros or add-ins from the trusted source. If you receive a new file from a known source and want to stop seeing the messages prompting you to enable the macros, you can add the certificate of the trusted source to the list of trusted sources.

Before you start

Internet Explorer 4.0 or later must be installed.

How to fix it

You need to set macro security to either Medium or High before you can add a macro developer to the trusted source list. If you suspect that macro security is disabled or set to Low, follow Steps 1 through 6. If you know that macro security is enabled, start with Step 7.

1. On the Tools menu, click Options.

2. Click the Security tab.

3. Click the Macro Security button.

4. Click the Security Level tab.

5. Click High or Medium, and click OK. ▶

6. Close Word.

7. Open Word and, if necessary, open the new file containing the macros.

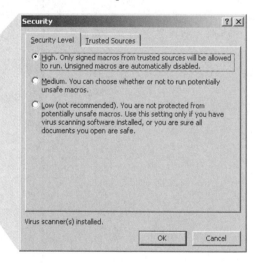

8. In the Security Warning box that appears, select the Always Trust Macros From This Source check box. ▶

9. Click Enable Macros.

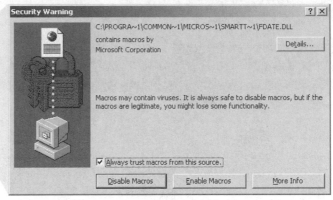

◎ Note

If you have installed an add-in that contains the macros, it will load when you open Word.

◎ Note

You can create digital certificates with the SelfCert tool that comes with Office XP; however, Word considers these certificates unauthenticated. As such, you can add these certificates to the list of trusted sources only on the computer on which the certificates were created.

◎ When you can't add a macro developer to the list of trusted sources

Even if you have Internet Explorer 4.0 on your computer, you might not be able to add a macro developer to the list of trusted sources because your system administrator might not permit you to add new macro developers. Or, the developer of the macro might not have digitally signed the macro. Or, the digital certificate might not be authenticated. Authentication is the process used to confirm that the developer of the macro is, indeed, the developer of the macro. What do we mean? Digital certificates can be created by anyone—and therefore, they can be forged to look like they come from someone other than the signer. Authentication helps eliminate bogus digital certificates. It's like having a handwriting analyst determine whether your signature is original or a forgery. Word accepts only authenticated digital certificates. You should expect professional software developers to sign their work with authenticated certificates.

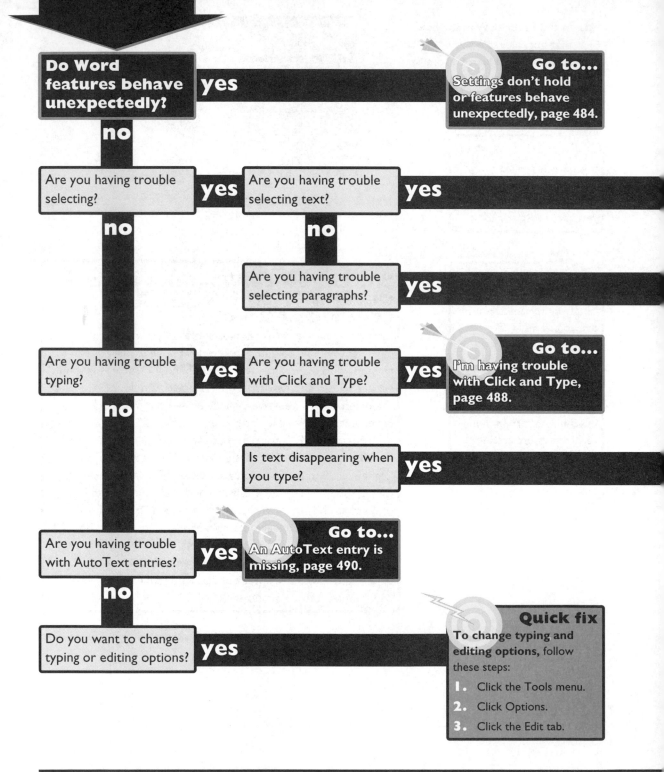

Do Word features behave unexpectedly? — **yes** →

Go to...
Settings don't hold or features behave unexpectedly, page 484.

no ↓

Are you having trouble selecting? — **yes** → **Are you having trouble selecting text?** — **yes** →

no ↓   **no** ↓

Are you having trouble selecting paragraphs? — **yes** →

Are you having trouble typing? — **yes** → **Are you having trouble with Click and Type?** — **yes** →

Go to...
I'm having trouble with Click and Type, page 488.

no ↓   **no** ↓

Is text disappearing when you type? — **yes** →

Are you having trouble with AutoText entries? — **yes** →

Go to...
An AutoText entry is missing, page 490.

no ↓

Do you want to change typing or editing options? — **yes** →

Quick fix
To change typing and editing options, follow these steps:
1. Click the Tools menu.
2. Click Options.
3. Click the Edit tab.

Quick fix

To stop selecting text when you click the mouse or press a key, press Esc to cancel Extend Selection mode (EXT appears on the status bar).

Quick fix

To stop selecting the paragraph mark when you select a paragraph, clear the Use Smart Paragraph Selection check box in the Options dialog box.

Quick fix

If text is disappearing as you type, turn off Overtype mode (OVR appears on the status bar) by pressing the Insert key on your keyboard.

If your solution isn't here, check this related chapter:

- Editing, page 32

Or see the general troubleshooting tips on page xix.

Settings don't hold or features behave unexpectedly

Source of the problem

No, you are *not* losing your mind. Weird things are happening. You like to display the Style area in Normal and Outline views, but it keeps disappearing. You turn on revision marks, and text you mark for deletion doesn't appear with strikethrough formatting; instead, it appears in the "add text" color and format. Strange things *are* happening. You are *not* imagining it.

When Word starts, it loads the following components in the order listed:

- Word auto macros
- Word Data key in the Windows Registry
- The Normal template (Normal.dot)
- Add-ins and templates in the Word and Office Startup folders
- COM add-ins
- Word Options key in the Windows Registry

Strange behavior in Word versions later than Word 6 usually can be traced to one of these sources.

> ### Before you start
>
> To fix this problem, you might need to edit the Registry, which, if done incorrectly, can make your computer unusable. Before you edit the Registry, back it up and make sure you understand how to restore it. View the "Backing Up Registry Files" and "Restoring the Registry" Help topics in regedit.exe.

How to fix it

Approach this fix by testing one component at a time.

Test the Normal template

The easiest component to test for flaky behavior is the Normal template. To test the Normal template, create a new Normal template. Follow these steps:

1. Close Word.

2. Click Start.

3. Point to Search (Find, in Windows 98 or Windows NT).

4. Click For Files And Folders.

5. In the Search For Files Or Folders Named box, type **Normal.dot**.

6. Set the Look In box to search your local hard disk.

7. Click Search Now.

8. Rename each Normal.dot file found by right-clicking each file, clicking Rename, and providing a new name.

9. Close the Search Results window or Find box and start Word.

Word will create a new Normal.dot template that won't contain any of your customizations. If Word doesn't behave strangely, your problem is resolved.

Disable auto macros

If Word is still behaving strangely, disable auto macros from running when you start Word. An *auto macro* is a macro that runs when you start Word. To disable auto macros, press and hold the Shift key while you click the icon to run Word. Then, test for strange behavior. If Word stops behaving strangely, auto macros are probably the source of your problem. If possible, you should delete any auto macros that exist in the template. On the Tools menu, point to Macros, and then click Macros. In the Macros dialog box, highlight each macro that begins with "Auto" and click the Delete button. If the Delete button is gray, you won't be able to delete the auto macro. But, auto macros are stored in a template, just like all other macros. The odds are good that the culprit is being loaded by a template in the Startup folder. See the next section to learn how to disable templates in the Startup folder—and thereby permanently disable auto macros.

Disable Startup folder items

If Word is still behaving strangely, remove add-ins and templates from the Word and Office Startup folders. Follow these steps:

1. Close Word (and Outlook if you use Word as your e-mail editor).

2. In either Windows Explorer or My Computer, find the Office Startup folder. The default location is C:\Program Files\Microsoft Office\Office10\Startup.

3. Rename each item in the folder or drag each item to a different folder.

4. Repeat Steps 2 through 3 for the items in the Word Startup folder. The Word Startup folder location is C:\Documents and Settings*User Name*\Application Data\Microsoft\Word\Startup.

Note

An auto macro could have been added by a Word add-in template. To determine which template contains the auto macro, change the Macros In box to a listed template. After you identify the template that contains the auto macro, you might want to remove that template from your system. Removing a template that was added by a Word add-in will remove the functionality the add-in provides.

Settings don't hold or features behave unexpectedly

(continued from page 485)

Restart Word. If Word doesn't behave strangely and you removed multiple items, add the items back in one at a time, opening and testing Word after each item you add to isolate the add-in or template that is causing the problem.

Re-create Registry keys

If Word is still behaving strangely, close Word (and all Office programs) and try deleting two Registry keys. When you reopen Word, Word will re-create fresh copies of these keys. Follow these steps:

1. Click Start, and then click Run.

2. Type **regedit** and click OK.

3. In the Registry Editor, find and click the following key: HKEY_CURRENT_USER\ Software\Microsoft\Office\ 10.0\Word\Data. ▶

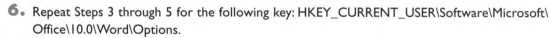

4. On the Edit menu, click Delete.

5. Click Yes to confirm deleting the Data key.

6. Repeat Steps 3 through 5 for the following key: HKEY_CURRENT_USER\Software\Microsoft\ Office\10.0\Word\Options.

7. Close the Registry Editor and start Word.

Disable COM add-ins

If Word is still behaving strangely, disable COM add-ins. COM add-ins are installed by programs that interact with Word and can be installed anywhere on your computer. To see a list of installed COM add-ins, follow these steps:

1. On the Tools menu, click Customize.

2. Click the Commands tab.

3. In the Categories list, click Tools. ▶

4. Drag the COM Add-Ins command to any toolbar.

5. Click Close.

6. Click the new COM Add-Ins button to view the COM add-ins that load with Word. ▼

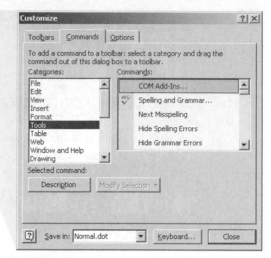

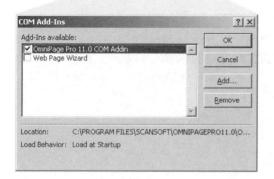

7. If add-ins appear in the COM Add-Ins dialog box, temporarily turn off each of the add-ins by clearing the check box next to each COM add-in.

8. Click OK.

9. Exit and restart Microsoft Word.

Word starts without loading the COM add-ins. If you disabled multiple add-ins and the problem is resolved, reenable them one at a time to determine which add-in is causing the problem. Remember to restart Word after enabling each add-in.

I'm having trouble with Click and Type

Source of the problem

The name implies that you don't need to do anything other than—well, click and type. But Click and Type can be tricky because contrary to what you might expect, it doesn't "just work." You need to check some settings and make sure that you understand the conditions under which Click and Type is available.

How to fix it

Follow these steps to use the Click and Type feature.

1. To make sure that the Click and Type feature is enabled, on the Tools menu, click Options. On the Edit tab, select the Enable Click And Type check box. ▶

2. Make sure that you're working in either Print Layout view or Web Layout view. Click and Type is not available in Normal view or Outline view.

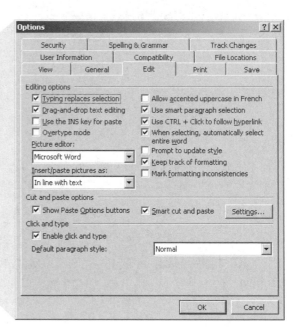

3. In the document, move the mouse pointer to a blank area. You should see the Click and Type pointer, which changes as you move the mouse pointer around the screen.

4. Double-click. Word positions the insertion point at the location where you double-clicked. As you type, the text will be formatted based on the shape of the Click and Type pointer. ▶

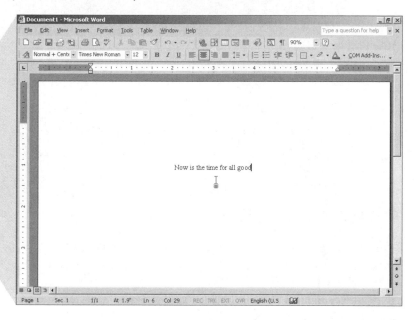

Places where you can't use Click and Type

There are places and situations where Click and Type doesn't work. You can't use Click and Type:

- In bulleted and numbered lists

- To the left or right of indents

- Next to floating objects

- To the left or right of pictures with top and bottom text wrapping

- While you're recording a macro

An AutoText entry is missing

Source of the problem

AutoText entries are supposed to speed up your typing and editing by letting you automatically insert text using an abbreviation for the text. But, if you can't *find* an AutoText entry, it can't help you.

You can trace missing AutoText entries to any of the following:

● The template you're using

● The style of the paragraph containing the insertion point

● The language of the paragraph containing the insertion point

How to fix it

Word stores AutoText entries in the current template. If you stored your AutoText entry in the Brochure template, it won't be available while you work on a document based on the Magazine template. But, you can copy AutoText entries from one template to another.

On the Tools menu, click Templates And Add-Ins. The current template's name appears in the Document Template box. Click the Organizer button, and then click the AutoText tab to copy the AutoText entries you want into the current template. ▶

Word displays a list of AutoText entries when you click the Insert menu and point to AutoText. However, this list can be incomplete because it only shows the AutoText entries that are available for the style of the paragraph containing the insertion point.

Tip

AutoText entries that you store in the Normal template are available while you work in any template.

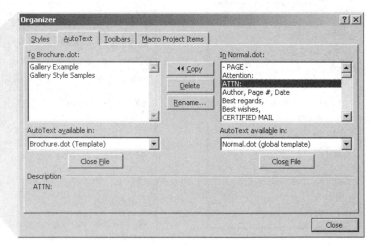

To see all AutoText entries available in the document template, on the Insert menu, point to AutoText, and then click AutoText. ▶

All AutoText entries in the template are listed on the AutoText tab of the AutoCorrect dialog box. ▼

If you have turned on automatic language detection, what you see isn't always what you get. The entries on the AutoText menu correspond to the language of the paragraph containing the insertion point. However, you'll see entries based on the language of the Normal template on the AutoText tab in the AutoCorrect dialog box. For example, suppose that you are using the English version of Word—therefore, your Normal template is in English—and you type one paragraph in Spanish. If you leave the insertion point in the Spanish paragraph and display the AutoText entries on the AutoText menu, the list will be in Spanish. But, if you open the AutoCorrect box, the AutoText entries will be in English.

Note

If you insert an AutoText field using the Field dialog box (on the Insert menu, click the Field command), the Field dialog box, like the AutoText tab in the AutoCorrect dialog box, reflects the language version of Word that you are using, not the language in which you are typing.

Are you having trouble with styles?

yes

no

Are you having trouble with character formatting?

yes

Are you trying to underline blanks?

yes

no

Go to...

I need to underline a blank line or a space, but I can't figure out how to do it, page 498.

Are you losing character formatting?

yes

Quick fix

To avoid changing or losing character formatting when you apply a style, apply the style first, and then format the characters.

Text formatting

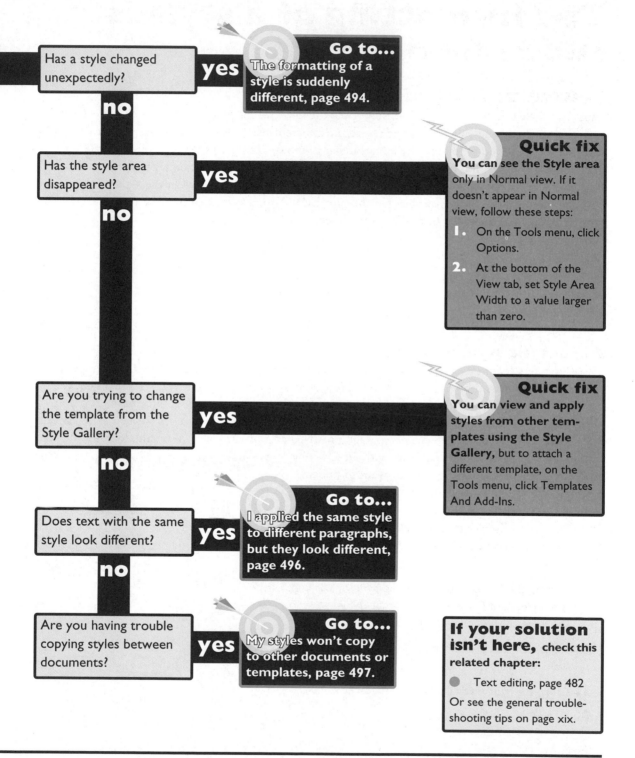

Has a style changed unexpectedly?

yes → **Go to...** The formatting of a style is suddenly different, page 494.

no

Has the style area disappeared?

yes → **Quick fix** You can see the Style area only in Normal view. If it doesn't appear in Normal view, follow these steps:
1. On the Tools menu, click Options.
2. At the bottom of the View tab, set Style Area Width to a value larger than zero.

no

Are you trying to change the template from the Style Gallery?

yes → **Quick fix** You can view and apply styles from other templates using the **Style Gallery,** but to attach a different template, on the Tools menu, click Templates And Add-Ins.

no

Does text with the same style look different?

yes → **Go to...** I applied the same style to different paragraphs, but they look different, page 496.

no

Are you having trouble copying styles between documents?

yes → **Go to...** My styles won't copy to other documents or templates, page 497.

If your solution isn't here, check this related chapter:
- Text editing, page 482

Or see the general trouble-shooting tips on page xix.

The formatting of a style is suddenly different

Source of the problem

Most people use styles to ensure that they apply the same formatting consistently. So, when a style that you've been using suddenly changes—for no apparent reason—you might get a bit frustrated.

There are several reasons a style might change unexpectedly. But you can relax, because all of them can be fixed. For example, either the style or the template might be set to automatically update whenever you make changes to a style—features you can turn off. Or, the style might be based on another style, and you changed the root style. Also, it's possible that the template containing the style is damaged or missing altogether.

How to fix it

Let's examine each possibility.

Automatic style updating

Word uses this feature to help you maintain consistency in your document formatting. Suppose that you've established bold and italics for a Note style and you've typed several notes. Then, you decide that you really want the Note style to include italics and underlining, but not bold. If you allow Word to automatically update the style, Word will change all occurrences of text styled in the Note style when you modify even one paragraph styled as Note. If you turn off the feature, you can modify one paragraph styled as Note without affecting any of the others. Then, when you *do* want to update all of the paragraphs styled as Note, you'll need to change the style itself instead of a particular paragraph styled as Note. You can turn off automatic updating for a particular style by modifying the style. Follow these steps:

1. Display the Styles And Formatting pane by clicking the Styles And Formatting button at the left edge of the Formatting toolbar. ▶

2. Right-click the style that you want to change, and then click Modify.

3. Clear the Automatically Update check box. ▶

4. Click OK.

Changing styles in a template

Suppose that you've created several documents using a particular template. Further suppose that you modified the appearance of a style in that template. When you reopen one of the documents you created prior to modifying the template, you might find that the styles in the document updated to reflect the changes you made in the template.

This phenomenon occurs because of a check mark in one little check box. With the document open, click the Tools menu, and then click Templates And Add-Ins. Clear the Automatically Update Document Styles check box, click OK, and save the document. Repeat this procedure for all the documents you want to retain their original formatting. Do this *before* you change the documents' template. ▶

Basing styles on styles

Styles can be based on other styles; if you change the root style, all of the styles based on that root style will assume the same changes. Suppose that you create a Tip style and you base it on the Note style we talked about earlier. When you change the Note style to include italics and underlining but not bold, you'll also change the Tip style. The most common surprise for most users occurs when they make a change to the font of the Normal style—because many styles (page numbers, headers, footers, and footnotes, to name a few) are based on the Normal style; changing the font of the Normal style changes the font of all those styles as well. To avoid changing other styles when you change a root style, define styles so that they are not based on other styles (unless, of course, you *want* a whole series of styles to change simultaneously). In the Styles And Formatting pane, right-click the style that is based on another style, and then click Modify. Open the Style Based On list, and click (No Style).

Missing template

Word stores the template upon which a document is based with the document. If you open the document and for some reason Word can't find the template, Word takes definitions for the template's styles from the Normal template. In this case, you only have two choices—restore a backup of the missing template or re-create the missing template.

I applied the same style to different paragraphs, but they look different

Source of the problem

Now here's a mystery—particularly when you consider that styles are designed to guarantee consistency. This makes no sense, right?

Well, this can happen if you formatted some text manually. The slick part of this solution is that Word's Reveal Formatting pane can actually identify the differences so that you can correct the problem.

How to fix it

1. On the Format menu, click Reveal Formatting.

2. Select one group of text that you want to compare.

3. Select the Compare To Another Selection check box in the Reveal Formatting task pane.

4. Select the second group of text that you want to compare.

In the Formatting Differences section of the task pane, you'll see a description of any differences between the two selections. ▶

Text formatting

My styles won't copy to other documents or templates

Source of the problem

Talk about frustration. You work very hard to make a style look just the way you want, and then you try to copy the style between documents or templates and can't! We know you're sitting there tearing your hair out while you contemplate re-creating the style many times for many documents and templates. Don't tear your hair out and don't re-create the style. The problem is probably related to restricted access to the document or template to which you want to copy styles.

How to fix it

Your access to the document or template to which you want to copy a style could be restricted. For example, the originator of the document or template might have protected it except for comments or tracked changes, or made it a read-only file, requiring a password to open the document or template. You can try to remove protection: on the Tools menu, click Unprotect Document. If the document is protected with a password, you must know the password before you can remove protection from the document.

If you don't know the password, you can open the document or template, but you can't save changes to it. You can, however, give it a different file name when you save it. ▶

There's one other way your access could be restricted: if the document or template you're trying to access is on a network, you might not have the user privileges necessary to save changes to it. In this case, you should check with your network administrator to obtain privileges.

Password   ? ✕

'MainMerge.doc' is reserved by Elaine Marmel

Enter password to modify, or open read only.

Password: _____

[Read Only]   [OK]   [Cancel]

I need to underline a blank line or a space, but I can't figure out how to do it

Source of the problem

You're trying to use the Underline button on the Formatting toolbar, right? If so, you're absolutely right—you *can't* underline a blank line or a space.

But, there are ways.

How to fix it

We have three possible solutions to your problem.

Solution #1

You can add a border to the bottom edge of the paragraph that contains the blank line or space. Select the paragraph, and then click the Bottom Border button on the Formatting toolbar.

Solution #2

You can use the underscore character (the uppercase compatriot of the hyphen).

Solution #3

You can type nonbreaking spaces, which look like blanks, where you want the underline to appear. Although nonbreaking spaces look like blanks, they are actually characters—and you know how to underline characters.

To type a nonbreaking space, press and hold the Ctrl and Shift keys, and then press the Spacebar. After you enter the nonbreaking spaces, select them, and click Underline on the Formatting toolbar.

> ### Note
> For inquiring minds: most people use nonbreaking spaces to prevent words that should appear together from breaking if they fall at the end of a line. For example, you might include a nonbreaking space between Mrs. and Smith to make sure that Mrs. Smith appears together on one line.

I'm having trouble with the alignment of underline formatting for subscript and normal text

You underlined some regular text. Then, you applied subscript formatting to a portion of the underlined text. In all probability, the underlines of the regular and subscripted text don't line up. Here's a trick to try. Don't underline the text; instead, draw a line under it using the Line button on the Drawing toolbar. To display the toolbar, right-click any toolbar, and then click Drawing. To draw a perfectly straight line, hold down the Shift key as you draw.

Are you having trouble with hyperlinks? **yes**

no

Do the horizontal scroll bars disappear when you display a Web frames page? **yes**

no

Do you see tags instead of content? **yes**

Go to...
Instead of my Web page content, <HTML> or other tags appear, page 502.

no

Are you having trouble positioning text or graphics on Web pages? **yes**

Go to...
When I save as a Web page, some text and graphics change positions, page 506.

no

Are you having trouble with frames? **yes** Does a document appear in the wrong frame? **yes**

no

Do you want to delete a frame? **yes**

Go to...
I'm having trouble with hyperlinks, page 504.

Quick fix
If horizontal scroll bars do not appear in your Web frames page, follow these steps:

1. On the Tools menu, click Options.
2. Click the View tab.
3. Select the Horizontal Scroll Bar check box.

Go to...
My document appears in the wrong place on the Web page, page 507.

Quick fix
You can't delete a frame with the Undo command. Instead, click the frame, and then click Delete Frames on the Frames toolbar.

If your solution isn't here, check this related chapter:

● Web publishing, page 116

Or see the general trouble-shooting tips on page xix.

Instead of my Web page content, <HTML> or other tags appear

Source of the problem

If you see letters in angle brackets, such as <HTML>, <HEAD>, and <P>, instead of the content of your Web page, it isn't Greek—nor is it any other foreign language. Unless, of course, you consider computer code a foreign language (and some could make a case for that).

You might be viewing the HTML source for this file instead of browser content. Or, you might be viewing HTML tags in the Microsoft Script Editor.

How to fix it

You might find yourself viewing the HTML source if you opened a file that contains Web page formatting but doesn't use a file name extension of .html, .htm, .htx, .asp, or .otm. You need to change your options if you see the HTML source for a file instead of browser content. To change your options and avoid this problem in the future, follow these steps:

1. On the Tools menu, click Options.

2. Click the General tab.

3. Select the Confirm Conversion At Open check box. ▶

4. Click OK.

5. Close the file, and then reopen it in Word.

6. In the Convert File dialog box, click HTML Document.

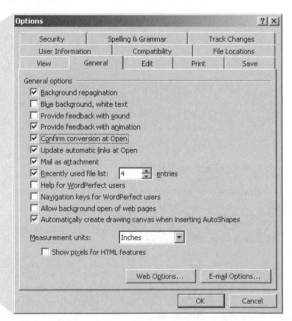

If your screen resembles the one in the figure, you're viewing HTML tags in the Microsoft Script Editor. You got here by opening a Web document, clicking the View menu, and then clicking HTML Source. To return to a world you recognize, on the File menu, click Exit. ▶

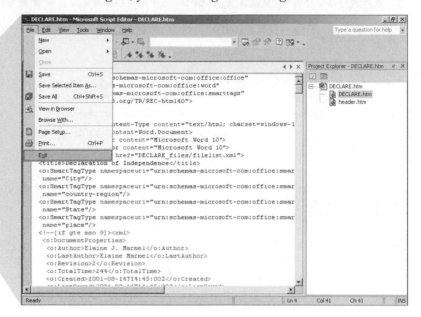

I'm having trouble with hyperlinks

Source of the problem

Hyperlinks can be tricky little rascals, behaving in unexpected ways. For example, you click a hyperlink and nothing happens, or a hyperlink goes to the wrong destination. Or, the hyperlink commands on the shortcut menu might seem to mysteriously disappear.

All of these problems can be resolved.

How to fix it

If nothing happens when you click a hyperlink or if a hyperlink takes you to the wrong place, it's possible that you can't connect to the destination. If the destination file is on the Internet, make sure your Internet connection is working. If the destination is on a network, make sure you're logged onto the network. Then, contact your network administrator to ensure you have rights to use the destination file.

It's also possible that you typed in the destination incorrectly when you created the link or that someone moved the destination since the time you created the hyperlink. Check the destination of the hyperlink. View the destination file in your Web browser if the file is on the Internet, or view it in Windows Explorer if the file is on your hard disk or a network. Then, check the hyperlink to make sure it is pointing to the location where you viewed the destination file. Follow these steps:

1. Right-click the hyperlink.

2. Click Edit Hyperlink.

3. Double-check the information that appears in the Look In box and in the Address box. ▶

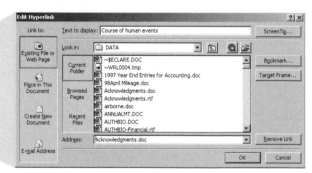

Now this next one might sound really weird, but if nothing happens when you click a hyperlink, it's possible that somebody formatted text to *look* like a hyperlink but didn't actually create a hyperlink. If you know the destination of the hyperlink, you can convert the formatted text into a hyperlink by selecting the text, clicking the Insert menu, and then clicking Hyperlink.

Okay, your hyperlink works, but you can't get the shortcut menu containing the Hyperlink commands to display. And you won't see the menu if Word is automatically checking for proofing errors and the text of the hyperlink contains a grammatical or spelling error. You need to correct the spelling or grammatical problem. To correct proofing errors, right-click the suspect text, and then accept the suggested correction or click Ignore Once.

Note

You can identify text with suspected spelling errors by the red wavy underline beneath them; you'll see a green wavy underline beneath text with suspected grammatical errors.

When I save as a Web page, some text and graphics change positions

Source of the problem

Believe it or not, the probable source of this problem is Word's abundance of formatting options. You probably used one or more formatting options that most Web browsers do not support. Therefore, when you save or view your document as a Web page, some text and graphics might look different.

How to fix it

You can avoid the problem if you only use those formatting options that are supported by Web browsers. To steer clear of the Word formatting features that most browsers don't support, save your document as a Web page.

When you create documents for the Web, work in Web Layout view. In this view, you'll see your text and graphics the way they will appear when you view them as Web pages in a Web browser.

> **Tip**
> If you need to precisely align graphics and text, use tables.

> ## When you save graphics and objects in a Web page, they change to GIF or JPEG format
> To view graphics in Web browsers, you must use a GIF, JPEG, or PNG format. The Word designers were clever; they were aware of this fact. So, when you save your document as a Web page, Word converts all graphics and objects to a GIF, JPEG, or PNG format in preparation for Web browser viewing. Don't panic, though. When you reopen the Web page in Microsoft Word, the graphics and objects are back in their original formats so that you can edit them.

My document appears in the wrong place on the Web page

Source of the problem

You created a hyperlink. It's supposed to display a document in a particular frame on the Web page when you click it (we call that particular frame the *target frame*). You test the hyperlink, and it works—kind of. You see the document, but it isn't where you want it to be on the Web page. When you see this kind of behavior, it's likely that the target frame for the hyperlink is not correct.

How to fix it

To change the target frame for a hyperlink, follow these steps:

1. Right-click the hyperlink.

2. Click Edit Hyperlink.

3. Click the Target Frame button.

4. Click the Select The Frame Where You Want The Document To Appear list. ▶

5. Click the frame where you want the document to appear.

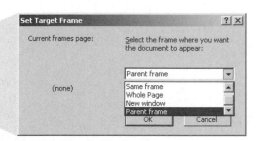

Glossary

3-D style A formatting setting you can apply to text or objects creating a three-dimensional effect.

absolute cell reference In Excel, the fixed address of a cell. An absolute cell reference takes the form $A$1. Absolute cell references are used in Excel formulas to ensure that a portion of a formula always points to a specific cell, even if the formula is copied to a different location.

action button In PowerPoint, a symbol you can draw on a slide and associate with an action, such as following a hyperlink.

active cell In Excel, the selected cell in which data is entered when you begin typing. Only one cell is active at a time. The active cell is bounded by a heavy border.

add-in A supplemental program that adds custom commands or custom features to Microsoft Office.

address The path to an object, document, file, or page. An address can be a URL (Web address) or a UNC path (network address) and can include a specific location within a file, such as a Word bookmark or an Excel cell range.

address book A collection of contact records in Outlook.

advance To move forward by one slide in a PowerPoint presentation.

alignment The arrangement of text or objects on a page. Typical alignment options include left or right aligned, centered, or justified.

animation In PowerPoint, animations are used to add movement to on-screen elements, such as text or graphics. Animations can be used to provide movement when elements first appear, when elements exit the slide, at a set time, or on a mouse click.

archive A process in Outlook that creates a backup copy of older e-mail messages and frees space in Outlook's public folders.

argument The values that a function uses to perform operations or calculations. Every function has its own specific arguments. Common arguments used within functions include numbers, text, cell references, and names.

authentication Process used to validate the source of a digital certificate for delivery of an e-mail attachment or used to signify a macro that is safe to run. If the security level enabled on the computer cannot authenticate the digital signature, the certificate is ignored or the user is prompted.

AutoContent   A wizard in PowerPoint that generates a presentation containing sample content based on user input regarding the type of presentation being created.

AutoCorrect   A feature in Microsoft Office programs that automatically corrects common typing and spelling errors or converts regular text characters to special symbols as you type.

AutoShapes   A group of ready-made shapes that includes basic shapes, such as rectangles and circles, plus a variety of lines and connectors, block arrows, flowchart symbols, stars and banners, and callouts.

background   The area of a PowerPoint slide behind the standard layout and any inserted elements to which you can apply a color or fill effect. Other Office programs can utilize backgrounds that add colors, pictures, or patterns behind the main material.

bookmark   In Word, a location or selection of text in a file that you name for reference purposes. Bookmarks identify a location within your file to which you can later refer or link.

broadcast   A live online presentation of PowerPoint slides that can include live narration and options for including audio and video streaming and can also be recorded for later playback.

cell reference   The letter and number combination that represents the row and column of a cell on a worksheet. For example, the reference of the cell that appears at the intersection of column B and row 3 is B3.

change history   In a shared workbook, information that is maintained about changes made in past editing sessions. The information includes the name of the person who made each change, when the change was made, and what data was changed.

chart area   The entire chart and all its elements.

chart sheet   A sheet in a workbook that contains only a chart. A chart sheet is beneficial when you want to view a chart or a PivotChart report separately from worksheet data or a PivotTable report.

Click and Type pointer shapes   In Word, these pointer shapes indicate which formatting will be applied when you double-click: a left-aligned, centered, or right-aligned paragraph; a left indent; or left or right text wrapping.

clip art   A collection of photos, line drawings, color illustrations, and other graphics that can be freely used in the creation of documents.

color scheme   In PowerPoint a predetermined set of colors that can be applied to slides in a presentation.

comma-separated file   Also called "comma-delimited file," a file containing data where individual field values are separated by a comma. Comma-separated files are most often used in importing and exporting operations, as are their cousins, the character-separated file and the tab-separated file.

comment   A note or annotation that an author or reviewer adds to a document. Microsoft Word displays the comment in a balloon in the margin of the document or in the Reviewing pane. PowerPoint displays a comment in a balloon on individual slides.

compare A feature that displays the differences between one document and another.

conditional format A format, such as cell shading or font color, that Excel automatically applies to cells if a specified condition is true.

connector A line used to connect objects in a diagram.

contact In Outlook, a contact is a saved record of a person or organization that includes information such as name, address, e-mail, phone, and fax number. Contacts are saved in address books.

Custom show A slide show assembled from one or more other slide shows that allows the creator to use only the slides needed in any order.

data label On an Excel chart, a label that provides additional information about a data marker, which represents a single data point or value.

data series Related data points that are plotted in a chart. Each data series in a chart has a unique color or pattern and is represented in the chart legend. You can plot one or more data series in a chart. Pie charts have only one data series.

data source In a Word mail merge operation, a file that contains the information to be merged into a document, such as the list of names and addresses you want to use in a mail merge. You must connect to the data source before you can use the information in it.

Database window The window that appears when you open an Access database or an Access project. It displays shortcuts for creating new database objects and opening existing objects.

design template A set of design elements on which the slides in a PowerPoint presentation can be based. Elements include font, color scheme, graphics, background effects, and so on.

digital certificate An attachment for a file, macro project, or e-mail message that vouches for its authenticity, provides secure encryption, or supplies a verifiable signature. To digitally sign macro projects, you must install a digital certificate.

digital signature An electronic, encryption-based, secure stamp of authentication on a macro or document. This signature confirms that the macro or document originated from the signer and has not been altered.

Distribute A drawing command that arranges two or more objects on a page or slide with equal spacing between them.

draft A saved version of an e-mail message in Outlook that has not yet been sent.

duplicate A copy of a slide in PowerPoint.

e-mail account An account established with an online provider that enables the account holder to send and access e-mail using Outlook after entering the e-mail account settings supplied by the online provider.

embedded chart A chart that is placed on a worksheet rather than on a separate chart sheet. Embedded charts are beneficial when you want to view or print a chart or a PivotChart report with its source data or other information in a worksheet.

embedded object Any object, such as a picture, chart, or spreadsheet, that is placed in a document, but originates from an external program. Once it is embedded, the object becomes part of the destination program. It can be edited by double-clicking it in the destination program. The tools from the source program then appear in the destination program to allow the object to be updated.

encoding The byte (or sequence of bytes) representing each character in an HTML or plain text file. Unicode encoding supports all characters in all languages and is readable in Microsoft Internet Explorer 4.0 or later and Netscape Navigator 4.0 or later.

export To save a document, database, or object to a file format other than the file format in which they were created so that another program can use (import) the contents. You can export documents to a variety of supported file formats.

external reference A reference to a cell, range, or defined name on a sheet in another Excel workbook.

Favorites The addresses of Internet sites that you save in order to easily access the sites from a list at a later time. Outlook maintains such a list of favorite online addresses.

field code A code that instructs Microsoft Word to insert text, graphics, page numbers, or other information into a document. For example, the DATE field inserts the current date. In a mail merge operation, field codes show where specified information from your data source will appear.

field results Text or graphics inserted in a document when Microsoft Word carries out a field's instructions. When you hide field codes, the field results replace the field codes.

fill color The color you select to fill the background of an object, such as an AutoShape or text box.

Fill handle In Excel, the small black square in the lower-right corner of the selection. When you point to the Fill handle, the pointer changes to a black cross and by dragging it, the cells selected can be filled with data derived from the original cells.

folder In Outlook, folders are used to store e-mail content. Public folders are accessible to several people sharing a network, based on the permissions they have to access them.

footer Text or graphics that appear at the bottom of every page. Footers often contain page numbers, chapter titles, dates, or author names.

Formula bar An area at the top of the Excel window that you use to enter or edit values or formulas in cells or charts. Displays the value or formula stored in the active cell.

formula A sequence of values, cell references, names, functions, or operators in a cell that together produce a new value. A formula always begins with an equal sign (=).

forward To send an e-mail you have received to another recipient.

frame A container that you can resize and position anywhere on the page. To position text or graphics that contain comments, footnotes, endnotes, or certain fields, you must use a frame instead of a text box. On Web pages, the named subwindow of a frames page. The frame appears in a Web browser as one of a number of window regions in which pages can be displayed. The frame can be scrollable and resizable, and it can have a border.

GIF   A graphics file format (.gif extension in Windows) used to display indexed color graphics on the World Wide Web. It supports up to 256 colors and uses lossless compression, meaning that no image data is lost when the file is compressed.

grayscale   A series of shades from black through white that delineate the details of computer graphics and images. Grayscale can represent a color document in a monochromatic environment such as a black and white monitor.

grid   In PowerPoint, a grid is a series of lines on a slide; you can set PowerPoint to snap objects you place on a slide to the nearest gridline.

group   To select multiple objects, usually graphics objects, and treat them as a single object for sizing, moving, and other editing functions.

guide   In PowerPoint, guides are movable horizontal and vertical lines used to position objects on a slide.

handout   In PowerPoint, a printing option that allows you to print out multiple slides on a page to hand out to an audience to follow along with your presentation.

Handout Master   *See* Master.

header   Text or graphics that appear at the top of every page in a section. Headers and footers often contain page numbers, chapter titles, dates, or author names.

heading style   Formatting applied to a heading. Microsoft Word has nine different built-in styles: Heading 1 through Heading 9.

hidden text   Character format that allows you to show or hide specified text. Microsoft Word indicates hidden text by underlining it with a dotted line.

History worksheet   A separate worksheet that lists changes made to a shared workbook. It includes the name of the person who made the change, when and where the change was made, what data was deleted or replaced, and how conflicts were resolved.

Hyperlink   Colored and underlined text or a graphic that you click to go to a file, a location in a file, an HTML page on the World Wide Web, or an HTML page on an intranet. Hyperlinks can also go to newsgroups and to Gopher, Telnet, and FTP sites.

Hypertext Markup Language (HTML)   The standard markup language used for documents on the World Wide Web. HTML uses tags to indicate how Web browsers should display page elements such as text and graphics and how to respond to user actions.

import   To bring a document, a database, or an object into one program from another program. You can import files created in a variety of supported file formats. In general, to bring any compatible content from one program or file format into another program or file format.

Inbox   The folder in Outlook where newly arrived e-mail is placed.

Journal A feature of Outlook that tracks activity involving documents, including documents attached to e-mail messages.

JPEG A graphics file format (.jpg extension in Microsoft Windows) supported by many Web browsers that was developed for compressing and storing photographic images. It is best used for graphics with many colors, such as scanned photos. The compression loses detail in the picture, but the amount of compression and loss can be selected for the circumstances.

kiosk A freestanding display booth often used in malls or trade shows. PowerPoint includes a slide show setting that allows you to run a presentation in a continuous loop on a computer in a kiosk.

layout The number and arrangement of placeholders on a PowerPoint slide.

linked file A file created in a source program and referenced in a destination document so that it appears in the destination document but maintains a link back to the original file. When the original file is updated, the linked object can also be updated in the destination document.

loop To continuously play a PowerPoint presentation over and over again until an operator stops it.

macro An action or a set of actions you can use to automate tasks. Macros are recorded in the Visual Basic for Applications (VBA) programming language.

macro project A collection of components, including forms, code, and class modules, that make up a macro. Macro projects created in Microsoft Visual Basic for Applications (VBA) can be included in add-ins and in most Microsoft Office programs.

main document In a mail merge operation in Word, the document that contains the text and graphics that are the same for each version of the merged document, such as a form letter to be sent to many different recipients.

Master A feature of PowerPoint that allows you to make global formatting and placement choices for slides in a presentation from a single location. PowerPoint includes a Slide Master, Notes Master, and Handout Master.

Meeting Minder A dialog box in PowerPoint from which you can take meeting notes, set action items, and schedule meetings.

Messaging Application Programming Interface (MAPI) The Microsoft interface specification that allows different messaging and workgroup applications (including e-mail, voice mail, and fax) to work through a single client, such as Microsoft Exchange.

MHTML A MIME encapsulated aggregate HTML document. A method for saving and sending an entire Web site as a single file or attachment to an e-mail message. Requires Internet Explorer 4.0 or later to open the file and browse the Web site.

multiple-level category labels Category labels in a chart, based on worksheet data, that are automatically displayed on more than one line in a hierarchy. For example, the heading Produce might appear above a row with subheadings Lettuce, Tomatoes, and Cucumbers.

Glossary

name   In Excel, a word or string of characters that represents a cell, range of cells, formula, or constant value. Use easy to understand names, such as Products to refer to hard to understand ranges, such as Sales!C20:C30.

narration   A prerecorded audio description that can be saved with a PowerPoint presentation and played back using preset timing.

nonbreaking space   A space used to prevent multiple words from breaking if they fall at the end of a line. For example, by using a nonbreaking space, you can prevent M. Poirot from separating at the end of a line; instead, the entire item moves to the beginning of the next line.

Normal style   The default paragraph style used in documents based on the Normal template (Normal.dot).

Normal template   In Word, the global template that you use for any type of document. You can modify this template to change the default document formatting or content.

Normal view   In Word, the view that shows text formatting and a simplified page layout. Normal view is convenient for most editing and formatting tasks. In PowerPoint, Normal view includes three elements: an individual slide, an Outline pane, and a Slide pane that displays all slides in the presentation in miniature.

Notes   Also known as Speaker's Notes. Comments and information attached to individual slides in a presentation. Notes can be selected as a printing option in PowerPoint

and printed out along with slides to aid a speaker in delivering the presentation. PowerPoint also includes a Notes Page view.

Notes Master   *See* Master.

object, drawing   Any graphic you draw or insert. Drawing objects can be changed and enhanced. Drawing objects include AutoShapes, curves, lines, and WordArt.

object, floating   A graphic object that is inserted in the drawing layer so that you can position it precisely on the page or in front of or behind text or other objects.

object, inline   A graphic object that is positioned directly in the text of a Microsoft Word document at the insertion point.

online collaboration   A set of PowerPoint features that allow more than one person to work together on creating a presentation.

Order   In Microsoft Draw, the feature that allows you to set the sequence of stacked objects that overlap, bringing objects to the front or moving them to the back to create a layered effect.

Outbox   The Outlook folder where outgoing e-mail is stored prior to being sent.

Outline view   A view that shows the headings of a document indented to represent their level in the document's structure. You can also use Outline view to work with Master documents. PowerPoint includes an Outline pane in Normal view; each major heading in the outline represents a slide in the presentation.

overtype To replace existing characters as you type. By default, Microsoft Word inserts characters as you type. OVR is displayed in black in the status bar when overtype is active.

Pack And Go A wizard included in PowerPoint that allows you to make settings to save a presentation that you want to take with you to present out of your office or from another computer.

page break The point at which one page ends and another begins. Microsoft Word inserts an "automatic" (or soft) page break for you, or you can force a page break at a specific location by inserting a "manual" (or hard) page break.

paragraph mark The nonprinting symbol (¶) that Microsoft Word inserts when you press Enter to end a paragraph. The paragraph mark stores the formatting you apply to the paragraph.

password A security method used to restrict access to computer systems and sensitive files. On the World Wide Web, passwords are strings of characters that allow visitors access to Internet services if authentication is required. Excel passwords can consist of letters, numbers, spaces, and symbols. You must type uppercase and lowercase letters correctly when you set and enter passwords.

Paste Special An editing feature included in Microsoft Office programs that allows you to control the retention of formatting when pasting text or objects from one document to another, or from one place to another within a document.

PivotChart report A chart that provides interactive analysis of data, like a PivotTable report. You can change views of data, see different levels of detail, or reorganize the chart layout by dragging fields and by showing or hiding items in fields.

plot area In a 2-D chart, the area bounded by the axes, including all data series. In a 3-D chart, the area bounded by the axes, including the data series, category names, tick-mark labels, and axis titles.

PNG A graphic file format that is supported by some World Wide Web browsers. PNG supports variable transparency of images (alpha channels) and control of image brightness on different computers (gamma correction). PNG file compression is lossless, like GIF and unlike JPEG, and it doesn't have the 256 color limit of GIF files.

Print Layout view A view of a document or other object as it will appear when you print it. For example, items such as headers, footnotes, columns, and text boxes appear in their actual positions.

Print Preview A view of a document as it will appear when you print it. You cannot edit a document in Print Preview like you can in Print Layout view.

read-only A setting that allows a file to be read or copied, but changes cannot be saved. If you change a read-only file, you can save your changes only if you give the document a new name.

rules Sets of controls you can create for how Outlook handles e-mail messages. With rules you can, for example, designate certain categories of messages to be moved into a specific folder, deleted, or forwarded to another person.

section   A portion of a document in which you set certain page formatting options. You create a new section when you want to change such properties as line numbering, number of columns, or headers and footers.

separator characters   Characters you choose to indicate where you want text to separate when you convert a table to text, or where you want new rows or columns to begin when you convert text to a table.

shared workbook   A workbook set up to allow multiple users on a network to view and make changes at the same time. Each user who saves the workbook sees the changes made by other users. You must have Excel 97 or later to modify a shared workbook.

shortcut menu   A menu that shows a list of commands relevant to a particular item. To display a shortcut menu, right-click an item or press Shift+F10.

Slide Master   *See* Master.

Slide Sorter   A view in PowerPoint that displays all slides in a presentation. Slide sorter is often used to move, delete, and duplicate slides to organize a presentation.

slide transition   An animation effect that can be applied to PowerPoint slides that controls how one slide blends into the next.

status bar   A horizontal bar at the bottom of the screen that displays information about the current condition of the program, such as the status of items in the window, the progress of the current task, or information about the selected item.

style   A combination of formatting characteristics, such as font, font size, and indentation, that you name and store as a set. When you apply a style, all of the formatting instructions in the style are applied at one time.

style area   In Word, the vertical area along the left edge of the document window that displays the name of the paragraph style that is applied to each paragraph.

symbol   A text character other than letters or numbers, such as a bullet or copyright symbol.

synchronization   The process of updating files on a "client" computer (a portable or network client machine) and a "server" computer (a desktop or server machine) so that the latest, most current file versions are copied to both locations. In Outlook, you can synchronize online and offline folders so that you can access and work with e-mail and other Outlook folders offline, and then copy the changed files back to the server computer when you're online again. Similarly, any files that were changed by others on the server computer while you were offline are copied to your computer.

table   A collection of data that is stored in records (rows) and fields (columns).

task   An item on a to-do list. In Outlook, tasks can be created as a single occurrence or as recurring tasks.

task pane   A window within an Office application that provides commonly used commands within certain categories. Its location and size allow you to use these commands while still working on your files.

template A file or files that contain the structure and tools for shaping such elements as the style and page layout of finished files. For example, Word templates can shape a single document, PowerPoint templates can shape a presentation, and FrontPage templates can shape an entire Web site.

text box A movable, resizable container for text or graphics. Use text boxes to position several blocks of text on a page or to give text a different orientation from other text in the document.

text wrap A feature that can be turned on or off that causes text to automatically move to the next line in a document at a preset measurement on a page or slide.

toolbar A bar with buttons and options that you use to carry out commands. To display a toolbar, right-click any toolbar and click a toolbar from the list that appears. To see more buttons, click the Toolbar Options arrow at the right end of each toolbar.

tracer arrows In Excel, arrows that show the relationship between the active cell and its related cells. Tracer arrows are blue when pointing from a cell that provides data to another cell, and red if a cell contains an error value, such as #DIV/0!.

tracked change A mark that shows where a deletion, insertion, or other editing change has been made in a document.

transition *See* slide transition.

Visual Basic for Applications (VBA) A macro-language version of Microsoft Visual Basic that is used to program Windows applications and is included with several Microsoft applications.

watermark A semitransparent image that, when printed, appears either on top of or behind existing document text. In currency, a watermark is visible when you hold a bill up to the light.

Web browser Software that interprets HTML files, formats them into Web pages, and displays them. A Web browser, such as Microsoft Internet Explorer, can follow hyperlinks, transfer files, and play sound or video files that are embedded in Web pages.

Web Layout view A view of a document as it will appear in a Web browser. For example, the document appears as one long page (without page breaks) and text and tables wrap to fit in the window.

Web Page Preview A display showing how a document saved as a Web page would look in a typical browser.

Web publishing To save a document in HTML format on the World Wide Web.

Windows Clipboard An area of the Microsoft Windows operating system where one or more sets of text or objects can be placed when cut or copied from a document and are ready to be pasted into another document or location.

WordArt Text objects you create with ready-made effects to which you can apply additional formatting options.

zoom To get a closer or more distant view of a document. Zooming in displays less of a document; zooming out displays more of a document.

Glossary

Quick fix index

Quick fix index

Index

animation, 509
  Excel cell borders, 144, 153
  PowerPoint
    animated GIF files, 314
    animation schemes, 386
    custom sequences, 325
    letters or words, 385, 390
    mouse-click animations,
      388–89
    Normal view and, 348
    order of effects, 386–87
    sound and, 340
    troubleshooting flowchart,
      384–85
  Web presentations, 390–91
  Word printing problems, 468
Animation Schemes
  command, 385
apostrophes (’), 136, 152
Apple QuickTime, 335, 336,
  338–39
applications. *See programs*
appointments at wrong times,
  286–87
archiving Outlook files, 218,
  509
arguments in functions, 173,
  509
arranging objects
  aligning or distributing, 298–99
  overlapping items, 296–97
  rotating or flipping, 300–301
  troubleshooting flowchart,
    294–95
arrow keys, 134, 143, 154, 294
.asc files, 95
.asd files, 9
ASK fields, 432
.asp files, 502
aspect ratios, 30
asterisks (*), 21, 80, 152, 171
attaching templates, 493
attachments to e-mail
  correct commands for, 68
  file formats, 216
  forwarding messages, 220–21
  missing changes in, 218–19
  printing, 214–15
  problems opening, 216–17
  troubleshooting flowchart,
    214–15
  Web slide shows, 393, 398

audio. *See sound*
Audio Video Interleaved files,
  336
auditing formulas, 73, 169
authentication, 268, 481, 509
auto macros, 485
AutoArchive feature, 280
AutoCaptions feature, 70
AutoContent Wizard, 510
AutoCorrect feature, 38–39,
  510
  adding words, 39
  AutoText entries, 491
  misspelled entries in, 98
  options, 38, 104, 344
  removing words from, 104
AutoFit feature, 344
AutoFormat feature, 344
automatic actions
  correcting text, 38–39
  envelope feed, 414–15
  Office Clipboard, 34
  page breaks, 452
automatic updates
  dates or times, 455
  links, 321
  styles, 494–95
AutoRecover feature
  enabling, 5
  finding recovered files, 8–9
  lost changes in files, 10–11, 449
  restoring damaged files, 6–7
  running at specified intervals, 10
  troubleshooting flowchart, 4–5
"AutoRecover save of..."
  files, 9
AutoShapes, 510
  borders, 26
  copying, 114
  fitting text into, 380–81
  resizing, 31, 380, 381
  rotating or flipping text in,
    378–79
  shadows, 141
  troubleshooting flowchart,
    376–77
  unlocking, 191
AutoText feature, 482,
  490–91
AVI format (.avi files), 336
axes on Excel charts, 126–27,
  130–31, 132

background colors, 27, 70, 403
Background command, 27,
  330, 403
background error checking,
  168
Background Printing feature,
  62
background processes, 276–77
background saving, 448
backgrounds on slides, 307,
  330, 510. *See also* Slide
  Masters
backgrounds on Word pages,
  403, 462, 465, 510
backing up files, 4, 116–17, 251,
  484
balloons in reviewed
  documents, 71
barcodes, 412, 418–19
Basic Search task pane, 78, 80
basing styles on existing ones,
  115, 495
.bat files, 216
binary e-mail formats, 216
bitmaps, 317
black-and-white printing, 350,
  352
blank lines
  deleting in handouts, 346–47
  mail-merged documents, 432–34
blank spaces, underlining, 492,
  498
blocking meeting responses,
  248–49
blue boxes under words, 38
bold text, 409
bookmarks, 510
borders
  drawing objects, 24, 26–27
  in Excel, 134, 140, 144, 153
  in PowerPoint, 350, 356
  in Word
    around pages, 406–7, 411, 465
    around paragraphs, 407
    around tables, 322, 323
    troubleshooting flowchart,
      402–3
    as underlining, 498

indexing fields in Access, 183
indexing files with Fast
	Searching, 78
Indexing Services, 78
inkjet printers, 406
inline objects, 515
Insert Address Block dialog
	box, 438
Insert Clip Art task pane,
	16–17, 21
Insert File icon, 221
Insert Object dialog box, 87
inserting objects. *See* clip art;
	drawing objects;
	embedding objects;
	exporting; importing;
	links and linked objects
insertion points, 489
inside borders on pages, 140
installing
	digital signature updates,
		476–77
	Fast Searching feature, 78
	file format converters, 445
	graphics filters, 446
	Office Assistant characters, 43,
		44–45
	Recover Text Converter, 6
	Visual Basic for Applications, 474
interactive triggers, 388
Internet. *See also* Web
	publishing
	e-mail providers, 227
	problems accessing help, 47
	SSL (Secure Sockets Layer), 66
Internet E-Mail Settings dialog
	box, 222, 227
Internet Explorer, 66
Internet Format dialog box,
	217
Internet Message Access
	Protocol (IMAP), 227,
	230
intervals for AutoRecover,
	10–11
intranet hyperlink
	destinations, 96
invalid digital IDs, 272
invalid number formats, 171

joining meetings, 242–43
journal feature, 514
JPEG format (.jpg files), 120,
	506, 514

keyboard settings, 38
keys on keyboard, 137, 143
keys in Registry, 486
keywords, 16–17, 20–21
kiosks, 514

labels
	barcodes, 412, 418–19
	on columns in data sources, 437
	on Excel charts, 129, 132
	on Excel columns, 137, 182, 234,
		427
	security, 266
landscape pages, 57, 60
language detection, 491
language settings, 51
laser printers, 406
last-saved files, 8
layers of objects, 296–97
layout, defined, 514
layout of pages
	headers and footers, 454–55,
		460
	line numbering, 458–59
	page breaks, 452–53
	page number problems, 456–57
	troubleshooting flowchart,
		450–51
layout of slides
	missing font styles, 370–71
	moving or deleting graphics,
		374–75
	reapplying layout, 333, 373

replacing fonts, 368–69
scaling pages to fit paper, 61
switching, 372
too many placeholders, 372–73
troubleshooting flowchart,
	366–67
LDAP directories, 208–9, 211
leading (line spacing), 28–29,
	450
letters, animating, 384, 385,
	390
Letters And Mailings
	command, 427
levels of security
	adding trusted sources, 480
	changing levels, 472, 473
	trust levels, 270–71
licensing fonts, 370
Lightweight Directory Access
	Protocol (LDAP),
	208–9, 211
limiting searches to
	properties, 80–81
limits
	Click and Type feature, 489
	conditional formatting, 161
	custom dictionaries, 103
	Office Clipboard, 35
	public folders, 251
	slide images on handouts, 343
line breaks, 453, 498
line numbering, 450, 458–59
line spacing, 28–29, 450
lines. *See also* borders
	around notes pages, 356
	border colors, 26
	deleting on handouts, 346–47
linking outline levels to styles,
	405
links and linked objects
	Access PivotTables, 178–79
	animation on Master slides, 386
	availability of linked files, 309
	changing sources, 91, 321
	in e-mail messages, 237
	Excel worksheets and charts,
		128–29, 308–9
	hyperlinks, 320, 504–5
	inserting files in Outlook, 232
	inserting portions of files,
		238–39

About the authors

Nancy Stevenson is the author of more than 30 books on topics ranging from distance education to the Internet and software technologies. She has taught technical writing at the university level and holds a certificate from the University of Washington in Distance Learning Design. Nancy has held management positions with software and book publishers including Symantec, Macmillan, and IDG Books. She is currently a full-time writer and consultant to the publishing industry.

Elaine Marmel is President of Marmel Enterprises, Inc., an organization that specializes in technical writing and software training. Elaine has an MBA from Cornell University and worked on projects to build financial management systems for New York City and Washington, D.C. This prior experience provided the foundation for Marmel Enterprises, Inc., to help small businesses implement computerized accounting systems.

Elaine left her native Chicago for the warmer climes of Florida (by way of Cincinnati, OH; Jerusalem, Israel; Ithaca, NY; and Washington, D.C.) where she basks in the sun with her PC and her cats, Cato, Watson, and Buddy, and her dog, Josh, and sings barbershop harmony.

Elaine spends most of her time writing. She has been a contributing editor to *Inside Peachtree for Windows* and *Inside QuickBooks* monthly magazines since 1994. She also has authored and co-authored over 30 books about Windows 98, Microsoft Project, Quicken for Windows, Quicken for DOS, Microsoft Excel, Microsoft Word for Windows, Microsoft Word for the Mac, 1-2-3 for Windows, and Lotus Notes.

The manuscript for this book was prepared and galleyed using Microsoft Word 2000 and Microsoft Word 2002. Pages were composed using Adobe PageMaker 6.52 for Windows, with text in ACaslon Regular and display type in Gill Sans. Composed pages were delivered to the printer as electronic prepress files.

Cover designer

Landor Associates

Interior graphic designer

James D. Kramer

Production services

Publishing.com

Project manager

Tory McLearn

Technical editor

Curtis Philips

Copy editor

Anne Marie Walker

Principal compositor

Lisa Bellomo

Principal graphic artist

Jordana Bravo

Principal proofreader

Andrea Fox

Indexer

Jan C. Wright

Get a **Free**
e-mail newsletter, updates,
special offers, links to related books,
and more when you

register on line!

Register your Microsoft Press® title on our Web site and you'll get
a FREE subscription to our e-mail newsletter, *Microsoft Press
Book Connections.* You'll find out about newly released and upcoming
books and learning tools, online events, software downloads, special
offers and coupons for Microsoft Press customers, and information
about major Microsoft® product releases. You can also read useful
additional information about all the titles we publish, such as detailed book descriptions, tables of contents and indexes, sample
chapters, links to related books and book series, author biographies,
and reviews by other customers.

Registration is easy. Just visit this Web page and fill in your information:

http://www.microsoft.com/mspress/register

Microsoft®
